HARBRACE

COLLEGE

HANDBOOK

REVISED
TWELFTH EDITION

JOHN C. HODGES

WINIFRED BRYAN HORNER
Texas Christian University

SUZANNE STROBECK WEBB
Texas Woman's University

ROBERT KEITH MILLER
University of St. Thomas

**HARCOURT
BRACE**

HARCOURT BRACE COLLEGE PUBLISHERS
Fort Worth ● Philadelphia ● San Diego ● New York ● Orlando ● Austin ● San Antonio
Toronto ● Montreal ● London ● Sydney ● Tokyo

Publisher • Ted Buchholz
Senior Developmental Editor • Sarah Helyar Smith
Project Editor • Nancy Lombardi
Production Manager • Erin Gregg
Senior Book Designer • Don Fujimoto
Software Consultant • Dave Roberts

Address for Editorial Correspondence: Harcourt Brace College Publishers,
301 Commerce Street, Suite 3700, Fort Worth, TX 76102.

Address for Orders: Harcourt Brace & Company, 6277 Sea Harbor Drive,
Orlando, FL 32887. 1-800-782-4479, or 1-800-433-0001
(in Florida).

Copyrights and acknowledgments appear on pages C-1–C-2 which
constitute a continuation of the copyright page.

ISBN: 0-15-503337-9

Library of Congress Catalog Card Number: 93-77628

Printed in the United States of America

56789012   039   987654321

This book was printed on paper
made from waste paper, containing
10% POST-CONSUMER WASTE
and
40% PRE-CONSUMER WASTE
measured as a percentage of
total fibre weight content.

PREFACE

The *Harbrace College Handbook* is a compact yet comprehensive guide for writers. Its approach is practical, its advice is clearly and concisely stated, and its purpose is to help students become more effective writers. Abundant, specific examples throughout the book demonstrate the principles of writing that are applicable to both coursework and professional tasks.

The Twelfth Edition is a complete revision of the Eleventh. To make the handbook even more helpful to students, we have followed several principles:

1. To emphasize revision rather than correction, we have reworded some chapter titles and many section rules.
2. We have explained, whenever possible, the reasons or purposes for specific elements of grammar and punctuation. Students learn faster and write better when they understand the reasons for the rules in the handbook.
3. We have updated and freshened the explanations and examples throughout, making sure to balance the representation of men and women and of ethnic and racial groups.

4. To reflect the changing demographics of composition students, we have addressed *in context* the writing difficulties common to dialect interference and ESL.
5. We have extensively revised the exercises by increasing the number that encourage students to write or revise in context; by making many exercises the focus of class discussion, thereby encouraging students to collaborate; and by providing exercises that give students more writing practice.
6. In many chapters we have created checklists of topics that students often need to glance at.

Further, we have carefully reorganized some chapters, adding some sections and deleting or combining others to address the current needs of students. For example, chapters **1** and **7** have been adjusted to clarify concepts that have proved difficult for students, chapters **8** and **18** emphasize with suitable cautions the word-processing technology now available to most students, and chapter **19** contains a new section on sexist language.

The Glossary of Usage (formerly **19i**) is now a separate glossary at the back of the book, and the Record of Revisions (formerly **8f**) and the list of Commonly Misspelled Words (formerly **18e**) are now located in the Instructor's Manual.

We have also clarified some terminology. For example, to follow current linguistic practice, and to avoid the confusion that many students experience with the terms *main* and *dependent,* we pair the term *independent clause* with *subordinate clause.*

We have reinforced the process orientation of chapters **31–35**. An expanded chapter **31** discusses critical reading within a framework of logical thinking, which are vital skills for chapters **32–35** and for other college and work assignments. As the new title suggests, chapter **34** emphasizes that researched papers must be written and not simply compiled. Chapter **34** also features an expanded discussion of plagiarism and greater coverage of both MLA and APA documentation styles, which are now called out by new color tabs and running heads. Further, because chapter **35** now includes a researched paper about literature, the new MLA style paper in chapter **34** provides a model for a short, persuasive essay of a type often expected of students in writing courses. Of the six student papers in the handbook, four are new to the Twelfth Edition.

To reinforce the handbook's function as a reference tool, we have also significantly revised the backmatter. We have expanded and updated the **Glossary of Usage** and, as noted earlier, moved it from **19i** to the back of the book to make it easier to find. The **Glossary of Terms** has been renamed to encompass computer words and phrases that are common in composition today. In addition to a detailed general index, which identifies issues common in dialect interference, we have included specific, color-coded ESL, MLA, and APA indexes for quick reference.

Like the Eleventh Edition, the four-color design displays the rules and the main structural elements of each chapter in red; the notes, cautions, and exceptions in yellow to alert the student; and the exercise directions in green. This color format allows the reader to locate the needed information quickly and to differentiate key points from finer points.

These additions to the Twelfth Edition of the handbook do not overshadow the solid, proven coverage of previous editions. The time-tested organization of the handbook, which allows instructors maximum flexibility in teaching the chapters, is still the same. We believe that the revisions demonstrate that the *Harbrace College Handbook* responds to the changing needs of instructors and students by reflecting the best of current research in rhetoric and composition.

Ancillaries

- Instructor's Manual by Mary Lee Donahue
- *The Resourceful Writer,* Third Edition (and its Instructor's Manual), by Suzanne S. Webb

- *Harbrace College Workbooks* (and their accompanying Instructor's Editions): Form 12A, "Diversity of Writers in America," by Larry G. Mapp; Form 12B, "Exploring the Cosmos," by Larry G. Mapp (available in 1995); Form 12C, "Writing for the World of Work," by Melissa Barth (available in 1995); and the *Harbrace ESL Workbook*, Second Edition, by Charles Hall and Jeffrey Gross
- Correction Chart
- Harbrace Instructor's Resource Package
- Harbrace Test Package, print and computerized versions, which include diagnostic tests as well as CLAST and TASP guidelines
- Harbrace software, which includes *Harbrace Online, PC-Write Lite* word-processing software, *Writing Tutor* for IBM and Macintosh, *GramPop* and *DocuPop* reference software, *ExamRecord* grade book

Acknowledgments We express our gratitude to those colleagues who assisted in the development of the Twelfth Edition: John M. Adair, *Cumberland County College;* Nancy G. Anderson, *Auburn University, Montgomery;* W. Steve Anderson, *University of Arkansas, Little Rock;* Rebecca Argall, *Memphis State University;* Margaret P. Baker, *Brigham Young University, Hawaii;* Miriam Baker, *Dowling College;* Dorothy Bankston, *Louisiana State University;* Mary V. Battle, *Memphis State University;* Jametha A. Beatty, *Embry-Riddle Aeronautical University;* Ann Begley, *Westmont College;* Linda Bensel-Meyers, *University of Tennessee, Knoxville;* Mary Jo Berger, *Randolph Macon College;* Julie Bertch, *Rio Salado Community College;* Vincent P. Betz, *Palm Beach Community College, North Palm Beach;* Clair Bigler, *University of Wisconsin;* Betsy A. Bowen, *Fairfield University;* Peggy S. Brent, *Hinds Community College;* Carolyn Smith Brown, *LDS Business College;* Mary Buckalew, *University of North Texas;* Paula R. Buck, *Florida Southern College;* Chris Burnham, *New Mexico State University;* Philip J. Burns, *Worcester*

State College; Don Bushman, *University of Arizona;* Sarah V. Clere, *Mount Olive College;* Arthur Coleman, *C. W. Post College;* Colleen Corless, *Saint Peter's College;* Gerald S. Coulter, *Central Connecticut State University;* Joseph T. Cox, *United States Military Academy;* Bill Crider, *Alvin Community College;* Lillian Cromey, *Northwestern Connecticut Community College;* Mary Cross, *Fairleigh Dickinson University;* Beth DeMeo, *Alvernia College;* Rosalie de Rosset, *Moody Bible Institute;* Marvin Diogenes, *University of Arizona;* Mary Lee Donahue, *Rowan College;* Veneta Edwards, *Hill College;* Carolyn Farkas, *Cecil Community College;* Larry Fink, *Hardin-Simmons University;* Loris D. Galford, *McNeese State University;* Linda S. Garcia; Ellen F. Gardiner, *University of Mississippi;* Marie M. Garrett, *Patrick Henry Community College;* David George, *Urbana University;* Susan Gilbert, *Meredith College;* Loren C. Gruber, *Northwest Missouri State University;* Huey Guagliardo, *Louisiana State University, Eunice;* Susan J. Hanna, *Mary Washington College;* Judy S. Hart, *Frank Phillips College;* W. Dale Hearell, *Stephen F. Austin State University;* Michael B. Herzog, *Gonzaga University;* John Meredith Hill, *University of Scranton;* Elizabeth S. Hodges, *Virginia Commonwealth University;* Sister Thomasita Homan, *Benedictine College;* Ronald G. Hoover, *Pennsylvania State University, Altoona;* Marcia L. Hurlow, *Asbury College;* Carol V. Johnson, *Virginia Wesleyan College;* Joyce Jolly, *Shelton State Community College;* Douglas Jones, *Jefferson State Community College;* Cletus Keating, *Weekend College of the University of Denver;* Colin K. Keeney, *University of Wyoming;* Sue B. Kelley, *Snead State Junior College;* M. Jimmie Killingsworth, *Texas A & M University;* Donald M. Lance, *University of Missouri;* Robert Lawrence, *York College;* David Lee, *Southern Utah University;* Han-Mook Lee, *Wiley College;* Allyn Leidig, *Mercy College;* Christopher Litten, *Columbia Union College;* Darrel Lloyd, *Hastings College;* Jan Luton, *Teikyo Marycrest University;* Michael Steven Marx, *Skidmore College;* James W. Mathews, *West Georgia College;* Mike Matthews, *Tarrant County Junior College;* Jane

McCormick, *United Wesleyan College;* Ann McCray, *Amarillo College;* Nellie McCrory, *Gaston College;* Jane McMillan-Brown, *Upsala College;* James A. Merrill, *Oxnard College;* Joan T. Mims, *West Chester University;* William D. Mowatt, *West Valley College;* Robert J. Nelson, *State University of New York College of Technology;* Scott Orme, *Spokane Community College;* Eleanora Overbey, *University of Tennessee, Knoxville;* Mary C. Padget, *Tennessee Technological University;* Jane Paznik, *Borough of Manhattan Community College;* Betsey L. Pender, *University of North Florida;* Julie Persinger, *Central Community College;* Robert Petersen, *Middle Tennessee State University;* Marianne Pollack, *Eastern New Mexico State University;* Kirk G. Rasmussen, *Utah Valley Community College;* Edward J. Rielly, *Saint Joseph's College;* Cheryl Roberts, *Tarrant County Junior College;* Sharon P. Robinson, *Russell Sage College;* Paula Ross, *Gadsden State Community College;* Carolyn Rude, *Texas Tech University;* Judy Ryan, *Fresno City College;* Florence P. Schenker, *Memphis State University;* Reinhold Schlieper, *Embry-Riddle Aeronautical Institute;* Richard J. Schneider, *Wartburg College;* James Scrimgeour, *Western Connecticut State University;* Georgeanna Sellers, *High Point College;* Terry Shellenberger, *Utah Valley Community College;* Deborah Sinnreich-Levi, *Stevens Institute of Technology;* Marilyn Smothers, *Union University;* Malinda Snow, *Georgia State University;* Mark Snowhite, *Crafton Hills College;* Isabel B. Stanley, *East Tennessee State University;* Ed Stieve, *Nova University;* Jack E. Surrency, *Florida Community College, Jacksonville;* Vivian Thomlinson, *Cameron University;* Peter Ulisse, *Housatonic Community College;* J.K. Van Dover, *Lincoln University;* Carolyn Wall, *Spokane Community College;* Ray Wallace, *Kennesaw State College;* Bernadette Waterman Ward, *State University of New York, Oswego;* Linda S. Weeks, *Dyersburg State Community College;* John O. White, *California State University, Fullerton;* Toby Widdicombe, *New York Institute of Technology;* Laura Winters, *College of Saint Elizabeth;* Joy P. Yarnall, *Okaloosa-Walton Community College.*

We thank Vivian Casper and William E. Tanner (*Texas Woman's University*) and instructors in the University of Tennessee Writing Center for their many helpful suggestions. We also thank the composition instructors at Texas Christian University and Texas Woman's University, who class tested some of the chapters, and the instructors and students at Northeastern State University of Oklahoma. Our work was greatly eased by the help of Kimberly Allison, Carol Johnson, Marilyn Keef, and Shelley Aley.

For over half its history, Mary E. Whitten labored lovingly to keep the *Harbrace College Handbook* current and authoritative. Just as she continued the work of John Hodges in the Fifth through Tenth Editions, we have strived to continue her work in the Eleventh and in this Twelfth Edition.

No set of acknowledgments would be complete without recognition of the staff of Harcourt Brace College Publishers: Sarah Helyar Smith, Nancy Lombardi, Don Fujimoto, Erin Gregg, Ilse Wolfe West, Tom Hall, and Ellen C. Wynn.

Winifred Bryan Horner
Suzanne Strobeck Webb
Robert Keith Miller

CONTENTS

MECHANICS

PUNCTUATION

_____EFFECTIVE SENTENCES_____

LARGER ELEMENTS

GRAMMAR

1

Sentence Sense

To think more clearly and write more effectively, understand how sentences work.

Writing a clear, precise sentence is an art, and you can master that art by developing your awareness of what makes sentences work. This chapter will show you the *functions* of English sentences and help you understand their *forms* by examining the relationships among sentence elements. Understanding the forms and functions of English sentences will help you revise your sentences so they say what you mean; knowing how to revise will help you become a more flexible and effective writer. (For explanations of any unfamiliar terms, see the **Glossary of Terms**.)

The parts of a sentence   The English sentence divides into two parts.

> **SUBJECT + PREDICATE.**
>
> The **voters** + **elected** the incumbent.
> The **peach** + **tastes** good.
> The **tomato** + **is** ripe.

These parts are the two essential elements of the English sentence, the subject and the predicate. The **subject** of a sentence is what the sentence is about or says something about (see **1b**). It is the part of the sentence that answers the questions "Who?" or "What?" The **predicate** of a sentence says something about the subject (see **1a**). It contains a word that expresses action, occurrence, or state of being. In the sentences above, *elected* expresses the action the voters took, *tastes* expresses an occurrence (what happens when the peach is eaten), and *is* expresses the state of being of the tomato.

The pattern of these sentences is **SUBJECT + PREDICATE**, the basic order of English sentences. A subject and a predicate together make a **clause** (see **1e**).

1a

Learn to recognize verbs and predicates.

A verb functions as the predicate of a sentence or as an essential part of the predicate. You can recognize a verb by observing its form as well as its function.

> Khalid **swims**. [verb by itself]
> Khalid **swims** a mile before breakfast. [verb plus modifiers]

Predicates may be compound:

> Khalid **swims** a mile before breakfast and
>   **arrives** at the office by eight.

A verb may consist of more than one word. These words may include two kinds of elements, those that precede the main verb and those that follow it. The **auxiliary**, a helping verb, precedes the verb. The verbs *have* and *be* are auxiliaries and follow the pattern of **AUXILIARY + VERB**. Since they precede the verb, auxiliaries are often called *verb markers*. **Modals** also precede the verb. (See chapter **7** for a complete discussion of verbs.)

> The fight **had started** by then.
> He **will be studying** late.
> Mara **should go** now.

Other words may intervene between the auxiliary and the verb:

> **Have** the members **paid** their dues?   [Compare "The members *have paid* their dues."]
> I **have** not **paid** mine.
> Television **will** never completely **replace** the radio.

Verbs with particles   Verbs with particles, sometimes called *phrasal verbs*, function grammatically just like single-word verbs and verbs with auxiliaries. Following the verb, the **particle** (a word such as *across, away, down, for, in, off, out, up,* or *with*) combines with it to create a meaning different from that of the verb as a single word. For example, the meaning of the verb *turned*, even when the modifier *out* occurs nearby, is different from the meaning of the combination *turned out*.

> Martha **turned** the car **out** of the way.   [single-word verb and modifier]
> Martha's essay **turned out** better than mine.   [verb with particle, meaning "achieved a result"]
> Martha was well **turned out**.   [verb with particle, meaning "well dressed"]
> Please **turn out** the lights.   [verb with particle, meaning "extinguish"]

■ **Exercise 1**   Underline the verbs (including any auxiliaries and particles) in the following sentences (adapted from *Reader's Digest*).

1. Developing nations are now facing many serious difficulties.
2. The flock of wheeling birds descended.
3. The Doberman has eaten up some of the finest sirloin we have.
4. Parts of the wreckage may never be found.
5. Phyllis's manner has given her statements the force of commands.
6. Is exercise important for healthy hearts and lungs?
7. There are approximately ten million college students.
8. Her own political history makes current promises questionable.
9. Parents and small children invaded the video store and rented all the Disney tapes.
10. He pulled the bike away from the rack, grasped the handlebars firmly, and swung his leg over the bar.

1b

Learn to recognize subjects, objects, and complements.

(1) Subjects of verbs

All grammatically complete sentences, except for imperatives (which are commands or requests in which the subject, *you*, may be understood), contain stated subjects of verbs. Subjects are nouns or pronouns (or word groups serving as nouns)—see **1c**. In the following sentences, the subjects are in boldface, and the verbs are in italics. The understood subject is in brackets.

> **Louisiana** *produces* delicious yams.
> *Doesn't* **North Carolina** also *grow* yams?
> [**You**] *Take*, for example, Louisiana and North Carolina.
> [imperative]

Subjects of verbs may be compound:

> **Louisiana** and **North Carolina** grow yams. [compound subject]

To identify the grammatical subject of a sentence, first find the verb; then use the verb in a question beginning with *who* or *what*, as shown in the following examples:

The runner leaped the hurdle.	The book was read by Nan.
Verb: **leaped**	Verb: **was read**
WHO leaped? **The runner** (not the hurdle) **leaped**.	WHAT was read? **book** (not Nan) **was read**.
Subject: **runner**	Subject: **book**

Subjects usually precede verbs in sentences. Common exceptions occur in questions and after the word *there* (which is never the subject). *There* is an expletive, a word that fills out a sentence without altering the meaning.

Was the **statement** true?   [verb + subject]
Did these refugees **survive**?   [auxiliary + subject + verb]
There **were** no **objections**.   [*there* + verb + subject]

(2) Objects of verbs

Verbs denoting action often require a **direct object** to receive or to show the result of the action. Such verbs are called **transitive** verbs. See chapter **7**. Sometimes a word that shows to whom or for whom the action occurred (**indirect object**) comes between the verb and the direct object. In the following sentences, the objects are in boldface.

> The clerk sold **her** the expensive **briefcase**.   [direct object: *briefcase*—indirect object: *her*]
> Felix owns a **dog** and a **cat**.   [compound direct object]

Like the subjects of verbs, direct and indirect objects are generally nouns or pronouns.

To identify a direct object, find the subject and the verb; then use them in a question ending with *whom* or *what*, as shown in the following example:

> Juana silently took his hand.
> Subject and verb: **Juana took**
> Juana took WHAT?   **hand**
> Direct object: **hand**

Notice that direct objects in sentences like the following are directly affected by the action of the verb.

> A tornado leveled a city in Nebraska.   [*Tornado*, the subject, acts. *City*, the object, receives the action.]

Knowing how to change from the *active* to the *passive voice* can also help you identify an object. When you make a verb passive, the word that was the object of the active verb becomes the subject of the passive verb. Also, the original subject is either omitted or incorporated in a phrase beginning with *by.* (See also examples on pages 79 and 88 of chapter **7** and **29d**.)

ACTIVE The Eagles finally **defeated** the **Lions**. [*Lions* is the direct object of *defeated*.]

PASSIVE The **Lions were** finally **defeated**. [*Lions* is the subject of *were defeated*; original subject omitted.]

The **Lions were** finally **defeated** by the Eagles. [original subject incorporated in a phrase]

Notice that a form of *be* (such as *is, are, was*) is added when an active verb is changed to a passive verb.

Some verbs (such as *give, offer, bring, take, lend, send, buy,* and *sell*) may have both a direct object and an indirect object.

Linda gave Felipe a new bicycle. [Subject + verb + direct object: **Linda gave bicycle**.]

Linda gave a bicycle TO WHOM? **Felipe** [Indirect object: **Felipe**]

Direct and indirect object of verbs may be compound.

She likes **peas** and **spinach**. [compound direct object]

We offered **Elena** and **Octavio** a year's membership. [compound indirect object]

■ **Exercise 2** Circle the subjects of the verbs in Exercise 1 on page 4. Then put a wavy line under the direct and indirect objects.

(3) Subject and object complements

Nouns, pronouns, and adjectives are used as subject and object complements (see **1c**). A **subject complement** refers to, identifies, or qualifies the subject. Subject complements help complete the meaning of the forms of *be* (*am, is, are, was, were, been*), of the linking verbs (such as *seem, become*), and of the sensory verbs (such as *feel, look, smell, sound, taste*). These verbs are often called **intransitive verbs**. See chapter **7**.

Leilani is my **sister**.   [*Sister* identifies *Leilani*, the subject.]
Some violence became **inevitable**.   [*Inevitable* describes or
  qualifies *violence*, the subject.]

An **object complement** refers to, identifies, or qualifies
the direct object. Object complements help complete the
meaning of verbs such as *make, name, elect, call, paint.*

We elected Jesse **president**.
The flaw made it **worthless**.
The churches of Guadalajara are **old** and **famous**.   [compound
  subject complement]
They will name the baby **Judah** or **Judith**.   [compound ob-
  ject complement]

(4) Word order

Becoming thoroughly aware of English word order—usually
SUBJECT + VERB + OBJECT or **COMPLEMENT**—will help you
recognize subjects, objects, and complements. Study carefully
the five most commonly used sentence patterns, observing
the importance of word order—especially in pattern 2—in
determining meaning.

PATTERN 1

SUBJECT + VERB.

The **children did** not **listen**.
The **lights** on the patrol car **flashed** ominously.

PATTERN 2

SUBJECT + VERB + OBJECT.

Mice frighten elephants.
Elephants frighten mice.
Kenya's **athletes** often **win** the marathon.

PATTERN 3

> **SUBJECT + VERB + INDIRECT OBJECT**
> **+ DIRECT OBJECT.**

Jan showed Karl the **book**.
The **company will** probably **send me** a small **refund**.

In some sentences—especially questions—the direct object does not always take the position indicated by these basic patterns.

> What **event do** Kenya's **athletes** often **win**? [direct object + auxiliary + subject + verb]

PATTERN 4

> **SUBJECT + LINKING VERB**
> **+ SUBJECT COMPLEMENT.**

My son's **name is Aaron**.
The **fence was white**.

PATTERN 5

> **SUBJECT + VERB + DIRECT OBJECT**
> **+ OBJECT COMPLEMENT.**

I named my **son Aaron**.
I painted the **fence white**.

■ **Exercise 3**   Label all subjects and objects of verbs, indirect objects, subject complements, and object complements in the quotations below. Be prepared to discuss the basic sentence patterns (and any variations) and the types of verbs used.

1. An idea has built a nation.   —NORMAN FORD
2. Cultural patterns once established seem to endure.
    —JOSEPH L. WHITE
3. Art and games need rules, conventions, and spectators.
    —MARSHALL McLUHAN
4. A rumor needs no true parent.   —GLORIA NAYLOR
5. In the *Odyssey*, Homer gives us detailed information of wind and stars.   —MAURICIO OBREGÓN
6. We must put down our old industrial tasks and pick up the tasks of the future.   —JOHN NAISBITT
7. There was one knot so complicated that it blinded the knot-maker.   —MAXINE HONG KINGSTON
8. America has not always been kind to its artists and scholars.
    —LYNDON B. JOHNSON
9. Good schooling requires that any student alter early childhood habits.   —RICHARD RODRIGUEZ
10. Modern English, especially written English, is full of bad habits which spread by imitation and which can be avoided if one is willing to take the necessary trouble.   —GEORGE ORWELL

1c

Learn to recognize the parts of speech and to understand their functions.

Recognizing the form of a word can help you to identify what part of speech it is and to understand how it functions in the sentence. This understanding will help you make appropriate grammatical and stylistic choices.

Words are traditionally grouped into eight classes or parts of speech: *verbs, nouns, pronouns, adjectives, adverbs, prepositions, conjunctions,* and *interjections.* Verbs, nouns, adjectives, and adverbs (called vocabulary or lexical words) make up more than 99 percent of all words listed in the dictionary. But pronouns, prepositions, and conjunctions—although small in number—are important because they are used over and over in our speaking and writing. Prepositions and conjunctions (called function or structure words) connect and relate other parts of speech. Prepositions and conjunctions, as well as interjections, are also the only word classes that do not change their form. For a summary of the form changes of the other parts of speech, see **inflection**, in the **Glossary of Terms**.

Carefully study the function and forms of each of the eight parts of speech that are shown in the chart below and discussed on the following pages. See also the corresponding entries in the **Glossary of Terms**. The chart shows the relationships among parts of speech, form, and function.

Compassionate friends generously offered her shelter from the Nazis' persecution.

	FORM	FUNCTION	PART OF SPEECH
Compassionate	-*ate* ending	modifier	adjective
friends	-*s* (plural)	subject	noun
generously	-*ly* ending	modifier	adverb
offered	-*ed* (past)	verb of predicate	verb
her	objective case	indirect object	pronoun
shelter	singular	direct object	noun
from	invariable	connector	preposition
the	invariable	modifier	adjective
Nazis'	*s'* (possessive)	modifier	noun
persecution	singular	obj. of prep.	noun

Notice here that one part of speech—the noun (a naming word that forms the plural with -*s* and the possessive with '*s*)—is used as a subject, a direct object, a modifier, and an object of a preposition.

A dictionary labels words according to their parts of speech. Some words have only one classification—for example, *notify* (verb), *sleepy* (adjective), *practically* (adverb). Other words have more than one label because they can function as two or more parts of speech. The label of a word therefore depends upon its use in a given sentence. The word *living*, for instance, is first treated as a form of the verb *live* (as in *are living*) and is then listed separately and defined as an adjective (*a living example*) and as a noun (*makes a living*). Another example is the word *up*:

> They dragged the sled **up** the hill.   [preposition]
> She follows the **ups** and downs of the market.   [noun]
> "They have **upped** the rent again," he complained.   [verb]
> Kelly ran **up** the bill.   [part of phrasal verb]
> The **up** escalator is jerking again.   [adjective]
> Hopkins says to look **up**, to "look **up** at the skies!"   [adverb]

(1) Verbs   *notify, notifies, is notifying, notified*
write, writes, is writing, wrote, has written

A verb functions as the predicate of a sentence or as an essential part of the predicate: see **1a**.

> Gabriel **writes**. He **has written** five poems.
> He **is** no longer **writing** those dull stories.

Two suffixes frequently used to make verbs are -*ize* and -*ify*:

> *terror* (noun)—*terrorize, terrify* (verbs)
> *real* (adjective)—*realize* (verb)

▲ Caution: Verbals (infinitives, participles, and gerunds) cannot function as the predicate of a sentence: see **1d**.

(2) Nouns   *nation, nations; nation's, nations'*
woman, women; kindness, kindnesses
Carthage, United States, William, NASA
breakthrough, buddy system, sister-in-law

Nouns function as subjects, objects, complements, appositives, and modifiers, as well as in direct address and in absolute constructions. See **noun**, in the **Glossary of Terms**. Nouns name persons, places, things, ideas, animals, and so on. The articles *a*, *an*, and *the* signal that a noun is to follow (a *chair*, an *activity*).

> **McKinney** drives a **truck** for the **Salvation Army**.

Suffixes frequently used to make nouns are *-ance, -ation, -ence, -ism, -ity, -ment, -ness,* and *-ship.*

> *relax, depend* (verbs)—*relaxation, dependence* (nouns)
> *kind, rigid* (adjectives)—*kindness, rigidity* (nouns)

Words such as *father-in-law, Labor Day,* and *swimming pool* are generally classified as *compound nouns.*

(3) Pronouns
> *I, me, my, mine, myself*
> *you, your, yours, yourself*
> *he, him, his; she, her, hers; it, its*
> *we, us, our; they, them, their*
> *this, these; who, whom, whose; which, that*
> *one, ones; everybody, anyone*

A pronoun is a word that can substitute for a noun in sentences. Pronouns change form according to their function (see chapter **5**).

> **They** bought **it** for **her**.   **Everyone** knows **that**.

(4) Adjectives
> *shy, sleepy, attractive, famous, historic*
> *three men, this class, another one*
> *young, younger, youngest; good, better, best*

Adjectives modify or qualify nouns and pronouns (and sometimes gerunds—see page 18). Generally, adjectives appear immediately before the words they modify.

> **These difficult** decisions, whether **right** or **wrong**, affect all of us.
>
> **Competitive** runners look **healthy**.

In the second of these two examples, *healthy* is a predicate adjective (subject complement), a word that modifies the subject and helps to complete the meaning of the sentence. See **4b** and **7**.

Suffixes such as *-al, -able, -ant, -ative, -ic, -ish, -less, -ous,* and *-y* may be added to certain verbs or nouns to form adjectives:

> *accept, repent* (verbs)—*acceptable, repentant* (adjectives)
> *angel, effort* (nouns)—*angelic, effortless* (adjectives)

The articles *a, an,* and *the* are often classified as adjectives.

(5) Adverbs   *rarely* saw, call *daily*, *soon* left, left *sooner*
very short, *too* angry, *never* shy, *not* fearful
practically never loses, *nearly always* cold

As the examples show, adverbs modify verbs, adjectives, and other adverbs. In addition, an adverb may modify a verbal, a phrase, a clause, or even the rest of the sentence in which it appears:

> I noticed a plane **slowly** circling overhead.
> **Honestly**, Jo wasn't speeding.

The *-ly* ending nearly always converts adjectives to adverbs:

> *rare, honest* (adjectives)—*rarely, honestly* (adverbs)

(6) Prepositions   *on* a shelf, *between* us, *because of* rain
to the door, *by* them, *before* class

A preposition always has an object, which is usually a noun or a pronoun. The preposition establishes a relationship such as space, time, accompaniment, cause, or manner between its object and another word in the sentence. The preposition with its object (and any modifiers) is called a *prepositional phrase*.

> ***With* great feeling**, Martin Luther King, Jr., expressed his dream *of* **freedom**.

The preposition may follow rather than precede its object, and it can be placed at the end of the sentence:

> What was he complaining **about**? [*What* is the object of the preposition. Compare "He was complaining about what?"]

Words commonly used as prepositions:

about	besides	inside	since
above	between	into	through
across	beyond	like	throughout
after	but	near	till
against	by	of	to
along	concerning	off	toward
among	despite	on	under
around	down	onto	underneath
at	during	out	until
before	except	outside	up
behind	excepting	over	upon
below	for	past	with
beneath	from	regarding	within
beside	in	round	without

Phrasal prepositions (two or more words):

according to	by way of	in spite of
along with	due to	instead of
apart from	except for	on account of
as for	in addition to	out of
as regards	in case of	up to
as to	in front of	with reference to
because of	in lieu of	with regard to
by means of	in place of	with respect to
by reason of	in regard to	with the exception of

(7) Conjunctions   cars *and* trucks, in the boat *or* on the pier
will try *but* may lose, *neither* Ana *nor*
Miguel

I worked *because* Dad needed money.
The river rises *when* the snow melts.

Conjunctions are connectors. The **coordinating conjunctions** (*and, but, or, for, nor, so,* and *yet*), as well as the correlatives (*both–and, either–or, neither–nor, not only–but also, whether–or*), join sentence elements (words, phrases, or clauses) of equal grammatical rank. See also chapter **26**. The **subordinating conjunctions** (such as *because, if, since, until, when, where, while*) join subordinate clauses to independent clauses: see **1d**, pages 17–21.

Words like *consequently, however, nevertheless, then,* and *therefore* (see the list on page 40) serve as conjunctive adverbs (or adverbial conjunctions):

Don seemed bored in class; **however**, he did listen and learn.

(8) Interjections   *Wow! Oh,* that's a surprise.

Interjections are exclamations. They may be followed by an exclamation point or by a comma.

■ **Exercise 4**   Using your dictionary as an aid, classify each word in the following sentences according to its part of speech. Then write five sentences of your own in which you use one word from each quotation but change its part of speech.

EXAMPLE   We just moved into a new house.
Many schools house *students off campus.*

1. He struts with the gravity of a frozen penguin. —*TIME*
2. Neither intelligence nor integrity can be imposed by law.
—CARL BECKER
3. They pick a President and then for four years they pick on him.
—ADLAI STEVENSON
4. She thought of her knotty, muscled limbs, her harsh, knuckly hands and drew herself up into an unhappy little ball in the middle of the big feather bed. —ZORA NEALE HURSTON

5. Quick to grasp at the excellent opportunities for making money in the city, the Chinese took to carpentering, washing and ironing, and operating restaurants and hotels.   —BETTY LEE SUNG

1d

Learn to recognize phrases.

A **phrase** is a word group that lacks a subject and/or a predicate and which functions as a single part of speech (noun, verb, adjective, or adverb). Observe how a short simple sentence can be expanded by adding modifiers, not only single words but also word groups that function as adjectives or adverbs.

> The ship had arrived. [subject (noun phrase) + predicate (verb phrase)]

Expansion:

> The **last** ship had **recently** arrived. [single-word modifiers added]
>
> The last ship **carrying passengers**, a large troop ship, had recently arrived **in the Ross Sea**. [verbal, prepositional, and appositive phrases added]

(1) Kinds of phrases

A phrase is a sequence of grammatically related words without a subject, a predicate, or both. The most common kinds of phrases are noun phrases, verb phrases, prepositional phrases, verbal phrases, and appositive phrases.

> The last ship   [noun phrases—no predicate]
>
> had arrived   [verb phrase—no subject]
>
> in the Ross Sea,   [prepositional phrase—neither subject nor predicate]
>
> carrying passengers   [verbal phrase—neither subject nor predicate]
>
> a large troop ship,   [noun phrase as appositive—neither subject nor predicate]

Noun phrases serve as subjects, objects, and complements. **Verb phrases** serve as predicates. **Prepositional phrases** may modify nouns, pronouns, adjectives, adverbs, or verbs. **Appositive phrases** substitute for and expand the meaning of noun phrases: Millicent, *my oldest sister*.

▲ Caution: As you learn to recognize phrases, give special attention to verb forms in word groups that are used as nouns, adjectives, or adverbs. Although such verb forms (called *verbals*) are much like verbs because they have different tenses, can take subjects and objects, and can be modified by adverbs, they cannot function as the predicate of a sentence. These verbal phrases may serve only as adjectives, adverbs, or nouns.

VERBAL PHRASES IN SENTENCES

Shoppers **milling around** did not buy much.   [participial phrase (see the **Glossary of Terms**) modifying the noun *shoppers*]
Some people win arguments by **just remaining silent**.   [gerund phrase (see the **Glossary of Terms**), object of the preposition *by*]
The group arrived in a van **loaded with heavy equipment**. [participial phrase modifying the noun *van*]
Vernon went to Boston **to visit relatives**.   [infinitive phrase (see the **Glossary of Terms**) modifying the verb *went*]

(2) Phrases used as nouns

VERBAL PHRASES

Verbals may be classified as participles, gerunds, and infinitives. *Verbals* and *verbal phrases* function as adjectives, nouns, or adverbs. *Gerund phrases* are always used as nouns. *Infinitive phrases* are often used as nouns (although they may also function as modifiers). Occasionally a *prepositional phrase* serves as a noun (as in "*After supper* is too late!").

NOUNS	PHRASES USED AS NOUNS
The **decision** is important.	**Choosing a major** is important. [gerund phrase—subject]
She likes the **job**.	She likes **to do the work**. [infinitive phrase—direct object]
He uses my room for **storage**.	He uses my room for **storing his auto parts**. [gerund phrase—object of a preposition]
He wants two things: **money** and **power**.	He wants two things: **to make money** and **to gain power**. [infinitive phrases in a compound appositive—see pages 57–58]

APPOSITIVE PHRASES

An **appositive phrase** identifies, explains, or supplements the meaning of the word it adjoins.

> Johnny cake, **a kind of cornbread**, is native to New England.

> Anthony Burgess, **one of the most prolific writers in the English-speaking world**, admits, "I might revise a page twenty times." —DONALD M. MURRAY

■ **Exercise 5** Underline the gerund phrases and the infinitive phrases (including any modifiers) used as nouns in the following sentences. Put a wavy line under any appositives.

1. Maintaining a daily exercise program is essential.
2. Angry and proud, Claire resolved to fight back.
3. To embrace the ideals of others to gain popularity is foolish.
4. All human acts—even saving a stranger from drowning or donating a million dollars to the poor—may ultimately be selfish.

5. Running along a crowded sidewalk, the boy, a danger to everyone, collided with an elderly woman.

(3) Phrases used as modifiers

Prepositional phrases nearly always function as adjectives or adverbs. *Infinitive phrases* are also used as adjectives or adverbs. *Participial phrases* are used as adjectives. *Absolute phrases* are used as adverbs. See also **sentence modifier**, in the **Glossary of Terms**.

ADJECTIVES	PHRASES USED AS ADJECTIVES
It was a **sad** day.	It was a day **for sadness**. [prepositional phrase]
A **destructive** riot erupted in the city.	**Destroying everything in its path**, a riot erupted in the city. [participial phrase containing a prepositional phrase]
My **wet** clothes felt cold.	**Drenched with water**, my clothes felt cold. [participial phrase containing a prepositional phrase]

ADVERBS	PHRASES USED AS ADVERBS
Drive **carefully**.	Drive **with care on wet streets**. [prepositional phrases]
She sang **joyfully**.	She sang **to express her joy**. [infinitive phrase]
Therefore, I could feel the warm sun on my face.	**My eyes closing against the glare**, I could feel the warm sun on my face. [see the **Glossary of Terms—absolute phrase**]

The preceding examples demonstrate how phrases function in the same way as single-word modifiers. Remember, however, that phrases are not merely substitutes for single words.

Phrases can express more than can be packed into a single word:

> The gas gauge fluttered **from empty to full**.
> He telephoned his wife **to tell her of his arrival**.
> The firefighters **hosing down the adjacent buildings** had very little standing room.

■ **Exercise 6** Underline each phrase in the following sentences. Then state whether the phrase functions as a noun, an adjective, an adverb, or an appositive.

1. I expect a job offer like that one only once in a lifetime.
2. Dazzled by Baryshnikov's speed and grace, the audience gave him a standing ovation.
3. Needing something to drink, I remembered the cola left over from the party.
4. The time for lavish spending is drawing to a close.
5. They answered carefully, one looking at the ceiling and the other gazing out the window.
6. A wave curling over the surfer swallowed him for a moment.
7. The skipper, a slender blond woman, swung the tiller sharply to starboard.
8. Not wanting to wait for the rest of us, Andrew went home in a cab.
9. She took the job to get a better salary and to move to a more pleasant area of the country.
10. My brother bought a second car, small but fuel efficient.

1e

Learn to recognize clauses.

A clause is a group of related words that contains a subject and a predicate.

(1) Independent clauses

Some clauses are independent units of expression and are called independent clauses or main clauses. An **independent clause** is an autonomous unit and can be punctuated as a sentence. (See **1f** and **3a**.) Every sentence contains at least one independent clause. The example below shows the subject in italics and the predicate in boldface.

My friend Maria **received the gold medal**.

(2) Subordinate clauses and conjunctions

Sentences may also contain subordinate or dependent clauses. A **subordinate clause** is a group of related words that contains a subject and a predicate and that begins with a word like *because, which,* or *who* (subordinate conjunction or relative pronoun—see list following). The wording of the subordinate clause prohibits it from standing independently.

Maria received the gold medal **because her performance was flawless**.

Subordinate clauses provide additional information about the independent clause and establish the relationship of the additional information to the independent clause. Unlike an independent clause, a subordinate clause is grammatically dependent and may function within a sentence as an adverb, an adjective, or a noun. It usually conveys less important information than the independent clause.

The last ship carrying passengers had recently arrived in the Ross Sea, **which was closed by ice most of the year**. [subordinate clause]

I had to leave the meeting early **because I became ill**. [adverb clause]

Simple illustrations, **which the instructor drew on the board**, explained the process. [adjective clause]

Geologists know **why earthquakes occur**. [noun clause—direct object]

The following conjunctions are commonly used to introduce, connect, and relate subordinate clauses to other words in the sentence.

Words commonly used as subordinating conjunctions:

after	inasmuch as	supposing that
although	in case that	than
as [far/soon] as	insofar as	though
as if	in that	till
as though	lest	unless
because	no matter how	until
before	now that	when, whenever
even if	once	where, wherever
even though	provided (that)	whether
how	since	while
if	so that	why

Relative pronouns also serve as markers of those subordinate clauses called *relative clauses* (see chapter **5**, page 55):

that	what	which	who, whoever
whom, whomever	whose		

SUBORDINATE CLAUSES USED AS NOUNS

NOUNS	NOUN CLAUSES
The **news** may be false.	**What the newspapers say** may be false. [subject]
I do not know his **address**.	I do not know **where he lives**. [direct object]
Give the tools to **Rita**.	Give the tools to **whoever can use them best**. [object of a preposition]
Karen's **protest** amazed me.	The fact **that Karen protested** amazed me. [appositive]

The conjunction *that* before a noun clause can be omitted when no confusion results.

I know **she is right**. [Compare "I know *that* she is right."]

SUBORDINATE CLAUSES USED AS MODIFIERS

Two types of subordinate clauses, the adjective clause and the adverb clause, serve as modifiers.

Adjective clauses   Any clause that modifies a noun or a pronoun is an adjective clause. Adjective clauses, which nearly always follow the words modified, usually begin with relative pronouns but may begin with words such as *when, where,* or *why.*

ADJECTIVES	ADJECTIVE CLAUSES
Everyone needs **loyal** friends.	Everyone needs friends **who are loyal**.
The **golden** window reflects the sun.	The window, **which shines like gold**, reflects the sun.
My sister lives in a **peaceful** town.	The town **where my sister lives** is peaceful.

If it is not used as a subject, the relative pronoun (*who, whom, that, which,* and so on) in an adjective clause may sometimes be omitted:

He is a man **I admire**.   [Compare "He is a man *whom I admire*."]

Adverb clauses   An adverb clause usually modifies a verb but may modify an adjective, an adverb, or even the rest of the sentence in which it appears. Adverb clauses are ordinarily introduced by subordinating conjunctions.

ADVERBS	ADVERB CLAUSES
Next, the disk controller failed.	**After I backed up my files**, the disk controller failed.
His popularity dropped **locally**.	His popularity dropped **where people knew him**.

24

The trip is **too** expensive for me.	The trip is more expensive **than I can afford**.
Figure the interest **very** carefully.	Figure the interest **as carefully as you can**.

Some adverb clauses may be elliptical. See also **25b**.

If I can save enough money, I'll go to Alaska next summer. **If not**, I'll take a trip to St. Louis. [Clearly implied words are omitted.]

■ **Exercise 7** Find the subordinate clauses in the following sentences (adapted from *Time* magazine), and label each as a noun clause, an adjective clause, or an adverb clause.

1. The candidate refused to endorse a policy that promised federal aid to the cities.
2. As the days grew shorter, her spirits darkened.
3. Both small nations claimed victory in the battle, which immediately became a symbol of the stalemated global war.
4. What excited scientists most was the unmistakable traces of dry riverbeds and deltas etched into the rocky Martian surface.
5. Some people think that if government agents were to enforce existing laws efficiently, the drug epidemic could be controlled.

■ **Exercise 8** Underline the independent clauses in the following paragraph by Anne Rivers Siddons (from *Outer Banks*). Put subordinate clauses in brackets.

¹We stood on the high green crown and looked down at the sea. ²A wooden walkway led from the porch down through the low, scrubby vegetation to the tan sand itself. ³The walkway was weathered to near-black like the house, and it snaked its way through drifts of sea oats, beach grass, and a dense, low matting of little running plants and flowers I could not name. ⁴The sand itself was powdery and soft, drifting like whipped cream and then melting into damp, packed flatness and finally a shining mirror where earth met water. ⁵The combers marched in stately and perfect, unhurried and unimpeded in their progress straight from Spain. ⁶The water, except where it broke white on the beach, was the deep true blue of gentians, or lapis lazuli. ⁷No one was on the beach below, and no sails broke the great, tossing blueness, and no sound but the hollow boom . . . hushhhh of the water and the bronze calling of gulls reached our ears. ⁸The wind was

straight off the sea and fresh and nearly chilly, blowing our hair straight back, but the sun on the backs of our necks and shoulders was still hot.

1f

Learn to recognize the forms and functions of sentences.

The form of a sentence is identified by the number and kinds of clauses it contains. The function of a sentence refers to its purpose.

(1) Think about sentences by examining their forms.

a. A **simple sentence** consists of a single independent clause:

> **I [subject] had lost my passport.**   [predicate containing verb and direct object]
>
> **I [subject] did** not **worry** about it.   [predicate containing verb and prepositional phrase]

b. A **compound sentence** consists of at least two independent clauses and no subordinate clauses:

> **I had lost my passport,** but **I did not worry about it**.   [A comma and a coordinating conjunction link the two independent clauses.]

c. A **complex sentence** has one independent clause and at least one subordinate clause:

> **Although I had lost my passport,** I did not worry about it.   [A subordinate clause—indicated here by *although* and followed by a comma (see **12b**)—precedes the independent clause.]
>
> I will not worry about my passport **unless I lose it**.   [The subordinate clause follows the independent clause, and *unless* signals a different relationship from *although*.]

d. A **compound–complex sentence** consists of at least two independent clauses and at least one subordinate clause:

When I lost my passport, **I ordered** a new one, but **I did** not **worry** about it. [*When* signals the subordinate clause; *but* connects the two independent clauses.]

(2) Think about sentences by examining their purposes or functions.

English sentences make statements (*declarative*), ask questions (*interrogative*), give commands or make requests (*imperative*), and make exclamations (*exclamatory*).

DECLARATIVE	She refused the offer. [statement]
IMPERATIVE	Refuse the offer! [request or command]
INTERROGATIVE	Did she refuse the offer? She refused, didn't she? She refused it? [questions]
EXCLAMATORY	What an offer! She refused it! [exclamations]

Be aware of the forms and functions of the sentences you read. Notice how writers use them to achieve particular effects (see also **30e**). In your own writing, think about what you want your readers to understand from each sentence, and make sure you have used the forms and functions that will express your thoughts most effectively.

■ **Exercise 9** Analyze the passage below, which has been adapted from the essay "Thinking as a Hobby" by William Golding: (1) Identify the form (simple, compound, complex, or compound–complex) and the function (declarative, interrogative, imperative, or exclamatory) of each sentence. (2) Underline the independent clauses. (3) Bracket subordinate clauses and identify whether they are noun, adjective, or adverb clauses.

¹Clearly there was something missing in me. ²Consider this: perhaps nature had endowed the rest of the human race with a sixth sense and left me out. ³This must be so, I mused, on my way back to the class, since whether I had broken a window, or failed to remember Boyle's Law, or been late for school, my teachers produced me one, adult answer: "Why can't you think?"
⁴As I saw the case, I had broken the window because I had tried to hit Jack Arney with a cricket ball and missed him; I could not remember

Boyle's Law because I had never bothered to learn it; and I was late for school because I preferred looking over the bridge into the river. [5]In fact, I was wicked! [6]Were my teachers, perhaps, so good that they could not understand the depths of my depravity? [7]Were they clear, untormented people who could direct their every action by this mysterious business of thinking? [8]I decided that the whole thing was incomprehensible.

■ **Exercise 10**   Write ten sentences of your own, constructing them so that you have written at least one simple sentence, two compound, three complex, and one compound–complex. Make sure that at least one of the sentences is declarative, one is interrogative, one is imperative, and one is exclamatory. Identify the main and subordinate clauses in your sentences, and label the subordinate clauses as noun, adjective, or adverb.

2

Sentence Fragments

Write complete sentences; revise ineffective fragments.

Although written as if it were a sentence, a **fragment** is only a part of a sentence—such as a phrase or a subordinate clause (see **1d–1e**).

FRAGMENTS	SENTENCES
Larry always working in his yard on Saturdays.	Larry always works in his yard on Saturdays.
Because he enjoys the flowers and shrubs.	He enjoys the flowers and shrubs.
Which help to screen his house from the street.	He enjoys the flowers and shrubs which help to screen his house from the street—
For example, a tall hedge with a border of petunias.	for example, a tall hedge with a border of petunias.

Fragments begin with a capital letter and end with a period. They can be effective in some writing situations, but complete sentences are usually easier to understand than fragments. Learn to revise fragments to make complete sentences.

Testing for and revising fragments   You can ask three questions to identify fragments in your writing:

1. Is there a verb? If not, supply one or attach the fragment to a related sentence (**2a**). Remember, a verbal is not a verb.
2. Is there a subject? If not, supply one or attach the fragment to a related sentence (**2a**).
3. Is there a subordinating conjunction? If so, remove it or attach the subordinate clause to a related sentence (**2b**).

Occasionally, writers deliberately use fragments for emphasis. For example, writing that mirrors speech often contains grammatically incomplete sentences or expressions. Similarly, exclamations and answers to questions are often single words, phrases, or subordinate clauses written as sentences.

> **Understand**?   [question with implied subject (*you*), informal use]

> **Unbelievable! No pain**, **no gain**.   [exclamation and phrases, informal use]

> Why does Camilla's radio always play classic rock? **Because that is her favorite kind of music**.   [subordinate clause, answer to question, informal use]

> I don't remember a world without language. From the time of my earliest childhood, there was language. **Always language, and imagination**, **speculation**, **utters of sound**. **Words**, **beginnings of words**. —SIMON J. ORTIZ [Phrases, literary use—note how repetition links the first fragment to the preceding sentence and telegraphs Ortiz's emphasis in the second fragment.]

> What I most remember is certain moments, revelations, epiphanies, in which the sensuous little savage that I then was came face to face with the universe. **And blinked**.
> —WALLACE STEGNER

▲ Caution: Have a good reason for any sentence fragment you allow to stand.

2a

Revise phrases punctuated as sentences.

Verbal phrases, prepositional phrases, parts of a compound predicate, and appositives are sometimes written as fragments. Revise them in one of the ways demonstrated below.

How to Revise Phrases Written as Sentences

FRAGMENTS IN CONTEXT

Archaeologists excavating ancient cities carefully brush dirt from the artifacts. *Using paintbrushes for that purpose.* [verbal (participial) phrase—no subject or verb]

Later, Raymond began to tap out the rhythm. *First on the table and then on the counter.* [prepositional phrase—no subject or verb]

Mai was the first woman to be elected president of her class. *And tapped for Mortar Board.* [part of a compound predicate—no subject]

My department is looking for a new teacher. *Preferably a writing teacher.* [appositive phrase—no subject or verb]

FRAGMENT   REVISION

1. Supply missing elements.

Using paintbrushes for that purpose.

They used paintbrushes for that purpose. [subject and verb supplied]

First on the table and then on the counter.

First **he tapped** on the table and then on the counter. [subject and verb supplied]

| And tapped for Mortar Board. | **She** was also tapped for Mortar Board. [subject supplied] |
| Preferably a writing teacher. | **We prefer** a writing teacher. [subject and verb supplied] |

2. Attach the fragment to a related existing sentence.

Using paintbrushes for that purpose.	Archaeologists excavating ancient cities carefully brush dirt from artifacts **using paintbrushes for that purpose**.
First on the table and then on the counter.	Later, Raymond began to tap out the rhythm, **first on the table and then on the counter**.
And tapped for Mortar Board.	Mai was the first woman to be elected president of her class **and tapped for Mortar Board**.
Preferably a writing teacher.	My department is looking for a new teacher, **preferably a writing teacher**.

■ **Exercise 1**   Revise each item below to eliminate the sentence fragment either by including it in the related sentence or by supplying missing information to make it into a sentence. Explain why you chose to revise as you did in each case. If any fragment does not require revision, explain your reason for allowing it to stand.

1. Trying to reduce my business expenses. I took a computer repair course.
2. The committee considered the proposal. Establishing a subcommittee.
3. Her hair stringy and her face smudged. Toni stumbled in the door.
4. Sexist language has a negative effect. Not only on women but also on men.
5. I smiled at the supervisor who insulted me. Against my nature, but necessary.

2b

Revise clauses punctuated as sentences.

Subordinate clauses are sometimes mistakenly written as sentences. You can revise these clauses by removing the subordinate conjunction, by attaching them to the sentence they logically belong with, or by reducing the clause to a single-word modifier (see chapter **4**).

How to Revise Clauses Written as Sentences

FRAGMENTS IN CONTEXT

After they understood the environmentalists' concerns. Thousands of people began to recycle their garbage.   [detached adverb clause]

Carol and I tried to follow Michael's map. *Which was sketchy and confusing.*   [detached adjective clause]

FRAGMENT	REVISION

1. Remove the subordinating conjunction.

After they understood the environmentalists' concerns. Which was sketchy and confusing.	They understood the environmentalists' concerns. It was sketchy and confusing. [*which* removed and subject supplied]

2. Attach the fragment to a related sentence.

After they understood the environmentalists' concerns.	**After they understood the environmentalists' concerns**, thousands of people began to recycle their garbage.
Which was sketchy and confusing.	Carol and I tried to follow Michael's map**, which was sketchy and confusing**.

3. *Reduce the fragment to single-word modifiers and include in the related sentence.*

Which was sketchy and confusing.	Carol and I tried to follow Michael's **sketchy**, **confusing** map.

■ **Exercise 2**   Revise each item below to eliminate the sentence fragment by following one of the three methods in **2b**. Explain why you chose to revise as you did in each case.

1. After I discovered I liked enchiladas. I decided to give burritos a try.
2. Demanding fines for owners who do not comply. Dudley claims that pets should be neutered.
3. Our campus recently endured the latest flu epidemic. Which affected class attendance.
4. I get sick. Whenever I smell exhaust fumes. And whenever I eat macadamia nuts.
5. Marilyn tried to send me a fax. Because she found the information I desperately needed.

■ **Exercise 3**   The paragraph below, altered from a passage in *Discover*, contains seven fragments. Follow the guidelines in **2a** and **2b** to revise the paragraph so it contains no fragments. Give your reasons for revising each fragment as you did.

[1]Most green things—frogs, leaves, army trucks—owe their emerald cast to pigments, chemicals that absorb less green light. [2]Not just reflecting more of it than they do any other wavelength. [3]The green solar flash, the green thunderstorms that turn up once in a while in the late afternoon, and the green icebergs occasionally seen by polar explorers. [4]These are a bit more complex. [5]The green flash isn't quite as spectacular as some people think. [6]Though it is memorable if you're lucky enough to see it. [7]You're not likely to forget it. [8]Some people report seeing a huge ray shooting up from the sun. [9]But that's really not what happened. [10]The atmosphere behaved like a prism. [11]Peeling apart full-spectrum sunlight and revealing its constituent colors. [12]The glass prism that we all know from junior high school science classes. [13]It refracts, or bends, light. [14]Light bending at the edges of the prism where it crosses the boundary between glass and air. [15]Light slows down upon entering the glass. [16]Because glass is denser than air.

3

Comma Splice and Fused Sentence

Join independent clauses with a coordinating conjunction or a semicolon to prevent misreading and to show relationships clearly.

A **comma splice** consists of two (or more) independent clauses joined simply by a comma. It is an error in punctuation that occurs only in compound or compound–complex sentences. A **fused sentence** (also called a *comma fault* or *run-on sentence*) occurs when neither a conjunction nor appropriate punctuation joins two independent clauses.

COMMA SPLICE   The wind was cold, they decided not to walk.
FUSED SENTENCE   The wind was cold they decided not to walk.

Correct comma splices or fused sentences either by separating the clauses or by joining and showing the relationship between them.

To separate:

1. Separate independent clauses by placing a period after each clause:

The wind was cold. They decided not to walk.

2. Separate independent clauses with a semicolon (see **14a**):

The wind was cold; they decided not to walk.

When you use the second method of revision, keep in mind that the semicolon relates but keeps separate two grammatically equal units of thought: **SUBJECT + PREDICATE; SUBJECT + PREDICATE**. As you check for comma splices and make revisions, do not overuse the semicolon or use it between parts of unequal grammatical rank: see **14c**.

To link and relate:

3. Insert a comma before the appropriate coordinating conjunction (*and, but, or, nor, for, so, yet*—see **12a**):

The wind was cold**, so** they decided not to walk.
They decided not to walk**, for** the wind was cold.

4. Make one clause subordinate to the other (see **12b**):

The wind was so cold **that** they decided not to walk.
Because the wind was cold**,** they decided not to walk.

5. Reduce one of the clauses to an introductory phrase (see **25b**):

Because of the cold wind, they decided not to walk.

If you cannot always recognize an independent clause and distinguish it from a phrase or a subordinate clause, study chapter **1**, especially **1d–1e**.

▲ Note: Contrary to American practice, British usage commonly links independent clauses with a comma.

■ **Exercise 1** Connect each pair of the following sentences in four ways: separate them with a semicolon, join them with a coordinating conjunction, make one subordinate, and reduce one to an introductory phrase.

EXAMPLE
They should have walked a mile every day. That would have improved their physical fitness.

a. *They should have walked a mile every day; that would have improved their physical fitness.*
b. *They should have walked a mile every day, and that would have improved their physical fitness.*
c. *If they had walked a mile every day, they would have improved their physical fitness.*
d. *To improve their physical fitness, they should have walked a mile every day.*

1. There used to be turtles in that pond. I remember seeing them when I was a child.
2. He may haggle fiercely over details. He also has the best interests of this project firmly in mind.
3. My sister likes to read. I sent her a book for her birthday.
4. Kim plans to buy a new computer. She has already researched which ones are the best buy.
5. I enjoy watching movies on television. I resent having to pay for cable service.

3a

Use a comma between independent clauses *only* when they are linked by a coordinating conjunction (*and, but, or, for, nor, so, yet*). See also **12a.**

COMMA SPLICE   Women's roles have changed radically in recent decades, women are now a larger percentage of the work force.

REVISED   Women's roles have changed radically in recent decades, **for** women are now a larger percentage of the work force.   [coordinating conjunction *for* added after the comma]

OR   Women's roles have changed radically in recent decades; women are now a larger percentage of the work force.   [A semicolon separates the independent clauses. See also the fused sentence examples on pages 38, 40, and **14a.**]

COMMA SPLICE   He was not an outstanding success at his first job, he was not a complete failure either.

REVISED   He was not an outstanding success at his first job, **nor** was he a complete failure.   [Note the shift in the word order of subject and verb after the coordinating conjunction *nor*.]

OR   He was **neither** an outstanding success at his first job **nor** a complete failure.   [a simple sentence with a compound complement]

COMMA SPLICE   I ran over some broken glass in the parking lot, it did not puncture my tires.

REVISED   I ran over some broken glass in the parking lot, **but** it did not puncture my tires.   [the coordinating conjunction *but* added after the comma]

OR   **Although** I ran over some broken glass in the parking lot, it did not puncture my tires.   [Addition of *although* makes the first clause subordinate: see **12b(1)**.]

To avoid a fused sentence, use a period or a semicolon between independent clauses not linked by a coordinating conjunction.

FUSED   She wrote him a love letter he answered it in person.

REVISED   She wrote him a love letter. **He** answered it in person.   [each independent clause written as a sentence]

OR   She wrote him a love letter; he answered it in person.   [independent clauses separated by a semicolon: see **14a**]

▲ **Exception:** Either a comma or a semicolon may be used between short independent clauses not linked by a coordinating conjunction when the clauses are parallel in form and unified in thought. The comma emphasizes similarity; the semicolon, difference.

School bores them, preaching bores them, even television bores them.   —ARTHUR MILLER

One is the reality; the other is the symbol.   —NANCY HALE

The comma is also used to separate a statement from a tag question.

You can come, can't you? He rides a bike, doesn't he?
They couldn't be wrong, could they—not all those millions!

—WILLIAM GOLDING

■ **Exercise 2** Use a subordinating conjunction (see the list on page 23) to combine each of the five pairs of sentences in Exercise 1. For the use of the comma, see above or refer to **12b**.

EXAMPLE
Because it would have improved their physical fitness, they should have walked a mile every day.

■ **Exercise 3** Read the following sentences (adapted from *Natural History* and *Omni*). Place a check mark after a sentence with a comma splice and an X after a fused sentence. Do not mark correctly punctuated sentences.

1. In this method, a drawing was made on a plank of hardwood, the wood was cut away around it.
2. Life requires critical thinking skills, the ability to express yourself, persuade, argue, and build. That is what we need to teach students.
3. The mammals are partial to peanut butter and rolled oats, which we used to lure them into our live traps.
4. Mathematics has always been applicable to nature this may express a deep link between our minds and nature.
5. Dave clattered down the steps and went across the concrete to the terminal, at the entrance a soldier checked his ID before waving him on.
6. The ringleaders abandoned the cub they had attacked we stayed with the dying cub to follow its fate.
7. Today almost 60,000 tourists a year come to the Galapagos Islands to gawk at the birds, and almost everybody shoots several rolls of film.
8. Lichens and mushrooms create a soft, spongy mat, larger plants slowly invade their territory.
9. Between the islands of North and South Bimini is a five-mile long, two-mile wide lagoon except for the deep waters near Alicetown, the lagoon averages about three feet deep.
10. One afternoon I was searching for sharks from an airboat, a flat-bottomed craft capable of operating in only a few inches of water, even with plugs of wax jammed deep in my ears, the roar of the engine behind my head was deafening.

■ **Exercise 4** Use various methods (see pages 35–38) to revise the comma splices or fused sentences in Exercise 3.

3b

Use a semicolon before a conjunctive adverb or transitional phrase that is placed between independent clauses. See also **14a.**

> COMMA SPLICE   Sexual harassment is not just a women's issue, after all, men can be sexually harassed too.
>
> REVISED   Sexual harassment is not just a women's issue; **after all**, men can be sexually harassed too. [INDEPENDENT CLAUSE; *transitional phrase*, INDEPENDENT CLAUSE.]
>
> FUSED SENTENCE   The nineteenth-century European imperialists left arbitrarily drawn boundaries in Africa therefore, each country is composed of a mix of languages and cultures.
>
> REVISED   The nineteenth-century European imperialists left arbitrarily drawn boundaries in Africa; **therefore**, each country is composed of a mix of languages and cultures. [INDEPENDENT CLAUSE; *conjunctive adverb*, INDEPENDENT CLAUSE.]

Below is a list of frequently used conjunctive adverbs and transitional phrases.

Conjunctive adverbs:

also	however	next
anyhow	incidentally	nonetheless
anyway	indeed	otherwise
beside	instead	similarly
consequently	likewise	still
finally	meanwhile	then
furthermore	moreover	therefore
hence	nevertheless	thus

Transitional phrases:

after all	even so	in the second place
as a result	for example	on the contrary
at any rate	in addition	on the other hand
at the same time	in fact	
by the way	in other words	

Unlike a coordinating conjunction, which has a fixed position between the independent clauses it links, many conjunctive adverbs and transitional phrases may either begin the second independent clause or take another position in it. See also **32b(4)**.

> She believed daily exercise has many benefits**; however,** she couldn't fit it in to her schedule.   [The conjunctive adverb begins the second independent clause. See also **14a**, page 147.]
>
> She believed daily exercise has many benefits; she couldn't**,** however, fit it in to her schedule.   [The conjunctive adverb (set off by commas) appears later in the clause.]

> COMPARE   She believed daily exercise has many benefits, **but** she couldn't fit it in to her schedule.   [The coordinating conjunction has a fixed position.]

■ **Exercise 5**   Write five correctly punctuated compound sentences using various conjunctive adverbs and transitional phrases to connect and relate independent clauses.

3c

Do not let a divided quotation trick you into making a comma splice. See also **16a**.

> COMMA SPLICE   "Who won the lottery?" he asked, "how much money was in the pot?"
>
> REVISED   "Who won the lottery?" he asked**.** "**H**ow much money was in the pot?"

COMMA SPLICE   "Injustice is relatively easy to bear," says
Mencken, "it is justice that hurts."

REVISED   "Injustice is relatively easy to bear," says Mencken;
"it is justice that hurts."

■ **Exercise 6** Divide the following quotations without creating a
comma splice, as shown in the example below.

EXAMPLE

COMMA SPLICE   W. C. Fields once said, "I am free of all prejudice, I hate everyone equally."

REVISED   "I am free of all prejudice," W. C. Fields once said.
"I hate everyone equally."

1. "The cartoonists, of course, have the best arrangement. If they
   don't like a character, they just tear it up," the director observed.
2. Abraham Lincoln is supposed to have said, "You can fool all of the
   people some of the time and some of the people all of the time.
   But you can't fool all of the people all of the time."
3. "I know of no successful surgical procedure that will replace maca-
   roni in the spine with a rigid backbone. This is strickly a do-it-
   yourself project," says Ann Landers.
4. According to Harrison E. Salisbury, "There is no shortcut to life. To
   the end of our days, life is a lesson imperfectly learned."
5. John Kenneth Galbraith commented, "Money is a singular thing. It
   ranks with love as man's greatest source of joy—and with death
   as his greatest source of anxiety."

■ **Exercise 7** Comma splices and fused sentences have been incorporated into the following paragraph based on an interview in which
TV Guide asked Vanessa Williams to comment upon what she watches
on television. Indicate how the comma splices and fused sentences
could be revised, and mark sentences that need no revision with a
check mark.

[1]"I really like game shows and talk shows, I watch *Jeopardy!, Scrab-
ble,* and *Wheel of Fortune* because they use my mind.   [2]I watch Sally,
Oprah, Phil, and Geraldo because the topics are either really informative
or so bizarre that it's hard to pull away.   [3]When I was pregnant, I
watched Lifetime's *What Every Baby Knows* so many child-rearing
shows focus on what can go wrong, this one was the only one that
explained what to expect, for instance, on your first visit to a pediatrician.

⁴I watch music videos it's a good way to evaluate directors I'd like to work with.   ⁵There's not one series or soap opera I watch religiously. ⁶My agent would like me to do a part on *L.A. Law* I've seen it, but I can't name the characters."

■ **Exercise 8** First review chapter **2** and study chapter **3**. Then identify and mark the sentence fragments (SF), comma splices (CS), and fused sentences (FS) in the following items. Next, write down why you classified them as you did, and finally make the appropriate revisions. Put a check mark after each sentence that needs no revision.

1. We sold our property, then we bought a motor home for touring the country.
2. The little convertible comfortably holds four people six are riding in it now. Not to mention all their packages and books.
3. Malcolm X was assassinated two years before Robert Kennedy was, however the assassinations occurred for different reasons.
4. Writers should avoid sexist language, it is usually easy to do so.
5. Wallace Stevens, the poet, walked to work at the insurance company where he was an executive.
6. Most of my professors require students to be on time for classes. The reason being that students who come in late disturb the other students.
7. Toni Morrison's newest novel ought to be made into a movie, if the studios can get permission.
8. The company surely has a policy against nepotism, this is defined as "hiring your relatives."
9. It was difficult. Almost impossible. An experiment that was doomed from the start.
10. During the summers, I used to work at a book store. Usually stocking shelves and running the cash register, but never getting to indulge my passion for reading.

4
Adjectives and Adverbs

Distinguish between adjectives and adverbs. Use the conventional forms.

Adjectives and adverbs are modifiers and make writing lively. Modifiers qualify, restrict, or intensify the meaning of other words. They also describe degrees of comparison. **Adjectives** modify nouns and pronouns, and **adverbs** modify verbs, adjectives, or other adverbs.

ADJECTIVES

a **quick** review
a **brief, dramatic** pause
armed squads
She looked **angry**.
the **best qualified** person

ADVERBS

reviewed **quickly**
a **briefly** dramatic pause
very heavily armed squads
She looked **angrily** at me.
saw **more clearly**

Adverbs commonly describe how (manner), where (place), or when (time) the action occurred.

MANNER   We proceeded **carefully**.
PLACE   We walked **there**.
TIME   Alex woke up **early**.

Adverbs may also modify verbals (gerunds, infinitives, participles) or even whole clauses; see **1c**, page 14. Whole clauses can even function as adverbs. See **1e**, page 24.

> *When my family visited my aunt's house in San Francisco*, my grandmother would search for me among my many cousins.
> —RICHARD RODRIGUEZ
> [an adverbial clause of time modifying the verb *would search*]

The *-ly* ending can be an adjective-forming suffix as well as an adverb-forming one.

NOUNS TO ADJECTIVES   cost–costly, hour–hourly
ADJECTIVES TO ADVERBS   correct–correctly, light–lightly

A number of words ending in *-ly* (such as *deadly, cowardly*), as well as many not ending in *-ly* (such as *far, fast, little, well*), may function either as adjectives or as adverbs. Some adverbs have two forms (such as *quick, quickly; slow, slowly; loud* and *clear, loudly* and *clearly*).

When in doubt about the correct form of a modifier, consult your dictionary. Look for the labels *adj.* and *adv.*, for examples of usage, and for any usage notes.

▲ Caution: Adjectives and adverbs are always singular in form: yellow (NOT yellows) daffodils.

4a

Use adverbs to modify verbs, adjectives, and other adverbs.

NOT   Leela played her part **perfect**.
USE   Leela played her part **perfectly**.   [The adverb *perfectly* modifies the verb *played*.]

NOT   The plane departs at a reasonable early hour.
USE   The plane departs at a **reasonably** early hour.   [The adverb *reasonably* modifies the adjective *early*.]

Most dictionaries still label the following as informal usage: *sure* for *surely*, *real* for *really*, and *good* for the adverb *well*.

INFORMAL   The Broncos played **real good** during the first quarter.

FORMAL   The Broncos played **very well** during the first quarter. [appropriate in both formal and informal usage—see also **19b**]

■ **Exercise 1**   In the phrases below, convert adjectives into adverbs, following the pattern of the examples.

EXAMPLE
careless laugh–*laughed carelessly*   [OR *carelessly laughed*]

1. prompt answer
2. abrupt reply
3. regular visit
4. calm reminder
5. special belief
6. belated reward

EXAMPLE
former prosperity–*formerly prosperous*

7. recent graduate
8. near possibility
9. total recall
10. complete happiness

■ **Exercise 2**   In the following sentences, convert any informal or unacceptable modifier into an adverb acceptable in college writing. Put a check mark after each sentence that needs no revision.

1. When I have to balance my checkbook, the pocket calculator surely does help.
2. They ran very swift.
3. Our national famous team played well but did not win.
4. They were lucky to escape as easy as they did.
5. I don't sleep as regular as I would like with my new schedule.
6. The storm hit very sudden.
7. I get all mixed up when I have to work that rapid.
8. Maria is exceptional intelligent.
9. He dances most graceful when the music is slow.
10. They were well-trained and swam good.

4b

Distinguish between adverbs used to modify the verb and adjectives used as subject or object complements.

NOT   Don tied the rope tight to the tree.
USE   Don tied the rope **tightly** to the tree.   [The adverb *tightly* modifies the verb *tied*.]

NOT   The lilacs smell sweetly.
USE   The lilacs smell **sweet**.   [The adjective *sweet* is a subject complement and modifies *lilacs*.]

NOT   Trina feels badly.
USE   Trina feels **bad**.   [Meaning "Trina feels ill," the adjective *bad* is a subject complement and modifies *Trina*.]

Subject complements (usually adjectives, nouns, or pronouns) refer to the subject, but they are part of the predicate and help to complete the meaning of linking verbs—such as the sense verbs *feel, look, smell, sound,* and *taste,* and forms of the verb *be.*

Eleanor's birthday cake smelled **good**.   [The adjective *good*, a subject complement, modifies the subject *cake*.]

I felt as intensely **Mexican** as I shall ever feel.
                     —ENRIQUE "HANK" LOPEZ
[The adjective *Mexican*, a subject complement, modifies the subject *I*.]

Object complements (usually adjectives or nouns) modify the direct object as they help to complete the meaning of such verbs as *make, name, elect, call, find, consider.*

They elected Collette **president**.   [The noun *president* refers to the direct object *Collette* and completes the meaning of the verb *elected*.]

Either an adverb or an adjective may follow a direct object; the choice depends on meaning, on the word modified:

Anne considered Morris **angrily**.   [The adverb *angrily* modifies the verb *considered*.]

Anne considered Morris **angry**.   [An object complement, *angry* modifies the noun *Morris*.]

▲ Caution: Do not omit the *-d* or *-ed* of a past participle as an adjective. (See also **7a**, page 83.)

Among these ritual activities is always included a number of speeches . . . specially **composed** for the occasion.
—S. I. HAYAKAWA

■ **Exercise 3**   Using adjectives as complements, write two sentences that illustrate each of the following patterns.

> **Subject + linking verb + subject complement.**
> **Subject + verb + direct object + object complement.**

■ **Exercise 4**   Look up each pair of the following modifiers in your dictionary. Give special attention to specific examples of usage and to any usage notes. Then write sentences of your own to illustrate the formal use of each modifier.

EXAMPLE
    bad, badly–*I felt bad. I played badly.*

1. slow, slowly
2. real, really
3. awful, awfully
4. good, well
5. most, mostly
6. quick, quickly

4c

Use the correct comparative and superlative forms of adjectives and adverbs. See also **22c**.

Many adjectives and adverbs change form to indicate degree of comparison. Generally, shorter adjectives (and a few adverbs) form their comparative degree by adding *-er* and the superlative by adding *-est*.

young, younger, youngest
quick, quicker, quickest

Most two-syllable adjectives with stress on the first syllable also form their comparative or superlative by adding *-er* or *-est*. (For words whose base form ends in *-y*, change the *-y* to *-i* when adding the comparative or superlative ending—see **18d[3]**.)

> sturdy, sturdier, sturdiest

Longer adjectives and most adverbs form the comparative by the use of *more* (or *less*) and the superlative by the use of *most* (or *least*).

> fortunate, more/less fortunate, most/least fortunate
> rapidly, more/less rapidly, most/least rapidly

A few common modifiers have irregular forms.

> little, less, least
> good/well, better, best
> bad/badly, worse, worst
> far, further/farther, furthest/farthest [See the **Glossary of Usage**.]

Consult your dictionary when you are not sure.

(1) Use the comparative to denote a greater degree or to refer to two in a comparison.

> The metropolitan area is much **bigger** now than it was five years ago.
> Bert can run **faster** than his father.
> Dried apples are **more** nutritious per pound than fresh apples. [a comparison of two groups]
>
> **More** embittered than ever, the chief demanded that Joseph halt the march in Rocky Canyon and hold a council.
> —DEE BROWN

Make sure to complete the comparison; always make clear what the subject is being compared with. Note in the examples how the conjunction *than* signals the second element being compared.

With the use of *other*, the comparative form may refer to more than two.

> Bert can run **faster** than the *other* players.

▲ **Note:** In certain expressions, no degree is intended although the comparative form is used: *outer* space, *higher* mathematics, *lower* Manhattan.

(2) Use the superlative to denote the greatest degree or to refer to three or more in a comparison.

> The interests of the family are **best** served by open communication.

> Bert is the **fastest** of the three runners.
> OR   Bert is the **fastest** runner of all.

The superlative occasionally refers to two, as in "Put your *best* foot forward!"

▲ **Note:** Usage, however illogical it may seem, accepts comparisons of many adjectives or adverbs with absolute meanings, such as "a *more perfect* society," "the *deadest* campus," and "*less completely* exhausted." But many writers make an exception of *unique*—using "*more nearly* unique" rather than "more unique." They consider *unique* an absolute adjective—one without degrees of comparison.

(3) Use a single comparative rather than a double comparative or superlative.

> NOT   Our swimming hole is much more shallower than Crystal Lake. [double comparative: *-er* and *more*]
> USE   Our swimming hole is **much shallower** than Crystal Lake. [a single comparative: *shallower*]
> NOT   That was the most funniest movie. [double superlative: *-est* and *most*]

USE   That was the **funniest** movie.   [a single superlative: *funniest*]

■ **Exercise 5**   Give the comparative and superlative forms of each adjective or adverb.

1. warm
2. slowly
3. thirsty
4. happy
5. ill
6. active
7. realistically
8. helpful
9. slow
10. hollow

■ **Exercise 6**   Provide the appropriate comparative or superlative form of the modifier given in parentheses.

[1]"This fish weighs (little) than the one I caught yesterday," Uncle Verne said as he reeled in his line.   [2]"But this isn't the (bad) day for fishing."   [3]Uncle Verne, a veteran fisherman, finds the silver shad the (useful) lure available for catching bass.   [4]A (lively) bait has never before been produced.   [5]Its movement attracts even the (tiny) of bass.   [6]Of course, Uncle Verne hopes to haul in the (big) fish of all; however, at times one must be prepared to deal with the (small) fish.   [7]When a big bass strikes at the bait, only the (strong) fisherman will be able to fight the battle.   [8]Although, physically, Uncle Verne appears to be the (weak) fisherman in the boat, when the catch is weighed at the end of the day, there is no doubt he is good.

4d

Avoid awkward or ambiguous use of a noun form as an adjective.

Many noun forms effectively modify other nouns (as in *reference* manual, *windfall profits* tax, *House Ways and Means* Committee), especially when appropriate adjectives are not available. Avoid such forms, however, when they are awkward or confusing.

AWKWARD   Many candidates entered the president race.

BETTER   Many candidates entered the presidential race.

CONFUSING   The Representative Landor recess maneuvers led to victory.

BETTER   Representative Landor's maneuvers during the recess led to victory.

4e

Use a single rather than a double negative.

The term **double negative** refers to the use of two negatives within a clause to express a single negation. Like the double comparison, the double negative is grammatically redundant. It should be avoided in formal written English.

NOT   He did not keep no records.   [double negative: *not* and *no*]

USE   He did **not** keep any records.   [one negative: *not*]

OR   He kept **no** records.   [one negative: *no*]

NOT   Nobody couldn't help him.   Couldn't nobody help him.   [double negative: *nobody* and *-n't*]

USE   **Nobody** could help him.   [one negative: *nobody*]

Because *hardly, barely,* and *scarcely* already denote severely limited or negative conditions, use of *not, nothing,* or *without* with these modifiers creates a double negative.

NOT   I couldn't hardly quit in the middle of the job.

USE   I **could hardly** quit in the middle of the job.

NOT   The motion passed with not scarcely a protest.

USE   The motion passed with **scarcely** a protest.

The occasional use of two negatives to express a positive meaning can be effective when used carefully.

We **cannot** afford to ask **nobody** from the commission.   [Compare: We must ask somebody from the commission.]

▲ **Note:** Many writers consider the idiom "*cannot help but disagree*" a regionalism (see page 202) and substitute "*cannot help disagreeing*" or "*cannot but disagree.*"

■ **Exercise 7** Eliminate double negatives in the following sentences.

1. I don't have no money.
2. It was so crowded I couldn't hardly move.
3. They never tried nothing new.
4. We needed money, but nobody didn't have none.
5. The team didn't scarcely have any money left.

4f

Follow a specific order for cumulative adjectives.

Writers often use up to three adjectives to modify a noun. English requires that the adjectives be placed in the following order: article or enumerator, value, size, shape, age, color, nation, faith, material, noun used as adjective.

> some dedicated Vietnamese students
> their faded antique quilt
> a granite kitchen counter

■ **Exercise 8** After you have reread rules **4a** through **4e** and have studied the examples, correct all errors in the use of adjectives or adverbs in the sentences below. Also eliminate any awkward use of nouns as adjectives. Put a check mark after any sentence that needs no revision.

1. She is short and fast and plays good.
2. Adding chopped onions and green fiery fresh jalapeño peppers to the chili makes it taste real well.
3. According to the National Weather Service, September is suppose to be our wettest month.
4. It was easy the largest deficit in history.
5. Although today's TV news was relatively unbias, it was more duller than usual.
6. The repair estimates person had left for the day.
7. It seems as though I have to study harder than I use to.
8. My friend Carlos is much contenter now that he has a best job.
9. A spelling match between fourth and fifth graders is usually close.
10. Detective novel authors like to make young petite innocent female characters look suspicious.

5

Case

Choose the case form that shows the function of nouns and pronouns in sentences.

Case refers to the form of a noun or pronoun that shows its relation to other words in a sentence. For example, the different case forms of the boldfaced pronouns below, all referring to the same person, show their different uses.

> **I** [the subject] believe that **my** [modifier] uncle will help **me** [direct object].

I, being the subject, is in the *subjective* (or nominative) case; *my,* showing possession, is in the *possessive* (or genitive) case; and *me,* being the object, is in the *objective* case.

The personal pronouns Personal pronouns identify the speaker (first person: *I, we*), the person spoken to (second person: *you*), and the person or thing spoken about (third person: *he, she, it*). As you study the following table, observe that the pronouns *I, we, he, she, they,* and *who* have distinctive forms for all three cases and for both singular and plural number. Note that *you* and *it* are the same in both singular and plural and change case form only in the possessive.

	SINGULAR	PLURAL
SUBJECTIVE	I	we
	you	you
	he, she, it	they, it
POSSESSIVE	my, mine	our, ours
	your, yours	your, yours
	his, her, its	their, theirs
OBJECTIVE	me	us
	you	you
	him, her, it	them

The pronouns *my, our, your, him, her, it,* and *them* combine with *-self* or *-selves* to become **intensive/reflexive pronouns** (see the **Glossary of Terms**). Formal English does not accept *myself* as a substitute for *I* or *me*.

John and **I** [NOT myself] work at the gas station.

▲ **Note:** *Hisself* and *theirselves,* although the logical forms for the reflexive pronouns (possessive plus *-self* as in *myself, yourself, herself*), are not accepted in formal English; use *himself, themselves.*

Bill lives by **himself**. [NOT hisself]
They live by **themselves**. [NOT theirselves]

The relative pronouns Relative pronouns (*who, whom, which, whose,* and *that*) introduce clauses that refer to a noun in the main clause.

Julieta, **who** is my sister, lives in Atlanta.

Who, whose, and *whom* ordinarily refer to people; *which* to things; and *that* to either. The possessive pronoun *whose* (in lieu of an awkward *of which*) sometimes refers to things:

The poem, **whose** author is unknown, has recently been set to music.

SINGULAR OR PLURAL

SUBJECTIVE	who, which, that
POSSESSIVE	whose, that
OBJECTIVE	whom, which, that

See also **1d** and **12d**.

Use of case The subject of a verb and the subject complement are in the **subjective case**.

SUBJECTIVE	**He** left early. **Who** noticed? [subjects of verbs]
	It was **I** on the phone. [subject complement— Compare "*I* was on the phone."]

▲ Caution: Do not omit a pronoun that is the subject of a sentence.

Modifiers that indicate ownership or a comparable relationship are in the **possessive case**. A few possessive pronouns (such as *mine* and *theirs*) take the position and function of nouns.

POSSESSIVE	**Their** dog likes **its** new food. [modifier]
	That book is **yours**. [subject complement]

Nouns and some indefinite pronouns (such as *everyone, anyone*) have a distinctive form only in the possessive case: *a student's opinion, the students' opinions, everyone's vote.* See **15a**.

▲ Caution: Use *their* not *they* to show possession: their book, NOT they book.

The object of a verb, verbal, or preposition is in the **objective case**.

OBJECTIVE	Marcella blamed **me**. [direct object]
	Telephoning **them** is a nuisance. [object of verbal]
	I gave **him** the book. [indirect object]
	To **whom** was it addressed? [object of preposition]

5a

Be aware of case forms for pronouns in compound constructions.

For *multiple subjects or subject complements,* use the subjective case.

> **She and her father** buy groceries on Saturday morning.
> I thought **he or Dad** would come to my rescue.
> It was **Maria and I** who solved the problem.   [See **5f.**]

As a matter of courtesy rather than emphasis, place first-person pronouns last in a compound construction.

> NOT   Me and Ricardo are good friends.
> USE   **Ricardo and I** are good friends.

For *multiple objects of prepositions,* use the objective case.

> between **Merrill and me**   [NOT between Merrill and I]
> with **Lesley and me**   [NOT with Lesley and I]

▲ Note: You can test the case of a pronoun after a preposition by eliminating the accompanying noun or pronoun.

> Gabriel gave it to (Edwyn and) **me**.

For *multiple objects of verbs or verbals* and *subjects of infinitives,* use the objective case.

> Clara may appoint **you or me**.   [direct object]
> They lent **Tom and her** ten dollars.   [indirect object]
> He gets nowhere by scolding **Bea or him**.   [object of gerund]
> Dad wanted **Sue and me** to keep the old car.   [subject of infinitive]

For *appositives,* use the same case as the noun they refer to. See **12d(1).**

> Two team players, **she and I**, helped the coach.   [Compare "*She and I* helped the coach."]

The coach called on two team players, **him and me**, to help Jim. [Compare "The coach called on *him and me* to help Jim."]

Let's just **you and me** help the coach. [Compare "*Let just me help the coach.*"]

Do not let an appositive following *we* or *us* cause you to choose the wrong form.

NOT   Us students need this.

USE   **We** students need this. [Compare "We need this."]

NOT   Don told we students about it.

USE   Don told **us** students about it. [Compare "Don told us about it."]

■ **Exercise 1**   Choose the correct pronoun within the parentheses in each of the following sentences. Explain your choice.

1. When choosing courses, students like Reuben and (I, me) have many options.
2. (She, Her) and (I, me) asked for a delay.
3. It was April and (he, him) who used the computer yesterday.
4. Are Mitch and (they, them) still going to the game?
5. Between Lana and (she, her) there is little cooperation.
6. Mr. Liu will hire a new assistant, either Sam or (he, him).
7. Leaving Ramon and (he, him) at the gym, we drove over to see Magdalena and (she, her).
8. My friends and (I, me, myself) expected Leopold and (she, her) to arrive at any moment.
9. Two students in our class, Neil and (he, him), talked with the professor before class.
10. After the meeting the chair talked with two members of the committee, Terese and (he, him).

5b

Determine the case of each pronoun by its use in its own clause.

(1) *Who* or *whoever* as the subject of a clause

The subject of a verb in a subordinate clause takes the subjective case, even when the whole clause is used as an object:

I forgot **who** won the game.   [*Who* is the subject of the clause *who won the game.* The clause is the object of the verb *forgot.*]

He has consideration for **whoever** needs his help.   [*Whoever* is the subject of the clause *whoever needs his help.* The clause is the object of the preposition *for.*]

(2) Situations with *who* or *whom* that often cause confusion

Such expressions as *I think, he says, she believes,* and *we know* may follow either *who* or *whom.* The choice depends on the position of *who* or *whom* in its own clause.

Walter picked Jan **who** he knows speaks well.   [*Who* is the subject of the verb *speaks.*]

Walter picked Jan **whom** he knows we all respect.   [*Whom* is the object of the verb *respect.*]

(3) Pronoun after *than* or *as*

In sentences that have implied (rather than stated) elements, the choice of the pronoun form is important to meaning:

She likes Clarice more than **I**.   [subjective case, meaning "more than I like Clarice"]

She likes Dana more than **me**.   [objective case, meaning "more than she likes me"]

He talks with Jerry as much as **her**.   [objective case, meaning "as much as he talks with her"]

■ **Exercise 2**   Using the case form in parentheses, convert each pair of the following sentences into a single sentence.

EXAMPLES

I remember that boy. He was in my history class last semester. (who)

I remember that boy who was in my history class last semester.

Susan consulted her project director. Susan had hired her specifically for this job. (whom)

Susan consulted her project director whom she had hired specifically for this job.

1. Lee Harvey Oswald was the prime suspect in the president's assassination. Jack Ruby killed him in front of millions as live television cameras recorded the event. (whom)
2. We got news of the president's assassination from Walter Cronkite. Walter Cronkite was the CBS news anchor. (who)
3. After the president had been shot, stunned bystanders stood around crying and rubbing their eyes. The bystanders had been cheering and calling to Kennedy as he rode by in the motorcade. (who)
4. People still wonder if Oswald was really guilty. The Warren Commission labeled Oswald the lone assassin. (whom)
5. Numerous authors have written on the subject of the president's murder. These authors have been labeled "assassination buffs" by the press. (who)

■ **Exercise 3** In the sentences below, insert *I think* after each *who*. (Notice that *who*, not *whom*, is still the correct case form.)

1. Joan Didion, who is a journalist, has written about cultural and political conflicts in such works as *Miami* and *Salvador*.
2. It was the Reverend Martin Luther King, Jr., who won the 1964 Nobel Peace Prize.
3. Mary Wollstonecraft Shelley, who is the author of *Frankenstein*, was married to poet Percy Bysshe Shelley.

In the following sentences, complete each comparison by using first *I* and then *me*. Explain the difference in each meaning.

4. Collette likes you as much as _____.
5. My parents praised her more than _____.

5c

Use *whom* for all pronouns used as objects in formal written English.

Use *whom* as the object of the verb or preposition in formal written English.

> NOT   They voted for the person **who** they trusted.
> USE   They voted for the person **whom** they trusted.   [object of the verb *trusted*]

NOT He is unsure **who** the message was intended for.
USE He is unsure **whom** the message was intended for.   [object of the preposition *for*]

In subordinate clauses use *whom* as the object of the verb or preposition:

NOT Richard told David who to call. Richard told David to call who?
USE Richard told David **whom** to call. Richard told David to call **whom**?   [object of the infinitive *to call*—see also **5e**.]

NOT The artist who she loved has gone away.
USE The artist **whom** she loved has gone away.   [object of the verb *loved* in the relative clause *whom she loved*]

NOT This is a friend who I write to once a year.
USE This is a friend **whom** I write to once a year.   [object of the preposition *to* in the relative clause]

Whom may be omitted (or *that* substituted) in sentences where no misunderstanding would result:

The friend he relied on moved away.
This is a person I try to avoid.

▲ **Note:** In informal English, the pronoun *who* is commonly used when it occurs as the first word in the sentence, even when it is the object of a verb or a preposition. As always, consider your audience.

Who do you want? Who is the gift for?

■ **Exercise 4** Following the guidelines for formal written English, change *who* to *whom* when the pronoun functions as an object. Put a check mark after sentences containing *who* correctly used as the subject of a verb or as a subject complement.

1. Who did you ask?
2. Who wants to go?
3. He knows who they will suggest for the position.
4. He knows who will be suggested for the position.
5. The woman who the reporter interviewed was very open.

6. Can you imagine who I saw at the meeting?
7. Someone must know who they are and where they came from.
8. In a tight situation, she knows exactly who to call on when.
9. To find out who murdered who, watch the end of the video.
10. At registration, whoever I asked for directions was very helpful.

■ **Exercise 5** In the following sentences the clauses in which *who* or *whom* appear are in boldface. Choose the appropriate form of the pronouns within the parentheses.

1. She is a woman (who/whom) **we hardly know**.
2. They were talking about (who/whom) **would succeed us**.
3. I gave it to the person (who/whom) **you indicated**.
4. Was she the actor (who/whom) **you read about**?
5. I am not sure (who/whom) **is responsible**.

5d

Use the possessive case immediately before a gerund. See the **Glossary of Terms**.

> NOT I appreciated him helping Shelley.
> USE I appreciated **his** helping Shelley. [Compare "I appreciated his help."]

> NOT Shelley refusing the help was a surprise.
> USE **Shelley's** refusing the help was a surprise. [Compare "Shelley's refusal of the help was a surprise."]

The *-ing* form of a verb can be used as a noun (gerund) or as an adjective (participle). The possessive case is not used before participles:

> **Alex's** radioing the Coast Guard solved our problem. [NOT "Alex radioing. . . ." *Radioing* is a gerund.]
> The **man** sitting at the desk solved our problem. [NOT "The man's sitting. . . ." *Sitting* is a participle.]

▲ Note: The *'s* to show possession is often not heard in rapid speech, but be careful not to omit it in writing.

Susan's street   [NOT Susan street]

5e

Use the objective case for the subject or the object of an infinitive.

They wanted Dave and **me** to do the dishes.   [subject of the infinitive *to do*]

I liked to help Guy and **him**.   [object of the infinitive *to help*]

5f

Use the subjective case for a subject complement. See the **Glossary of Terms**.

That certainly could be **she** sitting near the front.   [Compare "She could be sitting. . . ."]

It was **I** who first noticed the difference.   [Compare "I first noticed. . . ."]

Informal English accepts *It's me* (*him, her, us,* and *them*).

▲ Caution: Do not omit a linking verb before a subject complement.

She is angry.   [NOT She angry.]

■ **Exercise 6**   Find and revise all case forms that would be inappropriate in formal English. Put a check mark after each sentence that needs no revision.

1. As for my friend and I, we both like movies, but she likes them more than I.
2. There was no one who would listen to us, no one whom we could make understand.

3. It was April and he who I blamed for me being fired.
4. Julio racing the motor did not hurry Maurice or me.
5. It is true that the Staffords eat more sweets than us; no wonder they weigh more than us.
6. Do Aaron and she want you and I to go to the show with them?
7. Let's you and me tell Hervé who to telephone for help.
8. Just between you and me, I think that her friends and she could take care of the situation by themselves.
9. We students wanted higher standards in high school, but most of us graduating seniors did not speak up much.
10. The chairperson wanted us—Linda and I—to choose a book for the library.

6

Agreement

Make a verb agree in number with its subject; make a pronoun agree in number with its antecedent.

A verb and its subject or a pronoun and its antecedent agree when their forms indicate the same number and person. Notice below that the singular subject takes a singular verb and that the plural subject takes a plural verb. (If you cannot easily recognize verbs and their subjects, study **1a** and **1b**.)

SINGULAR   The **car** in the lot **looks** shabby.   [*car looks*]
PLURAL   The **cars** in the lot **look** shabby.   [*cars look*]

Lack of subject-verb agreement occurs chiefly in the use of the present tense. Except for forms of *be* and *have* (*you were, he has eaten*), verbs in other tenses do not change form to indicate the number and person of their subjects. For a list of various forms of *be* and the subjects they take, see page 78.

A pronoun must agree with its antecedent (the noun that the pronoun refers to) in number. (See also chapter **28**.)

SINGULAR   A **wolf** has **its** own language.   [*wolf–its*]
PLURAL   **Wolves** have **their** own language.   [*wolves–their*]

A pronoun also must agree with its antecedent in gender. See **6b(1)**.

the **boy** and **his** mother   [masculine antecedent]
the **girl** and **her** father   [feminine antecedent]
the **garden** and **its** weeds   [neuter antecedent]

6a

Make a verb agree in number with its subject.

As you study the following rules and examples, remember that *-s* (or *-es*) marks plural nouns but singular verbs (those present-tense verbs with third-person singular subjects).

subject + *s*	OR	**verb + *s***
The egotists like attention.		The egotist likes attention.
Tomatoes ripen best in the sun.		A tomato ripens best in the sun.

Be sure that you do not omit the *-s* on the third-person singular form of the verb:

> The counselor **speaks** quietly.   [NOT counselor speak]

(1) Do not be misled by subjects and verbs that have endings not clearly sounded in rapid speech.

> **Scientists** seem puzzled.   [NOT scientist seem]
> She **asks** Sybil first.   [NOT she ask or she ask's]

(2) Make the subject and verb agree when words intervene between them.

> The **rhythm** of the pounding waves **is** calming.
> **All** of the dogs in the neighborhood **were barking**.

The grammatical number of the subject does not change with the addition of expressions beginning with such words as *accompanied by, along with, as well as, in addition to, including, no less than, not to mention, together with.*

> The **economy** as well as taxes **influences** votes.
> **Taxes**, not to mention unemployment, **influence** votes.

(3) Subjects joined by *and* are usually plural.

My **friends** and my **mother like** each other.
The **team** and the **band were** on the field.

Building a good marriage and **building a good log fire are**
similar in many ways. —JOSEPHINE LOWMAN
[gerund phrases—Compare "Two actions are similar."]

▲ **Exception:** A compound subject takes a singular verb when
the subject denotes one person or a single unit.

The **flesh and blood** of the world **was** dead. —VIRGINIA WOOLF
Its **inventor** and chief **practitioner is** a native son of Boston,
Robert Coles. —MARTHA BAYLES

(4) Singular subjects joined by *or, either . . . or, neither . . .*
***nor* take a singular verb.**

John or Doris **writes** to us regularly.
Neither Carol nor Ted **is excluded** from the meeting.
Either Patty or Tom **was** asked to preside.

If one subject is singular and one is plural, the verb agrees
with the nearer subject.

Neither the basket nor the **apples were** expensive.
Neither the apples nor the **basket was** expensive.

The verb also agrees with the nearer subject in person.

Either Nat or **you were** ready for any emergency call.
Either you or **Nat was** ready for any emergency call.

(5) Do not let inverted word order (VERB + SUBJECT) or the
structure *there* [OR *here*] + VERB + SUBJECT cause you
to make a mistake in agreement.

VERB + SUBJECT

Hardest hit by the high temperatures and the drought **were**
American **farmers**. —*TIME*

Among our grandest and longest-lived illusions **is** the **notion** of the noble savage. —JOHN PFEIFFER

There + VERB + SUBJECT

There **are** a few unanswered **questions**.
There **were anger** and **hatred** in that voice. —JOHN CIARDI

(6) A relative pronoun (*who, which, that*) used as subject has the same number as its antecedent.

It is the **doctor who** often **suggests** a diet.
It is among the **books that are** out of print.
This is the only **store that gives** triple coupons. [Compare "Only one store gives triple coupons."]
It is not bigger discounts but **better service that makes** the store successful. [Compare "Better service (not bigger discounts) makes the store successful."]
He is one of **those who agree** with my decision. [*Who* refers to *those*, a plural pronoun. The plural form of the verb is necessary for agreement.]

(7) When used as subjects, such words as *each, either, one, everybody,* and *anyone* regularly take singular verbs. *All, any, some,* and *none* may take either a singular or a plural verb.

Neither of them **likes** going to the show.
Each has a good seat.
Everybody in the class **has** tickets.

Every or *each* preceding singular subjects joined by *and* calls for a singular verb:

Every silver knife, fork, and spoon **has** to be counted.
Each cat and each dog **has** its own toy.

Placed after a plural subject, *each* does not affect the verb form:

The cat and the dog each **have** their own toys.

Subjects such as *all, any, some,* and *none,* as well as *half* and *most,* may take a singular or a plural verb; the context generally determines the choice of the verb form.

Julie collects baseball cards; **some are** worth a great deal of money. [Compare "Some cards are worth a great deal of money."]

The milk was thrown away because **some was** sour. [Compare "Some milk was sour."]

(8) Collective nouns and phrases denoting a fixed quantity take a singular verb when they refer to the group as a unit and take a plural verb when they refer to individuals or parts of the group.

Singular (regarded as a unit):

The **committee is** meeting today.
Ten million gallons of oil **is** a lot of oil.
The **jury convenes** today.
The **number is** very small.

Plural (regarded as individuals or parts):

A **number were** absent.
Ten million gallons of oil **were spilled**.
The **majority** of us **are** in favor.

Although the use of *data* and *media* as singular nouns (for *datum* and *medium*) has gained currency in informal English, most writers still use *data* and *media* as plural nouns in formal written English.

FORMAL   The media have shaped television.
INFORMAL The media has shaped television.

FORMAL   The data are in the appendix.
INFORMAL The data is in the appendix.

(9) A linking verb agrees with its subject, not with its complement (predicate noun).

His **complaint is** allergies.
Allergies are his complaint.

▲ **Note:** Because the number of the pronoun *what* depends on the number of the word (or word group) referred to, the verb does agree with its complement in sentences like this:

What I do, at these times, **is** to change the way the system works. —LEWIS THOMAS [Compare "That is what I do."]

(10) Titles of single works, words spoken of as words, and nouns plural in form but singular in meaning usually take singular verbs. In all doubtful cases, consult a good dictionary.

Thelma and Louise **sticks** in the memory. [The movie, not the characters, sticks in the memory.]
"Autumn Leaves" **is** a beautiful song.
Kids **is** informal for *children.*
The kinds of evidence you have **are** what matter.

Nouns that are regularly treated as singular include *economics, electronics, measles, mumps, news,* and *physics.*

Measles **is** a serious disease.
Economics **is** important for a business major.

Some nouns (such as *athletics, politics, series, deer,* and *sheep*) can be either singular or plural, depending on meaning:

Statistics is an interesting subject. **Statistics are** often misleading.

A **series** of natural disasters **has** occurred recently. Two **series** of natural disasters **have** occurred recently.

The **sheep strays** when the gate is left open. **Sheep stray** when the gate is left open.

■ **Exercise 1** In the following paragraph, circle the correct form of the verbs in parentheses.

¹The timing for these classes (was/were) poorly planned. ²There (is/are) several days and three other periods that could have been chosen instead. ³Neither my opinion nor the teacher's choice (was/were) taken into account. ⁴Every one of my opinions, including the last, (has/have) been ignored. ⁵Dr. Closser was the only one of the administrators who (was/were) even listening.

■ **Exercise 2** Choose the correct form of the verb within parentheses in each sentence below. Make sure that the verb agrees with its subject according to the rules of formal English.

1. Neither Karla nor Kayle (think, thinks) that the problem is solved.
2. Attitudes about responsibility, of course, (vary, varies).
3. Every one of the items (was, were) inventoried last month.
4. A low wall and a high hedge (provide, provides) privacy for the entrance.
5. Neither of them even (know, knows) when to stop.
6. There (come, comes) to my mind now the names of the two or three people who were most influential in my life.
7. The grand prize (was, were) ten million dollars.
8. A drugstore, as well as a movie theater, (is, are) in the immediate neighborhood.
9. Such computers, which (stores, store) personal data, (jeopardizes, jeopardize) the privacy of millions.
10. An understanding of mathematics (is, are) facilitated by a knowledge of number theory.

6b

Make a pronoun agree in number and gender with its antecedent (see also **19j**).

SINGULAR	The puppy wants **its** breakfast.
PLURAL	Lawyers represent **their** clients.
MASCULINE	John represents **his** clients.
FEMININE	Mary represents **her** clients.

(1) Such singular antecedents as *man, woman, person, everybody, one, anyone, each, either, neither, sort,* and *kind* are referred to by a singular pronoun.

> Each of the books had **its** own cover.   [NOT their]
> One has to live with **oneself**.   [NOT themselves]
> A woman has a right to follow **her** conscience.   [feminine singular antecedent]

Make your writing inclusive, not sexist. Avoid the use of pronouns that exclude either sex or that stereotype male or female roles.

> NOT   As a **person** grows up, **he** must assume responsibilities.
> [excludes females]
> NOT   As a **person** grows up, **she** must assume responsibilities.
> [excludes males]
> USE   As **people** grow up, **they** must assume responsibilities.
> [includes both sexes]

The following sentences also stereotype male and female roles:

> A **professor** should be thoroughly familiar with **his** material.
> A **secretary** should be thoroughly familiar with **her** filing system.

Include both sexes by using one of the following options, which are listed in order of preference:

Options to Avoid Stereotyping

1. Recast the sentence so the subject and verb are plural.

   Professors should be thoroughly familiar with **their** material.

2. Recast the sentence in the passive voice (but see also **29d**).

   The filing system should be carefully examined by the secretary.

3. Avoid the pronoun altogether.

> A **secretary** should be thoroughly familiar with **the** filing system.

4. Substitute a compound phrase.

> A **professor** should be thoroughly familiar with **his or her** material.

Be aware that any of these inclusive options may change your meaning; some work more effectively in a given situation than others. Decide carefully which meaning makes your point most clearly.

Many people consider the compound phrase *his or her* to be stylistically awkward, so use the phrase sparingly. Many also find the forms *his/her* and *he/she* to be ugly and bureaucratic; you can always rewrite your sentence to avoid them.

(2) Two or more antecedents joined by *and* are referred to by a plural pronoun; two or more singular antecedents joined by *or* or *nor* are referred to by a singular pronoun.

> **Fern and Velma** won **their** game.
> Did **Fern or Velma** win **her** game?

If one of two antecedents joined by *or* or *nor* is singular and one is plural, the pronoun agrees with the nearer antecedent.

> Neither the net nor the **balls** were returned to **their** place.
> Abandoned puppies or even a grown **dog** has **its** problems surviving.

▲ Note: When following this rule is awkward or makes the meaning unclear, recast the sentence to avoid the problem.

| UNCLEAR | Roger or Maria will bring her book. [Is the point who will bring the book or that the book must be Maria's?] |
| BETTER | Roger will bring his book, or Maria will bring hers. |

(3) Collective nouns are referred to by singular or plural pronouns, depending on whether the collective noun has a singular or plural sense. See also **6a(8).**

CONSISTENT	The committee **is** casting **its** vote. [both singular]
CONSISTENT	The committee **are** casting **their** votes. [both plural]
INCONSISTENT	The committee is casting their votes. [singular verb, plural pronoun]

In informal speech, when such words as *everyone* clearly refer to many separate individuals, they are often treated as collective nouns.

INFORMAL	**Everyone** turned in **their** papers on time.
FORMAL	**All** turned in **their** papers on time.

■ **Exercise 3** Following formal usage, choose the correct pronoun or verb form in parentheses in each sentence.

1. A number of employees (has/have) expressed (his, his and her, his/her, their) concern about sexual harassment.
2. If any one of the girls (needs/need) money for lunch, (she/they) can ask Principal Holland.
3. Neither the owner nor the employees mentioned the incident when (she/they) talked to the inspectors.
4. The Missouri team (was/were) brilliant; (it/they) afforded no opportunity for failure.
5. If the House Committee (controls/control) the decision, (it/they) may vote (itself/themselves) more power.

■ **Exercise 4** Revise the following sentences to make them inclusive, not sexist. Use one of the four options listed on pages 72–73.

1. A drunk driver is a menace to himself and everyone else on the road.
2. A nurse looks efficient in her starched, white uniform.
3. Each professor should turn in his grades by Friday.
4. A teacher must give her report to the social worker, who will put it on her desk so that it will be ready for the psychiatrist when he gives his testimony.

5. A chair of a committee should have his agenda organized ahead of time.
6. If he follows proper procedures, an officer always thoroughly questions the victim.
7. They called for a secretary, and they wanted her to start work immediately.
8. Every lawyer should make sure his receptionist knows which parking place is hers.
9. A poet is especially sensitive to his world.
10. A doctor usually does not treat members of his own family.

■ **Exercise 5** All of the following sentences are correct. Change them as directed in parentheses, revising other parts of the sentence to secure agreement of subject and verb, pronoun and antecedent.

1. A sign in the lab was put up by some frustrated students who were having trouble with their computer manuals. (Change *some frustrated students* to *a frustrated student.*)
2. The sign reads: "This computer does only what you tell it to, not what you want it to." (Change *this computer* to *these computers.*)
3. The sign in the lab reminds me of similar problems. A chef, for example, whose vegetables or casserole is ruined in a microwave might think: "This oven reads buttons, not minds." (Change *vegetables or casserole* to *casserole or vegetables.* Change *This oven* to *These ovens.*)
4. All too often what comes out of our mouths is the very opposite of what we intend to say but exposes what we really think. (Change *what* to *the words that.* Change *our* to *one's.*)
5. Two of my instructors, together with a few of my classmates, were talking about such Freudian slips the other day. (Change *Two* to *One.*)
6. Who knows what kind of label is attached to one's computer errors! (Change *kind* to *kinds.*)
7. Then there is the mirror. (Change the *mirror* to *mirrors.*) There are times when people don't like to face mirrors. (Change *people* to *a person.*)
8. At such times a person has to face how he or she actually looks, not how he or she wants to look. (Change *a person* to *people.*)
9. There is another thought that comes to mind. (Change *another thought* to *other thoughts.*)
10. Mirrors reflect images in reverse, so not even in a mirror do we ever see ourselves as we really are. (Change *we* to *one.*)

7
Verbs

Use the appropriate form of the verb.

Verbs express existence, action, or occurrence and are an essential part of the predicate (see **1a**). Verb forms indicate not only the number and person of their subjects (see **1b**, **6a**) but also tense, voice, and mood.

Tense **Tense** refers to the form of the verb that indicates time. The usual practice is to distinguish six tenses in English: three simple tenses and three perfect tenses.

> SIMPLE TENSES
> *Present:* We often **ask** questions.
> *Past:* After the class we **asked** questions.
> *Future:* We **will ask** questions if we do not understand.

> PERFECT TENSES
> *Present:* We **have asked** questions whenever we have not understood.
> *Past:* We **had asked** questions, so we understood the material.
> *Future:* We **will have asked** questions before then.

A **perfect tense** refers not only to the time in which the action began but also to the time in which the action is completed. The six tenses are based on primary forms called principal parts (*ask, asked, asked, asking*). See **7a**, **7b(2)**.

Regular and irregular verbs The way a verb forms its past tense determines its classification as regular or irregular. A **regular verb** takes the -*d* or -*ed* ending to denote the past tense.

REGULAR   *laugh (laughs), laughed*
believe (believes), believed

Irregular verbs do not take the -*d* or -*ed* ending. They form their past tense in other ways (see pages 83–85).

IRREGULAR   *eat (eats), ate*
run (runs), ran
cut (cuts), cut

Auxiliary verbs **Auxiliary verbs** (or helping verbs) combine with other verbs to indicate tense, voice, or mood. **Modal auxiliary verbs** join the present form of the verb to express obligation or possibility. The following words are commonly used as auxiliaries:

AUXILIARY VERBS		MODAL AUXILIARIES	
be	have	will	may
am	has	shall	might
are	had	can	must
is			
was	do	would	
were	does	should	
been	did	could	
being			

As shown in the discussion of tense, *will* joins the present form of a verb to show the future tense. (See the **Glossary of Usage** for the limited use of *shall*.) *Have* joins the past form of a verb to show the perfect tense. *Be* joins the past participle of a verb to form the passive voice (page 79). *Be* also joins the present participle (the -*ing* form—**7a**, **7b[2]**) of a verb to show the progressive (an action in progress). *Do* joins the present form of the verb to express emphasis or to form questions.

> She **will** go. [future tense]
> She **has** gone. [perfect tense]
> She **is** laughing. [present progressive]
> She **was** laughing. [past progressive]
> She **will be** laughing. [future progressive]
> The book **is** read often. [passive voice—present tense]
> The book **has been** read often. [passive voice—present perfect tense]
> I **do** like that chocolate pie. [emphasis—present tense]
> **Did** she like chocolate pie? [question—past tense]
> I **should** study tonight. [obligation]
> I **might** study tonight. [possibility]

Although the auxiliary always precedes the basic verb, other words may intervene between them.

> **Have** the members **paid** their dues?
> Television **will** never completely **replace** the radio.

▲ Note: In formal writing, *can* refers to ability; *may* refers to permission. See the **Glossary of Usage**.

> I **can** skate fast. [ability]
> **May** I borrow the car? [permission]

Forms of the verb *be* The most irregular verb in the English language is *be*. It has eight forms: *am, are, is, was, were, be, been, being.*

> That may **be** true. He **was being** difficult.

The following is a list of forms of *be* used with various subjects in the present and the past tense.

	First	*Second*	*Third*	
PRESENT	I am	you are	he/she/it is	[singular]
	we are	you are	they are	[plural]

| PAST | I was | you were | he/she/it was | [singular] |
| | we were | you were | they were | [plural] |

The verb *be* may serve as a linking verb between a subject and its complement. See **1b**.

Gabriel **is** a very good student.

▲ **Note:** Some dialects use the infinitive *be* in place of the present form of the verb *be*. Some dialects also use *be* with the present participle to indicate habitual action. In formal written English, use the conventional forms of the verb *be*, as shown in the list above.

| NOT | She be a fine hockey player. |
| BUT | She **is** a fine hockey player. |

| NOT | He be walking to class. |
| BUT | He **is** walking to class. |

Voice **Voice** indicates the relationship between the action of the verb and the subject of the verb. Two kinds of relationships are possible: active and passive. **Active voice** emphasizes the subject as the *doer* of the action. **Passive voice** emphasizes the subject as the *receiver* of the action. (See also **27a**, **29d**, and the **Glossary of Terms**.) To make an active verb passive, use the auxiliary verb *be* with the base verb.

| ACTIVE | The dog **chases** the cat. [The subject *dog* acts on the object *cat*.] |
| PASSIVE | The cat **is chased** by the dog. [The subject *cat* is acted upon. The prepositional phrase identifying the doer of the action could be omitted.] |

Most writers choose the active voice because it is clearer, more precise, more concise, and more vigorous than the passive voice. Use passive voice only when you have good reason (see **29d**).

Transitive and intransitive verbs   Notice in the voice examples above that the object of the active verb becomes the subject of the passive verb. This transformation is possible only with transitive verbs. A **transitive verb** takes a direct object and can be made passive. An **intransitive verb** does not take a direct object (although it may take a subject complement) and cannot be made passive. (See the **Glossary of Terms**.)

TRANSITIVE	The figures **deceive** many people. [The direct object is *people*.]
INTRANSITIVE	The figures **seem** reliable. [The subject complement is *reliable*.]
	The figures **rise** annually. [Intransitive complement—the adverb *annually* modifies the verb.]

Some verbs may be transitive or intransitive, depending on the sentence.

TRANSITIVE	Claudia **studies** the book.
INTRANSITIVE	Claudia **studies** all night.

A dictionary will indicate if a verb is transitive, intransitive, or both.

Mood   Mood indicates the attitudes of speakers or writers toward what they are saying. The **indicative mood** makes assertions, the **imperative mood** commands or requests, and the **subjunctive mood** expresses hypothetical or conditional situations (see also **7c**).

The following conjugation of the verb *see* (*sees, saw, seen, seeing*) shows the relationships among tense, person, voice, and mood. It also shows how the auxiliary verbs help to make a verb passive and help to form the perfect tense.

The Conjugation of a Verb

INDICATIVE MOOD

Active Voice		*Passive Voice*	

PRESENT TENSE

Singular	*Plural*	*Singular*	*Plural*
1. I see	we see	I am seen	we are seen
2. you see	you see	you are seen	you are seen
3. one (he/she/it) sees	they see	one (he/she/it) is seen	they are seen

PAST TENSE

1. I saw	we saw	I was seen	we were seen
2. you saw	you saw	you were seen	you were seen
3. one saw	they saw	one was seen	they were seen

FUTURE TENSE

1. I shall (will) see	we shall (will) see	I shall (will) be seen	we shall (will) be seen
2. you will see	you will see	you will be seen	you will be seen
3. one will see	they will see	one will be seen	they will be seen

PRESENT PERFECT TENSE

1. I have seen	we have seen	I have been seen	we have been seen
2. you have seen	you have seen	you have been seen	you have been seen
3. one has seen	they have seen	one has been seen	they have been seen

PAST PERFECT TENSE

1. I had seen	we had seen	I had been seen	we had been seen
2. you had seen	you had seen	you had been seen	you had been seen
3. one had seen	they had seen	one had been seen	they had been seen

FUTURE PERFECT TENSE (seldom used)

1. I shall (will) have seen	we shall (will) have seen	I shall (will) have been seen	we shall (will) have been seen
2. you will have seen	you will have seen	you will have been seen	you will have been seen
3. one will have seen	they will have seen	one will have been seen	they will have been seen

IMPERATIVE MOOD

PRESENT TENSE

See.   Be seen.

SUBJUNCTIVE MOOD

Active Voice   *Passive Voice*

PRESENT TENSE

Singular: if I, you, one see   if I, you, one be seen
Plural: if we, you, they see   if we, you, they be seen

PAST TENSE

Singular: if I, you, one saw   if I, you, one were seen
Plural: if we, you, they saw   if we, you, they were seen

PRESENT PERFECT TENSE

Singular: if I, you, one have seen   if I, you, one have been seen
Plural: if we, you, they have seen   if we, you, they have been seen

PAST PERFECT TENSE (Same as the Indicative)

7a

Use the principal parts of verbs properly, and distinguish between confusing similar verbs.

(1) Use the principal parts of verbs precisely.

As shown in the preceding conjugation, the principal parts of a verb include the present or simple form (*see*), which is also the stem of the infinitive (*to see*), the past form (*saw*), and the past participle (*seen*). (See **Principal Parts of Verbs**.) The present participle (*seeing*) is often considered a fourth principal part.

The **present form** may function as a single-word verb (*ask*) or may be preceded by auxiliaries (*will ask*) or modals (*might ask*). The **past form** functions as a single-word verb with *-d* or *-ed* except in the case of irregular verbs. See page 77. It also functions with auxiliaries as a verb phrase (*have been asking*). Use a **present participle** when the subject causes the action, a past participle when the subject is affected by the action. When used as part of a simple predicate, the past participle and the present participle always have at least one auxiliary.

> She was prejudicing the jury. [subject acts]
> The jury was prejudiced. [subject acted upon]

> He **has asked** them. I **was asked**. I **will be asking** questions.
> They **have begun**. **Had** he **begun**? It **is beginning** to snow.

Both the past and the present participle serve not only as parts of a simple predicate but also as modifiers: "pastries *baked* last week," "heat waves *rising* from the road." Note that nouns modified by participles are not sentences: see **2a**.

▲ Caution: For a past tense or past participle form, do not omit a needed -*d* or -*ed* because of pronunciation. For example, although it is easy to remember a clearly pronounced -*d* or -*ed* (*added, repeated*), it is sometimes difficult to remember a needed -*d* or -*ed* in such expressions as *supposed to* when the sound is not emphasized in speech. (See **19d–e**.)

> Yesterday I ask**ed** myself: "Is the judge prejudice**d**?" [NOT Yesterday I ask myself is the judge prejudice?]
> He use**d** to smoke. [NOT He use to smoke.]
> I am not suppose**d** to be the boss. [NOT I am not suppose to be the boss.]
> She talk**ed** to Ellen yesterday. [NOT She talk to Ellen yesterday.]

The following list of principal parts includes both regular and irregular verbs that are sometimes misused.

Principal Parts of Verbs

PRESENT	PAST	PAST PARTICIPLE
arise	arose	arisen
ask	asked	asked
attack	attacked	attacked
awaken	awakened OR awoke	awakened
bear	bore	borne/born
begin	began	begun
blow	blew	blown
break	broke	broken

Principal Parts of Verbs

PRESENT	PAST	PAST PARTICIPLE
bring	brought	brought
burst	burst	burst
choose	chose	chosen
cling	clung	clung
come	came	come
dive	dived OR dove	dived
do	did	done
drag	dragged	dragged
draw	drew	drawn
drink	drank	drunk
drive	drove	driven
drown	drowned	drowned
eat	ate	eaten
fall	fell	fallen
fly	flew	flown
forgive	forgave	forgiven
freeze	froze	frozen
get	got	got OR gotten
give	gave	given
go	went	gone
grow	grew	grown
hang (things)	hung	hung
hang (people)	hanged	hanged
happen	happened	happened
know	knew	known
ride	rode	ridden
ring	rang	rung
rise	rose	risen
run	ran	run
see	saw	seen
shake	shook	shaken
shrink	shrank OR shrunk	shrunk OR shrunken
sing	sang OR sung	sung
sink	sank OR sunk	sunk
speak	spoke	spoken
spin	spun	spun

Principal Parts of Verbs

PRESENT	PAST	PAST PARTICIPLE
spit	spat	spat
spring	sprang OR sprung	sprung
steal	stole	stolen
sting	stung	stung
stink	stank OR stunk	stunk
strive	strove OR strived	striven OR strived
swear	swore	sworn
swim	swam	swum
swing	swung	swung
take	took	taken
tear	tore	torn
throw	threw	thrown
wake	woke OR waked	waked OR woken
wear	wore	worn
weave	wove	woven
wring	wrung	wrung
write	wrote	written

▲ Caution: Mistakes with verbs sometimes involve spelling errors. Use care when you write troublesome verb forms such as the following:

PRESENT	PAST	PAST PARTICIPLE	PRESENT PARTICIPLE
lead	led	led	leading
loosen	loosened	loosened	loosening
lose	lost	lost	losing
pay	paid	paid	paying
study	studied	studied	studying

■ **Exercise 1** Respond to the questions written in the past tense with a past tense verb; respond to the questions in the future tense with a present perfect verb (*have* or *has* + past participle). Follow the pattern of the examples.

EXAMPLES
Did it really happen? *Yes, it really happened.*
Will the bubble burst? *Yes, the bubble will burst.*

1. Will they run a mile?
2. Did she give it to you?
3. Will it happen?
4. Did he do that?
5. Did the cat die?
6. Will you begin now?
7. Did the river flood?
8. Will they arrive early?
9. Did they really go home?
10. Will the battery die?
11. Did he eat the grits?
12. Will Maurice decide to go?
13. Did the daffodil bloom?
14. Will the pond freeze?
15. Did they bake the pie?
16. Will they bring spaghetti?
17. Did Fern hit a home run?
18. Will Maria cling to her ideas?
19. Did you go to the movie?
20. Will Edwyn be at home?

(2) Do not confuse *set* with *sit* or *lay* with *lie*.

Sit means "be seated," and *lie down* means "rest in [or get into] a horizontal position." To *set* or *lay* something down is to place it or put it somewhere. Learn the distinctions between the forms of *sit* and *set* and those of *lie* and *lay*.

PRESENT	PAST	PAST PARTICIPLE	PRESENT PARTICIPLE
sit	sat	sat	sitting
set	set	set	setting
lie	lay	lain	lying
lay	laid	laid	laying

The verbs *sit* and *lie* (and their verbal forms) are intransitive: they do not take objects. The verbs *set* and *lay* are transitive: they do take objects. (If you cannot easily recognize objects of verbs, see **1b**.)

SIT: **Sit** down. **Sitting** down, I thought it over. He **sat** up.

SET: I **set** the clock. It **had been set** there.

LIE: **Lie** down. **Lying** down, I fell asleep. He **lay** there for hours.

LAY: We **laid** these aside. These **had been laid** aside.

■ **Exercise 2**   Substitute the correct forms of *sit* and *lie* for the italicized word in each sentence. Follow the pattern of the example. Do not change the tense of the verb.

EXAMPLE
The lawn mower has been *rusting* in the yard.
The lawn mower has been *sitting* in the yard.
The lawn mower has been *lying* in the yard.

1. My little brother never seems to *slow* down.
2. Lottie's dog *stayed* in his house all night.
3. Melody *remained* in that position for half an hour.
4. Caleb often *sleeps* in the car.
5. Have they *been* there all along?

■ **Exercise 3**   Without changing the tense of the italicized verb, substitute the correct form of one of the verbs in parentheses at the end of each sentence.

1. Last year they *established* the ground rules for the contest. (lie/lay)
2. I often *stand* there and watch the tide come in. (sit/set)
3. After he weeded the garden, Chen decided to *sleep* on the couch. (lie down/lay down)
4. Ron was *sprawling* on the couch. (sit/set)
5. Velma was *putting* up the Christmas tree. (sit/set)

7b

Learn the meaning of tense forms, and use them logically.

(1) Learn the meaning of tense forms.

Although tense refers to time (see page 76), the tense forms do not always agree with divisions of actual time. The present tense form, for example, is by no means limited to the present time. As you study the following examples, observe that auxiliaries as well as single-word verbs indicate time and that time may be indicated by other words in the sentence.

Present tense (now, at the present time)

I **see** what you meant by that remark.
Dana **uses** common sense. [habitual action]
Mistakes **are** often **made**. [passive verb, habitual action]
Blind innocence **sees** no evil. [universal or timeless truth]
In 1939 Hitler **attacks** Poland. [historic present]
Joseph Conrad **writes** about what he **sees** in the human heart. [literary present]
The store **opens** next week. [present form, used with the adverbial *next week* to denote future time]
I **am trying** to form an opinion. [a progressive form denoting past, present, and (probably) future]

Past tense (past time, not extending to the present)

I **ate** the cake.
They **played** a good game.
We **were continuing** our work. [continuing action in the past]
The paper **was collaborated on** by two people. [passive]
Adolpho **used to be** happy. [Compare "was happier then."]

Future tense (at a future time, sometime after now)

We **will see** the movie.
Shall we **try** a different road?
He **will be having** his dinner. [progressive]
A different color **will be employed**. [passive]

Present perfect tense (sometime before now, up to now)

I **have taken** the prize.
She **has broken** her previous records consistently.
Has Michelle **been using** her talents?
Deer **have been seen** in those woods.

Past perfect tense (before a specific time in the past)

Terese **had planned** to meet with me before school.
After Shawn **had left** for work, he realized it was a holiday.
Had they **been sailing** along the coast?
At his death their home **had been** on the market for ten years.

Future perfect tense (before a specific time in the future)

Ten hours **will have passed** by that time.

▲ Note: Sometimes the simple past tense is used for the past perfect.

Carla **talked** to me before the game started.

Far more frequently the simple future replaces the future perfect:

The top executive **will see** the report by next week.
In another ten years I **will be seeing** my dreams come true.

■ **Exercise 4** For each sentence, explain the differences in the meaning of the tense forms separated by slashes.

1. It *has rained/had rained* for days.
2. Jean *cut/did cut/was cutting* her hair.
3. Rondel *speaks/is speaking* French.
4. He *wrote/has written* to the president about this.
5. My mother-in-law *had bought/will have bought* the car by then.
6. Time *flies/does fly/has flown/had been flying* by rapidly.
7. In 1821 Percy Bysshe Shelley *declares/declared* "poets are the unacknowledged legislators of the world."

(2) Use tense forms in logical sequence.

Verbs Notice in the following examples the relationship of each verb form to actual time:

When John **sang**, everyone **applauded**. [Both actions took place at the same definite time in the past.]

Mary **has stopped** drinking the water, because she **had heard** that it was dangerous.   [Both forms indicate action at some time before now.]

When I **had been** there two weeks, I **decided** that I **had been cheated**.   [The *had* before *been* indicates a time prior to that of *decided*.]

Infinitives   Use the present infinitive to express action occurring at the same time as, or later than, that of the main verb; use the present perfect infinitive for action prior to that of the main verb:

I want **to show** you my new trick.   [present infinitive—for the same time as the main verb, *want*]

He preferred **to go** home.   [present infinitive—for time later than *preferred*]

I would like **to have won** first place.   [present perfect infinitive—for time prior to that of the main verb. Compare "I wish I *had won*."]

Participles   Use the present form of participles to express action occurring at the same time as that of the main verb; use the present perfect form for action prior to that of the main verb:

Studying for the exam, he thought of many new ideas.   [The studying and thinking were simultaneous.]

Having built the house themselves, they felt a real sense of pride.   [The building took place first; then came their sense of pride.]

■ **Exercise 5**   Choose the verb form inside parentheses that is the logical tense form.

1. When the song (ended, had ended), the jukebox stopped.
2. The winners cheered when the legislation (had been passed, was passed).
3. I plan (to move, to have moved) tomorrow.
4. We should have planned (to have gone, to go) by bus.
5. (Having finished, Finishing) the project, Leslie went home.

6. (Having asked, Asking) the question, Dario couldn't go back on his offer.
7. The president had left the meeting before it (had adjourned, adjourned).
8. It is customary for students (to register, to have registered) early for summer classes.
9. Patrice had not expected (to meet, to have met) our group until Thursday.
10. It is autumn and the leaves (were, have been) falling.

7c

Use the appropriate form of the verb for the subjunctive mood.

Although the subjunctive mood is alive in fixed expressions such as *so be it*, *be that as it may*, *as it were*, and *God bless you*, it has been largely displaced by the indicative. But a few distinctive forms for the subjunctive still occur.

Forms for the subjunctive   For the verb *be*:

> PRESENT, singular or plural: **be**
> PAST, singular or plural: **were**

(Contrast the indicative forms of *be* with various subjects on pages 78–79.)
   For all other verbs with third-person singular subjects:

> PRESENT, singular only: **see**   [The -*s* ending is dropped.]

Examples
It is necessary that Ron **see** him first.
Suppose he **were** to die before she does.
One debater insisted that the other not **avoid** the question.

Alternatives
Ron **has to see** him first.
Suppose he **dies** before she does.
One debater urged the other not **to avoid** the question.

Should and *would* (past forms of *shall* and *will*) are also used for the subjunctive.

(1) Use the subjunctive in *that* clauses after such verbs as *demand, recommend, urge, insist, request, suggest, move*.

I move that the nominations **be** closed.
I urge that he **be** assisted.
The president insisted that he **resign**.   [Compare "The president told him *to resign*."]

(2) Especially in formal English, use the subjunctive to express wishes or (in *if* or *as if* clauses) a hypothetical, highly improbable, or contrary-to-fact condition.

I wish I **were** in Madison. **Would I were** there now!
If I **were** you, I'd accept the offer.
Drive as if every other car on the road **were** out to kill you.
                                                        —*ESQUIRE*

Especially in formal English, *should* is still used in conditional clauses:

If she **should** resign, we **would** have grave difficulty locating a competent replacement.
OR   If she **resigns**, we **will** have grave difficulty locating a competent replacement.

The indicative is displacing this use of the subjunctive, just as *will* is displacing *shall*—except in questions such as "*Shall we go?*"

(3) Use *had* rather than *would have* in an *if* clause that expresses an imagined condition.

If he **had** [NOT *would have*] arrived earlier, he wouldn't have lost the sale.
OR   **Had** he arrived earlier, he wouldn't have lost the sale.

■ **Exercise 6** Explain the use of the subjunctive in the following sentences in each of these situations: (a) a formal letter of application and (b) an informal letter to a friend.

1. Had Linda been here, she would have explained everything.
2. She insisted that Victor be heard.
3. I wish that Inez were here.
4. If there should be a change in policy, we would have to make major adjustments.

■ **Exercise 7** Compose five sentences illustrating various uses of the subjunctive.

7d

Avoid needless shifts in tense or mood. See also **27a.**

INCONSISTENT   He *came* to the meeting and *tries* to take over. [shift in tense from past to present]

CONSISTENT   He **came** to the meeting and **tried** to take over.

INCONSISTENT   It is necessary to restrain an occasional foolhardy park visitor. If a female bear *were* to mistake his friendly intentions and *supposes* him a menace to her cubs, he would be in trouble. [shift in mood from subjunctive to indicative] But females with cubs *were* only one of the dangers.   [a correct sentence if standing alone, but here inconsistent with present tense of preceding sentence and therefore misleading] All bears are wild animals and not domesticated pets. It *is* therefore an important part of the park ranger's duty to watch the tourists and above all *don't* let anyone try to feed the bears.   [shift in mood from indicative to imperative]

BETTER   It is necessary to restrain an occasional foolhardy park visitor. If a female bear **were** to mistake his friendly intentions and **suppose** him a menace to her cubs, he would be in trouble. But females with cubs **are** only one of the dangers. All bears are wild animals and not domesticated pets. It **is** therefore an important part of the park ranger's duty to watch the tourists and above all not **to let** anyone try to feed the bears.

■ **Exercise 8**   In the following passage correct all errors and inconsistencies in tense and mood as well as any other errors in verb usage.

[1]Elizabeth Barrett Browning was one of the most renowned poets of the Victorian period and remained so to this day.   [2]Even now, most people could have recognized her poem "How Do I Love Thee? Let Me Count the Ways."   [3]Born in 1806, Elizabeth Barrett had suffered from a childhood spinal injury, had laid in bed, seemingly restricted to the isolated life of an invalid.   [4]In 1845, however, she meets Robert Browning, one of the most outstanding poets of the day.   [5]Though Elizabeth's father protests the union, the two decide to eloped the following year.

[6]Because Elizabeth's father had opposed the marriage and encourage her poor health, the couple moves to Italy.   [7]Elizabeth and Robert will remain in Italy until 1861, when Elizabeth will have died.   [8]The dramatic story of the Brownings' romance was presented in Rudolf Besier's *The Barretts of Wimpole Street*, which were written in 1930.   [9]If she was less of an invalid, Elizabeth Barrett Browning might have wrote more than her nine collections of poetry.   [10]Though her literary reputation was often overshadowed by her husband's, many of her contemporaries acclaim her as the superior poet of the two.

MECHANICS

8

Manuscript Form

Prepare and proofread a neat, well-formatted manuscript.

A neat, well-arranged, and scrupulously accurate manuscript contributes to your credibility with your reader. A messy manuscript suggests haste, carelessness, and incompetence. Take the trouble to show that you care about your work.

Manuscripts prepared outside of class should contain few, if any, mistakes (see chapter **33** on *revision*). With the increased availability and use of computers for word processing, more options are available for producing your final draft. A word-processing program can ease your writing process and help you produce a clean, clear, coherent paper.

Manuscripts prepared in class or when time is limited should be as neat as possible. When necessary, carefully cross out words and passages you wish to delete, and clearly indicate insertions of words or even sentences. Do not use valuable time recopying your responses unless your instructor has specifically requested you do so, but always proofread carefully (see **8c**). For a detailed discussion of in-class essays and essay tests, see **35b**.

8a

Use the proper materials.

Unless you are given other instructions, follow these general practices for producing final drafts.

(1) Handwritten papers Follow your instructor's recommendations for submitting handwritten papers. Generally, write with blue or black ink on only one side of regular notebook paper, size $8\frac{1}{2} \times 11$ inches.

(2) Typewritten papers Use a good grade of white typing paper, size $8\frac{1}{2} \times 11$ inches (neither onionskin nor erasable bond). Use a fresh black ribbon, and type on only one side of the paper.

(3) Word-processed papers Use good quality, letter-sized cut sheets or equally good quality pin-feed paper. Separate any continuous sheets and remove any perforated edging. Make sure the printer ribbon is fresh enough to type clear, dark characters. Print from a good ink jet or laser printer is always acceptable. If you have a dot matrix printer, set the word-processing program (or the printer) for letter-quality or near-letter-quality print; most readers find print that shows the separate dots hard to read.

Although laser and ink jet printers are capable of printing different sizes and styles of letters (fonts) on a single page, most academic papers should be printed using a font that looks like typewriter type such as Courier or Times Roman. In addition, you can also set your software to underline words or print them in italics and boldface.

8b

Arrange your writing in a clear and orderly fashion on the page.

(1) **Legibility** Whether handwritten, typed, or word-processed, papers should be easy on the reader's eye. Avoid fancy letters, artful flourishes, hard-to-read script, strike-overs, and tiny letters. If your handwriting is large, consider skipping every other line. If it is not easily legible, print.

(2) **Layout** Follow your instructor's directions about margins and other matters of formatting. Generally, leave one-inch margins on all sides of the text to give your reader room for comments and to prevent a crowded appearance. The ruled vertical line on notebook paper marks the left margin for handwritten papers. You can adjust the margin control on a typewriter to provide the margins you need.

A word-processing program can also be set to provide proper margins. In addition, word-processing software can lay out pages of your manuscript exactly to your specifications: it can number your pages, print a certain number of lines per page, and suggest appropriate word divisions. Word-processing software will also allow you to vary the spacing between lines, but unless your instructor agrees to different spacing, observe the conventions of academic writing and double-space all papers except those you write by hand.

(3) **Indention** Indent the first lines of paragraphs uniformly, about an inch in handwritten copy and five spaces in typewritten or word-processed copy. Indent block quotations ten spaces. See **16a(4)**.

(4) Paging   Place Arabic numerals—without parentheses or periods—at the right margin, one-half inch from the top of each page. Put your last name immediately before the page number or, if your instructor prefers, give a short running title (see **34h and k**).

(5) Title and heading   Do not put quotation marks around the title or underline it (unless it is a quotation or the title of a book), and use no period after the title unless it is a complete sentence. Capitalize the first and last words of the title and all other words except articles, coordinating conjunctions, prepositions, and the *to* in infinitives. See also **9c**.

Unless your instructor requests a title page, type your name, your instructor's name, the course and section number, and the date in the top left-hand corner (one inch from the top and one inch from the left edge of the page), double-spacing after each line. Center the title and double-space between the lines of a long title. Double-space after the title. Begin your first paragraph on the fourth line below the title. (See the models in **34h and k**.) If you use a title page, follow your instructor's directions about the form.

(6) Quoted lines   When you quote over four lines (or over forty words) of another's writing to explain or support your ideas, set off the entire quotation by indenting it ten spaces: see **16a(4)**. Acknowledge the source of quotations: see **34e**.

(7) Punctuation   Never begin a line with a comma, a colon, a semicolon, a hyphen, a dash, or a terminal mark of punctuation; similarly, never end a line with the first of a set of brackets, parentheses, or quotation marks. Most word-processing software automatically prevents these mistakes, but check to be sure you have set it to print out correctly.

Leave one space after a comma, a semicolon, a colon, a period, a question mark, or an exclamation point. To indicate a dash, use two hyphens without spacing before, between, or after. Use a pen to insert marks that are not on your machine, such as accent marks or mathematical symbols. (See also chapter **17**.)

(8) Justification   If you print your paper with word-processing software, resist the impulse to justify (make straight) your right margins. Unless a printer has proportional spacing, justification inserts spaces between words so that every line is the same length; the irregular spacing within the line can be distracting and at times misleading to readers. For information about breaking a word at the end of a line, see **18f**.

(9) Binding   Unless your instructor tells you otherwise, staple or paper clip the pages of your paper; do not use pins or brads.

8c

Proofread your manuscript carefully before submitting it to readers.

Proofreading is different from revising or editing (see **33g**). **Revising** requires you to reconsider and possibly to reorganize your ideas. **Editing** makes sure your prose is as clear, accurate, and stylistically consistent as possible; it also pays particular attention to the conventions of grammar, mechanics, punctuation, and spelling. **Proofreading** checks for and corrects typographical errors of layout, spelling, punctuation, and mechanics.

Proofread your paper after you have revised and edited it. Follow the Proofreading Checklist below whether you proofread manually or with the word processor. First, check the format of the paper as specified in the layout section. Next, check the items listed in each of the other three sections by reading your paper one sentence at a time, starting with the last sentence and progressing up the paper. Read the words slowly, looking at and pronouncing each syllable carefully. If you find it difficult to look for each of the items simultaneously, then repeat the process several times, looking for only one or two of the items each time. Keep a good college dictionary at your elbow (**18**, **19a**), and use it. Refer also to the chapters and sections cross-referenced in this handbook.

Proofreading Checklist

Layout

1. Are all margins one inch wide or according to your instructor's specifications?
2. Is each page numbered?
3. Does the first page have the appropriate title and heading?
4. Is the first line of each paragraph indented five spaces (or one inch if handwritten)?
5. Is the type (or handwriting) dark, clean, clear, and legible?
6. Are the lines double-spaced?
7. Are all listed items numbered sequentially?

Spelling (18)

1. Are all words spelled correctly?
2. Have you double-checked the words you frequently misspell?
3. Are any letters transposed (*form/from*)?

    4. Are you consistent in spelling words that have more than one acceptable spelling (*theater/theatre*)?

    5. Are all foreign words spelled correctly?

Punctuation

1. Do all sentences have appropriate closing punctuation (**17a–c**)?
2. Is all punctuation within sentences appropriately used and correctly placed (comma, **12–13**; semicolon, **14**; apostrophe, **15**; other internal marks of punctuation, **17d–i**; hyphen, **18f**)?
3. Are quotations carefully and correctly punctuated (**16, 34e(2)**)?

Capitalization and Italics

1. Does each sentence begin with a capital letter (**9e**)?
2. Are all proper names, people's titles, and titles of published works correctly capitalized (**9a–d**)?
3. Are quotations properly capitalized (**16a, 34e(2)**)?
4. Are italics used properly (**10**)?

Word processing   In addition to making revising and editing easier, a word-processing program can help you proofread and prepare a clean, error-free, and attractive manuscript. You can verify your spelling and find typographical errors with the spelling checkers most word-processing programs include, but be aware that no program can find misused homophones—a frequent source of spelling errors—such as *hole* for *whole* (see **18b**). Nor can it find typographical errors that produce legitimate words which do not fit the sentence: for instance, if you mistakenly type *the* when you meant to type *she*.

    Usually these proofreading programs operate by highlighting or otherwise isolating on the screen the word that may be misspelled. Word processing makes proofreading easier, but you must still make the final spelling decisions.

Using word-processing programs does not make proofreading the printed-out manuscript unnecessary. Remember to read your manuscript with care. Word-processing programs are only a mechanical means for manipulating language you create yourself. They cannot think for you; they only remind you to think for yourself.

9
Capitals

**Capitalize words according to standard conventions.
Avoid unnecessary capitals.**

Capital letters denote such things as proper names, peoples
and their languages, geographical names, and certain organizations. No overall rule for capitalization exists, but the following guidelines will help in certain specific cases. When special
problems arise, consult a good, recent college dictionary. Dictionaries list not only words and abbreviations that begin with
capitals but also acronyms that have full capitals.

> Civil War, NASA, FORTRAN, Hon., Bastille Day

If usage is divided, dictionaries also give options:

> sunbelt OR Sunbelt, old guard OR Old Guard, nos. OR Nos.

A recent dictionary is an especially useful guide when the
capitalization of a word depends upon a given meaning: "*mosaic* pictures" but "*Mosaic* laws," "on *earth*" but "the planet
Earth."

9a

Capitalize proper names and, usually, their derivatives and their shortened forms (abbreviations and acronyms).

PROPER NAMES

As you study the following examples, observe that common nouns like *college, company, memorial, park,* and *street* are capitalized when they are essential parts of proper names.

▲ Note: Occasionally, a common noun is capitalized for emphasis or clarity, as in "The motivation for many politicians is Power."

(1) Names and nicknames of persons or things, trademarks

> Buffalo Bill, Gandhi, Skylab, Flight 224, Zora Neale Hurston, Pepsi, Nike, Richard II, Academy Award, Garden of Eden, Alamo, Broadway, Chevrolet Lumina

(2) Geographical names

> Ellis Island, Estes Park, Japan, Zimbabwe, Northwest, Arctic Circle, Korea, Middle West, Havana, Iowa, Great Divide, Moscow, Mississippi River, Nigeria, Germany, New Jersey

(3) Peoples and their languages

> Asians, Mayans, Eskimos, Indians, Latinos, Poles, Irish, African Americans, Sikhs
> German, Chinese, Spanish, Yiddish, French, English, Swahili

▲ Options: Blacks or blacks; native Americans or Native Americans

(4) Organizations, government agencies, institutions, companies

Phi Beta Kappa, B'nai B'rith, National Endowment for the Arts, Howard University, National Organization for Women, Ford Motor Company, Congress for Racial Equality, Act Up, International Red Cross

(5) Days of the week, months, holidays

Veterans Day, Wednesday, August, Ramadan, Tet, Thanksgiving, Groundhog Day

▲ Note: The names of the seasons are not capitalized: spring, summer, fall, winter.

(6) Historical documents, periods, events

Bill of Rights, Stone Age, Declaration of Independence, Gulf War

(7) Religions and their adherents, holy books, holy days, words denoting the Supreme Being

Christianity, Hinduism, Islam, Judaism
Christian, Hindu, Moslem, Jew
The Bible, Book of Mormon, Koran, Talmud
Easter, Yom Kippur, Hannukkah   OR   Chanukah
Allah, God, Vishnu, Buddha, Yahweh

▲ Option: Some writers always capitalize pronouns (except *who, whom, whose*) referring to the Deity. Other writers capitalize such pronouns only when the capital is needed to prevent ambiguity, as in "The Lord commanded the prophet to warn *His* people."

(8) Personifications (See also **20a[4]**.)

Can Honor's voice provoke the silent dust,
Or Flattery soothe the dull cold ear of Death?   —THOMAS GRAY

DERIVATIVES

(9) Words derived from proper names

Anglicize [verb];   Israelite, Christmas, Leninism [nouns];
French, Orwellian [adjectives]

When proper names and their derivatives become names of
a general class, they are no longer capitalized.

zipper   [originally a capitalized trademark]
blarney   [derived from Blarney stone, said to impart skill in flattery
to those who kiss it]

ABBREVIATIONS AND ACRONYMS

(10) Shortened forms of capitalized words (See also **11** and
17a[2].)

IRS CBS CST L.A. NBC AT&T OPEC UNESCO
NOW Y.M.C.A. AMEX JFK B.A. [words derived from
the initial letters of capitalized word groups]

▲ Common exceptions: a.m. OR A.M.

9b

**Capitalize titles of persons that precede the name but not
those that follow it.**

Governor Ann Richards, Captain Machado, Uncle Verne
Ann Richards, the governor; Machado, our captain; Verne,
my uncle
President Lincoln; the president of the United States

Words denoting family relationship are usually capitalized when serving as substitutes for proper names:

> Tell **M**other I'll write soon.   [Compare: My mother wants me to write.]

9c

In titles and subtitles of books, plays, student papers, and so on, capitalize the first and last words and all other words except articles, coordinating conjunctions, prepositions, and the *to* in infinitives.

The articles are *a, an, the*; the coordinating conjunctions are *and, but, or, nor, for, so, yet*. (Formerly, longer prepositions like *before, between,* or *through* in titles were capitalized; MLA style, however, favors lowercased prepositions, whatever the length.) See **34g**.

> *Howards End*
> "Why Women Are Paid Less Than Men"
> "What It Takes to Be a Leader"
>
> *Straight on Till Morning*
> "Trouble in Paradise"

In a title, capitalize the first word of a hyphenated compound. As a rule, capitalize the word following the hyphen if it is a noun or a proper adjective or if it is equal in importance to the first word.

> *The Arab-Israeli Dilemma*   [proper adjective]
> *A Substitute for the H-Bomb*   [noun]
> *Stop-and-Go Signals*   [words of equal importance]

Usage varies with respect to the capitalization of words following such prefixes as *anti-, ex-, re-,* and *self-*:

> *The Anti-Poverty War*   OR   *The Anti-poverty War*

In all cases, use the style appropriate to your discipline, or ask your instructor. See **10**, **16**, and **34g–h**.

9d

Capitalize the pronoun *I* and the interjection *O* (but not *oh*, except when it begins a sentence).

If **I** forget thee, **O** Jerusalem, let my right hand forget her cunning.   —PSALMS

9e

Capitalize the first word of every sentence (or of any other unit written as a sentence) and of directly quoted speech.

Humorists often describe their zany relatives.

Oh, really! **D**o such jokes have a point? **N**ot at all.

Most first drafts, in fact, can be cut by fifty percent without losing anything organic. (**T**ry it; it's a good exercise.)
   —WILLIAM ZINSSER   [a parenthetical sentence]

But a voice called out, "**H**alloo, Ben, my boy!"

One thing is certain: **W**e are still free.   [an optional capital after the colon—see also **17d**.]

She often replies, "**M**aybe tomorrow, but not today."
OR   "**M**aybe tomorrow," she often replies, "but not today."
OR   "**M**aybe tomorrow," she often replies. "**B**ut not today."
   [See also **3c**.]

For the treatment of directly quoted written material, see **16a(1)**, **16a(3)**.

9f

Avoid unnecessary capitals.

Do not capitalize common nouns preceded by the indefinite articles *a* and *an* and by such limiting modifiers as *every* or *several*.

a speech course in theater and television
COMPARE   Speech 324: Theater and Television

a university, **several** high schools
COMPARE   University of Michigan, Hickman High School

Always capitalize proper nouns, even when preceded by *a* or *an* or by modifiers like *every* or *several*. In such cases, capitalized nouns name one or many of the members of a class: *several* Canadians, *a* St. Bernard, *a* Missourian.

Style Sheet for Capitalization

CAPITALS	NO CAPITALS
Revolutionary War	a war in history
a Chihuahua, a Ford tractor	a poodle, a farm tractor
Washington State University	a state university
Declaration of Independence	a declaration of independence
May, Memorial Day	spring, holiday
the South, Southerners	to drive south, the southern regions
Italian, German, Japanese	the language requirement
the P.T.A. [OR the PTA]	organization for parents and teachers
Parkinson's disease	flu, asthma, leukemia
the U.S. Army	a peace-time army
two Democratic candidates	democratic procedures
Dr. Catherine Kadohata	every doctor, my doctor

■ **Exercise 1**   Write brief sentences using each of the following words correctly.

1. president   3. college   5. east   7. avenue   9. restaurant
2. President   4. College   6. East   8. Avenue   10. Restaurant

■ **Exercise 2**   Supply capitals wherever needed.

[1]i am looking forward to the holidays although i must do a great deal of studying french and biology in order to offset the grade i expect in economics.   [2]mother encouraged me to travel in the west this holiday

since my uncle lives in denver near pike's peak, the rocky mountains, estes park, and the royal gorge. ³uncle bill, a minister, preaches on god's glory in nature, the law of moses in the bible, and often proclaims himself "free from the politics of democrats and republicans," although he did quite a bit of campaigning when President Reagan ran for re-election. ⁴my uncle wrote the book *preaching in the rocky mountains: life in the wilderness in communion with god's majesty, might, and mayhem.* ⁵i may go to visit uncle bill this holiday, but before the end of january i will probably be back in springfield at southwest missouri state university.

10

Italics

Use italics (underlining) according to conventional practices. Use italics (underlining) sparingly for emphasis.

In handwritten or typewritten papers, italics are indicated by underlining. Although typesetters put underlined words in italic type and even though word processing programs enable you to use italic type, most teachers and publishers prefer that you show italics by underlining , because italic type does not aways show punctuation clearly.

It was on <u>60 Minutes</u>.   It was on *60 Minutes*.

10a

Italicize (underline) titles of separate publications (books, magazines, newspapers, pamphlets) and titles of plays, films, television and radio programs, entire recordings, works of art, long poems, comic strips, genera, species, and software programs.

As you study the following examples, note that punctuation forming a part of the title is also italicized.

BOOKS	*Memory of Kin* *Where Are the Children?*
MAGAZINES	*Reader's Digest* *Smithsonian*
NEWSPAPERS	*USA TODAY* the *Wall Street Journal*

PLAYS, FILMS	*Cats* *Last of the Mohicans*
TV, RADIO SHOWS	*Nightline* *All Things Considered*
RECORDINGS	*No Fences* *Great Verdi Overtures*
WORKS OF ART	Michelangelo's *Pieta* Grant Wood's *American Gothic*
LONG POEMS	*Paradise Lost*
COMIC STRIPS	*Peanuts* *Doonesbury*
GENERA, SPECIES	*Homo sapiens*
SOFTWARE	*WordPerfect* *The Writing Tutor*

Occasionally short works such as essays, songs, short poems, episodes of a television series, and short stories are italicized, particularly when many such titles appear in a single paper. The usual practice, however, is to place those titles in quotation marks. (See **16b**.)

> "Can Anything Be Done?" is the most thought-provoking section of David Burnham's *The Rise of the Computer State*.

> Jane Alexander starred in "Testament" on *American Playhouse*.

▲ Exceptions: Neither italics nor quotation marks are used in references to legal documents or to major religious texts, such as books of the Bible.

> The Declaration of Independence marked a turning point in history.

> Matthew, Mark, Luke, and John are the first four books of the New Testament.

10b

Italicize (underline) foreign words and phrases in the context of an English sentence.

> I tell her I know Chinese. *"Beyeh fa-foon,"* I say. *"Shee-veh, Ji nu,"* meaning "Stop acting crazy. Rice gruel, Soy sauce."
> —GISH JEN

> "Ah! Sixty-two, *cabrón*! And you, naa! You would break your back!" —JIMMY SANTIAGO BACA

Countless words borrowed from other languages are a part of the English vocabulary and are therefore not italicized. The more familiar the word becomes, the less likely it is to be italicized.

cliché (French)	pizza (Italian)	versus (Latin)
bayou (Choctaw)	amigo (Spanish)	karate (Japanese)

10c

Italicize (underline) names of specific ships, satellites, and spacecraft.

U.S.S. *Picking*   the space shuttle *Challenger*

Names of trains and names of a general class or a trademark are not italicized: Orient Express, a PT boat, a Boeing 747, Telstar, ICBMs.

10d

Italicize (underline) words, letters, or figures spoken of as such or used as illustrations, statistical symbols, or algebraic formulas.

Finally he told my mother to put an *H* in that blank. "For *human* race," he said.   —ELIZABETH GORDON

$c = r^2$

In APA style italicize volume numbers in reference lists. See **34j(2)**.

Memory & Cognition, *3*, 635–647.

▲ **Note:** Quotation marks may be used to identify words used in a special or ironic sense (see also **16c**).

10e

Use italics (underlining) sparingly for emphasis. Do not italicize the title of your own paper.

Writers occasionally use italics to show stress, especially in dialogue, or to emphasize the meaning of a word.

> When he sees the child dragging a rotten tomato on a string, Bill Cosby asks, "What *are* you doing?"
>
> If they take offense, then that's *their* problem.
>
> No one can imagine a *systematic* conversation.
>
> —JACQUES BARZUN

But overuse of italics for emphasis (like overuse of the exclamation point) defeats its own purpose. If you tend to overuse italics to stress ideas, study section **29**. Also try substituting more specific or more forceful words for those you are tempted to underline.

A title is not italicized when it stands at the head of a book or article. Accordingly, the title at the head of your paper (unless it is also the title of a book or it includes the title of a book) should not be underlined. See also **8b(5)**.

■ **Exercise 1** Underline all words that should be italicized in the following sentences.

1. NotaBene is a word-processing program designed especially for use in colleges and universities.
2. I looked up the New Yorker in the library in order to read Mousetrap, a story by Jane Shapiro.
3. The St. Louis Post Dispatch reported that the Titanic, a luxury oceanliner that sank in 1912, had been photographed under water.
4. Carlos enjoys watching classic films like Casablanca.
5. I like to find appropriate quotations in The New Quotable Woman.

11

Abbreviations, Acronyms, and Numbers

Use abbreviations only when appropriate for the audience, the purpose, and the occasion. Spell out the first-time use of abbreviations and acronyms, and spell out numbers that can be expressed simply.

Abbreviations and figures are desirable in tables, notes, and bibliographies and in some kinds of special or technical writing. In ordinary writing, however, only certain abbreviations and figures are appropriate. All the principles in this section apply to ordinary writing, which of course includes the kind of writing often required in college.

> Behaviors that rate high on the Sensation Seeking Scale (SSS) include engaging in risky sports, occupations, or hobbies; seeking variety in sexual and drug experiences; behaving fearlessly in common phobic situations; and preferring exotic foods.

ABBREVIATIONS

11a

In ordinary writing, designations such as *Miss, Ms.* (or *Ms*), *Mr., Mrs., Dr.,* and *St.* precede a proper name, and those such as *Jr., Sr., II,* and *MD* follow.

> Ms. Joyce Lee Mr. Juan Ramirez
> *Dr.* Alice Holt BUT Alice Holt, *MD*
> E. M. Booker, III James Chou, Sr.

Do not use redundant titles:

> Dr. Carol Ballou or Carol Ballou, MD [NOT Dr. Carol Ballou, MD]

Omit periods in abbreviations of academic titles: *MA, PhD, MD*. To form plurals of most abbreviations add *-s* alone, without an apostrophe: *PhDs*. For punctuation conventions about designations that follow the proper name, see **15a(3)**.

Use abbreviations such as *Prof., Sen., Capt.,* or *Rev.* only before initials or full names. In formal writing *Reverend* or *Rev.* is an adjective and is preceded by *the* and followed by title, full name, or initials.

> NOT Reverend Campbell
> USE the Reverend Dr. Campbell OR the Reverend George Tyler Campbell OR Rev. G. T. Campbell

11b

Spell out names of states, countries, continents, months, days of the week, and units of measurement in formal writing.

> On Sunday, October 10, we drove eighty-seven miles to Tulsa, Oklahoma; the next day we flew to South America.

▲ Note: For addresses in correspondence, however, use appropriate postal abbreviations. Note that no period follows the abbreviation.

Postal Abbreviations

AL	Alabama	MT	Montana
AK	Alaska	NE	Nebraska
AZ	Arizona	NV	Nevada
AR	Arkansas	NH	New Hampshire
CA	California	NJ	New Jersey
CO	Colorado	NM	New Mexico
CT	Connecticut	NY	New York
DE	Delaware	NC	North Carolina
DC	District of Columbia	ND	North Dakota
FL	Florida	OH	Ohio
GA	Georgia	OK	Oklahoma
GU	Guam	OR	Oregon
HI	Hawaii	PA	Pennsylvania
ID	Idaho	PR	Puerto Rico
IL	Illinois	RI	Rhode Island
IN	Indiana	SC	South Carolina
IA	Iowa	SD	South Dakota
KS	Kansas	TN	Tennessee
KY	Kentucky	TX	Texas
LA	Louisiana	UT	Utah
ME	Maine	VT	Vermont
MD	Maryland	VA	Virginia
MA	Massachusetts	VI	Virgin Islands
MI	Michigan	WA	Washington (state)
MN	Minnesota	WV	West Virginia
MS	Mississippi	WI	Wisconsin
MO	Missouri	WY	Wyoming

11c

Spell out *Street, Avenue, Road, Park, Company* and similar words used as an essential part of proper names in formal writing.

Montgomery Avenue is east of Forest Park.

Writers often abbreviate such words when used as part of an address in correspondence: *1255 Montgomery Ave.*

11d

Spell out the words *volume, chapter,* and *page* and the names of courses of study.

I read pages 46–48 of chapter 12 in volume 2 for my psychology course.

Volume, chapter, and *page* are commonly abbreviated in bibliographies (see **34g–k**).

Special Usage Regarding Abbreviations

The following abbreviations and symbols are permissible and usually desirable. See also **11a**.

1. *Clipped forms of words*

   Some clipped forms—such as *info, rep, exec,* or *porn*—are avoided in formal writing. Others—such as *math, lab, exam,* and *Cal Tech*—are so commonly used that they are becoming acceptable.

2. *Certain words used with dates or figures*

58 BC	AD 70	8:00 a.m. OR A.M.	
8:31 EST OR E.S.T.	No. 13 OR no. 13	$4.25	
25.5 MPG OR mpg			

3. *The* District of Columbia *and the* United States *used adjectivally:*

   Washington, DC; the U.S. Navy.

4. *The names of organizations, agencies, countries, persons, or things usually referred to by their capitalized initials*

USMC	FDA	MIT	NBC	NFL	USSR
JFK	VCRs	IQ	TV		

5. *Certain common Latin expressions* (the English equivalent is spelled out in brackets)

cf.	[compare]		etc.		[and so forth]
e.g.	[for example]		i.e.		[that is]
et al.	[and others]		vs.	OR v.	[versus]

▲ Note: Avoid using the ampersand (&) except in copying official titles or names of firms and in APA parenthetical documentation. See section **34j**. The abbreviations *Inc.* and *Ltd.* are usually omitted in ordinary writing.

   U.S. News & World Report   Motorola   [NOT Motorola, Inc.]

ACRONYMS

11e

Spell out the meaning of any acronym that may not be familiar to your reader the first time that you use it.

Acronyms are words formed from the initial letters of other words or from the combination of syllables of other words: *AIDS* (**a**cquired **i**mmuno**d**eficiency **s**yndrome), *sonar* (**so**und **na**vigation **r**anging).

FEMA (the Federal Emergency Management Administration) was criticized for its slow response to the victims of Hurricane Andrew.

OR The Federal Emergency Management Administration (FEMA) was criticized. . . .

Your reader will probably be familiar with such terms as *NASA, NATO, laser, radar,* and *SAT* scores but perhaps not with those such as *modem, VAT.*

■ **Exercise 1** Strike out any form that is inappropriate in formal writing.

1. Ms. Shelly Aley; a prof. but not a saint.
2. 21 mpg; on TV; in Calif. and Ill.
3. on Greenwood Ave.; on Greenwood Avenue
4. on Aug. 31; on August 31
5. for Jr.; for John Evans, Jr.
6. before 6 A.M.; before six in the A.M.

NUMBERS

11f

Follow accepted practices for writing numbers; be consistent.

When you use numbers infrequently in a piece of writing, spell out those that can be expressed in one or two words and use figures for the others. When you use numbers frequently, spell out those from one to nine and use figures for all others. Very large numbers may be expressed by a combination of words and numbers. Consult your instructor when in doubt.

ALWAYS   over three inches
BUT   three-quarters of an inch   OR   .75 inches

ALWAYS	after 124 years
BUT	after twenty-two years OR after 22 years

ALWAYS	563 voters
BUT	five hundred voters OR 500 voters

ten million bushels   OR   10,000,000 bushels   OR   10 million bushels

▲ **Note 1:** In a discussion of related items that contains both single- and double- or triple-digit numbers, use figures for all numbers.

Lana ate **7** cookies but Julio ate **12**.

▲ **Note 2:** If a sentence begins with a number, spell out the number.

Three hundred forty-two runners competed in the marathon.

Special Usage Regarding Numbers

1. *Specific time of day*

   5 p.m.   OR   5:00 p.m.   OR   five o'clock in the evening
   7:30 a.m.   OR   half-past seven in the morning

2. *Dates*

   December 28, 1951   OR   28 December 1951 [NOT December 28th, 1951]
   October fifth   OR   the fifth of October   OR   October 5   OR   October 5th
   the sixties   OR   the 1960s
   the nineteenth century
   in 1800   in 1859–1860   OR   the winter of 1859–60
   from 1890 to 1895   OR   1890–1895   OR   1890–95 [NOT OR from 1890–95]

3. *Addresses*

> 6800 Tremont Drive, Apartment 301, Fort Worth, Texas
> 76133   [OR   6503 Sienna Dr., Apt. 301, Fort Worth, TX 76133]
> 18 Ninth Street
> 505 East 135 Street   OR   505 East 135th Street

4. *Identification numbers*

> Channel 12   Interstate 70   Charles I   Room 114

5. *Pages and divisions of books and plays*

> page 10   chapter 7   part 1
> in act 1, scene 2   OR   in Act I, Scene ii

6. *Decimals and percentages*

> a 3.5 average $5\frac{1}{2}$ percent   0.502 metric tons

7. *Large round numbers*

> sixty billion dollars   OR $60 billion   OR
> $60,000,000,000   [Figures are used for emphasis only.]

8. *Repeated numbers* (in legal or commercial writing)

> The player's fee will not exceed three million (3,000,000)
> dollars.   OR   The player's fee will not exceed three million
> dollars ($3,000,000).

■ **Exercise 2**   Using accepted abbreviations and figures, change each
item to a shortened form.

1. on the third of January
2. Doctor Carla Estevez
3. three million dollars
4. Joseph Walley, a certified public accountant
5. two o'clock in the afternoon
6. before the fifteenth of April, 1973
7. at the top of the fifteenth page
8. four years before Christ
9. in the second scene of the third act
10. twenty-five-year tax pay-back plan (from 1973 to 1998)

PUNCTUATION

12

The Comma

Apply basic principles governing comma usage.

Just as pauses and variations in voice pitch help to convey the meaning of spoken sentences, punctuation helps to convey the meaning of written sentences.

> After the professor answered, Martin Keith left the room.
> After the professor answered Martin, Keith left the room.

The use of the comma depends primarily on the structure of the sentence and signals a small interruption. Inflexible rules governing the use of the comma are few, and the styles of different publications vary. Whatever approach you use, follow basic principles and be consistent.

Commas

    a. precede coordinating conjunctions when they link independent clauses;
    b. follow introductory adverb clauses and, usually, introductory phrases;
    c. separate items in a series (including coordinate adjectives);
    d. set off nonrestrictive and other parenthetical elements.

12a

A comma ordinarily precedes a coordinating conjunction that links independent clauses.

```
                        CONJUNCTION
                         ⎛ and ⎞
                         ⎜ but ⎜
   INDEPENDENT           ⎜ or  ⎜      INDEPENDENT
   CLAUSE,          ⎨  for  ⎬       CLAUSE.
   Subject + predicate,    ⎜ nor ⎜      subject + predicate.
                         ⎜ so  ⎜
                         ⎝ yet ⎠
```

The minutes would pass, and then suddenly Einstein would stop pacing as his face relaxed into a gentle smile.
—BANESH HOFFMANN

Fanny Lou Hamer was a Black woman who pioneered civil rights organizing in the South, but few Americans know of Hamer's work.   —META GAIL CARSTARPHEN

Justice stands upon Power, or there is no Justice.
—WILLIAM S. WHITE

From one point of view their migration was the fruit of an old prophecy, for indeed they emerged from a sunless world.
—N. SCOTT MOMADAY

I am not complaining, nor am I protesting either.
—RALPH ELLISON

I wanted to be as they were telling me I should be, so I had ceased to exist; I had renounced my soul's private obligations.   —ROSARIO FERRÉ

There was no voice apart from his, yet he appeared to be chatting in friendly, excited tones with some other person.
—WOLE SOYINKA

The rule also applies to coordinating conjunctions that link the independent clauses of a compound–complex sentence.

> It has been ambitious and plucky of me to attempt to describe what is indescribable, and I have failed, as I knew [that] I would. —E. B. WHITE [two independent clauses and three subordinate clauses]

When the clauses are short, the comma may be omitted before *and*, *but*, or *or*, but seldom before *for*, *nor*, *so*, *yet*.

> I liked the haircut and it made me actually look forward to my future fame. —AMY TAN

Sometimes, especially when the second independent clause reveals a contrast or when one independent clause contains commas, a semicolon separates independent clauses. See also **14a**.

> We do not, most of us, choose to die; nor do we choose the time or conditions of our death. —JOSEPH EPSTEIN

▲ Note: As a rule, do not use a comma before a coordinating conjunction that links parts of a compound predicate.

> He snapped the locker door open and kicked his shoes off without sitting. —REGINALD McKNIGHT [compound predicate— no comma before *and*]

Only occasionally do writers use a comma to emphasize a distinction between the parts of the predicate, as in E. M. Forster's "Artists always seek a new technique, and will continue to do so as long as their work excites them."

▲ Caution: Do not place a comma after a coordinating conjunction linking independent clauses.

> NOT   I found Ellen intimidating at first but, I grew to love her.
> USE   I found Ellen intimidating at first, but I grew to love her.

■ **Exercise 1**   Using the punctuation pattern of **12a** link the sentences in the following items with an appropriate *and*, *but*, *or*, *nor*, *for*, *so*, or *yet*.

> EXAMPLE
> We cannot win the battle.   We cannot afford to lose it.
> *We cannot win the battle, nor can we afford to lose it.*

1. A physician is accused of performing unnecessary surgery. Another hospital investigation is launched.
2. Nonsmokers do not like to have smoke blown in their faces. They also dislike eating in smoke-filled restaurants.
3. Familes can choose to have their elderly relatives live with them at home. They may choose to house them in retirement centers.
4. We decided to drive along the coast road. We wanted to see the ocean.
5. They had tried to call us several times on Thanksgiving. We were out of town.

■ **Exercise 2** Follow **12a** as you insert commas before conjunctions linking independent clauses in these sentences. (Remember that not all coordinating conjunctions link independent clauses and that *but, for, so,* and *yet* do not always function as coordinating conjunctions.)

1. Everyone in our class was assigned to an editing group but only three of the groups could work together efficiently.
2. There are many customs for us to learn about for our society has finally begun to appreciate its diversity.
3. She planned to travel to Hawaii so that she could see an active volcano but she had to get an extra job to pay for the trip.
4. We had heard the bands on compact disk and seen them on television but the live performance was still the best of all.
5. Some cultures see women as having enormous power and treat them with great respect and our country could benefit from their example.

12b

A comma usually follows introductory words, phrases, and clauses.

> **ADVERB CLAUSE, INDEPENDENT CLAUSE.**

> **INTRODUCTORY PHRASE,** } subject + predicate.
> **INTRODUCTORY WORD,**

(1) Adverb clauses before independent clauses (see 1e.)

When you write, you make a sound in the reader's head.
—RUSSELL BAKER

The expansion phase is a demanding one, but if the choice is made for life and for following our true convictions, our energy level is intensified. —GAIL SHEEHY [adverb clause preceding the second independent clause]

▲ Note: A writer may omit the comma after an introductory adverb clause especially when the clause is short, if the omission does not make reading difficult.

If you look to the history of Europe you find that homelessness first appears (or is first acknowledged) at the very same moment that bourgeois culture begins to appear. —PETER MARIN

When the adverb clause follows the independent clause, there is usually no need for a comma. But a comma may be used if the adverb does not affect the meaning of the independent clause.

The young Japanese doctor in Los Angeles shook his head when Charley listed his symptoms. —HISAYE YAMAMOTO [*When* is a subordinating conjunction introducing an adverbial clause.]

I have had no difficulties establishing my citizenship in the tribe because my grandmother's name can be found on the Dawes roll. —SARAH HAWKSBILL HARRIS [*Because* is a subordinating conjunction introducing an adverbial clause.]

Perhaps in this way the reign of women is approaching, when the enigma of her anthropological superiority will be deciphered. —STEPHEN JAY GOULD [The adverb clause does not affect the meaning of the independent clause.]

(2) Introductory phrases before independent clauses

Prepositional phrases:

From the deck, I could not see my father, but I could see my mother facing the ship, her eyes searching to pick me out.
—JAMAICA KINCAID

Omit the comma after introductory prepositional phrases when no misreading would result:

> In a crisis we choose Lincoln and FDR. In between we choose what's-his-name. —JOHN NAISBETT

> COMPARE   Because of this, beauty differs radically from truth and goodness in one very important aspect.
> —MORTIMER J. ADLER   [comma added to prevent misreading]

Other types of phrases:

> Having attempted nothing, I had no sense of my limitations; having dared nothing, I knew no boundaries to my courage.
> —TREVANIAN   [participial phrases before both independent clauses—See also **1d** and **1e**]

> Wordsworth aside, the early British romantic poets seem unnecessarily difficult. —ANA FLORES   [absolute phrase—see also **12d(3)**]

(3) Introductory transitional expressions, conjunctive adverbs, interjections, and an introductory *yes* or *no*

> Furthermore, benefits include maternity leave of eight weeks and other child-care leave which either parent can take until the child's first birthday. —KATHRYN STECHERT   [transitional expression—see the lists on pages 40–41]

> Well, move the ball or move the body. —ALLEN JACKSON

> Yes, I bought my tickets yesterday. No, I didn't pay cash.

▲ Caution: Do not use a comma after phrases that begin inverted sentences. (See also **29f**.)

> With prosperity came trouble. —MALACHI MARTIN   [Compare "Trouble came with prosperity."]

> Of far greater concern than censorship of bad words is censorship of ideas. —DONNA WOOLFOLK CROSS

■ **Exercise 3** Insert a comma where needed after adverb clauses or after phrases that begin the following sentences. Put a check mark after any sentence in which a comma is not needed.

1. If you are trying to collect a small nest egg by paying your taxes early so you can get a refund don't count on it.
2. As far as he is concerned all politicians are corrupt.
3. At the same time I recognize that they had good intentions.
4. Before noon the voting lines were two blocks long.
5. While passing three gravel trucks going downhill the driver lost control of his car.
6. Trying to outwit competitors is the concern of almost every company.
7. With one hand on the wheel and the other on the gear shift the driver guided the car expertly around the curves and up the steep hill.
8. Under the back seat is an extra heater as well as some storage space.
9. The race far from over the reporters began to announce the results.
10. When you can help someone less fortunate than yourself.

12c

Commas separate items in a series (including coordinate adjectives).

A series is a succession of three or more parallel elements. See chapter **26**. The punctuation of a series depends on its form:

> The melon was *pink*, *sweet*, and *juicy*.   [**a, b,** and **c**—a preferred comma before *and*]

> The melon was *pink*, *sweet* and *juicy*.   [**a, b** and **c**—an acceptable omission of comma before *and* when there is no danger of misreading—compare "Leila was my mother's sister, my aunt and my friend," a compound appositive indicating two elements: **a, a** and **b**.]

> The melon was *pink*, *sweet*, *juicy*.   [**a, b, c**]

> The melon was *pink* and *sweet* and *juicy*.   [**a** and **b** and **c**]

(1) Words, phrases, and clauses in a series

> He taught me, nevertheless, to believe in hard work, to mistrust easy inspiration, to write and rewrite.   —ADRIENNE RICH

My ideas of womanhood, passed on largely by my mother and grandmothers, Laguna Pueblo women, are about practicality, strength, reasonableness, intelligence, wit, and competence.
—PAULA GUNN ALLEN

▲ Exception: If items in a series contain internal commas, make them clear by separating them with semicolons: see **14b**. For special emphasis, writers sometimes use commas to slow the pace when coordinating conjunctions link all the items in a series.

We cannot put it off for a month, or a week, or even a day.

(2) Coordinate adjectives

Use a comma between coordinate adjectives that are not linked by a coordinating conjunction. One test for coordinate adjectives is to interchange them; another is to put *and* between them. If the meaning remains similar, the adjectives are coordinate.

It is a waiting, silent, limp room. —EUDORA WELTY [*Waiting, silent,* and *limp* all modify *room.* Compare "It is a silent, limp waiting room."]

Swinging onto the narrow, poorly paved road, I gunned the motor and sped toward the town I'd been singing about almost since infancy. —ENRIQUE "HANK" LOPEZ [*Narrow* and *poorly paved* modify *road.*]

Along the trail to Telescope Peak—at 10,000 feet—appear thin stands of limber pine and the short, massive, all-enduring bristlecone pine, more ancient than the Book of Genesis.
—EDWARD ABBEY

■ **Exercise 4** Using commas as needed, write sentences supplying coordinate adjectives to modify any five of the following ten word groups.

EXAMPLE
metric system *Most countries use the familiar, sensible metric system to measure distances.*

1. onion bagel	6. community college
2. classical music	7. baseball parks
3. cheddar cheese	8. office buildings
4. metal sculpture	9. sports car
5. computer software	10. state highway

12d

Commas set off nonrestrictive and other parenthetical elements as well as contrasted elements, items in dates, and so on.

Nonrestrictive clauses or phrases give nonessential information about a noun or pronoun. They can be omitted without changing the meaning. **Restrictive clauses** or phrases are essential to the clear identification of the word or words they refer to. They limit (rather than describe) those words by making them refer to a specific thing or person or to a particular group.

To set off a nonrestrictive word or word group with commas, use two commas unless the element is placed at the beginning or the end of the sentence. (Expressions that come at the beginning of a sentence are also treated in **12b**.)

> For those who fail to achieve an effective personal identity**,** **according to Peter Loewenberg,** racial prejudice may meet the need for emotional strength and personal control.

> **According to Peter Loewenberg,** for those who fail to achieve an effective personal identity, racial prejudice may meet the need for emotional strength and personal control.

> For those who fail to achieve an effective personal identity, racial prejudice may meet the need for emotional strength and personal control**,** **according to Peter Loewenberg**.

(1) Nonrestrictive clauses or phrases and nonrestrictive appositives are set off by commas. Restrictive elements are not set off.

Adjective Clauses or Phrases Adjective clauses or phrases that limit the noun or pronoun they modify are restrictive;

those that describe are nonrestrictive. As you study the following examples, read each sentence aloud and notice not only differences in meaning but also your pauses and intonation.

NONRESTRICTIVE	RESTRICTIVE OR ESSENTIAL
Clauses:	
My mother, **who listened to his excuses,** smiled knowingly.	Any mother **who listened to such excuses** would smile knowingly.
We will explore Mammoth Cave, **which has twelve miles of undergound passageways**.	We will explore a cave **that has twelve miles of underground passageways**.
Phrases:	
In July these mountains, **covered with snow,** seem unreal.	In July mountains **covered with snow** seem unreal.
The old Renault, **glistening in the rain,** looked brand new.	An old car **glistening in the rain** looked brand new.
Such noise, **too loud for human ears,** can cause deafness.	A noise **too loud for human ears** can cause deafness.

▲ **Note:** Sometimes only the omission or the use of commas indicates whether a modifier is restrictive or nonrestrictive and thus signals the writer's exact meaning. Although many writers prefer to use *that* at the beginning of restrictive clauses, *which* has become acceptable if it does not cause confusion.

Appositives   Because appositives rename a noun, they may be nonrestrictive (set off by commas) or restrictive (not set off by commas). A nonrestrictive appositive supplies additional but nonessential details about the noun or pronoun. A restrictive appositive limits the meaning of the noun or pronoun by pointing out which one (or ones). See also **5a**, **24a**, and **30b–c**.

NONRESTRICTIVE	RESTRICTIVE OR ESSENTIAL
Even Zeke Thornbush, **my friend,** let me down.	Even my friend **Zeke Thornbush** let me down.
Voyager photographed Saturn, **the ringed planet**.	Voyager photographed the planet **Saturn**.

Abbreviations after names are treated as nonrestrictive appositives: "Was the letter from Frances Evans, **PhD,** or from F. H. Evans, **MD**?"

■ **Exercise 5** Use commas to set off nonrestrictive adjective clauses or phrases and nonrestrictive appositives in the following sentences. Put a check mark after any sentence that needs no commas.

1. I was able to interview Michael Jackson who plays basketball.
2. I was able to interview the Michael Jackson who plays basketball.
3. One of my older sisters Arlene takes out the trash twice a week.
4. Lilacs which have a beautiful fragrance are my favorite flowers.
5. Few people around here have ever heard of my home town a little place called Bugtussle.
6. All players who broke the rules had to sit on the bench.
7. The word *malapropism* is derived from the name of a character in Sheridan's *The Rivals* a Mrs. Malaprop.
8. The woman who is waving the red scarf is Sally.
9. Spokane Falls which was founded in 1871 was renamed Spokane in 1891.
10. Charles M. Duke Jr. and astronaut John W. Young landed their lunar vehicle near Plum Crater.

(2) Contrasted elements, geographical names, and most items in dates and addresses are set off by commas.

Contrasted Elements

Aerobic dance affords cardiovascular fitness, **not just improved muscle tone**. —ARLESE MARTIN

Women, **but not men,** use a questioning tone in answering questions. —MARILYN FRENCH

Human beings, **unlike oysters,** frequently reveal their emotions. —GEORGE F. WILL

Usage is divided regarding the placement of a comma before *but* in such structures as the following:

Other citizens who disagree with me base their disagreement, not on facts different from the ones I know, but on a different set of values. —RENÉ DUBOS

Today the Black Hills are being invaded again, not for gold but for uranium. —PETER MATTHIESSEN

Geographical Names, Items in Dates and Addresses

Boston, Massachusetts, is the cradle of American liberty.

The letter was addressed to Ms. Kelly Capwell, Santa Barbara, CA 93108. [no comma between the state abbreviation and the zip code]

Tracy applied for the job on April 13, 1993, and accepted it on Monday, May 24, 1993.

OR

Tracy applied for the job in April 1993 and accepted it on Monday, 24 May 1993. [Note that commas are omitted when the day of the month is not given or when the day of the month precedes rather than follows the month.]

■ **Exercise 6**   Insert commas where needed in the following sentences.

1. Those are wildflowers not weeds.
2. The publisher's address is 301 Commerce Street Fort Worth Texas 76102.
3. The meeting will be held in Denver Colorado and will begin on 21 March 1991.
4. Paul Revere Jones was born in Grand Forks Kansas on April 24 not on April 18.

5. On January 20 1993 the forty-second President of the United States was inaugurated.

(3) Parenthetical words, phrases, or clauses (inserted expressions), mild interjections, words in direct address, and absolute phrases are set off by commas.

Parenthetical Expressions

Language, **then,** sets the tone of our society. —EDWIN NEWMAN

To be sure, beauty is a form of power. —SUSAN SONTAG

Order, **I suggest,** is something evolved from within, not something imposed from without. —E. M. FORSTER

Much of the court and, **thus,** a good deal of the action are often invisible to a basketball player, so he needs more than good eyesight. —JOHN MCPHEE

Guard your enthusiasms, **however frail they may be**.
                                —ARDIS WHITMAN [parenthetical clause]

The Age of Television has dawned in China, **a generation later than in the West**. —LINDA MATHEWS [appended element]

"Well Granny," **he said,** "you must be a hundred years old and scared of nothing." —EUDORA WELTY

When they cause little or no pause in reading, expressions such as *also, too, of course, perhaps, at least, therefore,* and *likewise* are seldom set off by commas.

Our ideas about gender roles have **perhaps** changed in recent decades. —LAWRENCE SACHS

Adolescents are **at least** as confused in the nineties as they were in the fifties. —PILAR O'BRIEN

Mild Interjections and Words Used in Direct Address

Ah, that's my idea of a good meal. [interjection]
Now is the time, **animal lovers,** to protest. [direct address]

Absolute Phrases

> **His temper being what it is,** I don't want a confrontation.
>
> He was thumping at a book, **his voice growing louder and louder.** —JOYCE CAROL OATES

12e

Occasionally a comma (although not required by any of the major principles already discussed) may be needed for ease in reading.

Some commas are necessary to prevent misreading. Without commas the following sentences would confuse the reader, if only temporarily.

> Still, water must be transported to dry areas.   [Compare "Still water. . . ."]
>
> The day before, I had talked with her on the phone.   [Compare "I had talked with her the day before."]
>
> Someone predicted that by the year 2000, 3.5 million employees would be on the federal payroll.   [Compare "Someone predicted that by the year 2000 3.5. . . ."]
>
> The earth breathes, in a certain sense.   —LEWIS THOMAS   [Compare "The earth breathes in moisture."]

Sometimes a comma replaces a clearly understood word or group of words.

> Politicians sometimes make controversial remarks; bureaucrats, never.   —MARGARET McCARTHY

■ **Exercise 7**   Commas have been deleted from the following sentences. Insert commas where they are needed. Explain the reason for each comma used, and point out where optional commas might be placed as a matter of stylistic preference.

1. When I was six we moved closer to civilization but by then the twig had been bent.   —MARGARET A. ROBINSON

2. It was a middle-class neighborhood not a blackboard jungle; there was no war no hunger no racial strife. —RALPH A RAIMI
3. My guess is that as the family breaks down friendships will grow in importance. —SUSAN LEE
4. But alas I do not rule the world and that I am afraid is the story of my life—always a godmother never a God. —FRAN LEBOWITZ
5. If all else fails try doing something nice for somebody who doesn't expect it. —GEORGE BURNS
6. On March 31 1968 Lyndon Johnson gave his televised speech to the nation restricting the bombing of North Vietnam and renouncing any possibility of another term as president in order to hold the country together in the time he had left. —NEIL SHEEHAN
7. If women speak and hear a language of connection and intimacy while men speak and hear a language of status and independence then communication between men and women can be like cross-cultural communication prey to a clash of conversational styles.
   —DEBORAH TANNEN
8. Whatever she planted grew as if by magic and her fame as a grower of flowers spread over three counties. —ALICE WALKER
9. His trainer was a woman of about forty and the two of them horse and woman seemed caught up in one of those desultory treadmills of afternoon from which there is no apparent escape. —E. B. WHITE
10. I had once tried to write had once reveled in feeling had let my crude imagination roam but the impulse to dream had been slowly beaten out of me. —RICHARD WRIGHT

■ **Exercise 8** For humorous effect the writer of the following paragraph deliberately omits commas that can be justified by rules **12a**, **12b**, or **12d**. Edit the paragraph by putting in commas to contribute to ease of reading. Compare your version with someone else's, and comment on any differences you find.

¹The commas are the most useful and usable of all the stops. ²It is highly important to put them in place as you go along. ³If you try to come back after doing a paragraph and stick them in the various spots that tempt you you will discover that they tend to swarm like minnows into all sorts of crevices whose existence you hadn't realized and before you know it the whole long sentence becomes immobilized and lashed up squirming in commas. ⁴Better to use them sparingly, and with affection precisely when the need for one arises, nicely, by itself. —LEWIS THOMAS, *The Medusa and the Snail*

13

Superfluous Commas

Remove superfluous commas.

Unnecessary or misplaced commas are false or awkward signals that may confuse the reader. If you tend to use too many commas, remember that although the comma ordinarily signals a pause, not every pause calls for a comma. As you read each sentence in the following paragraph aloud, you may pause naturally at places other than those marked by a period, but no commas are necessary.

> *Bailout* has replaced *rescue* in bizbuzz: A dispute is raging among etymologists about its derivation. One school holds that it is from the act of a pilot donning a parachute and leaping out of a falling airplane; another points to the frenzied activity of a fisherman bailing out a boat that is taking in water.
>
> —WILLIAM SAFIRE

To avoid using unnecessary commas, first review chapter **12** and then study and observe the following guidelines.

13a

Delete commas that separate the subject from its verb or the verb from its object.

Remove the circled commas.

> Most older, married students⊙ must hold a job in addition to going to school.   [separation of subject (*students*) and verb (*must hold*)]

The lawyer said⊙ that I could appeal the speeding ticket.
[separation of verb (*said*) and direct object (a noun clause: *that I could . . .*)]

13b

Delete commas that immediately precede or follow coordinating conjunctions unless they link independent clauses.
See **12a** and **3**.

Remove the circled commas.

I fed the dog⊙ and put it out for the night.   [separation of compound verbs (*fed . . . and put out*)]

For three decades the surgeon-general's office has warned about the dangers of smoking, but⊙ millions of people still smoke.
[separation of conjunction (*but*) and subject of clause (*millions of people*)]

13c

Delete commas that set off words and short phrases that are not clearly parenthetical.

Remove the circled commas.

Martha was born⊙ in Miami⊙ in 1959.
Perhaps⊙ the valve is not correctly calibrated.

13d

Delete commas that set off restrictive (necessary) clauses, phrases, or appositives. See **12d(1)**.

Remove the circled commas.

Everyone⊙ who owns an automobile⊙ needs to have collision insurance.

With strains of bagpipes in the background, crowds watched two men⊙ carrying lances as they charged each other on horseback.

13e

Delete commas that precede the first or follow the last item of a series (including a series of coordinate adjectives).

Remove the circled commas.

Field trips were required in a few courses, such as⊙ botany, geology, and sociology.

I've always wanted a low-slung, fast, elegant⊙ convertible.

■ **Exercise 1** Study the structure of the following sentences; then answer the question that follows by giving a specific reason for each item. Be prepared to explain your answers in class.

[1]At the age of eighty my mother had her last bad fall, and after that her mind wandered free through time. [2]Some days she went to weddings and funerals that had taken place half a century earlier. [3]On others she presided over family dinners cooked on Sunday afternoons for children who were now gray with age. [4]Through all this she lay in bed but moved across time, traveling among the dead decades with a speed and ease beyond the gift of physical science.

—RUSSELL BAKER

Why is there no comma after the following words: (1) *eighty,* (2) *and* (sent. 1), (3) *that,* (4) *weddings,* (5) *and* (sent. 2), (6) *others,* (7) *dinners,* (8) *this* (sent. 4), (9) *bed,* (10) *and* (sent. 4)?

■ **Exercise 2** Change the structure and the punctuation of the following sentences according to the pattern of the examples.

EXAMPLE

A fishing boat saw their distress signal, and it stopped to offer aid. [an appropriate comma: see **12a**]

A fishing boat saw their distress signal and stopped to offer aid. [second main clause reduced to a part of compound predicate—comma no longer needed]

1. Our employers gave us very good annual evaluations, and they also recommended us for raises.
2. Much modern fiction draws upon current psychological knowledge, and it presents very believable characters.
3. Kim has several jobs to put herself through college, and she works hard at all of them.

> EXAMPLE
> If a person suffers physical abuse, he or she should notify the police.   [an appropriate comma: see **12b**]
> *Any person who suffers physical abuse should notify the police.* [introductory adverb clause converted to restrictive clause—comma no longer needed]

4. When people make requests rather than give orders, they generally get cooperation.
5. If older folks want younger folks to take advice, they would do well to listen to what the young people say.

■ **Exercise 3**   In the following paragraph (modified from *Time* magazine), some of the commas are needed and some are superfluous. Circle all unnecessary commas. Explain (see chapter **12**) each comma that you allow to stand.

¹Yet, punctuation is something more than a culture's birthmark; it scores the music in our minds, and gets our thoughts moving to the rhythm of our hearts. ²Punctuation, is the notation in the sheet music of our words, telling us when to rest, or when to raise our voices. ³It acknowledges that the meaning of our discourse, as of any symphonic composition, lies, not in the units, but in the pauses, the pacing, and, the phrasing. ⁴Commas adjust things, such as, the tone, the color, and the volume, till the feeling comes into perfect focus. ⁵A world, which has only periods, is a world without shade. ⁶It has a music without sharps, and flats. ⁷It has a jackboot rhythm. ⁸Words cannot bend, and curve. —PICO IYER

14

The Semicolon

Use the semicolon between independent clauses not linked by a coordinating conjunction and between coordinate elements containing commas.

The semicolon has two uses. Having the force of a coordinator, it can link closely related independent clauses. A stronger mark of punctuation than the comma, it can also separate coordinate sentence elements that contain internal commas. If you can distinguish between independent and subordinate clauses and between phrases and clauses (see **1d** and **1e**), you should have little trouble using the semicolon.

14a

Use a semicolon to connect independent clauses not linked by a coordinating conjunction.

Link two or more related independent clauses with a semicolon unless they are already joined by a coordinating conjunction (*and, but, for, or, nor, so, yet*).

> Some French fries are greasy. Others are not. I like them any way you fix them.   [three simple sentences—can be either emphatic or choppy depending on context]

Some French fries are greasy; others are not. I like them any way you fix them.   [a semicolon showing the relationship between the more closely related ideas]

The dark is not mysterious; it is merely dark.
—ARCHIBALD MACLEISH

Small mammals tick fast, burn rapidly, and live for a short time; large mammals live long at a stately pace.
—STEPHEN JAY GOULD

This principle also applies in compound–complex sentences (see also **14b**):

When you discover yourself lying on the ground, limp and unresisting, head in the dirt, and helpless, the earth seems to shift forward as a presence; hard, emphatic, not mere surface but a genuine force—there is no other word for it but *presence.*
—JOYCE CAROL OATES

COMPARE   When you discover yourself lying on the ground, limp and unresisting, head in the dirt, and helpless, the earth seems to shift forward as a presence. Hard, emphatic, not mere surface but a genuine force— there is no other word for it but *presence.*

Sometimes a semicolon (instead of the usual comma) precedes a coordinating conjunction when a sharp division between the two independent clauses is desired. See also **12a**, page 128.

Politicians may refrain from negative campaigning for a time; but when the race gets close, they can't seem to resist trying to dredge up personal dirt to use on their opponents.

▲ **Note:** Occasionally, a comma separates short, very closely related main clauses.

We are strengthened by equality, we are weakened by it; we celebrate it, we repudiate it. —THOMAS GRIFFITH   [a semicolon used between pairs of independent clauses joined by commas]

Use a semicolon before conjunctive adverbs only when they come between independent clauses. (See **3b** and the list on page 40.)

> Some French fries are greasy; **however**, others are not. I like them any way you fix them.

> OR   Some French fries are greasy, others are not; **however**, I like them any way you fix them.

The comma after a conjunctive adverb or transitional expression is often omitted when the adverb is not considered parenthetical or when the comma is not needed to prevent misreading.

> New Orleans is unique among American cities; indeed in many ways it is scarcely American.   —PHELPS GAY

When the second main clause explains or amplifies the first, a colon may be used between main clauses. See **17d**, page 168.

▲ Caution: The semicolon is characteristic of formal or literary writing. Do not overwork it: see **14c**. Often it is better to revise compound sentences according to the principles of subordination: see **24**.

■ **Exercise 1**   Use semicolons where needed to eliminate errors in punctuation. Indicate sentences that need no revision by a check mark.

1. A parent is a person who provides advice and direction a child is a person who needs that advice and direction.
2. Surely all families have at least one peculiar member, for instance, my sister hoards food against the day when California becomes an island.
3. Cartoons do, nevertheless, distort reality and glorify violence.
4. He took a course in Chinese cooking, later, while showing us how to slice vegetables rapidly, he cut his thumb.
5. The motor in my car blew up, as a result, I had to use the city bus for a month.

14b

Use the semicolon to separate elements which themselves contain commas.

I subscribe to several computer magazines which include reviews of new, better-designed hardware; descriptions of inexpensive, commercial software programs; advice from experts; and actual utility programs which make keeping track of my files easier.

■ **Exercise 2** Substitute a semicolon for any comma that could result in misreading.

1. Dennis based his conclusions on statements by Carl Rogers, a clinical psychologist interested in counseling, Noam Chomsky, the father of transformational linguistics, and Bertrand Russell, the famous logician, philosopher, and pacifist.
2. Many of the most interesting current authors are physicists and geologists, experts in various social sciences, such as sociology and psychology, and politicians and their advisers.

14c

Semicolons do not connect parts of unequal grammatical rank.

Semicolons do not connect clauses and phrases (see **1d** and **1e**):

NOT   I admired Mr. Grimes; the computer repair wizard.

USE   I admired Mr. Grimes, the computer repair wizard.   [appositive phrase—see **12d**]

NOT   We drove two cars to Colorado; it being perhaps the most spectacular state in the country.

USE   We drove two cars to Colorado, perhaps the most spectacular state in the country.   [absolute phrase—see **12d**]

NOT   Problems for residents of our inner cities are increasing; expanding unemployment, rising costs of housing, and uninhibited crime, not to mention an intensification of racism.

USE   Problems for residents of our inner cities are increasing: expanding unemployment, rising costs of housing, and uninhibited crime, not to mention an intensification of racism. [noun phrases—see **17d**]

Semicolons do not connect a main clause and a subordinate clause:

NOT   If the government ignores the situation; the cities will erupt in violence this summer.

USE   If the government ignores the situation, the cities will erupt in violence this summer. [introductory adverb clause—see **1e**]

NOT   I learned that she had lost her job; which really surprised me.

USE   I learned that she had lost her job, which really surprised me. [adjective clause—see **1e**]

NOT   This suit is really too tight; although I can still wear it.

USE   This suit is really too tight, although I can still wear it. [adverb clause—see **1e**]

■ **Exercise 3** Find the semicolons used between parts of unequal rank and punctuate appropriately. Do not change properly used semicolons.

1. Stella always got her produce at little country stands; no store-bought vegetables for her; then she prepared the best fried green tomatoes I have ever eaten.
2. Although I know I should finish my papers a week early; I still wind up writing them the night before they are due.
3. I dislike only two kinds of people; those who tell me what to do and those who don't do anything themselves.
4. Many times I've pushed the up button; after I've waited for as long as five minutes; the doors of two elevators open at once.
5. Eating hot, cheesy, thick-crust pizza; swooping down a snow-covered mountain; watching old Bogart movies—these are some of my favorite activities.

■ **Exercise 4** Compose four sentences to illustrate various uses of the semicolon.

■ **Exercise 5** This is an exercise on the comma and the semicolon. Study the following examples, which illustrate chapters **12** and **14**. Using these examples as guides, punctuate sentences 1–10 appropriately.

12a Sara neglected to label all the connections in the computer before unplugging them, for she had not read the directions that came with the new motherboard.

12b Since Sara had not read the directions that came with the new motherboard, she neglected to label all the connections before she unplugged them.

In very large print, the directions explain why labeling is necessary.

12c Sara did not read the directions that came with her new motherboard, observe the warning, or label the connections.

Sara was a smug, impatient, overconfident person.

12d Sara did not read the motherboard directions, which warned against unplugging connectors before labeling them.

Sara, an impatient person, unplugged all the connectors before labeling them.

First, read the directions.

12e When she bought the motherboard, she had asked how to install it.

14a Sara ignored the directions that came with her new motherboard; she unplugged the connections without labeling them.

Sara unplugged the connections without labeling them; thus, she was unable to put the computer back together.

14b Sara told the technician that she forgot to read the directions; that she had, of course, been careless; and that having to pay a technician had taught her never, ever, to forget to read the directions.

1. Students today are more intent than ever on making good grades in their courses for they know that those grades can mean the difference between a good job and a mediocre one.
2. Professor Mikoyama a noted Japanese scientist invented a new kind of microchip.
3. The fruit stand where we stopped displayed baskets overflowing with fresh snap beans rosy peaches mounds of home-grown tomatoes and heads of leafy lettuce.
4. Five or six healthy energetic little boys splashed merrily in the water.
5. While Adriana was taking care of the baby and Ana fixed dinner Mama finished painting the bathroom.

6. After climbing the forty-seven steps to Tom's front door I was out of breath.
7. In high school we were asked to memorize dates and facts such as 1066 the Battle of Hastings 1215 the signing of the Magna Carta 1917 the Russian revolution and 1945 the bombing of Hiroshima and Nagasaki.
8. They often talk about their dream of sailing to Hawaii on a large sloop to tell the truth however they seem perfectly happy with their small boat on Lake Minnetonka.
9. I complained about how long we had to wait Rudy thought I was angry.
10. The Chungs were waiting for us at La Cantina Laredo however we thought we were to meet them at the Cafe Lorenzo.

15

The Apostrophe

Use the apostrophe to show possession (except for personal pronouns), to mark omissions in contractions, and to form certain plurals.

15a

Use the apostrophe to show possession for nouns (including acronyms) and indefinite pronouns.

The possessive (or genitive) case shows ownership or a comparable relationship: *Tonya's* car, three *years'* experience. The possessive case of nouns and of indefinite pronouns may be indicated by the use of **'s** (see **15a[1]**) or by the apostrophe alone (see **15a[2]**).

  everybody's friend   the students' laughter

Occasionally, the possessive is indicated by the use of both an *of* phrase and **'s** (often called a double possessive):

  that book of LaShonda's [LaShonda owns or wrote the book.]
  COMPARE that book of LaShonda [The book describes
        LaShonda.]

A possessive may follow the word it modifies:

> Is that new computer Ana's or Kim's? [Compare "Ana's or Kim's computer."]

(1) For singular nouns (including acronyms) and indefinite pronouns, add the apostrophe and -s.

> Nan's idea   a day's work   NASA's aim   anyone's guess
> Keats's house   box's lid   horse's blanket

When the **'s** results in awkward repetition of an *s*, *x*, or *z* sound, omit the *s*: Moses' city.

(2) For plural nouns ending in *s*, add only the apostrophe. For plurals not ending in *s*, add the apostrophe and -*s*.

> her sons' room   ten dollars' worth   the Ameses' home
> BUT   men's watches   women's names   children's rights

(3) For compounds or to show joint ownership, add the apostrophe and -*s* only to the last word.

> Mac and Fil's house [Compare "Mac and Fil's houses"—they own more than one house jointly.]
>
> his father-in-law's job   anyone else's idea
>
> the Dean of Students' rules   Ian James, Jr.'s book [To avoid confusion no comma follows *Jr.'s* although *Jr.* is normally set off by commas.]

(4) To indicate individual ownership, add the apostrophe and -*s* to each name.

> Tamiko's and Sam's apartments
> Christina's and Geraldo's mail [Compare "Christina's mail" and "Geraldo's mail"; *mail* is a collective noun. "Christina and Geraldo's mail" indicates mail belonging jointly to Christina and Geraldo.]

▲ Note: Proper names (organizations, geographical locations, and so on) sometimes do not use the apostrophe or the apostrophe and -s. Follow local usage.

Devil's Island   Devils Tower   Devil Mountain

■ **Exercise 1** Change the modifier after the noun to a possessive form before the noun, following the pattern of the examples.

EXAMPLES
the laughter of the crowd   *the crowd's laughter*
suggestions made by James   *James's suggestions*
                                 OR *James' suggestions*

1. the acreage belonging to John L. Field III
2. the house built by the Weinbergs
3. the voices of Yoshi and Sofia
4. the hopes of my sister-in-law
5. the home of Malcolm X
6. worth a dollar
7. a turn belonging to somebody else
8. poems by Langston Hughes
9. coats for men
10. a book written by Laura and Carol
11. the index of the book
12. the syllabus of the course
13. a mistake made by the president of the company
14. the agents of the IRS
15. the wishes of the people

15b

Use the apostrophe to mark omissions in contractions and in numbers.

didn't   he'll   they're   there's   she'd   class of '98
o'clock   [contraction of *of the clock*]

"Well, Curley's pretty handy," the swamper said skeptically. "Never did seem right to me. S'pose Curley jumps a big guy an' licks him. Ever'body says what a game guy Curley is."
                                    —JOHN STEINBECK [See also **19b**.]

15c

Use the apostrophe and -s to form only certain plurals.

Use the apostrophe and -s for the plural forms of lowercase letters and of abbreviations followed by periods.

his *e*'s and *o*'s   no more *ibid.*'s [The **'s** is not italicized (underlined). See also **10d**.]

When needed to prevent confusion, use **'s** to show the plural of capital letters and of words referred to as words.

too many I**'s**   several A**'s**   two plus**'s**   the ha ha**'s**

When no confusion would result, use either **'s** or **-s** to form such plurals as the following:

the 1900**'s** OR the 1990**s**   his 7**'s** OR his 7**s**
her and**'s** OR her and**s**   the VFW**'s** OR the VFW**s**
the &**'s** OR the &**s**

▲ Caution: Never use **'s** to indicate plurals of words not referred to as words: The Smith**s** are home, two television**s** (NOT the Smith's are home, two television's).

15d

Personal pronouns and plural nouns that are not possessive do not take an apostrophe.

A personal pronoun (*I, we, you, he, she, it, they*) has its own form to show possession (*my, our, your, his, hers, its, theirs*).

A friend of **theirs** knows a cousin of **yours**.

▲ Caution: Do not confuse *it's* with *its* or *who's* with *whose*. *It's* is a contraction for *it is*. *Its* is the possessive form of *it*. Used with a personal pronoun, *'s* always indicates a contraction.

Its motor is small.   **It's** [it is] a small motor.
The dog enjoys **its** bone.   **It's** [it is] the dog's bone.
The board made **its** plan.   **It's** [it is] the board's plan.

Who's is the contraction of *who is*. *Whose* is the possessive form of the relative pronoun *who*.

Who's [Who is] responsible?   **Whose** responsibility is it?

■ **Exercise 2**   Insert apostrophes where needed. Indicate sentences that need no revision by a check mark.

1. Many students attitudes changed in the early 1990s.
2. Two of Mr. Charles students won awards for their essays.
3. My bosss unpredictable rages are bad for company morale.
4. Ahmad dislikes football: its roughness disturbs him.
5. Snapshots of the class of 97 cover Alicias bulletin board.
6. "Its just one MDs opinion, isnt it?" Jehan asked.
7. There are four is and four ss in Mississippi.
8. Theres a world of difference between Toms ability and theirs.
9. NATOs stability is still a political analysts concern.
10. Computers often confuse his account with someone elses.

16

Quotation Marks

Use quotation marks for direct quotations (other than those in indented blocks), for some titles, and for words used in a special sense. Place other marks of punctuation in proper relation to quotation marks.

Quotation marks, like scissors, are always used in pairs. The first mark indicates the beginning of the quotation, and the second mark indicates the end.

16a

Use quotation marks for direct quotations and in all dialogue. Set off long quotations by indention without quotation marks. See **34e**.

(1) Use double quotation marks for direct quotations but none for indirect quotations. Use single quotation marks to enclose a quotation within a quotation.

Direct quotation:

> "People are trapped in history," writes James Baldwin, "and history is trapped in them." [Quotation marks enclose only the quotation, not expressions like *she said* or *he replied*. Place the period within the quotation marks. See **16e**.]

Indirect quotation:

> James Baldwin claims that people cannot escape history and that history cannot exist without people.   [Quotation marks are not used for indirect quotations.]

Quotation within a quotation:

> "Jennifer keeps telling me to 'get a life,'" Mark complained. [The comma appears in the quotation within a quotation; the period goes at the end of the sentence. See page 160 for how to punctuate a quotation within a quotation presented as an indented block.]

In direct quotations, reproduce all quoted material exactly as it appears in the original, including capitalization and punctuation. If the quoted material contains an error, insert "sic" within brackets immediately after the error. If the quoted material contains a reference that would be unclear once the material is taken out of context, explain the reference in one or two words immediately after the reference. (See **17g** and **34e**.) Indicate an omission within a quotation by the use of ellipsis points. (See **17i**.)

(2) Use quotation marks for dialogue (directly quoted conversation).

In dialogue, write what each person says, no matter how short, as if it were a separate paragraph. Include expressions such as *he said,* as well as closely related bits of narrative, in the same paragraph as the direct quotation.

> Through an interpreter, I spoke with a Bedouin man tending nearby olive trees.
> "Do you own this land?" I asked him.
> He shook his head. "The land belongs to Allah," he said.
> "What about the trees?" I asked. He had just harvested a basket of green olives, and I assumed that at least the trees were his.

"The trees, too, are Allah's," he replied.

I marveled at this man who seemed unencumbered by material considerations . . . or so I was thinking when, as if in afterthought, he said, "Of course, I own the *olives.*"

—HARVEY ARDEN, "In Search of Moses"

▲ Note: When quoting more than one paragraph by a single speaker, put quotation marks at the beginning of each new paragraph but at the end of only the last paragraph.

(3) Set off thoughts with double quotation marks, just as if they were stated.

"Here we go again," I thought.

(4) Set off long quotations of prose and poetry by indention. Run short quotations into the text.

Prose When using the MLA style of documentation (**34g**), set off any quotation consisting of more than four lines by indenting all lines ten spaces. When using the APA style (**34j**), set off quotations of more than forty words by indenting all lines five spaces. When using either MLA or APA style, double space the lines within the block.

If you quote one or more complete paragraphs, indicate each paragraph by indenting its first line an additional three spaces in MLA style and an additional five spaces in APA style. If you quote only part of a paragraph, do not indent its first line the additional spaces.

Introduce the long quotations usually with a colon. Use internal quotation marks only if they appear in the original.

```
Metal coins replaced bartering. Then paper money
became more convenient to use than metal coins not
only because it is easy to handle but also because,
```

as Cetron and O'Toole say in <u>Encounters with the
Future</u>, it has other advantages:

> Printing more zeros is all it takes on a
> bill to increase its value. Careful
> engraving makes it easy to recognize and
> difficult to counterfeit. The fact that
> private individuals cannot create it at
> will keeps it scarce. Karl Marx once said
> that paper money was valued "only insofar
> as it represents gold" but that may never
> have been true. (188)

Today, checks and credit cards are even more
convenient than paper money.

Poetry Except for very special emphasis, treat a quotation
of three (or fewer) lines of poetry as a short quotation—that
is, run in with the text and enclosed in quotation marks.
Indicate the divisions between lines by a slash with a space
on each side (see **17h**). Set off passages of more than three
lines—double-spaced and indented ten spaces from the left
margin unless unusual spacing is part of the poem. Use quotation marks only if they appear in the original. (Numbers in
parentheses—placed two spaces after the close of the quotation—may be used to indicate line numbers of the poem.)

In "London" William Blake expressed his horror of
institutional callousness:

> How the Chimney-sweeper's cry
> Every black'ning Church appalls;
> And the hapless Soldier's sigh
> Runs in blood down Palace walls.   (9-12)

■ **Exercise 1** Change each indirect quotation to a direct quotation and each direct quotation to an indirect one.

1. My brother says that he doesn't understand me.
2. "Although running helped me to become more energetic," Amy claimed, "it also helped me to sleep better."
3. Jamaica asked, "Do you want to go out for pizza?"
4. Luis explained that he enjoys music the most when he can listen to it when he is alone.
5. Connie said that she thought that Joe's motto ought to be "I'll do it tomorrow!"

16b

Use quotation marks for minor titles (short stories, essays, short poems, songs, episodes of a radio or television series, articles in periodicals) and for subdivisions of books.

Lon Otto's *Cover Me* contains such wonderful stories as "Winners" and "How I Got Rid of That Stump." [short stories]

"Nani" is my favorite of the poems by Alberto Rios that we studied this semester. [poem]

I always want to laugh when I hear "Big Girls Don't Cry." [song]

Coral Browne starred in "An Englishman Abroad," part of the *Great Performances* series. [episode in a television series]

Did you read Lemann's "Stressed Out in Suburbia" when it appeared in *The Atlantic*? [article in a periodical]

Use double quotation marks to enclose a minor title appearing in a longer italicized (underlined) title. Use single marks for one within a longer title enclosed in double quotation marks.

Modern Interpretations of "My Last Duchess"
"An Introduction to 'My Last Duchess' "

16c

Used sparingly, quotation marks may enclose words intended in a special or ironic sense.

His **"**gourmet dinner**"** tasted as if it had come out of a grocer's freezer.

OR   His so-called gourmet dinner tasted as if it had come out of a grocer's freezer. [The use of *so-called* eliminates the need for quotation marks.]

And I do mean good and evil, not **"**adjustment and deviance,**"** the gutless language that so often characterizes modern discussions of psychological topics. —CAROL TAVRIS

▲ **Note:** Either quotation marks or italics may be used in definitions. See also **10d**.

Ploy means **"**a strategy used to gain an advantage.**"**
Ploy means *a strategy used to gain an advantage.*

16d

Do not overuse quotation marks.

Do not use quotation marks to enclose a cliché (see **20c**). Doing so calls attention to the cliché and shows that you were unwilling to use your own words.

NOT   A good debater does not "beat about the bush."
USE   A good debater does not beat around the bush.
BETTER   A good debater comes directly to the point.

Do not use quotation marks for a *yes* or *no* in indirect discourse or for diction that you may consider questionable.

NOT   A "wimp" can't say "no" to anyone.
USE   A wimp can't say no to anyone.

■ **Exercise 2** Edit the following sentences by inserting quotation marks or by eliminating the need for quotation marks.

1. In a short story called Everyday Use, Alice Walker explores the meaning of family heritage.
2. Here, stoked means fantastically happy on a surfboard.
3. *Women's Ways of Knowing* begins with a chapter entitled To the Other Side of Silence.
4. Teynae could "swim like a fish."
5. I became interested in country music after hearing a tape of Patsy Cline singing Crazy and I Fall to Pieces.

16e

When using various marks of punctuation with quoted words, phrases, or sentences, follow the conventions of American printers.

(1) Place the comma within the quotation marks. Place the period within the quotation marks if the quotation ends the sentence.

"Jenny," he said, "let's have lunch."
She replied, "OK, but first I want to finish 'The Machine Stops.'"
This poem illustrates what Hopkins called "inscape."

If words follow the quotation in the sentence, place the period at the end of the sentence. If a parenthetical citation follows a sentence ending with a quotation, place the period after the citation. For example, in the MLA style of documentation, a page number in parentheses follows a quotation (see **34g**).

"Nancy, thanks for your help," she said.

In his well-respected book *On Writing Well*, William Zinsser writes, "One of the bleakest moments for writers is the one when they realize that their editor has missed the point of what they are trying to do" (270).

For block quotations see p. 159.

(2) Place the semicolon and the colon outside the quotation marks.

> She spoke of "the protagonists"; yet I remembered only one in "The Tell-Tale Heart": the mad murderer.

(3) Place the question mark, the exclamation point, and the dash within the quotation marks when they apply only to the quoted matter. Place them outside when they do not.

Within the quotation marks:

> Pilate asked, "What is truth?"
> Gordon replied, "No way!"
> "Achievement—success!—" states Heather Evans, "has become a national obsession."
> Why do children keep asking "Why?" [a question within a question—one question mark inside the quotation marks]

Outside the quotation marks:

> What is the meaning of the term "half-truth"?
> Stop whistling "All I Do Is Dream of You"!
> The boss exclaimed, "No one should work for the profit motive!"—no exceptions, I suppose.

■ **Exercise 3** Write a page of dialogue between two friends who are disagreeing about songs or stories. Punctuate the quotations carefully.

■ **Exercise 4** Insert quotation marks where they are needed.

1. Have you read Amy Tan's essay Mother Tongue?
2. For my poetry class I have to write a paper on a poem by Adrienne Rich; I can choose At a Bach Concert, Diving into the Wreck, or Living in Sin.
3. I was disturbed by the editorial Does Professional Hockey Have a Future?
4. Get aholt, instead of get hold, is still used in that region.
5. Andy said, Have people ever asked me Do you revise what you write? Yes, lots of times, and when they do, I tell them that my motto is A writer's work is never done!

17

The Period and Other Marks

Use the period, question mark, exclamation point, colon, dash, parentheses, brackets, slash, and ellipsis points appropriately. For the use of the hyphen, see **18f.**

Notice how the marks in color below signal meaning and intonation.

> The days are dark. Why worry? The sun never stops shining!

> In *Lady Windermere's Fan* **(**1892**)** is this famous line**:** "I **[**Lord Darlington**]** can resist everything except temptation."

> According to *Consumer Reports,* "The electronic radio**/** clock **• • •** is extremely complicated**—**enough so to require five pages of instruction in the owner's manual**.**"

Type two spaces after the period, question mark, exclamation point, and the last dot of four-dot ellipsis points; type one space after the colon, the ending parenthesis and bracket, and each of the dots in ellipsis points. No spaces precede or follow the hyphen or dash.

17a

Use the period as an end mark and with some abbreviations.

(1) Use the period to mark the end of a declarative sentence and a mildly imperative sentence.

We each need to respect our ethnic heritage. [declarative]

Respect your ethnic heritage. [mild imperative]

She asks how people can belittle the ethnic heritage of others. [declarative sentence containing an indirect question]

"How can people belittle the ethnic heritage of others?" she asked. [declarative sentence containing a direct quotation]

"I'm as good as you are!" he shouted. [declarative sentence containing an exclamation]

(2) Use periods after some abbreviations.

Dr., Jr. a.m., p.m. vs., etc., et al.

Periods are not used for all abbreviations (for example, *MVP,* *mph, FM*—see page 120). When in doubt about whether to punctuate an abbreviation, consult a college dictionary. Dictionaries often list options, such as *USA* or *U.S.A., CST* or *C.S.T.*

Use only one period after an abbreviation that ends a sentence:

The study was performed by Ben Werthman et al.

17b

Use the question mark after direct (but not indirect) questions.

What has Sandra Cisneros written? [direct question]

She asked what Sandra Cisneros has written. [indirect question]

Did you hear her ask, "What has Sandra Cisneros written?"
[A direct question within a direct question is followed by one
question mark inside the closing quotation mark: see 16e(3).]

Does Sandra Cisneros write short stories? plays? poems? [A
series of questions having the same subject and verb may be
treated as elliptical; that is, only the first item need include both
subject and verb.]

Declarative sentences may contain direct questions:

Did he say, "Cisneros published a collection of stories in 1991"?
[No period precedes the quotation mark; the question mark
follows the quotation mark.]

He asked, "Did Cisneros publish a collection of stories in 1991?"
[Put a question mark inside quotation marks when it concludes
a direct question. See 16e(3).]

When we ask ourselves, Why does evil happen? we seek a
logical explanation for the irrational. [A question mark follows
the interpolated question not enclosed in quotation marks.
Capitalize the word beginning a formal question.]

A question mark within parentheses expresses the writer's
uncertainty about the correctness of the preceding word, figure, or date: Chaucer was born in 1340 (?) and died in 1400.

▲ Caution: Do not write an indirect question as a direct question: She asked him if he would go. NOT She asked him would
he go.

17c

**Use the exclamation point after an emphatic interjection
and after other expressions to show strong emotion, such
as surprise or disbelief.**

Boo! What a game! Look at that windshield!

Do not put a comma or a period after an exclamation point.

"Watch out!" he yelled. Jo exclaimed, "It's snowing!"

Use the exclamation point sparingly; overuse diminishes its value. A comma is better after mild interjections, and a period is better after mildly exclamatory expressions and mild imperatives.

> Oh, look at that windshield.   How quiet the lake was.

■ **Exercise 1** Illustrate the chief uses of the period, the question mark, and the exclamation point by composing and punctuating brief sentences of the types specified.

1. a direct question
2. a mild imperative
3. a declarative sentence containing a quoted exclamation
4. a declarative sentence containing an indirect question
5. a declarative sentence containing an interpolated question

17d

Use the colon as a formal introducer to call attention to what follows and as a mark of separation in time and scriptural references and between titles and subtitles.

(1) The colon directs attention to what follows: an explanation or summary, a series, or a quotation.

> Surprisingly enough, my first impression of Nairobi was that it was just like any American city: skyscrapers, movie theaters, discos, and crime.   —JAY FORD

The colon may introduce a second independent clause that explains or amplifies the first independent clause.

> For I had no brain tumor, no eyestrain, no high blood pressure, nothing wrong with me at all: I simply had migraine headaches, and migraine headaches were, as everyone who did not have them knew, imaginary.   —JOAN DIDION

Similarly, a colon occasionally follows one sentence to introduce the next.

> The sorrow was laced with violence: In the first week of demolition, vandals struck every night.   —*SMITHSONIAN*

Style manuals vary about whether to capitalize a complete sentence after a colon. MLA permits use of a lowercase letter; APA does not. All style manuals, however, use a capital letter to begin a quoted sentence that follows a colon.

> Claire Safran points out two of the things that cannot be explained: "One of them is poltergeists. Another is teenagers."

▲ Caution: Within a single sentence, use only one colon to direct attention.

(2) Use the colon between figures in time references and between titles and subtitles.

> At 2:15 a.m. the phone rang.
>
> I just read *Textual Carnivals: The Politics of Composition*.

▲ Note 1: Many writers prefer to use a colon in scriptural references: He quoted from Psalms 3:5. MLA recommends periods (Psalms 3.5), and recent Biblical scholarship follows this practice.

▲ Note 2: The colon is also used after the salutation of a business letter and in bibliographical data: see **34g**, **34h**, and **35b(1)**.

(3) Do not use superfluous colons.

Be especially careful not to use an unnecessary colon between a verb and its complement or object, between a preposition and its object, or after *such as*.

> NOT The winners were: Pat, Lydia, and Jack.
> USE There were three winners: Pat, Lydia, and Jack.
>   OR The winners were as follows: Pat, Lydia, Jack.
>   OR The winners were Pat, Lydia, and Jack.

NOT   Many vegetarians do not eat dairy products, such as: butter, cheese, yogurt, or ice cream.

USE   Many vegetarians do not eat dairy products, such as butter, cheese, yogurt, or ice cream.

■ **Exercise 2** Punctuate the following sentences by adding colons. Put a check mark after any sentence that needs no change.

1. At 1230 a.m. he was still repeating his favorite quotation "TV is the opiate of the people."
2. The suburbs were clean, tidy, and boring.
3. Three states noted for their vacation areas are these Hawaii, Florida, and California.
4. During our tour of the library, our guide recommended that we find one of the following periodicals *Intellect, Smithsonian, Commentary,* or *The Chronicle of Higher Education*.
5. For years women have been insisting on this principle equal pay for equal work.

■ **Exercise 3** Decide whether to use a colon or a semicolon between the main clauses of the following sentences. See also **14a**.

1. The riots had a positive result they got the attention of Washington.
2. Some acts of violence had a positive result others were simply destructive.
3. Few results of the riots are positive perhaps none of them are.
4. There is one positive result people are paying attention.

17e

Use the dash to mark a break in thought, to set off a parenthetical element for emphasis or clarity, and to set off an introductory series (see also 17f, pages 172–73).

Use dashes sparingly, not as easy or automatic substitutes for commas, semicolons, or end marks. Indicate a dash on the typewriter or printer by two hyphens without spacing before, between, or after them. In handwriting, show a dash as an unbroken line about the length of two hyphens.

(1) Use the dash to mark a sudden break in thought, an abrupt change in tone, or faltering speech.

A hypocrite is a person who—but who isn't? —DON MARQUIS

When I was six I made my mother a little hat—out of her new blouse. —LILY DACHÉ

But perhaps Miss—Miss—oh, I can't remember her name—she taught English, I think—Miss Milross? She was one of them. —GARRISON KEILLOR

(2) Use the dash to set off a parenthetical element for emphasis or (if it contains commas) for clarity.

The primary feature of the racially prejudiced personality is authoritarianism—a preoccupation with issues of power such as who is strong and who is weak. —T. W. ADORNO

Local governments—with the encouragement of cable operators—have thrown up nearly insurmountable barriers to the entry of more than one firm into each market. —JOHN MERLINE

Sentiments that human shyness will not always allow one to convey in conversation—sentiments of gratitude, of apology, of love—can often be more easily conveyed in a letter —ARISTIDES

(3) Use the dash after an introductory list or series.

Notice that in the main part of each of the following sentences a word like *all, these, that, such,* or *none* points to or sums up the meaning of the introductory list.

Keen, calculating, perspicacious, acute and astute—I was all of these. —MAX SHULMAN

Farmer, laborer, clerk—that is a brief history of the United States. —JOHN NAISBITT

17f .

Use parentheses to set off parenthetical, supplementary, or illustrative matter and to enclose figures or letters when used for enumeration.

> Through the use of the Thematic Apperception Test (TAT) they were able to isolate the psychological characteristic of a *need to achieve*. —MATINA HORNER   [a first-time use of an acronym in an article—see **11e**]

> Bernard Shaw once demonstrated that, by following the rules (up to a point), we could spell fish this way: ghoti.
> —JOHN IRVING   [an explanatory parenthetical expression]

> In contrast, a judgment is subject to doubt if there is any possibility at all (1) of its being challenged in the light of additional or more accurate observations or (2) of its being criticized on the basis of more cogent or more comprehensive reasoning. —MORTIMER J. ADLER   [In long sentences especially, the enumeration highlights the points.]

Notice in the next example that an entire sentence may be parenthetical. See also **9e**.

> If we refuse to talk "like a lady," we are ridiculed and criticized for being unfeminine. ("She thinks like a man" is, at best, a left-handed compliment.) —ROBIN LAKOFF

▲ Note: Use parentheses sparingly and remember that the elements they enclose should still read smoothly within the sentence as a whole.

PUNCTUATION OF PARENTHETICAL MATTER

Dashes, parentheses, commas—all are used to set off parenthetical matter, but they express varying degrees of emphasis. Dashes set off parenthetical elements sharply and usually emphasize them:

> But in books like Piri Thomas's *Down These Mean Streets* and
> Pedro Pietri's *Puerto Rican Obituary*, there was suddenly a
> literature by Puerto Ricans, in English and decidedly in—and
> against—the American grain. —JUAN FLORES

Parentheses usually de-emphasize the elements they enclose:

> But in books like Piri Thomas's *Down These Mean Streets* and
> Pedro Pietri's *Puerto Rican Obituary*, there was suddenly a
> literature by Puerto Ricans, in English and decidedly in (and
> against) the American grain.

Commas separate elements, usually without emphasizing
them:

> But in books like Piri Thomas's *Down These Mean Streets* and
> Pedro Pietri's *Puerto Rican Obituary*, there was suddenly a
> literature by Puerto Ricans, in English and decidedly in, and
> against, the American grain.

> That face has moved men and women to poetry, and to tears.
> —MAURICE SHADBOLT

17g

**Use brackets to set off interpolations in quoted matter and
to replace parentheses within parentheses.**

> The *Home Herald* printed the beginning of the mayor's speech
> "My dear fiends [sic] and fellow citizens."   [A bracketed *sic*—
> meaning "thus"—tells the reader that the error appears in the
> original. See **16a(4)**]

> Deems Taylor has written "Not for a single moment did he
> [Richard Wagner] compromise with what he believed, with
> what he dreamed."   [An unclear pronoun reference is explained
> by the bracketed material.]

> Not every expert agrees. (See, for example, Malachi Martin's
> *Rich Church, Poor Church* [New York: Putnam's, 1984].)

17h

Use the slash between terms to indicate that either is applicable and to mark line divisions of quoted poetry. See also **16a(4)**.

Note that the slash is used unspaced between terms, but with a space before and after it between lines of poetry.

> Today visions of the checkless/cashless society are not quite as popular as they used to be.   —KATHRYN H. HUMES

> Equally rare is a first-rate adventure story designed for those who enjoy a smartly told tale that isn't steeped in blood and/or sex.   —JUDITH CHRIST

> When in "Mr. Flood's Party" the hero sets down his jug at his feet "as a mother lays her sleeping child / Down tenderly, fearing it may awake," one feels Robinson's heart to be quite simply on his sleeve.   —WILLIAM H. PITCHARD

Extensive use of the slash to indicate that either of two terms is applicable (as in *and/or, he/she*) can make writing choppy.

■ **Exercise 4**   Punctuate each of the following sentences by supplying commas, dashes, parentheses, brackets, or slashes. Prepare to explain the reason for all marks you add, especially those you choose for setting off parenthetical matter.

1. Mohandas K. Gandhi or is it Mahatma Gandhi? is supposed to have said "There is more to life than increasing its speed."
2. A family vacation which is supposed to be fun is often stressful.
3. "What I dislike most about Leon is" she began but she stopped when she saw him approaching her.
4. Praise, recognition, understanding these are the most powerful weapons in an employer's arsenal.
5. He is the young fellow who seems to have everything brains, sense of humor, ambition.
6. In the half century between 1560 and 1610, two of the greatest writers who ever lived were born William Shakespeare 1564 and John Milton 1608.

7. This ridiculous sentence appeared in the school paper: "Because of a personal fool sic the Cougars failed to cross the goal line during the last seconds of the game."
8. Body language a wink or yawn nose-rubbing or ear-pulling folded arms or crossed legs can often speak much louder than words.
9. Two of the TV networks specifically NBC and ABC have successful early morning programs *Today* and *Good Morning America* respectively.
10. Some recipes for example those for ceviche and sashimi do not require you to cook the fish.

17i

Use ellipsis points (three equally spaced periods) to mark an omission from a quoted passage and to mark a reflective pause or hesitation.

(1) Use ellipsis points to indicate an omission within a quoted passage.

ORIGINAL To bring rowing to minorities, it's important to first understand why they aren't rowing. The first clue is that not long ago programs spent as much energy keeping minorities out of rowing as they now expend to attract them. (From Tina Fisher Forde, "Breaking Down Barriers," *American Rowing*, November/December 1992: 19.)

Omission within a quoted sentence

Noting that "programs spent • • • energy keeping minorities out of rowing," Tina Fisher Forde explains one reason for the small numbers of minorities in rowing.

Omission at the beginning or end of a quoted sentence   Do not use ellipsis points at the beginning of a quotation, whether it is run in to the text or set off in a block.

If an omission at the end of the quoted sentence coincides with the end of your sentence, use a period in addition to the three ellipsis points, leaving no space immediately after the last letter in your sentence. If you cite a parenthetical reference, place the period after the second parenthesis instead.

> Tina Fisher Forde claims that in the past rowing programs worked hard at "keeping minorities out of rowing. . . ." [OR rowing . . ." (19).]

Omission of a sentence or more   Use a period before ellipsis points (that is, use four dots) to mark omissions within a quoted passage if a complete sentence stands on either side of the ellipsis. Also use a period before ellipsis points to mark the omission of a sentence or more (even a paragraph or more) within a quoted passage. If the quoted material ends with a question mark or exclamation point, retain the mark and add *three* ellipsis points.

ORIGINAL   There's an uncertainty in our minds about the engineering principle of an elevator. We've all had little glimpses into the dirty, dark elevator shaft and seen the greasy cables passing each other. They never look totally safe. The idea of being trapped in a small box going up and down on strings induces a kind of phobia in all of us. (From Andrew A. Rooney, *Pieces of My Mind* [New York: Atheneum, 1984], 121.)

Of the common fear of riding in an elevator, Andrew A. Rooney writes, "We've all had little glimpses into the dirty, dark elevator shaft. . . . The idea of being trapped in a small box going up and down on strings induces a kind of phobia in all of us."
[Thirteen words have been omitted from the original, but a sentence comes before and after the period and ellipsis points.]

Andrew A. Rooney writes about the fear of riding in an elevator: "We've all had little glimpses into the dirty, dark elevator shaft and seen the greasy cables passing each other. They never look totally safe. The idea of being trapped . . . induces a kind of phobia in all of us." [Ten words have been omitted from the original, all within a single sentence.]

To indicate the omission of a full line or more in quoted poetry, use spaced periods covering the length either of the line above it or of the omitted line.

I love people who harness themselves, an ox to a heavy cart,
who pull like water buffalo, with massive patience,
. . . .
who do what has to be done, again and again.
—MARGE PIERCY, "To Be of Use"

(2) Use ellipsis points sparingly to mark a reflective pause or hesitation.

Love, like other emotions, has causes . . . and consequences.
—LAWRENCE CASTER

Ellipsis points to show a pause may also come after the period at the end of a sentence:

All channels are open. The meditation is about to begin. . . .
—TOM ROBBINS

■ **Exercise 5** Beginning with "According to John Donne," or with "As John Donne has written," quote the following passage, omitting the words placed in brackets. Use three or four periods as needed to indicate omissions.

No man is an island [entire of itself]; every man is a piece of the continent, a part of the main. [If a clod be washed away by the sea, Europe is the less, as well as if a promontory were, as well as if a manor of thy friend's or of thine own were.] Any man's death diminishes me because I am involved in mankind [and therefore never send to know for whom the bell tolls; it tolls for thee]. —JOHN DONNE

■ **Exercise 6** First, replace the dashes, commas, and italicized words in the following sentences with ellipsis points. Then, observing the differences in meaning and emphasis indicated by each mark of punctuation, write two sentences of your own to illustrate the use of ellipsis points to mark a pause or hesitation.

1. The rivers are polluted—*and, I believe,* prompt action is called for.
2. The rivers can be cleaned up *if people will work at it.*

■ **Exercise 7** Punctuate the following sentences by supplying appropriate end marks, commas, colons, dashes, and parentheses. Do not use unnecessary punctuation. Be prepared to explain the reason for each mark you add, especially when you have a choice of correct marks (for example, commas, dashes, or parentheses).

1. Too many cities are all the same glass buildings neon signs crowded sidewalks
2. "Are we are we leaving now" I sputtered
3. I keep remembering what he said "Rock music from the sixties is just as popular with young people as Heavy Metal"
4. The convicts demanded the following concessions better food longer exercise periods unrestricted access to television
5. "Judy" she exploded "Judy that's an awful thing to say" She raised an arm to slap her daughter but it wouldn't reach
6. Maxine, formerly my father's nurse, took my mother's hand where no one could see and squeezed it gently and compassionately
7. The secret of happiness is to count your blessings—not your birthdays　—SHANNON ROSE
8. My own guess is that sociobiology will offer no comfort to thinkers conservatives or liberals who favor tidy ideas about what it means to be human
9. As one man put it "Rose Bowl Sugar Bowl and Orange Bowl are all gravy bowls"
10. "Good and" can mean "very" "I am good and mad" and "a hot cup of coffee" means that the coffee not the cup is hot

SPELLING AND DICTION

18
Spelling
and Hyphenation

Spell every word according to established usage as shown by your dictionary. Hyphenate words in accordance with current usage.

SPELLING

Spelling problems are highly visible, and misspellings may make a reader doubt whether the writer can present information clearly and correctly. Therefore, always proofread to detect misspellings or typographic errors (see **8c**).

One way to improve spelling is to record the words that you have misspelled and study their correct spellings. Another way is to use mnemonic devices. For example, you might remember the spelling of "separate" by reminding yourself that it has "a rat" in it or the spelling of "attendance" by remembering that it includes "dance."

Most word-processing programs have spell checkers that will help detect spelling errors by checking a single word, a block of text, a page, or the entire document. Be aware, however, of the limitations of a computer spell checker. For example, it will not find the error in frequently confused words such as *principal* and *principle* since it cannot know the meaning that determines the correct spelling of these words. Make sure to proofread your document after you have used the spell checker to catch such errors.

If you have any doubt about a correct spelling, consult your dictionary. Watch for restrictive labels such as *British* or *chiefly British*. In general use the American form.

AMERICAN	theater	fertilize	color	connection
BRITISH	theatre	fertilise	colour	connexion

In ordinary writing, do not use spellings labeled *obsolete* or *archaic, dialectal* or *regional, nonstandard* or *slang*.

NOT	afeard	heighth	chaw	boughten
BUT	afraid	height	chew	bought

If your dictionary lists two unlabeled alternatives, either form is correct—for example, *fulfil* or *fulfill, symbolic* or *symbolical, girlfriend* or *girl friend*. The first option listed is usually the more common or preferred form.

18a

Do not misspell a word because of mispronunciation.

Mispronunciation often leads to misspellings. In the following words, trouble spots are in boldface.

accident**all**y	congra**tul**ations	gover**n**ment	**per**spire
a**thl**ete	February	mod**er**n	realtor
can**di**date	gen**er**ally	nuc**le**ar	stren**gth**

As you check pronunciation in the dictionary, notice carefully which letters represent /ə/, *schwa*, the symbol for a neutral vowel sound in unaccented syllables, usually an indistinct *uh* sound, as in *confidence*.

A word that is difficult to spell, such as *often*, may have alternate pronunciations (ôf′ən, ôf′tən). Of these, one may be a better guide to spelling. Here are examples of other such words:

every**b**ody	literat**u**re	vet**e**ran
int**e**rest	soph**o**more	w**h**ich

Be careful when spelling words like *and*, *than*, and *have* since they are often not stressed in speech: I would have (NOT *of*) preferred fish rather than (NOT *then*) soup and (NOT *an*) salad.

18b

Distinguish between words of similar sound; use the spelling required by the meaning.

Words such as *forth* and *fourth* or *sole* and *soul* are homophones: they sound alike but have vastly different meanings and spellings. Be sure to choose the right word for your context. A spell checker will not identify such an error.

Many frequently confused spellings may be studied in groups:

Contractions and possessive pronouns (See **15b, 15d.**)

It's my turn next.	Each group waits **its** turn.
You're next.	**Your** turn is next.
There's no difference.	**Theirs** is no different.

Single words and two-word phrases (See **Glossary of Usage.**)

He wore **everyday** clothes.	He wears them **every day**.
Maybe we will go.	We **may be** going.
You ran **into** my car.	We can run **in to** check it.
Nobody was there.	The police found **no body**.

Singular nouns ending in *-nce* and plural nouns ending in *-nts*

Assistance is available.	I have two **assistants**.
For **instance**, Jack can go.	They arrived **instants** ago.
My **patience** is frayed.	Some **patients** waited hours.

As you study the following list, use the **Glossary of Usage** or your dictionary to check the meaning of words you are not thoroughly familiar with. You may find it helpful to devise examples of usage such as these:

accept—have accepted	**except**—anything except money
its—enjoy its warmth	**it's**—it is warm
passed—passed the test	**past**—a lurid past

Words Whose Spellings Are Frequently Confused

accept, except	began, begin
access, excess	believe, belief
adapt, adopt	board, bored 20
advice, advise	break, brake
affect, effect	breath, breathe
aisles, isles	buy, by, bye
alley, ally	canvas, canvass
allusion, illusion	capital, capitol
already, all ready	censor, censure, sensor
altar, alter 10	choose, chose
altogether, all together	cite, site, sight
always, all ways	clothes, cloths
angel, angle	coarse, course 30
ascent, assent	complement, compliment
ask, ax	conscience, conscious
assistance, assistants	council, counsel
baring, barring, bearing	cursor, curser

dairy, diary
decent, descent, dissent
desert, dessert
dominant, dominate
dyeing, dying
elicit, illicit   40
envelop, envelope
fair, fare
faze, phase
formerly, formally
forth, fourth
forward, foreword
gorilla, guerrilla
have, of
hear, here
heard, herd   50
heroin, heroine
hole, whole
holy, wholly
horse, hoarse
human, humane
instance, instants
its, it's
later, latter
led, lead
lesson, lessen   60
lightning, lightening
lose, loose
maybe, may be
minor, miner
moral, morale
of, off
passed, past

patience, patients
peace, piece
persecute, prosecute   70
personal, personnel
perspective, prospective
plain, plane
pray, prey
precede, proceed
predominant, predominate
presence, presents
principle, principal
prophecy, prophesy
purpose, propose   80
quiet, quit, quite
respectfully, respectively
right, rite, write   50
road, rode
sense, since
shown, shone
stationary, stationery
straight, strait
than, then
their, there, they're   90
threw, through, thorough
to, too, two
tract, track   60
waist, waste
weak, week
weather, whether
were, wear, where
which, witch
who's, whose
your, you're   100

18c

Distinguish between the prefix and the root.

The root is the base to which prefixes and suffixes are added. Prefixes usually change the meaning of the root word, whereas suffixes change the part of speech of the root word. Notice in the following examples that no letter is added or dropped when the prefix is added to the root.

im-	**im**mobile, **im**moral	mis-	**mis**spell, **mis**state
dis-	**dis**respect, **dis**prove	re-	**re**gain, **re**join
un-	**un**natural, **un**lucky	ir-	**ir**regular, **ir**resolute

18d

Follow spelling conventions when adding suffixes.

(1) Dropping or retaining a final unpronounced *e*

Drop the *-e* before a suffix beginning with a vowel:

bride, brid**al**	combine, combin**ation**
come, com**ing**	prime, prim**ary**

Retain the *-e* before a suffix beginning with a consonant:

rude, rude**ness**	entire, entire**ly**
sure, sure**ly**	place, place**ment**

▲ Some exceptions: *likable, acreage, ninth, truly, duly, awful, wholly*

To keep the sound /s/ of *ce* or /j/ of *ge*, do not drop the final *e* before *-able* or *-ous*:

notic**eable**   manag**eable**   courag**eous**

(2) Doubling a final consonant before a suffix

Double a final consonant before a suffix beginning with a vowel if both (a) the consonant ends a word of one syllable or a stressed syllable and (b) the consonant is preceded by a single vowel.

> drop, dro**pp**ing   BUT   droop, droo**p**ing
> admit, admi**tt**ed   BUT   figure, figu**r**ed

(3) Changing or retaining a final *y* before a suffix

Change the *y* to *i* before suffixes—except *-ing*.

> defy: def**ies**, def**ied**, def**iance**   BUT   def**ying**
> modify: modif**ies**, modif**ier**, modif**ied**   BUT   modif**ying**

▲ **Exceptions:** Most verbs ending in *y* preceded by a vowel do not change the *y* before *-s* or *-ed: stay, stays, stayed.* Similarly, nouns like *joys* or *days* retain the *y* before *-s*. The following irregularities in spelling are especially troublesome: *lays, laid; pays, paid; says, said.*

(4) Retaining a final *l* before *-ly*

Do not drop a final *l* when you add *-ly*:

> usual, usual**ly**   real, real**ly**   cool, cool**ly**
> formal, formal**ly**

■ **Exercise 1**   Add the designated suffixes to the following words.

> EXAMPLES
> -ing: rise, lose, guide   *rising, losing, guiding*
> -ly, -er, -ness: late   *lately, later, lateness*
> -ed, -ing: rebel   *rebelled, rebelling*

1. -ing, -ment, -ed: manage
2. -ment, -ed, -ing: conceal
3. -able: desire, notice, manage
4. -ful, -ing, -ed: hope, care, use
5. -ous: continue, courage

6. -er, -ing, -ed: jog, play
7. -ly: safe, like, sure
8. -ing, -ed: plan, pay
9. -ance, -ing, -ed: admit
10. -ly, -ed, -ing: complete

(5) Adding -*s* or -*es* to form the plural of nouns

Form the plural of most nouns by adding -*s* to the singular:

> toys, scientists, tables
> the Smiths [proper names], sisters-in-law [chief word pluralized]

For nouns ending in an *f* or *fe*, change the ending to *ve* before adding -*s* when the plural changes from an *f* sound to a *v* sound: *thief, thieves; life, lives;* BUT *roof, roofs.*

For nouns ending in *s, z, ch, sh,* or *x,* add -*es* when the plural adds another syllable:

> box, box**es**   peach, peach**es**   crash, crash**es**   the Rodriguez**es**

For nouns ending in *y* preceded by a consonant, add -*es* after changing the *y* to *i*:

> company, compan**ies**   ninety, ninet**ies**

For most nouns ending in *o* preceded by a consonant, add -*es*, although usage varies. Consult a dictionary if you have a question.

ech**oes**	her**oes**	potat**oes**	vet**oes** [-*es* only]
autos	memos	pimentos	pros [-*s* only]
nos/n**oes**	mottos/mott**oes**	zeros/zer**oes** [-*s* or -*es*]	

▲ **Exceptions:** Certain irregular nouns, including retained foreign spellings, do not add -*s* or -*es* to form the plural. Consult a dictionary if you have questions.

SINGULAR	woman	goose	analysis	datum	species
PLURAL	wom**e**n	g**ee**se	analys**es**	dat**a**	species
SINGULAR	criterion	alumnus	alumna		
PLURAL	criteri**a**	alumn**i**	alumn**ae**		

■ **Exercise 2** Supply plural forms (including any optional spelling) for the following words. (If a word is not covered by the rules, use your dictionary.)

1. life	6. bath	11. scarf	16. phenomenon
2. theory	7. hero	12. half	17. halo
3. church	8. story	13. leaf	18. woman
4. radius	9. bush	14. speech	19. passer-by
5. Kelly	10. genius	15. tomato	20. potato

18e

Apply the rules to avoid confusion of *ei* and *ie*.

When the sound is /ē/ (as in *me*), write *ie* (except after *c*, in which case write *ei*):

> chief   yield   priest
> [BUT after c] receive   perceive   conceit

When the sound is other than /ē/, usually write *ei*:

> eight   heir   rein   their   weight   foreign

▲ Exceptions: either, neither, friend, species.

■ **Exercise 3**   Fill in the blanks with the appropriate letters: *ei* or *ie*.

1. bes____ge	6. conc____ve	11. w____rd
2. dec____t	7. n____ce	12. y____ld
3. fr____ght	8. sh____ld	13. p____ce
4. r____gned	9. f____nd	14. rec____ve
5. s____ve	10. pr____st	15. th____r

■ **Exercise 4**   Write a list of five reminders that help you remember certain difficult spellings. Share your mnemonic devices with other members of the class.

HYPHENATION

18f

Hyphenate words to express the idea of a unit, to avoid ambiguity, and to divide words at the end of a line.

Notice in the following examples that the hyphen links (or makes a compound of) two or more words that function as a single word.

We planted forget-me-nots and Johnny-jump-ups.   I wore my favorite T-shirt.   [nouns]

He hand-fed them.   I double-parked.   Hard-boil an egg.   [verbs]

Was it an eye-to-eye confrontation?   [adjective]

Consult a good recent dictionary when you are not sure of the form of compounds, since some are connected with hyphens (*eye-opener, cross-examine*), some are written separately (*eye chart, cross fire*), and others are written as one word (*eyewitness, crossbreed*).

▲ Caution: Do not confuse the hyphen with the dash, which is typed as a double hyphen with no spaces before and after. See **17e**.

(1) Hyphenate two or more words serving as a single adjective before a noun.

a well-built house   BUT   a house that is well built

"I reject get-it-done, make-it-happen thinking," he says.
—*THE ATLANTIC*

In a series, carry over hyphens from one item to the next.

eighteenth- and nineteenth-century rhetoric

▲ Exceptions: Omit the hyphen in the following situations:

(a) after an adverb ending in *-ly* (*quickly frozen foods*),
(b) in a compound using a comparative or superlative adjective (*a better built house*),
(c) in chemical terms (*sodium chloride solution*),
(d) in a modifier using a letter or numeral as the second element (*Group C homes, Type IV virus*).

(2) Hyphenate spelled-out fractions and compound numbers from twenty-one to ninety-nine (or twenty-first to ninety-ninth).

one-eighth   eighty-four   twenty-third

Also hyphenate combinations of figures and letters (*mid-1990s*) as well as zip codes that include the additional four digits (Dallas, TX 75392-0041).

(3) Hyphenate to avoid ambiguity or an awkward combination of letters or syllables between prefix and root or suffix and root.

re-sign the petition   [Compare "resign the position."]
a dirty movie-theater   [Compare "a dirty-movie theater."]

(4) Hyphenate the prefixes *ex-* ("former"), *self-*, *all-*; the suffix *-elect*; and between a prefix and a capitalized word.

president-elect   ex-husband   all-important   self-made
non-British   anti-American   mid-August

■ **Exercise 5:** Refer to **18f** and to your dictionary as you convert each phrase (or words within each phrase) to a compound or to a word with a prefix. Use hyphens when needed.

EXAMPLES
an ordeal lasting two months   *a two-month ordeal*
glasses used for water   *water glasses* OR *waterglasses*

1. a weekend lasting three days
2. an automobile five years old
3. a light used at night
3. a hangar for three airplanes
4. metal chairs covered with rust
5. a freeway with eight lanes
6. a brush for teeth
7. videos costing thirty dollars

8. mediators that solve problems
9. engineer that does research
10. in the shape of a T

■ **Exercise 6** Edit the following paragraph for misspellings and correct usage of the hyphen.

[1]I sat in silence viewing *Grand-Canyon*, a film that is principly about the decedent twentieth-century environment of America's big cities, and I found that it communicats better than all of the scientific datum now available. [2]For too hours, viewers sit on the edges of their seats in wonderous suspense as they watch hair raising encounters with urban violence. [3]After suffering empathy for people trapped in their artificial environment—Los Angeles with it's towering buildings of concrete, glass, and steel; it's madness of drive-by shootings, muggings, and foreboding, hovering police helicopters—the audience shoulders the burden of what it means to live in the twentieth and twenty first centurys. [4]What really surprised me about the film, though, was the ending. [5]What the Grand Canyon offers to two beleaguered familys who manage to escape the City of Lost Angels does not relinquish itself easily to words, and it doesn't readly respond to reason. [6]In the film's final scene, on the lip of the Grand Canyon, human woe sighes out in relief and shrinks against a backdrop of a monument millions of years since it began. [7]I guess I shouldn't have been so surprised that a film maker would realize something that I have been aware of all my life: nature in its grandure is sacred, and people have always raelized that it has important lessens to teach.

(5) If you must break a word at the end of a line, hyphenate it according to standard practice.

You will seldom need to divide words if you leave a reasonably wide right margin. If you must divide a word at the end of a line, however, use a hyphen to mark the separation of syllables. In dictionaries, dots usually divide the syllables of words: **re • al • ly, pre • fer, pref • er • ence, sell • ing, set • ting**. But not every division between syllables is an appropriate place for dividing a word at the end of a line. The following principles are useful guidelines:

(a) Abbreviations, initials, capitalized acronyms, or one-syllable words Do not divide these:

p.m. [NOT p.•m.] USAF [NOT US•AF]
UNESCO [NOT UNES•CO] through [NOT thr•ough]

(b) One-letter syllables Do not put the first or last letter of a word at the end or beginning of a line:

omit [NOT o•mit] able [NOT a•ble] boa [NOT bo•a]

(c) Two-letter endings Do not put the last two letters of a word at the beginning of a line:

dated [NOT dat•ed] doesn't [NOT does•n't] safely
[NOT safe•ly] gravel [NOT grav•el] taxis [NOT tax•is]

The vertical lines in the following examples mark appropriate end-of-line divisions.

(d) Hyphenated words Divide hyphenated words only at the hyphen:

mass-| produce
father-| in-law OR father-in-| law

(e) Consonants between vowels Divide words between two consonants that come between vowels—except when the division does not reflect pronunciation:

pic-| nic dis-| cuss thun-| der BUT co-| bra

(f) *-ing* words Divide words between those consonants that you double when adding *-ing*:

set-| ting jam-| ming plan-| ning [Compare "sell-| ing."]

▲ **Note:** Many word-processing programs include an automatic hyphenation feature, but these features sometimes hyphenate words incorrectly. Check each hyphenation and make corrections as needed.

■ **Exercise 7** First, put a check mark after the words that should not be divided at the end of a line. Then, with the aid of your dictionary, write out the other words by syllables and insert the hyphens followed by a vertical line to indicate appropriate end-of-line divisions.

1. cross-list
2. political
3. fourteenth
4. FEMA
5. tripped
6. tripping
7. guessing

8. against
9. present (gift)
10. present (give)
11. seacoast
12. eventual
13. decline
14. IRS

15. mystical
16. KOMU-TV
17. matches
18. disappear
19. cobwebs
20. patron

19
Good Usage

Choose words appropriate to the audience, the purpose, and the occasion. Use a good dictionary to select words that express your ideas.

Your vocabulary includes words and phrases from the formal language of the classroom as well as from the informal, casual language of everyday conversation. For example, you may use regional or dialectal expressions (also called localisms or provincialisms). In formal writing for college and the workplace, however, choose words that are meaningful to a general audience of educated readers, and avoid those that are colloquial.

A dictionary is an excellent reference tool to help you distinguish between the informal language of conversation and the formal language of writing. Through special usage labels, defined in their introductions, dictionaries can aid in the selection of appropriate words. Ordinarily, if a word has no usage label, it is appropriate for formal writing. Avoid those words labelled *nonstandard, archaic,* or *obsolete.* Also consult the **Glossary of Usage** for the most commonly confused or misused words.

College dictionaries

Rely upon a recent college dictionary, such as one of the following:

The American Heritage Dictionary
Funk & Wagnalls Standard College Dictionary
The Random House Dictionary
Webster's New Collegiate Dictionary
Webster's New World Dictionary

Unabridged dictionaries

Occasionally you may need to refer to an unabridged or to a special dictionary.

The Oxford English Dictionary. 2nd ed. 20 vols. 1989–.
Webster's Third New International Dictionary. 1981.

Special dictionaries

Bryson, Bill. *The Facts on File Dictionary of Troublesome Words.* 1985.
Cowie, A. P., and R. Mackin. *Oxford Dictionary of Current Idiomatic English.* Vols. 1–2. 1975, 1983.
Follett, Wilson. *Modern American Usage: A Guide.* 1966.
Morris, William, and Mary Morris. *Harper Dictionary of Contemporary Usage.* 2nd ed. 1985.
Onions, C. T. *Oxford Dictionary of English Etymology.* 1966.
Partridge, Eric. *Dictionary of Catch Phrases.* Rev. ed. 1986.
———. *Dictionary of Slang and Unconventional English.* 8th ed. 1985.
Roget's International Thesaurus. 4th ed. 1977.
Webster's Dictionary of English Usage. 1989.
Webster's Collegiate Thesaurus. 1976.

Some dictionaries and reference works are also offered on CD-ROM (computer disk) and are available in many libraries.

19a

Use a good dictionary intelligently.

Examine the introductory matter as well as the arrangement and presentation of material in your dictionary so that you can easily find the information you need. Note meanings of any special abbreviations your dictionary uses.

(1) Understand the information that a dictionary can provide.

Note the various kinds of information provided in the sample dictionary entries below.

Part of speech

Syllabication   Pronunciation

Forms

Spelling —— **ex·cite** (ĭk-sīt′) *tr.v.* **-cit·ed, -cit·ing, -cites.** **1.** To stir to activity
    2. To call forth (a reaction or emotion, for example): elicit: *odd*
Usage   *noises that excited our curiosity.* **3.** To arouse strong feeling in:
example   *speakers who know how to excite a crowd.* See Synonyms at **pro-**
    voke. **4.** *Physiology.* To produce increased activity or response   Two
Technical   in (an organ, a tissue, or a part); stimulate. **5.** *Physics.* **a.** To   relat
meanings   increase the energy of. **b.** To raise (an atom, for example) to a   mea
    higher energy level. [Middle English *exciten,* from Latin *excitāre,*
    frequentative of *excitēre: ex-,* ex + *ciēre,* to set in motion; see   Etym
    kei-² in Appendix.]

    pro·voke (prə-vōk′) *tr.v.* **-voked, -vok·ing, -vokes.** **1.** To incite
    to anger or resentment. **2.** To stir to action or feeling. **3.** To give
    rise to; evoke: *provoke laughter.* **4.** To bring about deliberately;
    induce: *provoke a fight.* [Middle English *provoken,* from Old French
    provoquer, from Latin *prōvocāre,* to challenge: *prō-,* PRO-¹; see
    PRO-¹ + *vocāre,* to call (see **wekʷ** in Appendix.] **-pro·vok′ing·ly**
    adv.

    SYNONYMS: *provoke, incite, excite, stimulate, arouse, stir.* These
    verbs are compared in the sense of moving a person to action or
    feeling or summoning something into being by moving a person in
    this way. *Provoke,* the least explicit with respect to means, frequently   Distir
    does little more than state the consequences produced: *"Let my*   amor
    presumption not provoke thy wrath" (Shakespeare). *"A situation*   synor
    which in the country would have provoked meetings" (John Galswor-
    thy). To *incite* is to provoke and urge on: *The insurrection was*
    incited by members of the outlawed opposition. Excite especially
    implies the provoking of a strong reaction or powerful emotion:
    The play is bound to fail; the plot excites little interest or curiosity.
    To *stimulate* is to excite to activity or to renewed vigor of action as
    if by spurring or goading: *"Our vigilance was stimulated by our*
    finding traces of a large . . . encampment" (Francis Parkman). *Arouse*
    and *rouse* suggest awakening, as from inactivity or apathy; *rouse,*
    the stronger term, often implies incitement to vigorous or animated
    activity or excitement of strong emotion: *"In a democratic society*
    like ours, relief must come through an aroused popular conscience
    that sears the conscience of the people's representatives" (Felix

Frankfurter). *"His mother . . . endeavored to rouse him from his passive state"* (Washington Irving). *"The oceangoing steamers . . . roused in him wild and painful longings"* (Arnold Bennett). To *stir* is to prompt to activity, to arouse strong but usually agreeable feelings, or to provoke trouble or commotion: *"It was him as stirred up th' young woman to preach last night"* (George Eliot). *"I have seldom been so . . . stirred by any piece of writing"* (Mark Twain). *"Men blame you that you have stirred a quarrel up"* (William Butler Yeats). See also Synonyms at **annoy**.

Spelling, syllabication, and pronunciation   The dictionary describes both written and spoken language. You can check spelling and word division (syllabication) as well as pronunciation of unfamiliar words. A key to sound symbols appears at the bottom of the entry pages as well as in the introduction. Alternative pronunciations usually represent regional differences. The first one listed is considered the more common.

Parts of speech and inflected forms   The dictionary also labels the possible uses of words in sentences—for instance, *tr. v., adj.* It identifies the various ways that nouns, verbs, and modifiers change form to indicate number, tense, and comparisons.

Definitions and examples of usage   The definitions are ordered according to how commonly they are used. Examples of the connotations in context, in a sentence or phrase, help to clarify subtleties of usage.

Synonyms and antonyms   Lists of synonyms often help to explain the meaning of a word. Note the subtle differences in meaning among the synonyms listed under *provoke*. Before using a synonym from a thesaurus, verify its meaning in the dictionary. Lists of antonyms help by providing words that have opposite meanings.

Most dictionaries are also printed in concise paperback forms, which provide less information but are useful for spellings, pronunciations, parts of speech, definitions, and abbreviated derivations.

■ **Exercise 1** Study the pronunciations of the following common words in your dictionary, and determine how you might pronounce them in your own region. Be prepared to discuss your pronunciations with those of your classmates.

1. either   2. orange   3. news   4. which   5. wash

■ **Exercise 2** With the aid of your dictionary or thesaurus, list two synonyms for each of the following words, and use each synonym in a sentence.

1. hatred   2. false   3. pleasure   4. oppose   5. stingy

■ **Exercise 3** Study definitions of the following pairs of words, and write a sentence for each pair to illustrate the subtle differences in meaning.

1. rot–putrefy
2. sensual–sensuous
3. innocent–ingenuous
4. free–liberate
5. necrophile–vampire
6. viable–practicable
7. excite–provoke
8. charisma–charm
9. mercy–clemency
10. fearless–courageous

(2) Etymologies: The origin and development of the language

Knowledge of the origin of a word—also called its derivation or etymology—can be useful in understanding its meaning. Such information is available in most dictionaries. For example, knowing that *caterpillar* is derived from two Latin words that mean "cat" and "hairy" provides a vivid picture of the larva. College dictionaries show the origin of a word in brackets at the beginning or end of the citation. Special etymological dictionaries give more detailed information.

English belongs to the Indo-European group of languages derived from a common source that was spoken in parts of Europe about six thousand years ago. By the beginning of the common era (1 A.D.), the original Indo-European had developed into eight or nine language families. Of these, the chief ones that influenced English were the Germanic in northwestern Europe (from which English is descended) and the Hellenic (Greek) and Italic (Latin) groups in the Mediterranean basin. Most modern English words show these influences.

The study of the history of the English language is customarily divided into three main periods. The first is the Old English period, which began about the middle of the fifth century when the language was largely Anglo-Saxon, with a small mixture of Old Norse as a result of the Scandinavian (Viking) invasions and a few words borrowed from Latin.

The Middle English period began with the Norman conquest in 1066 when the Norman French conquered the English, moved across the channel, and made French the language of the ruling classes. Although the peasants and workers still spoke English, the business of the church and the government was conducted in French. The Norman influence is still evident in modern English words such as *parliament* and the *"Oyez, oyez"* (Old French for "Hear ye, hear ye") which law courts in the United States customarily open with even today. By the end of the fourteenth century English began to prevail. It had lost much of its Anglo-Saxon word endings and taken on thousands of French words, but it was still basically English, not French, in its structure. This reemergence of the English language marked the beginning of Modern English.

The kinds of changes that have occurred during the development of the English language (until it was partly stabilized by printing, introduced in London in 1476) are suggested in the following passages. The first is from Old English, the second is from Middle English, and the third is from Modern English—the seventeenth-century King James version of the Bible.

Ǣlc þāra þe þās mīn word gehīerþ, and þā wyrcþ, biþ gelīc
Thus each who hears these my words, and does them, is like

þǣm wīsan were, sē his hūs ofer stān getimbrode.
a wise man, who builds his house on a stone.

[Matthew 7:24–25, tenth century]

Therfor ech man that herith these my wordis, and doith hem,
shal be maad lijk to a wise man, that hath bildid his hous on
a stoon.   [Matthew 7:24–25, fourteenth century]

Therefore whosoever heareth these sayings of mine, and doeth
them, I will liken him unto a wise man, which built his house
upon a rock.   [Matthew 7:24–25, seventeenth century]

English has always been open to borrowing from other
languages. As a result, a striking feature of Modern English
is its immense and varied vocabulary. Old English used fifty
or sixty thousand words; Middle English perhaps a hundred
thousand, many taken from French through Latin; and unabridged dictionaries today list over four times as many. As
the English people pushed out to colonize in many parts of
the globe, they brought home new words as well as goods.
For example, from India came *bungalow* and *dungaree,* from
Spain *patio* and *barbeque.* From North America, the English
borrowed *teepee* and *succotash* and from Africa, *okra* and
zombie. Modern English continues to borrow from the peoples who bring their native tongues to the English-speaking
countries. Such words as *tabouli, baklava,* and *reggae* are
recent additions. More and more, English is becoming the
language through which the world's business is conducted.
English etymologies involve not only the study of word meanings and derivations, but also the study of the many diverse
peoples who find their homes in the English speaking countries.

■ **Exercise 4**   With the aid of a dictionary, give the etymology of each
of the following words. You may need to consult other dictionaries
besides your own.

1. dexterity
2. youth
3. OK
4. velcro
5. lunatic
6. cute
7. hysterical
8. hallmark
9. sinister
10. laugh

19b

Use informal words only when appropriate to the audience, the purpose, and the occasion.

Words or expressions labeled *informal* or *colloquial* (meaning "characteristic of speech") in college dictionaries are used by writers every day, particularly in informal writing, especially dialogue. On occasion, informal words can be used effectively in formal writing, for example to add emphasis, but they are usually inappropriate. Unless an informal expression is specifically called for, use the unlabeled words in your dictionary.

INFORMAL	dopey	gypped	bellybutton
FORMAL	stupid	swindled	navel

Contractions are common in informal English, especially in dialogue: see **15b**. But contracted forms (like *won't* or *there's*) are usually avoided in college writing, which is not as casual as conversational English is.

■ **Exercise 5** Make a list of ten words or phrases that you would ordinarily consider informal and prepare for a class discussion on whether you would use them (a) in a job interview, (b) in a conversation with a friend, (c) in a conversation with the Dean of Students, (d) in a letter of application, and (e) in an essay. Check your dictionary to see how each word is labeled.

19c

Use newly coined words or slang only when appropriate to the audience, the purpose, and the occasion.

Newly coined words are usually fresh and interesting but may be unfamiliar to your reader since they are often regional or technical. A few years ago no one had heard of a *computer virus,* and even today many would find *hypertext* meaningless.

Define words that may be unfamiliar to the reader or, better yet, find another term.

Slang words, including certain coinages and figures of speech, are variously considered as breezy, racy, excessively informal, facetious, taboo, or vigorous and colorful. On occasion, slang can be used effectively, even in formal writing. Below is an example of the effective use of the word *spiel*, still labeled by dictionaries as *slang*:

> Here comes election year. Here comes the hopefuls, the conventions, the candidates, the spiels, the postures, the press releases, and the TV performances. Here comes the year of the hoopla. —JOHN CIARDI

A few years ago the word *hoopla* was also generally considered as slang, but now dictionaries disagree: one classifies this word as *standard* (unlabeled); another, *colloquial;* still another, *slang.* Like *hoopla,* words such as *spiel, uptight, schlep, dork,* and *wimp* have a particularly vivid quality; they soon may join former slang words such as *sham* and *mob* as part of the general English vocabulary. Or they may disappear from common usage.

Slang can easily become dated—which is a good reason to be cautious about using it in writing. Also, much slang is trite, tasteless, and imprecise. For instance, when used to describe almost anything approved of, *awesome* becomes inexact and flat.

19d

Use regional words only when appropriate to the audience.

Regional or dialectal usages should normally be avoided in writing outside the region where they are current since their meanings may not be widely known. Speakers and writers, however, may safely use regional words known to the audience they are addressing.

REGIONAL   We were **fixing** to swim in Joe's **tank**.
FORMAL   We were ready to swim in Joe's pond.   [OR *lake*]

19e

Avoid nonstandard words and usages.

Words and expressions labeled by dictionaries as *nonstandard* should not be used in formal writing, except possibly in direct quotations. For example, *ain't* should not be used for *am not*, nor should "He's done eaten" be used for "He has finished eating."

19f

Avoid archaic and obsolete words.

All dictionaries list words (and meanings for words) that have long since passed out of general use. Such words as *rathe* (early) and *yestreen* (last evening) are still found in dictionaries because, once the standard vocabulary of great authors, they occur in our older literature and must be defined for the modern reader.

A number of obsolete or archaic words—such as *worser* (for *worse*) or *holp* (for *helped*)—are still in use but are now nonstandard.

19g

Use technical words only when appropriate to the audience, the purpose, and the occasion.

When writing for the general reader, avoid all unnecessary technical language. The careful writer will not refer to an organized way to find a subject for writing as a *heuristic* or a need for bifocals as *presbyopia*. (Of course, the greater precision of technical language makes it desirable when the audience can understand it, as when one physician writes to another.)

Jargon is technical language tailored specifically for a particular occupation. Technical language can be an efficient shortcut for specialized concepts, but you should use jargon only when (1) you can be sure that both you and your readers understand it and (2) the purpose of the writing is of a technical nature.

19h

Use a simple, straightforward style. Avoid overwriting.

An ornate or flowery style makes reading slow and difficult, and it calls attention to the words rather than to the ideas. Keep your writing simple and straightforward.

> ORNATE   The majority believes that the approbation of society derives primarily from diligent pursuit of allocated tasks.
>
> SIMPLE   Most people believe success results from hard work.

■ **Exercise 6**   Rewrite the following passages for the audience and purpose specified (adapted from Stuart Chase, *Power of Words*).

1. **In a persuasive letter to members of the City Council:** It is obvious from the difference in elevation with relation to the short depth of the property that the contour is such as to preclude any reasonable developmental potential for active recreation.

2. **In a verbal, informational report to the Dean of Arts and Sciences:** Realization has grown that the curriculum or the experiences of learners change and improve only as those who are most directly involved examine their goals, improve their understandings, and increase their skill in performing the tasks necessary to reach newly defined goals.

3. **In an instructional brochure distributed by the Public Health Service to all of its clinics:** Vouchable expenditures necessary to

provide adequate dental treatment required as adjunct to medical treatment being rendered a pay patient in in-patient status may be incurred as required at the expense of the Public Health Service.

19i

Consider your purpose and your audience as you consult the Glossary of Usage.

Consult the **Glossary of Usage** for words and expressions most frequently confused or misused. Distinguish between the informal language that you might use in conversations with friends or in personal letters and the formal language that you should use for most college writing.

■ **Exercise 7** Refer to the **Glossary of Usage** and list the words or phrases that you might confuse or misuse.

19j

Avoid sexist language. (See also 6b.)

To avoid sexist usage, make your language inclusive; always give equal treatment to both men and women. Avoid the generic use of *man* to refer to both men and women, and do not stereotype sex roles—for example, assuming that all secretaries are women and all doctors are men.

INAPPROPRIATE	APPROPRIATE
authoress	author
the common man	the average person, ordinary people
lady doctor	doctor
male nurse	nurse
mankind	humanity, human beings, people

policeman	police officer
weatherman	meteorologist, weather forecaster
Have your *mother* send a snack.	Have your **parent** send a snack.
The law should prohibit an alcoholic from driving *his* car.	The law should prohibit an alcoholic from driving.
My *girl* will call the members.	My **assistant** will call the members.
The professors and their *wives* attended.	The professors and their **spouses** attended.

■ **Exercise 8** Rewrite the following sentences to remove all sexist language. Before you begin, review **6b**.

1. Every congressman cast his vote.
2. Men's laws have resulted in the establishment of a society where every person can realize his potential.
3. The executives had a meeting while the ladies had a tour of the city.
4. When everyone contributes his ideas, the discussion will be successful.
5. She was a fine actress as well as a published authoress.
6. The insurance policy covers all employees and their wives.
7. The reporter interviewed President Berrier and his secretary, Rosa Gonzales.
8. My uncle has never married and his sister is a spinster.
9. Melinda is a career woman.
10. Both Erik, an accomplished artist, and Mary, an attractive blonde, displayed their work.

■ **Exercise 9** Rewrite the following sentences in standard English appropriate for a theme in an English composition class. Consult the **Glossary of Usage** to determine appropriate usages.

1. As far as his grades go, he is well qualified.
2. If he had known John was coming, he would have waited longer.
3. Carlos owned alot of land.
4. It didn't effect the students that much.
5. The man was confused as to the price of the property.

6. He kept a large amount of bills in his pocket.
7. Most everyone wanted a ticket.
8. He had read in a magazine where the problem was pollution.
9. They were only hurting theirselves.
10. She was nauseous all morning.

20

Exactness

Choose words that are exact, idiomatic, and fresh.

When drafting, choose words that closely express your ideas and feelings. When revising, make those words exact, idiomatic, and fresh. Use effectively the words you already know. Good writing often consists of short, familiar words precisely used.

> The ball was loose, rolling free near the line of scrimmage. I raced for the fumble, bent over, scooped up the ball on the dead run, and turned downfield. With a sudden burst of speed, I bolted past the line and past the linebackers. Only two defensive backs stood between me and the goal line. One came up fast, and I gave him a hip feint, stuck out my left arm in a classic straight-arm, caught him on the helmet, and shoved him to the ground. The final defender moved toward me, and I cut to the sidelines, swung sharply back to the middle for three steps, braked again, and reversed my direction once more. The defender tripped over his own feet in confusion. I trotted into the end zone, having covered seventy-eight yards on my touchdown run, happily flipped the football into the stands, turned and loped casually toward the sidelines. Then I woke up.
>
> —JERRY KRAMER, *Farewell to Football*

Adding to your vocabulary, however, increases your options for choosing the exact word to suit your purpose, occasion, and audience. So make valuable new words your own by mastering their denotations and their connotations.

20a

Select the words that exactly express your ideas.

(1) Choose words that denote precisely what you mean. Avoid inaccurate, inexact, or ambiguous usage.

The *denotation* of a word indicates what it names, not what it suggests. For example, the noun *beach* denotes a sandy or pebbly shore, not suggestions of summer fun. Inaccurate usage misstates your point. Inexact usage diminishes your point. Ambiguous usage confuses your reader about your point. Select words that state your point exactly.

INACCURATE	The figures before me inferred that our enrollment had increased significantly this year. [*Infer* means "to make a conclusion from evidence." Compare "From the figures before me, I inferred that. . . ."]
ACCURATE	The figures before me **implied** that our enrollment had increased significantly this year. [*Imply* means "to suggest."]
INEXACT	Phyllicia spends too much money, and she earns it herself. [*And* adds or continues.]
EXACT	Phyllicia spends too much money, **but** she earns it herself. [*But* contrasts.]
AMBIGUOUS	I knew enough German to understand I would have to drive six miles—but no more. ["No more" can refer to number of miles to drive or adequacy of the writer's German.]
CLEAR	**I knew only enough** German to understand that I would have to drive six miles. OR I knew enough German to understand that I would have to **drive only** six miles.

■ Exercise 1 The italicized words in the following sentences are inaccurate, inexact, or ambiguous. Replace such words with exact ones.

1. The faculty was concerned about the *affects* of the new admission standards.
2. My father's curly hair and dimples gave him a *childish* appearance.
3. Ingrid *flouts* her wealth.
4. Bart *procrastinated* about where he ate dinner.
5. Luis worked hard to *obtain* a higher position in the company.
6. After you finish writing, go back and *adjust* your paper.
7. I frequently consult the classified ads, *and* I can seldom find what I want.
8. She didn't say it but she *intimidated* it.
9. Hurricanes are *seasonable*.
10. Petrina was worried even though she found her story *incredulous*.

■ Exercise 2 With the aid of your dictionary, give the exact meaning of each italicized word in the quotations below. (Italics have been added.) Pay particular attention to any usage notes.

1. Ignorance of *history* is dangerous. —JEFFREY RECORD

   Those who cannot remember *the past* are condemned to repeat it. —GEORGE SANTAYANA

2. The *cosmic* Zora emerges. I belong to no race nor time. I am the eternal feminine. . . . —ZORA NEALE HURSTON

   Malcolm did not invent the new *cosmology*—black power, black is beautiful, think black—or the mystique of Africanism.
   —PETER SCHRAG

3. And if you weren't going to *resign* on the spot, you might as well stay on till you were sixty-five, for all the effect it was going to have on management. —EDWARD RIVERA

   This is the type of negative freedom and *resignation* that often engulfs the life of the oppressed. —MARTIN LUTHER KING, JR.

4. Securing legislation was *a crucial step* in making the country more democratic. —JUAN WILLIAMS

   Study and planning are *an absolute prerequisite* for any kind of intelligent action. —EDWARD BROOKE

5. We had a *permissive* father. He *permitted* us to work.
   —SAM LEVENSON

(2) Choose the word that accurately connotes your idea.

The *connotation* of a word is what the word suggests or implies. *Beach,* for instance, may connote natural beauty, warmth, surf, water sports, fun, sunburn, crowds, or even gritty sandwiches. Context has much to do with which connotations a word evokes; in a treatise on shoreline management, *beach* evokes scientific, geographic connotations, whereas in a fashion magazine it evokes images of bathing suits.

■ **Exercise 3** Give one denotation and one connotation for each of the following words.

1. golden	3. star	5. liberal	7. aerobics	9. success
2. valley	4. Alaska	6. computer	8. justice	10. baboon

■ **Exercise 4** After the first quotation below are several series of words that the author might have used but did not select. Note the differences in meaning when an italicized word is substituted for the related word at the head of each series. Supply your own alternatives for each of the words that follow the other four quotations and be prepared to defend your choices.

1. Creeping gloom hits us all. The symptoms are usually the same: not wanting to get out of bed to start the day, failing to smile at ironies, failing to laugh at oneself. —CHRISTOPHER BUCKLEY
   a. gloom: *sadness, depression, melancholy*
   b. hits: *strikes, assaults, infects, zaps*
   c. usually: *often, frequently, consistently, as a rule*
   d. failing: *too blue, unable, neglecting, too far gone*
2. It was a night of still cold, zero or so, with a full moon—a night of pure magic. —WALLACE STEGNER
   a. night   b. still   c. pure   d. magic
3. The morning tides are low, the breeze is brisk and salty, and the clams squirt up through the sand and tunnel back down almost faster than you can dig. —ANN COMBS
   a. morning   b. brisk   c. squirt   d. tunnel
4. The stalks elbowed one another like gossips in a dense little village. —CYNTHIA OZICK
   a. elbowed   b. gossips   b. dense   d. village

5. Going away to college gives us a chance to rinse off part of our past, to shake off our burdensome reputations.

—JENNIFER CRICHTON

   a. college   b. chance   c. rinse   d. burdensome
   e. reputations

(3) Choose a specific and concrete word rather than a general and abstract one.

A *general* word is all-inclusive, indefinite, sweeping in scope. A *specific* word is precise, definite, limited in scope.

GENERAL	SPECIFIC	MORE SPECIFIC/CONCRETE
food	fast food	pizza
prose	fiction	short stories
place	city	Cleveland

An *abstract* word deals with concepts, with ideas, with what cannot be touched, heard, or seen. A *concrete* word signifies particular objects, with the practical, with what can be touched, heard, or seen.

ABSTRACT	democracy, loyal, evil, hate, charity
CONCRETE	mosquito, spotted, crunch, grab

Often writers tend to use too many abstract or general words, leaving their writing drab and lifeless. As you select words to fit your context, avoid combining an abstract word for subjects with a linking verb and an abstract word for the complement. Find more concrete words for the subject or the complement or use a transitive verb. Be as specific and concrete as you can. For example, instead of the word *bad,* consider using a more precise adjective.

bad planks: rotten, warped, scorched, knotty, termite-eaten
bad children: rowdy, rude, ungrateful, selfish, perverse
bad meat: tough, tainted, overcooked, contaminated

To test whether or not a word is specific, ask one or more of these questions about what you want to say: Exactly who?

Exactly what? Exactly when? Exactly where? Exactly how? As you study the following examples, notice what a difference specific, concrete words can make in the expression of an idea. Notice, too, how specific details can expand or develop ideas.

VAGUE	It seems to me that most Americans are uncertain about success, not because they are crazy, but because it's too hard to get.
SPECIFIC	It seems to me that most Americans harbor ambivalence toward success, not for neurotic reasons, but out of a realistic perception of what it demands.
	—ELLEN GOODMAN
VAGUE	She has kept no reminders of performing in her youth.
SPECIFIC	She has kept no sequined costume, no photographs, no fliers or posters from that part of her youth.
	—LOUISE ERDRICH
VAGUE	I remember my pleasure at discovering new things about language.
SPECIFIC	I remember my real joy at discovering for the first time how language worked, at discovering, for example, that the central line of Joseph Conrad's *Heart of Darkness* was in parentheses. —JOAN DIDION

All writers use abstract words and generalizations when these are vital to the communication of ideas, as in the following sentence:

> He is immortal, not because he alone among creatures has an inexhaustible voice, but because he has a soul, a spirit capable of compassion and sacrifice and endurance.   —WILLIAM FAULKNER

To be effective, however, use abstract words to express only clearly understood and well-thought-out ideas.

■ **Exercise 5**   Replace the general words and phrases in italics with specific ones.

1. I always think of a shopping mall as *very big*.
2. *Cities* have a *lot of problems* today.

3. The *new band* was *really great*.
4. Aunt Grace served *the same thing every Sunday*.
5. I explained my overdraft to my parents by telling them I had bought *some things I needed*.
6. I thought about the *numerous advantages* of my major.
7. The dog *walked* over to his *food*.
8. My parents always have *some kind of comment* about *my grades*.
9. There were *various aspects* of the plan that I didn't like.
10. The police searched *the whole area* thoroughly.

(4) Use figurative language appropriately.

Commonly found in nonfiction prose as well as in fiction, poetry, and drama, figurative language uses words in an imaginative rather than a literal sense. Simile and metaphor are the chief *figures of speech*. A *simile* is the comparison of dissimilar things using *like* or *as*. A *metaphor* is an implied comparison of dissimilar things not using *like* or *as*.

Similes

> And her fingers felt like a dead person's, like an old peach I once found in the back of the refrigerator; the skin just slid off the meat when I picked it up. —AMY TAN

> She sat like a great icon in the back of the classroom, tranquil, guarded, sealed up, watchful. —REGINALD McKNIGHT

> Seven bobwhite chicks marched behind their mother like nervous recruits. —GEOFFREY NORMAN

> The two men passed through the crowd as easily as the Israelites through the Red Sea. —WILLIAM X. KIENZLE

> He was like a piece of rare and delicate china which was always being saved from breaking and which finally fell.
> —ALICE WALKER

Metaphors

> His money was a sharp pair of scissors that snipped rapidly through tangles of red tape. —HISAYE YAMAMOTO

We refuse to believe that the bank of justice is bankrupt.
—MARTIN LUTHER KING, JR.

The white spear of insomnia struck two hours after midnight, every night. —GAIL SHEEHY

It was gurgling out of her own throat, a long ribbon of laughter, like water. —SANDRA CISNEROS [a metaphor and a simile]

Single words are often used metaphorically:

These roses must be **planted** in good soil. [literal]

A man's feet must be **planted** in his country, but his eyes should survey the world. —GEORGE SANTAYANA [metaphorical]

We always **sweep** the leaves out of the garage. [literal]

She was letting her imagination **sweep** unchecked round every rock and cranny of the world that lies submerged in the depths of our unconscious being. —VIRGINIA WOOLF [metaphorical]

Similes and metaphors are especially valuable when they are concrete and point up essential relationships that cannot otherwise be communicated. (For faulty metaphors, see **23c**.) Similes and metaphors can also be extended throughout a paragraph of comparison. See **32d(5)**.

Other common figures of speech contribute to lively writing. *Personification* is the attribution to the nonhuman (objects, animals, ideas) of characteristics possessed only by the human.

Time talks. It speaks more plainly than words. . . . It can shout the truth where words lie. —EDWARD T. HALL

Paradox is a seemingly contradictory statement that actually makes sense when thoughtfully considered.

That I may rise and stand, o'erthrow me. . . . —JOHN DONNE [in seeking religious salvation]

Overstatement (also called *hyperbole*) and *understatement* are complementary figures of speech often used for ironic or humorous effect.

> I for one, don't expect till I die to be so good a man as I am at this minute, for just now I'm fifty thousand feet high—a tower with all the trumpets shouting. —G. K. CHESTERTON
> [overstatement]

> You have a small problem; your employer has gone bankrupt.
> [understatement]

Irony is a deliberate incongruity between what is stated and what is meant (or what the reader expects). Verbal irony expresses the opposite of what the writer means; for example, in Shakespeare's *Julius Caesar,* Marc Antony stirs a mob to anger against Brutus by repeatedly stating, "Brutus is an honorable man." An *allusion* is a brief reference to a work or a person, place, event, or thing (real or imaginary) which serves as a kind of shorthand to convey a great deal of meaning compactly. The administration of President John F. Kennedy was often referred to as "Camelot," an allusion to the domain of the legendary King Arthur. An *image* expresses a sensory impression in words; for example, Tennyson describes the sea as seen from the point of view of an eagle as "wrinkled."

■ **Exercise 6** Write sentences containing the specified figure of speech or write down an example of it that you find in your reading.

1. Metaphor   2. Simile   3. Personification   4. Overstatement or understatement   5. Allusion

20b

Choose expressions that are idiomatic.

An *idiom* is an expression whose meaning is peculiar to the language or differs from the individual meanings of its elements. Be careful to use idiomatic English, not unidiomatic approximations. *She talked down to him* is idiomatic. *She talked under to him* is not. Occasionally the idiomatic use of prepositions may prove difficult. If you are uncertain which preposition to use with a given word, check the dictionary. For instance, *agree* may be followed by *about, on, to,* or *with.* The choice depends on the context. Writers often have trouble with expressions such as these:

> according **to** the plan   [NOT with]
> accuse **of** perjury   [NOT with]
> bored **by** it   [NOT of]
> comply **with** rules   [NOT to]
> conform **to/with** standards   [NOT in]
> die **of** cancer   [NOT with]
> in accordance **with** policy   [NOT to]
> independent **of** his family   [NOT from]
> inferior **to** ours   [NOT than]
> happened **by** accident   [NOT on]
> jealous **of** others   [NOT for]

Many idioms—such as *all the same, to mean well, playing possum, eating crow*—cannot be understood from the individual meanings of their elements. Some are metaphorical: *turning something over in one's mind.* Such expressions cannot be meaningfully translated word for word into another language. Used every day, they are at the very heart of the English language. As you encounter idioms that are new to you, master their meanings just as you would any new word.

■ **Exercise 7** Write sentences using each of the following idioms correctly. Use your dictionary when necessary.

1. burn out, burn up, burn down
2. differ from, differ with, differ about
3. wait on, wait for
4. get even with, get out of hand
5. on the go, on the spot

20c

Choose fresh expressions instead of trite, worn-out ones.

Such expressions as *bite the dust, breath of fresh air,* or *smooth as silk* were once striking and effective. Excessive use, however, has drained them of their original force and made them clichés. Some euphemisms (pleasant-sounding substitutions for more explicit but possibly offensive words) are not only trite but wordy and/or awkward—for example, *correctional facility* for *jail* or *pre-owned* for *used.* Many political slogans and the catchy phraseology of advertisements soon become hackneyed. Faddish or trendy expressions like *interface, impacted, paradigm, input,* or *be into* (as in "I am into dieting") are so overused that they quickly lose their force.

Nearly every writer uses clichés from time to time because they are so much a part of the language, especially of spoken English. But experienced writers will often give a fresh twist to an old saying or a well-known literary passage.

> If a thing is worth doing, it is worth doing badly.
> —G. K. CHESTERTON

> I am as pure as the fresh driven slush. —TALULAH BANKHEAD

> Washington is Thunder City—full of sound and fury signifying power. —TOM BETHELL [Compare Shakespeare's "full of sound and fury, / Signifying nothing."—*Macbeth*]

Proverbs and familiar expressions from literature or the Bible, many of which have become a part of everyday language, can often be used effectively in your own writing.

> Slowly but steadily, in the following years, a new vision began gradually to replace the dream of political power—a powerful movement, the rise of another ideal to guide the unguided, another pillar of fire by night after a clouded day.
> —W. E. B. DU BOIS [Compare Exodus 13:21: "And the Lord went before them . . . by night in a pillar of fire, to give them light."]

Good writers, however, do not rely too heavily on the words of others; they choose their own words to communicate their own ideas.

■ **Exercise 8**   From the following list of trite expressions—only a sampling of the many in current use—select ten that you often use or hear and replace them with carefully chosen words or phrases. Use six of them in sentences.

EXAMPLES
A bolt from the blue: *a shock*
beyond the shadow of a doubt: *undoubtedly*

1. a crying shame
2. after all is said and done
3. as hot as a firecracker
4. at the crack of dawn
5. bored to tears/death
6. to make a long story short
7. drop a bombshell
8. howl like a banshee
9. hoping against hope
10. horse of a different color
11. in the last anaylsis
12. flat as a pancake
13. launch a campaign
14. over and done with
15. soft as a baby's breath
16. shun like the plague
17. slept like a log
18. smell a rat
19. stick to your guns
20. the agony of defeat
21. the powers that be
22. the spitting image of
23. in this day and age
24. the bitter end

■ **Exercise 9**   Choose five of the ten items below as the basis for five original sentences. Use language that is exact, idiomatic, and fresh.

EXAMPLES
the appearance of her hair
Her hair poked through a broken net like stunted antlers.
—J. F. POWERS

OR

Her dark hair was gathered up in a coil like a crown on her head.
—D. H. LAWRENCE

1. the look on his face
2. the air in the country
3. the way she walks
4. the condition of the streets
5. spring in the air
6. the noises of the city
7. the view from upstairs
8. the scene of the accident
9. the final minutes of play
10. the approaching storm

■ **Exercise 10**   Comment upon the authors' choice of words—their use of exact, specific language to communicate their ideas—in the two paragraphs following. Be prepared to explain your comments.

¹Eating artichokes is a somewhat slow and serious business.   ²You must concentrate, focusing on each leaf as you break it off at its fleshy base, dip it in its sauce and draw it carefully to your mouth (being careful not to drip).   ³Between your front teeth it goes, and you scrape off the deliciously blanketed flesh.   ⁴Languorously you work this combination of flavors and sensations to the back of your mouth, where all the subtleties of the artichoke unfold and mingle with the sharp, rich sauce; and now your taste buds get the full, exciting impact.   ⁵Down it goes, and you pluck another leaf, sometimes methodically, working around the base of this thistle bud, sometimes with abandon.   ⁶Yet you can never really "bolt" an artichoke; there is always a measure of pause with each leaf, as it is torn, dipped, and tasted.

—MARTHA ROSE SHULMAN, "An Artichoke Memoir"

¹The basement was cold and dreary, dimly illuminated by two 40-watt bulbs which were screwed into the side walls above the dais.   ²This platform was made out of rough planks of various woods and dimensions, thrown together without so much as a hammer and nails; it stood seven or eight inches above the floor, and it supported the tin firebox and the crescent altar.   ³Off to one side was a kind of lectern, decorated with red and yellow symbols of the sun and moon.   ⁴In back of the dais there was a screen of purple drapery, threadbare and badly faded.   ⁵On either side of the aisle which led to the altar there were chairs and crates, fashioned into pews.   ⁶The walls were bare and gray and streaked with water.   ⁷The only windows were small, rectangular openings near the ceiling, at ground level; the panes were covered over with a thick film of coal oil and dust, and spider webs clung to the frames or floated out like smoke across the room.   ⁸The air was heavy and stale; odors of old wood smoke and incense lingered all around.   ⁹The people had filed into the pews and were waiting silently.

—N. SCOTT MOMADAY, "January 26"

21

Conciseness: Avoiding Wordiness and Needless Repetition

Be concise. Repeat a word or phrase only when it is needed for emphasis, clarity, or coherence.

Conciseness—using words economically—is fundamental to clear writing.

WORDY   In the early part of the month of August, a hurricane was moving threateningly toward Houston.

CONCISE   In early August, a hurricane threatened Houston.

Needless repetition of words or phrases distracts the reader and blurs meaning.

REPETITIOUS   This interesting instructor makes an uninteresting subject interesting.

CONCISE   This instructor makes a dull subject interesting.

For the effective use of repetition in parallel structures, for emphasis, and as a transitional device, see **26b**, **29e**, and **32b(3)**, respectively.

21a

Make every word count; omit words or phrases that add nothing to the meaning.

(1) Avoid the use of different words that say the same thing (tautology).

WORDY   Ballerinas auditioned in the tryouts for *The Nutcracker.*

CONCISE   Ballerinas auditioned for *The Nutcracker.*

WORDY   Each actor has a unique talent and ability that he or she uses in his or her own acting.

CONCISE   Each actor has a unique talent.

In the common phrases listed below, useless words appear in brackets.

yellow [in color]
at 9:45 p.m. [that night]
[basic] essentials
bitter[-tasting] salad
but [though]
connect [up together]
because [of the fact that]
[really and truly] fearless
fans [who were] watching TV

circular [in shape]
return [back]
rich [and wealthy] nations
small[-size] potatoes
to apply [or utilize] rules
[true] facts
was [more or less] hinting
by [virtue of] his authority
the oil [that exists] in shale

Avoid grammatical redundancy, such as double subjects (my sister [she] is), double comparisons ([more] easier than), and double negatives (could[n't] hardly).

(2) Omit unnecessary words. Use only as many words as will express the idea well.

WORDY   *In the event that* the electoral system is changed, expect complaints *on the part of* the voters.

CONCISE   **If** the electoral system is changed, expect complaints **from** the voters.   [Two words, *if* and *from,* take the place of eight.]

One or two words can replace expressions such as these:

at this point in time	**now**
made contact by personal visits	**visited**
on account of the fact that	**because**
somewhere in the neighborhood of $2500	**about $2500**
in spite of the fact that	**although**

One exact word can say as much as many. (See also **20a**.)

spoke in a low and hard-to-hear voice	**mumbled**
persons who really know their particular field	**experts**

(3) Remove unnecessary and wordy expletive constructions.

There followed by a form of *to be* is an *expletive*—a word that signals you will put the subject after the verb. (See also **29f**.) This weak construction can rob the subject of the force it gains from being first in the sentence.

WORDY   There were three squirrels playing in the yard.
CONCISE   Three squirrels played in the yard.

It also is an expletive when it lacks an antecedent and is followed by a form of *be*.

WORDY   It is easy to learn to type.
CONCISE   Learning to type is easy.

▲ Note: In a few instances, no logical subject exists and the impersonal *it* construction is necessary: It is going to snow.

▲ Caution: Avoid substituting *it* for *there*: USE There were (not it was) two cars in the garage.

■ **Exercise 1**   Revise each sentence to make it concise.

1. There are three possible dates that they might release the film on.
2. During the last electoral campaign, many ridiculous things happened that were really funny.

3. Many seriously ill patients in need of medical attention were diagnosed by physicians on the medical staff of the hospital.
4. Obesity in people who are overweight can be cured by diet and exercise as a remedy.
5. The tall skyscraper buildings form a dark silhouette against the evening sky.

■ **Exercise 2**   Substitute one or two words for each item.

1. in this day and age
2. has the ability to sing
3. was of the opinion that
4. in a serious manner
5. prior to the time that
6. did put in an appearance
7. located in the vicinity of
8. has a tendency to break
9. during the same time that
10. involving too much expense

■ **Exercise 3**   Delete unnecessary words below.

1. It looked to me as if it could be dangerous because it might not be safe.
2. Because of the fact that Larry was there, the party was lively.
3. Other things being equal, it is my opinion that all of these oil slicks, whether they are massive or not so big, do damage to the environment.
4. In the frozen wastes of the southernmost continent of Antarctica, meteorites from outer space that fell to earth thousands of years ago in the past were exposed to view by erosion of the deteriorating ice.

21b

Combine sentences or simplify phrases and clauses to eliminate needless words.

Note differences in emphasis as you study the following examples.

WORDY   The grass was like a carpet. It covered the whole playground. The color of the grass was blue-green.

CONCISE   A carpet of blue-green grass covered the entire playground.

WORDY	Some phony unscrupulous brokers are taking money and savings from elderly old people who need that money because they planned to use it as a retirement pension.
CONCISE	Some unscrupulous brokers are cheating old people out of their pensions.

■ **Exercise 4** Following the pattern of the examples below, condense the following sentences.

EXAMPLE
These were events that were, in essence, concerned with athletics.
These were athletic events.

1. This was a problem that was, of course, a result of political actions.
2. These were decisions which, in truth, partake of the nature of business.

EXAMPLE
It was a garden planned with a great deal of care.
It was a carefully planned garden. OR *The garden was carefully planned.*

3. He was a man with a great deal of compassion.
4. It was a remark charged with a lot of emotion.

EXAMPLE
The stories written by Carson McCullers are different from those composed by Flannery O'Connor.
Carson McCullers's stories are different from Flannery O'Connor's.

5. Sam picks nicer restaurants than the ones we choose.
6. Research shows that most women place a higher value on communication skills than the value most men put on communication skills.

EXAMPLE
It is inevitable. Corporations produce goods so that they can make a profit.
Inevitably, corporations produce goods to make a profit.

7. It is logical. People obey laws so they can avoid being arrested.
8. It is predictable. Before an election legislators reduce taxation so that they can win the approval of voters.

EXAMPLE

The forces that were against gun control ran an advertisement that covered two pages.

The anti-gun control forces ran a two-page advertisement.

9. A group that is in favor of labor wants vacations that last two months.
10. One editorial against "nukes" stressed the need for plants that are state controlled.

■ **Exercise 5**   Restructure or combine the following sentences to reduce the number of words.

1. These children are talented, and they need special educational programs, many of which are enriched.
2. America has two main kinds of business. Americans need to pay attention to getting justice for all, and they also need to be sure everyone is treated alike.
3. Because of the fact that my parents thought my fiancé was really a terrific guy, I put a lot of effort into trying to love him.
4. Our skating coach made the recommendation saying that my pairs partner and I should put more time and effort into our practicing.

21c

Repeat words or phrases only when necessary for emphasis, clarity, or coherence. (See also 26b, 29e, and 32b.)

NEEDLESS   His father is not like her father. Her father takes more chances.

REVISED   Her father takes more chances than his father.

NEEDLESS   She hoped that he understood that the complaint was not the way that she really felt about things.

REVISED   She hoped he understood that her complaint did not reflect her real feelings.

21d

Use pronouns and elliptical constructions to eliminate needless repetition.

Use a pronoun instead of needlessly repeating a noun or substituting a clumsy synonym. If the reference is clear, several pronouns may refer to the same antecedent.

NEEDLESS   The hall outside these offices was empty. The hall
           had dirty floors, and the walls of this corridor were
           full of gaudy portraits.
REVISED   The hall outside these offices was empty. It had
           dirty floors, and its wall were full of gaudy portraits.

An elliptical construction (the omission of words that will be
understood by the reader without being repeated) helps the
writer of the following sentence to be concise.

> Prosperity is the goal for some people, fame [is the goal] for
> others, and complete independence [is the goal] for still
> others. . . .   —RENÉ DUBOS

Sometimes, as an aid to clarity, commas mark omissions that
avoid repetition.

> Family life in my parents' home was based upon a cosmic order;
> Papa was the sun; Mamma, the moon; and we kids, minor
> satellites.   —SAM LEVENSON

To use repetition for emphasis, see **29e**.

■ **Exercise 6**   Revise each sentence to eliminate wordiness and needless repetition.

1. The manager returned the application back because of illegible
   handwriting that could not be read.
2. In this day and time, it is difficult today to find in the field of science
   a chemist who shows so much promise for the future as Tamara
   Black shows.
3. A distant hurricane or a sea quake can cause a tidal wave. This
   wave can form when either occurs.
4. A comedy of intrigue (or a situation comedy) is a comedy that relies
   on action instead of characterization for its comedy.
5. The bricks on our new house are red in color and in spite of the
   fact that they are new the look of these bricks is a used, beat-
   up appearance.

22

Clarity and Completeness

Include all the words or phrases necessary to complete the meaning of the sentence.

If you omit necessary words as you write, your mind may be racing ahead of your pen, or your writing may reflect omissions in your spoken English. Rapid speech often omits necessary words.

> The analyst talked about the tax dollar goes.   [The writer thought "talked about where" but did not write "where."]
> We better study hard.   [The speaker omitted "had" before *better*.]

Make your meaning clear by including all necessary words in your writing. Proofread your compositions carefully (**8c**) and study sections **22a–22c**.

22a

Include all articles, pronouns, conjunctions, or prepositions necessary for clarity and completeness. See also **26b**.

(1) Omitted article or pronoun

> INCOMPLETE   The first meeting was held on other campus.
> COMPLETE   The first meeting was held on **the** other campus.

INCOMPLETE	I know a man had a house like that.
COMPLETE	I know a man **who** had a house like that.

To avoid ambiguity, it is often necessary to repeat a pronoun or an article before a second part of a compound.

AMBIGUOUS	A friend and helper stood nearby. [one person or two?]
CLEAR	A friend and **a** helper stood nearby. [two persons clearly indicated by repetition of *a*]
ALSO CLEAR	My mother and father were there. [clearly two persons—repetition of *my* before *father* not necessary]

(2) Omitted conjunction or preposition

CONFUSING	Zelda saw the police officer who was following her had sped up. [The reader may be momentarily confused by "saw the police officer."]
BETTER	Zelda saw **that** the police officer who was following her had sped up.
INFORMAL	We had never tried that type film before.
BETTER	We had never tried that type **of** film before.

When two verbs require different prepositions, do not omit the first preposition. See also **20b**.

INCOMPLETE	I neither believe nor approve of those attitudes.
COMPLETE	I neither believe **in** nor approve **of** those attitudes.

In sentences such as the following, if you omit the conjunction (or relative pronoun), use a comma in its place.

The English used the paints chiefly on churches at first, then later on public buildings and the homes of the wealthy. —E. M. FISHER   [Compare "on churches at first and then later on public buildings."]

The fact is, very few people in this society make a habit of thinking in ethical terms. —HARRY STEIN   [Compare "The fact is *that* very few people. . . ."]

■ **Exercise 1** Insert needed words below.

1. Gary reminded Stella Richard might not approve.
2. What kind car to buy is the big question.
3. Winter and spring breaks the campus is dead.
4. She lent me a dollar then decided to take it back.
5. The trouble was my good pair shoes got stolen.
6. Boynton will not ask or listen to any advice.
7. People had known for years were no longer our friends.
8. The book which he referred was not in our library.
9. It is the exception proves the rule.
10. We need to use only a pinch pepper.

22b

Include necessary verbs and auxiliaries. (See also chapter **2.)**

AWKWARD	Dieting has never and will never be a complete solution to obesity.
BETTER	Dieting has never **been** and will never be a complete solution to obesity.
INCOMPLETE	As long as I been a student, I never cut a class.
COMPLETE	As long as I **have** been a student, I **have** never cut a class.
INCOMPLETE	This problem easy to solve.
COMPLETE	This problem **is** easy to solve.

▲ **Option:** In sentences such as the following, omitting or including the second verb is optional (see **21d**).

The sounds were angry, the manner violent. —A. E. VAN VOGT
[omission of second verb]

The sounds were angry, the manner was violent. [inclusion of second verb]

22c

Form complete comparisons.

INCOMPLETE	Noncooperation with evil is as much a moral obligation as cooperation with good.
COMPLETE	Noncooperation with evil is as much a moral obligation as **is** cooperation with good.

—MARTIN LUTHER KING, JR.

INCOMPLETE	Good communication skills are no more important in your job than personal relationships.
COMPLETE	Good communication skills are no more important in your job than **in** personal relationships.

INCOMPLETE	He is taller.
COMPLETE	He is taller **than I am**. [BUT Of the two brothers, he is the taller. OR He is taller than he was last year.]

INCOMPLETE	After I started believing in myself, the world offered me more challenges.
COMPLETE	After I started believing in myself, the world offered me more challenges **than before**. [Note that the reader could complete this comparison easily.]

INCOMPLETE	Most people think television is better.
COMPLETE	Most people think television is better **than it used to be**.
	OR Most people think television is better **than radio**. [two logical ways to complete the comparison]

In a comparison such as the following, the word *other* may indicate a difference in meaning.

O'Brien runs faster than any player on the team.   [O'Brien is apparently not on the team. In context, however, this may be an informal sentence meaning that O'Brien is the fastest of the players on the team.]

O'Brien runs faster than any other player on the team.   [*Other* clearly indicates that O'Brien is on the team.]

■ **Exercise 2**   Supply needed words in verb phrases and in comparisons.

1. They been trying to make small cars safe.
2. The consumers better listen to these warnings.
3. Mr. Flores loves his children more than his wife.
4. Kimesa enjoys talking to Professor Souris more than Jeff.
5. Laptop computers are better.
6. We always have and always will find fishing boring.
7. The scenery here is as beautiful as any place.
8. One argument was as bad, maybe even worse than, the other.
9. The ordinance never has and never will be enforced.
10. The crusty old man irritates his roommate more than the cranky young nurse.

22d

When used as intensifiers in formal writing, *so, such,* and *too* are generally (but not always) followed by a completing phrase or clause.

> The line was **so** long **that we decided to skip lunch**.
> Bill has **such** a hearty laugh **that it is contagious**.
> Laura was **too** angry **to think straight**.

■ **Exercise 3**   Insert words where needed.

1. I had a strange type virus my senior year.
2. As far as Boston, I could see the people were proud of their history.
3. The group is opposed and angered by these attempts to amend the Constitution.
4. It is good to talk with a person has a similar problem.
5. The rain in parts of Hawaii is as heavy as Brazil.
6. My sister older than my brother.
7. The lawyer had to prove whatever the witness said was false.
8. Here is the hole which the rabbit escaped.
9. The concert we attended last night was so wonderful.
10. The stadium was already filled with people and still coming.

EFFECTIVE SENTENCES

23

Sentence Unity

Write unified sentences.

Good writing is unified: it sticks to its purpose. A sentence may lack unity because it combines unrelated ideas (see **23a**) or because it contains unrelated details (**23b**), mixed metaphors, mixed constructions (**23c**), or faulty predication (**23d**). Clear, precise definitions (**23e**) often depend upon careful attention to sentence unity. The unity of a sentence contributes to the unity of a paragraph (see **32**) and of a whole composition (see **33**).

23a

Make the relationship of ideas in a sentence immediately clear to the reader.

UNRELATED	Alaska has majestic glaciers, but most Americans must travel great distances. [unity thwarted by a gap in the thought]
RELATED	Alaska has majestic glaciers, but **to see them** most Americans must travel great distances.
UNRELATED	I hate strong windstorms, and acorns pelt my bedroom roof all night.
RELATED	I hate strong windstorms **because they make** acorns pelt by bedroom roof all night.

234

■ **Exercise 1**   All the sentences below contain ideas that are apparently unrelated. Adding words when necessary, rewrite each of the sentences to indicate clearly a logical relationship between the ideas. If you cannot establish a close relationship, put the ideas in separate sentences.

1. Ian sent his sister a dozen red roses, and she sang on a fifteen-minute program on public TV.
2. Birds migrate to the warmer climates in the fall and in summer get food by eating worms and insects that are pests to the farmer.
3. The food in the cafeteria is notoriously poor, and most college students do not look underfed.
4. Professor Wong has different and refreshing ideas, and I missed his lecture on September 30.
5. There are many types of bores at parties, but I like to stay at home and watch television or read a good book.

23b

Avoid excessive or poorly ordered detail.

EXCESSIVE   When I was only sixteen, I left home to attend a college that was nearby and that my uncle had graduated from twenty years earlier.

CLEAR   I left home when I was only sixteen to attend a nearby college.   [If the detail about the uncle is important, include it in another sentence. If not, delete it.]

As you strive to eliminate ineffective details, remember that length alone does not make a sentence ineffective. Your purpose sometimes requires a long, detailed sentence. If the details all contribute to the central thought, then parallel structure, balance, rhythm, effectively repeated connectives, and careful punctuation can make a sentence of even paragraph length coherent. (See **32c[1]**.)

The rediscovery of fresh air, of home-grown food, of the delights of the apple orchard under a summer sun, of the swimming pool made by damming the creek that flows through the meadow, of fishing for sun perch or catfish from an ancient rowboat, or of an early morning walk down a country lane when the air is cool—all of these things can stir memories of a simpler time and a less troubled world.

—CASKIE STINNETT, "The Wary Traveler"

■ **Exercise 2** Revise each sentence to eliminate excessive detail.

1. When I was only four years old, living in an old colonial house, little of which remains today, because of the mall that was built there, I could walk the two miles that separated the house from the library.
2. The boat, considered seaworthy ten years ago, but now in need of paint and repairs, as is so often true of things that have not been maintained, moved out into the bay.
3. A course in business methods helps students get a job in order that they may prove whether they are fit for business and thus avoid postponing the test, as so many do, until it is too late.
4. I have never before known a man who was so ready to help a friend who had got into difficulties which pressed him so hard.
5. At last I returned the book that I had used for the report which I made Tuesday to the library.

23c

Revise mixed metaphors and mixed constructions.

(1) Do not mix metaphors. See also **20a(4)**.

A **mixed metaphor** combines different images, creating an illogical comparison.

MIXED   Playing with fire can get you into deep water.
REVISED   Playing with fire can burn your fingers.

MIXED   Her climb up the ladder of success was nipped in the bud.
REVISED   She slipped on her climb up the ladder of success.
          OR   Before her career could blossom, it was nipped in the bud.

▲ Note: Metaphors like these have become clichés; that is, people use them without thinking about their meanings. You can avoid mixing metaphors by creating fresh ones. See **20c**.

(2) Do not mix constructions.

A sentence that begins with one kind of construction and shifts to another kind is a **mixed construction.** (See also **23d**.) Mixed constructions may omit the subject or the predicate.

MIXED   When Win plays the accordion attracts the audience's attention.   [adverb clause + predicate; no subject]

REVISED When Win plays the accordion, she attracts the audience's attention.   [adverb clause + main clause]

OR   Win's playing of the accordion attracts the audience's attention.   [subject + predicate]

MIXED   It was an old ramshackle house but which was quite livable.

REVISED It was an old ramshackle house, but it was quite livable.

OR   It was an old ramshackle house which was quite livable.   [noun + adjective clause]

▲ Note: Sometimes a sentence is flawed by the use of a singular noun when a plural noun is needed: "Hundreds who attended the convention drove their own **cars** [NOT car]."

Similarly, do not allow speech habits to trick you into omitting a necessary plural: "Two **contestants** [NOT contestant] want to play."

23d

Avoid faulty predication.

Verbs should indicate actions that are possible for your subjects. Faulty predication occurs when the subject and predicate do not fit each other logically.

FAULTY   One book I read believes in eliminating subsidies.
         [A person, not a thing, believes.]

REVISED The author of one book I read believes in eliminating subsidies.

FAULTY   An example of discrimination is an apartment owner, especially after he has refused to rent to people with children.   [The refusal, not the owner, is an example of discrimination.]

REVISED An example of discrimination is an apartment owner's refusal to rent to people with children.

■ **Exercise 3**   Revise each sentence to eliminate a faulty predication, a mixed construction, or a mixed metaphor.

1. One example of a rip-off would be a butcher, because he could weigh his heavy thumb with the steak.
2. Another famous story from Scottish history is Bonnie Prince Charlie.
3. When people really try avoiding hurting people means they have compassion.
4. Fern was always busy as a bee and surefooted in her business dealings.
5. Could anyone be certain why Kyle resigned or where did he find a better job.
6. For Norlene, money seems to grow on trees, but it also goes down the drain easily.
7. Because she is so small explains the difficulty she has finding clothes that fit.
8. I felt like a grain of sand crying out in the wilderness.
9. When children need glasses causes them to make mistakes in reading and writing.
10. The forecast of subnormal temperatures in late March was predicted by the National Weather Service.

23e

Define words or expressions precisely.

(1) In formal writing avoid faulty *is-when, is-where,* or *is-because* constructions.

Constructions combining *is* with the adverbs *when, where,* or *because* are often illogical since forms of *to be* signify identity or equality between the subject and what follows.

FAULTY	Banishing a man is where he is driven out of his country. [Banishing is an act, not a place.]
REVISED	Banishing a man is driving him out of his country.
FAULTY	Unlike a fact, a value judgment is when you express personal opinions or preferences.
REVISED	Unlike a fact, a value judgment is a personal opinion or preference.
FAULTY	The reason the package arrived so late is because he didn't mail it soon enough.
REVISED	The package arrived so late because he didn't mail it soon enough.

(2) Write clear, precise definitions. See also **32d(7)**.

A short dictionary definition may be adequate when you need to define a term or a special meaning of a word that may be unfamiliar to the reader.

Here *galvanic* means "produced as if by electric shock."   [See also the note following **16c**.]

Giving a synonym or two may clarify the meaning of a term. Often such synonyms are used as appositives.

A *dolt* is a dullard, a blockhead.

Magendo, or black-market corruption, is flourishing.
—KEN ADELMAN

Writers frequently show—rather than tell—what a word means by giving examples.

Many homophones (*be* and *bee, in* and *inn, see* and *sea*) are not spelling problems.

Words often have a number of meanings. Make clear to the reader the meaning that you are using.

In this paper, I use the word *communism* in the Marxist sense of social organization based on the holding of all property in common.

By stipulating your meaning in this way, you control the discussion on your own terms.

You may formulate your own definitions of the concepts you wish to clarify.

> Questions are windows to the mind. —GERARD I. NIERENBERG
> [use of a metaphor—see also 20a(4)]

> Clichés are sometimes thought of as wisdom gone stale.
>   —JOSEPH EPSTEIN

A formal definition first states the term to be defined and puts it into a class, then differentiates the term from other members of its class.

> A phosphene [term] is a luminous visual image [class] that results from applying pressure to the eyeball [differentiation].

■ **Exercise 4**   Define any two of the following terms in full sentences using first (a) a short dictionary definition, then (b) a synonym, and finally (c) an example.

1. neurotic	3. bowie knife	5. integrity	7. wetlands	9. beagle
2. humanism	4. cedar	6. uncanny	8. lumber	10. peer

24
Subordination and Coordination

Use subordination to relate ideas concisely and effectively. Use coordination to give ideas equal emphasis. See also **1e, 2b.**

Subordination and coordination establish clear relationships among the writer's ideas and help the reader follow the train of thought. See also **1e** and **2b**.

Subordinate means "being of lower structural rank." In the following sentence, the italicized subordinate elements are grammatically dependent on the sentence base, the boldfaced independent clause.

> *Since the editor's father, Captain Arch Brown, was still piloting river steamboats,* **The Press recorded boat schedules too.**
> —WILLIAM H. BRYAN

Although an idea may be important, subordinating it establishes its connection to the independent clause and draws attention to the principal idea.

Coordinate means "being of equal structural rank." Coordination gives equal grammatical emphasis to two or more ideas that you want your reader to consider. In the following sentence, both main clauses (subject + predicate, and subject

+ predicate) are equally important to the writer's meaning: they are coordinate elements.

> He had a habit of pausing to fix his gaze on part of the congregation as he read, and that Sunday he seemed to be talking to a small group of strangers who sat in the front row.
>
> —ANDREA LEE

Coordination gives equal emphasis not only to two or more clauses but also to two or more words, phrases, or sentences. See also chapter **26**.

> a **horrible**, **debilitating** disease   [coordinate adjectives]
> **on the roof** or **in the attic**   [compound prepositional phrases]
> **I have not gone on a diet.** Nor **do I intend to.**   [sentences linked by coordinating conjunction]

A study of this chapter should help you use subordination effectively when you revise a series of short, choppy simple sentences (see **24a**) or stringy compound ones (**24b[1]**). It should also help you use coordination to secure the grammatical emphasis you want (**24b[2]**) and to eliminate faulty subordination (**24c**). If you cannot distinguish between phrases and clauses and between subordinate and main clauses, see **1d** and **1e**.

24a

Use subordination to combine a series of related short sentences into longer, more effective units.

CHOPPY   He stood there in his buckskin clothes. One felt in him standards and loyalties. One also felt a code. This code is not easily put into words. But this code is instantly felt when two men who live by it come together by chance.

BETTER   As he stood there in his buckskin clothes, one felt in him standards, loyalties, a code which is not easily put into words, but which is instantly felt when two men who live by it come together by chance.

—WILLA CATHER

When combining a series of related sentences, first choose a sentence base (subject + predicate); then use subordinate elements to relate the other ideas to the base. See **24a(4)** for the meaning of subordinate conjunctions. (Coordination is also used to combine short sentences, but inexperienced writers tend to use too much of it: see **24b**.)

(1) Use adjectives and adjective phrases.

CHOPPY — The limbs were covered with ice. They sparkled in the sunlight. They made a breathtaking sight.

BETTER — **Sparkling in the sunlight**, the **ice-covered** limbs made a breathtaking sight.   [participial phrase and hyphenated adjectival]

(2) Use adverbs or adverb phrases.

CHOPPY — Season the chicken livers with garlic. Use a lot of it. Fry them in butter. Use very low heat.

BETTER — **Heavily** season the chicken livers with garlic, and **slowly** fry them in butter.   [Note the use of both subordination and coordination.]

OR   **After heavily seasoning the chicken livers with garlic, slowly** fry them in butter.

CHOPPY — His face was covered with white dust. So were his clothes. The man looked like a ghost.

BETTER — **His face and clothes white with dust**, the man looked like a ghost.   [first two sentences combined in an absolute phrase]

(3) Use appositives and contrasting elements.

CHOPPY — These kindnesses were acts of generosity. They were noticed. But they were not appreciated.

BETTER   These kindnesses—**acts of generosity**—were noticed **but not appreciated.**

(4) Use subordinate clauses.

Subordinate clauses are linked and related to main clauses by markers (subordinating conjunctions and relative pronouns) which signal whether a clause is related to the sentence base by **time** (*after, before, since, until, when, while*), **place** (*where, wherever*), **reason** (*as, because, how, so that, since*), **condition** (*although, if, unless, whether*), or **additional information** (*that, which, who, whose*). See page 23 for a list of these markers.

CHOPPY   The blizzard ended. Then helicopters headed for the mountaintop. It looked dark and forbidding.

BETTER   **As soon as the blizzard ended**, helicopters headed for the mountaintop, **which looked dark and forbidding**.   [adverb clause and adjective clause]

■ **Exercise 1**   Combine the following short sentences by using effective subordination and coordination. (If needed, keep a short sentence or two for emphasis: see **29h**.)

[1]I have just read *Lakota Myth* by James R. Walker.   [2]I am especially interested in the accounts related by Little Wound and No Flesh.   [3]Both narratives have the character of a lyric.   [4]The lyrical quality is a visionary projection.   [5]This projection takes us into the spiritual realm of Lakota celebration.   [6]The celebration involves the feast.   [7]The accounts narrate the story of creation.   [8]Little Wound and No Flesh show that feasting and gift giving are wellsprings of creativity.   [9]Their approach is simple and direct.   [10]In the narratives, elements of nature are personified.

24b

To avoid stringing main clauses together, relate them by using subordination and coordination.

Do not overuse coordinating connectives like *and, but, or, so, then, however,* and *therefore.* For ways to revise stringy or loose compound sentences, see **30c**. Methods of subordination that apply to combining two or more sentences (**24a**) also apply to revising faulty or excessive coordination in a single sentence.

(1) Use subordination to show how some ideas are more important than others.

AWKWARD   Jim lost the election but the vote was rigged and he really didn't mind.   [three main clauses joined by *but* and *and*]

BETTER   Since it was a rigged vote, Jim didn't really mind losing the election.   [one subordinate clause and one main clause]

AWKWARD   I intensely dislike swimming. They always tried to throw me in the water. They thought it was funny.   [three loosely related sentences]

BETTER   Since I intensely dislike swimming, they always thought throwing me into the water was funny.   [one subordinate clause and one main clause]

(2) Use coordination to give ideas equal emphasis.

The dam broke, and the town was destroyed.   [equal grammatical emphasis on the dam and the town]

COMPARE   The town was destroyed when the dam broke.
        [emphasis on the town]

     OR   The dam broke, causing the town to be destroyed.   [emphasis on the dam]

■ **Exercise 2**   Revise the following passage using effective subordination and coordination.

¹Yesterday I was walking down the street and found a purse containing twenty-five dollars. ²Thousands of people were on the street. ³It was the lunch hour so I looked around for the owner, but no one claimed it. ⁴I went into the neighboring stores. ⁵But the shopkeepers were busy, and no one could say who had lost the money. ⁶I didn't know what to do, but I figured that the money belonged to me. ⁷My friends

disagreed, and they thought I should call the police. [8]I did. [9]The police held it, but still no one came forward. [10]After two months the police gave the money to me.

(3) Subordinate and coordinate clauses logically. Avoid making faulty connections between two ideas.

ILLOGICAL	The gasoline tank sprang a leak, when all hope of winning the race was lost.
BETTER	When the gasoline tank sprang a leak, all hope of winning the race was lost.
FAULTY	You can walk to school, and you can take the letter.
BETTER	You can take the letter when you walk to school.
FAULTY	Leela is a musician and who can play several instruments. [Do not use *but* or *and* before *which, who,* or *whom* when introducing a single adjective clause.]
BETTER	Leela is a musician who can play several instruments.

24c

Avoid faulty or excessive subordination.

FAULTY	Chen was only a substitute pitcher, winning half of his games.
BETTER	Although Chen was only a substitute pitcher, he won half of his games. [*Although* establishes the relationship between the ideas.]
EXCESSIVE	Some people who are insecure when they are involved in personal relationships worry all the time, at least when they are not busy with things they have to do, about whether their friends truly love them.
BETTER	Some insecure, idle people worry about whether their friends truly love them. [two subordinate clauses reduced to adjectives]

■ **Exercise 3** Observing differences in emphasis, convert each pair of sentences below to (a) a simple sentence, (b) a compound sentence consisting of two main clauses, and (c) a complex sentence with one main clause and one subordinate clause. Be prepared to discuss the most effective revision.

EXAMPLE
Your letter came this morning. It was long overdue.

    a. *Your long overdue letter came this morning.* [simple sentence]
    b. *Your letter came this morning, but it was long overdue.* [compound sentence]
    c. *Your letter, which was long overdue, came this morning.* [complex]

1. Merrill was hurrying to the library. On the way back, she lost her room key.
2. The room was very grim and lonesome. It was a large deserted place set in the middle of nowhere.
3. The men couldn't function in the heat doing the kind of work that they had to do. They stopped work and went home.
4. David spends most of his afternoons after work fishing in the lake. He is a patient and skillful fisherman.
5. After the commissioners heard the report they condemned the property. Then they ordered the owner to pay a fine.

■ **Exercise 4** Revise the following paragraph to show the relationship of the ideas through effective coordination and subordination. Adapted from the Fort Worth *Star Telegram*.

¹Patmos is in the Aegean Sea and it is a rocky island. ²It is Greek and in the Dodecanes chain of islands. ³It is nearer Turkey than the mainland of Greece since it is a 12-hour ferry boat ride from Athens. ⁴There is little vegetation. ⁵The island is 34 miles square and has a stark appearance. ⁶Patmos has good, dark sand beaches. ⁷It has villages of white square houses. ⁸There are outdoor cafes which are roofed with grapevines. ⁹The Monastery of St. John is on a hill. ¹⁰It overlooks the village.

25

Coherence: Misplaced Parts, Dangling Modifiers

Keep related parts of the sentence together. Avoid dangling modifiers.

25a

Keep related parts of the sentence together.

To make your meaning clear to readers, place modifiers near the words they modify. Note how the meaning of the following sentences changes according to the position of the modifiers:

> Natasha went out with **just** her coat on.
> Natasha **just** went out with her coat on.
> **Just** Natasha went out with her coat on.

> The man **who drowned** had tried to help the child.
> The man had tried to help the child **who drowned**.

(1) In formal English, place modifiers such as *almost, only, just, even, hardly, nearly,* and *merely* immediately before the words they modify.

The truck costs **only** $450.   [NOT only costs]
He works **even** during his vacation.   [NOT even works]

■ **Exercise 1**   Revise the following sentences, placing the modifiers in correct relation to the words they modify.

1. The new truck cost nearly fourteen thousand dollars.
2. José polished his 1966 Mustang almost until he could see his face in the door panels.
3. Chocoholics hardly turn down any desserts with chocolate in them.
4. She even sleeps late when she has a class that she needs to go to.
5. The hurricane only killed seven people.
6. My brother asked me Wednesday to go with him.
7. He only works when someone is around.
8. Feeling keenly about football, relations between the schools were strained.
9. The Browns returned this morning from their vacation in the mountains on the bus.
10. The books on the first shelf are only reserved for three days.

(2) Place a modifying prepositional phrase to indicate clearly what the phrase modifies.

MISPLACED	Arne says that he means to leave the country in the first stanza.
BETTER	Arne says **in the first stanza** that he plans to leave the country.
MISPLACED	Heated arguments had often occurred over technicalities in the middle of a game.
BETTER	Heated arguments **over technicalities** had often occurred **in the middle of a game**.

■ **Exercise 2**   Circle each misplaced prepositional phrase below; draw an arrow to its proper position.

1. My friend wrapped presents for Charlie's birthday with papers from the comic section of the newspaper.
2. In the cafeteria the school serves spaghetti to hungry customers on paper plates.

3. Shalanda went to sleep with her long blonde hair on the couch.
4. The instructor made it clear what the penalties for plagiarism are on Monday.

(3) Place adjective clauses near the words they modify.

MISPLACED I put the chair in the middle of the room which I had recently purchased.

BETTER I placed the chair, **which I had recently purchased**, in the middle of the room.

(4) Revise "squinting" constructions—modifiers that may refer to either a preceding or a following word.

SQUINTING I agreed on the next day to help him.

BETTER I agreed to help him **on the next day**.

OR **On the next day** I agreed to help him.

(5) Revise awkward constructions that separate the sentence base or split an infinitive.

AWKWARD *I had* in spite of my not living in a neighborhood as fine as Jane's a healthy *measure* of pride.
[awkward separation of a verb from its object]

BETTER In spite of my not living in a neighborhood as fine as Jane's, **I had** a healthy **measure** of pride.

AWKWARD Hawkins is the man *to*, if we can, *nominate* for governor. [awkward splitting of an infinitive]

BETTER Hawkins is the man **to nominate** for governor if we can.

Sometimes, splitting an infinitive is not only natural but desirable.

He forgot to **completely** close the gate. [Compare: He forgot **completely** to close the gate.]

■ **Exercise 3** Revise the sentences to eliminate squinting modifiers or needless separation of related sentence parts.

1. Fernando said last week that he had gone.
2. The game warden warned Arne not to carry a gun in a car that was loaded.
3. The puppy advertised in last night's paper which is already eight weeks old is a bargain.
4. Arlene promised when she was going to the store to buy some bread.
5. Jim failed to, because he was careless, wash his clothes.

25b

Revise dangling modifiers.

Although any misplaced word, phrase, or clause can be said to dangle, the term **dangling modifier** applies primarily to verbal phrases that do not refer clearly and logically to other words or phrases in the sentence. To correct a dangling modifier, rearrange the words in the sentence to make the modifier clearly refer to the right word, or add words to make the meaning clear and logical.

(1) Revise dangling participial phrases. See 1d.

DANGLING   *Taking our seats*, the game started. [no clear word for the phrase to refer to]

REVISED   *Taking our seats*, **we** started the game. [word supplied—participants]

OR *Taking our seats*, **we waited** for the game to start. [words supplied—observers]

Placed after the sentence base, the participial phrase in the revision below refers to the subject.

DANGLING   The evening passed very pleasantly, *munching* popcorn and *watching* a late movie. [no clear reference]

REVISED   **We** passed the evening very pleasantly, *munching* popcorn and *watching* a late movie. [reference supplied]

(2) Revise dangling phrases containing gerunds or infinitives. See **1d(1).**

DANGLING	On *entering* the stadium, the size of the crowd surprised Theo. [no clear subject]
REVISED	On *entering* the stadium, Theo was surprised at the size of the crowd. [subject supplied]
DANGLING	*To write* well good books must be read. [no clear subject]
REVISED	*To write* well, **I** must read good books. [subject supplied]

(3) Revise dangling elliptical adverb clauses. See **1e(2).**

Elliptical clauses imply some words rather than state them.

DANGLING	*When only a small boy,* my father took me with him to Chicago.
REVISED	*When* **I was** *only a small boy,* my father took me with him to Chicago.

▲ Note: Sentence modifiers (see the **Glossary of Terms**) are considered standard usage, not danglers.

In the first place, he was only ten years old.
Considering his age, he is in good shape.

■ **Exercise 4** Revise the following sentences to eliminate dangling modifiers. Put a check mark after any sentence that needs no revision.

1. Even though anticipating difficulties, the motion passed easily.
2. After sitting there awhile, it began to snow.
3. By selecting the judges from both parties, the decisions are likely to give general satisfaction.
4. To grow good tomatoes, the vines should be supported.
5. Entering the room, the light was turned on.
6. Darkness having come, we stopped for the night.
7. The meeting was adjourned by standing and repeating the pledge.
8. Having taken his seat, we began to question the witness.
9. In drawing up any system of classification, it is likely that there will be some overlapping.
10. Knowing how to swim is required before entering the deep water.

26
Parallelism

Use parallel structure to express matching ideas.

Parallelism reinforces grammatically equal elements, contributes to ease in reading, and provides clarity and rhythm. Parallel elements regularly appear in lists or series, in compound structures, in comparisons using *than* or *as,* and in contrasted elements.

> Getting a language in this way, **word by word**, has a charm that may be set against the disadvantages. It is like gathering a posy **blossom by blossom**. —MARY ANTIN [paired descriptive elements]

> But the oral tradition has prevented the **complete destruction of the web**, the **ultimate disruption of tribal ways**.
> —PAULA GUNN ALLEN [noun phrases serving as objects]

Many parallel elements are linked by a coordinating conjunction (such as *and, or, but*) or by correlatives (such as *neither . . . nor, whether . . . or*). Others are not. In the following examples, verbals used as subjects and complements are parallel in form.

> **To define** flora is **to define** climate. —*NATIONAL GEOGRAPHIC*
> **Seeing** is **believing**.

Parallel structures are also used in outlines to indicate elements of equal importance. See **33e**, page 370.

Faulty parallelism disrupts the balance of coordinate elements:

FAULTY   We are not so much what we eat as the thoughts we think. [The coordinate elements differ in grammatical form.]

REVISED   We are not so much **what we eat** as **what we think**. OR   We are not so much **the food we eat** as **the thoughts we think**.

If elements are not parallel in thought, do not try to make them parallel in grammatical structure. Rethink the sentence.

FAULTY   We can choose ham, tuna salad, cottage cheese, or television. [The first three elements are foods; the last is an activity.]

REVISED   **We can eat** or **we can watch television**.

26a

For parallel structure, balance similar grammatical elements: nouns with nouns, prepositional phrases with prepositional phrases, clauses with clauses.

As you study the parallel structures that follow, notice how repetition emphasizes the balanced structure.

(1) Parallel words and phrases

The Africans carried with them a pattern of kinship
that emphasized ‖ **collective survival,**
mutual aid,
cooperation,
mutual solidarity,
interdependence,
and ‖ **responsibility for others.**
—JOSEPH L. WHITE

She had ‖ **no time to be human,**
no time to be happy.   —SEAN O'FALLON

(2) Parallel clauses

I remember Iyatiku's sister, Sun Woman,
‖ **who held so many things in her bundle**,
‖ **who went away to the east**.   —PAULA GUNN ALLEN

(3) Parallel sentences

‖ **When I breathed in**, I squeaked.
‖ **When I breathed out**, I rattled.   —JOHN CARENEN

■ **Exercise 1** Underline the parallel structures in the following sentences.

1. There might be some people in the world who do not need flowers, who cannot be surprised by joy, but I haven't met them.
   —GLORIA EMERSON
2. Think before you speak. Read before you think. —CHRIS WELLES
3. But integration speaks not at all to the problem of poverty, only to the problem of blackness. —KWAME TOURE
4. The earth's nearest neighbor has mountains taller than Everest, valleys deeper than the Dead Sea rift, and highlands bigger than Australia. —*NEWSWEEK*
5. They must accept the criticism of others and be suspicious of it; they must accept the praise of others and be even more suspicious of it. —DONALD M. MURRAY

■ **Exercise 2** Write five sentences: one containing parallel words, one containing parallel phrases, one containing parallel clauses, and two that are themselves parallel.

26b

To make the parallel clear, repeat a preposition, an article, the *to* of the infinitive, or the introductory word of a phrase or clause.

For about fifteen minutes I have been sitting chin in hand in front of the typewriter,
‖ **trying to** be honest with myself,
‖ **trying to** figure out why writing this seems to be so dangerous
‖ an act.   —ADRIENNE RICH

The reward rests not ‖ **in** the task
           but ‖ **in** the pay. —JOHN K. GALBRAITH

I was happy in the thought
        ‖ **that** our influence was helpful
and ‖ **that** I was doing the work I loved
and ‖ **that** I could make a living out of it. —IDA B. WELLS

■ **Exercise 3** Insert or alter words as necessary to create parallel structures in the following sentences.

1. Failure is due either to lack of preparation or inability to master the subject.
2. She spends all her time working and on her studies.
3. William MacCracken is a man of the highest principles and with a good mind.
4. She took up drinking, gambling, and smoked cigarettes.
5. They knew that I was ill and hated dances.
6. He couldn't decide whether to go into business for himself or take the job.
7. He was silent and in a serious mood after the lecture.
8. The real worth of a person should be living rather than in words.
9. He discovered that the farm is well adapted to grazing cattle and it yields good hay.
10. I admire Anzio for his ideals but not his lifestyle.

26c

Use parallel structures with correlatives (*both . . . and; either . . . or; neither . . . nor; not only . . . but also; whether . . . or*).

FAULTY   Either they work or are fired.
PARALLEL Either ‖ **they work**
          or ‖ **they are fired**.

FAULTY   Whether at home or when at work he was always busy.
PARALLEL Whether ‖ **at home**
         or ‖ **at work**, he was always busy.

FAULTY   Not only practicing at 6 a.m. during the week, but
the team also scrimmages on Sunday afternoons.

PARALLEL   The team
not only ‖ **practices at 6 a.m. during the week**
but also ‖ **scrimmages on Sunday afternoons**.

OR   Not only does the team **practice at 6 a.m.
during the week**, but also it **scrimmages on
Sunday afternoons**. [The *also* may be
omitted.]

■ **Exercise 4** Revise each sentence using parallel structures to express parallel ideas.

1. He was not only kind but also knew when to help people in trouble.
2. I debated whether I should telephone or to run home.
3. He was respected by his associates and his employees loved him.
4. The professor said that she would give us a test on Friday and for us to review the first ten chapters of our textbook.
5. He has not only preserved but treasured his family's heritage.
6. The debates will enable you to differentiate the sincere candidates from those just saying something for effect.
7. Let us consider the origin of engineering and how engineering has progressed.
8. Walking and to swim are good exercise.
9. The sentences are difficult to understand, not because they are long but they are obscure.
10. She is strong but a fool.

■ **Exercise 5** First study the parallelism in the sentences below. Then use one of the sentences as a structural model for a sentence of your own.

1. These reporters felt no urge to inform their readers about how Lincoln stood, what he did with his hands, how he moved, vocalized, or whether he emphasized or subdued any parts of the address.
—CARL SANDBURG
2. The day I liked best in New York was the fall evening when the lights went out. The elevators stopped, the subways stopped, the neon stopped. Factories, presses, and automatic doughnut fryers— everything ground to a halt. —MARGARET A. ROBINSON

3. What is true of coral and of all other forms of marine life is also true of whales. —JACQUES-YVES COUSTEAU

4. Calm, relaxed people get ulcers as often as hard-pressed, competitive people do, and lower-status workers get ulcers as often as higher-status ones. —CAROL TAVRIS

5. Each word has been weighed, each thought has been evaluated, and each point carefully considered. —ZIG ZIGLAR

27

Consistency: Avoiding Shifts

Make grammatical structures, tone and style, and viewpoint consistent.

Abrupt, unnecessary shifts—for example, from past to present, from singular to plural, from formal diction to slang, from one perspective to another—obscure meaning and make reading difficult.

27a

Keep tense, mood, and voice consistent. See also chapter **7**.

SHIFT	While they waited, George argued against nuclear power while his brother discusses the effects of acid rain. [shift from past to present tense]
CONSISTENT	While they waited, George **argued** against nuclear power while his brother **discussed** the effects of acid rain. [both verbs in the past tense]
SHIFT	If I were truly naive and if I was as stupid as you think, I would never have discovered his scam. [shift from subjunctive to indicative mood]

CONSISTENT	If I **were** truly naive, and if I **were** as stupid as you think, I would never have discovered his scam. [both verbs in subjunctive mood]
SHIFT	My grandmother had to enter a nursing home when she was ninety-nine, but it was not liked by her. [shift from active to passive voice]
CONSISTENT	My grandmother **had to enter** a nursing home when she was ninety-nine, but she **did not like** it. [both verbs in active voice]

When using the literary present, as in summarizing plots of novels and plays, avoid slipping from the present into the past tense.

Romeo and Juliet **fall** in love at first sight, **marry** secretly, and **die** [NOT *died*] together in the tomb within the same hour.

27b

Be consistent in the use of person and number. See also **6b**.

SHIFT	If a person is going to improve, *you* should work harder. [shift from third person to second person]
CONSISTENT	If **you** are going to improve, **you** should work harder. [second person] OR If **people** are going to improve, **they** should work harder. [third person] OR If **we** are going to improve, **we** should work harder. [first person]
SHIFT	The senior class *is* planning to ask six faculty members to *their* spring dance. [shift from singular to plural]
CONSISTENT	The senior class **is** planning to ask six faculty members to **its** spring dance.

■ **Exercise 1**   Correct all needless shifts in tense, mood, voice, person, and number.

1. When she saw him, she thinks immediately that she is in the wrong class.
2. Jane moved that the election be held in March and that it will be a mail ballot.
3. If one is going to win the race, you will have to train harder.
4. Every witness was questioned, and they were taken to police headquarters.
5. Before the game began, Mabel comes over to our seats and asked us to wait for her later.

27c

Avoid shifts between direct and indirect discourse. See also **26a**.

SHIFT	Janet wondered *how the thief got the computer out* and *why didn't he steal the silver?* [shift from indirect to direct discourse]
CONSISTENT	Janet wondered **how the thief got the computer out** and **why he didn't steal the silver.** [two indirect questions]
	OR Janet asked, "**How did the thief get the computer out? Why didn't he steal the silver?**" [two direct questions]
SHIFT	Her assistant said "She's out" and would I please wait. [shift from direct to indirect discourse]
CONSISTENT	Her assistant **said that she was out** and **asked me please to wait**. [indirect discourse]

27d

Keep tone and style consistent.

SHIFT	It seemed to Romeo, as he gazed up at the balcony, that Juliet's face was as white as the underside of a fish.
CONSISTENT	It seemed to Romeo, as he gazed up at the balcony, that Juliet's face was as pale as **the snow**.

27e

Keep perspective and viewpoint consistent.

FAULTY	Standing in the valley, I could see our troops at the crest of the hill and, on the other side of the ridge, the enemy in full retreat. [shift in perspective from the valley to the top of the hill]
CONSISTENT	**From the airplane**, I could see our troops at the crest of the hill and, on the other side of the ridge, the enemy in full retreat.
FAULTY	The underwater scene was dark and mysterious; the willows lining the shore dipped gracefully into the water. [The perspective abruptly shifts from beneath the surface of the water to above it.]
CONSISTENT	The underwater scene was dark and mysterious; **above**, the willows lining the shore dipped gracefully into the water.

■ **Exercise 2**   Correct all needless shifts. Put a check mark after any sentence that needs no revision.

1. A big jazzy moon bathed the sea in mellow light.
2. No matter what her friend may say, she always took the opposite view.
3. If there is little enthusiasm, we might ask, "Why should they be enthusiastic?"
4. The students closed their books and hurry away to the gym.
5. First grab the bat and then you should place your feet properly.
6. James likes fishing but hunting is also liked by him.
7. Eleanor took summer courses and her leisure hours were devoted to swimming.
8. We have reached a point where it is difficult for one to resign.
9. My friend asked whether I knew the coach and will she be with the team.
10. Pick the daisies in the morning, and then they should be placed in water.

■ **Exercise 3**   Revise the following paragraph to eliminate all needless shifts.

[1]He was an adept old man, it always seemed to me. [2]He has a deceptively open face, and his manner is that of an innocent young boy. [3]He tried to appear ingenuous and said that "I am opposed to all bribes." [4]Nevertheless he will let it be known that he is not above taking small gifts. [5]Take these thoughts for what they are worth; it may help one in understanding this person.

28

Reference of Pronouns

Make a pronoun refer unmistakably to its antecedent.
See also **6b** and **19j**.

Each boldfaced pronoun below clearly refers to its italicized antecedent, a single word or a word group:

> Perhaps it is the same survival instinct that makes *women* amenable to change that also tends to make **them** vulnerable.
> —ROSE M. NOLEN

> A cow-calf operation keeps *cattle* year-round in the same pastures where **they** are bred, born, and raised.

> Thus, *being busy* is more than merely a national passion; **it** is a national excuse. —NORMAN COUSINS

Without any loss of clarity, a pronoun can often refer to a noun that follows:

> Unlike **their** predecessors, today's *social workers* cannot exclusively seek middle-class, home-owning, two-parent, one-career families for the children they want to place. —MARSHA TRUGOT

As you edit your compositions, check to see that the meaning of each pronoun is immediately obvious. If there is any chance of confusion, repeat the antecedent, use a synonym for it, or recast your sentence.

28a

Make antecedents clear.

When a pronoun could refer to either of two possible antecedents, the ambiguity confuses the reader. Recast the sentence to make the antecedent clear, or replace the pronoun with a noun.

AMBIGUOUS	Juan told Pete that he had made a mistake. [Whom does *he* refer to?]
CLEAR	In talking with Pete, *Juan* admitted that **he** had made a mistake.
AMBIGUOUS	The books were standing on the shelf, which needed sorting. [Did the books or the shelf need sorting? See also **25a(3)**.]
CLEAR	The *books*, **which** needed sorting, were standing on the shelf.

▲ Note: A pronoun may clearly refer to two or more antecedents: "*Jack* and *Jill* met **their** Waterloo."

28b

Make references clear.

Placing a pronoun too far away from its antecedent may force your reader to backtrack to get your meaning. Making a pronoun refer to a modifier can obscure your meaning. Recast the sentence to bring a pronoun and its antecedent closer together or substitute a noun for the obscure pronoun.

REMOTE	The *freshman* found herself the unanimously elected president of a group of animal lovers, *who*

was not a joiner of organizations. [*Who* is too far removed from the antecedent *freshman*. See also 25a(3).]

BETTER The **freshman who** was not a joiner of organizations found herself the unanimously elected president of a group of animal lovers.

OBSCURE Before Ellen could get to the jewelry store, *it* was all sold. [reference to a modifier]

BETTER Before Ellen could get to the jewelry store, all the **jewelry** was sold.

■ **Exercise 1** Revise each sentence below to eliminate any ambiguous, remote, or obscure pronoun references.

1. Shana's dislike for Collette did not end until she asked her to go to a movie with her.
2. On the keyboard, the many function keys often confuse a computer novice that are not clearly identified.
3. Professor Connelly spoke to Maureen as she was walking into class.
4. In Maria's book she does not say what to do.
5. Vinh got there too late to buy the book. It was a big disappointment.

28c

Use broad or implied reference only with discretion.

Pronouns such as *it, this, that, which,* and *such* may refer to a specific word or phrase or to the sense of a whole clause, sentence, or paragraph.

SPECIFIC REFERENCE The glow was enough to read by, once my eyes adjusted to it. —MALCOLM X [*It* refers to *glow*.]

BROAD REFERENCE Some people think that the fall of man had something to do with sex, but that's a mistake. —C. S. LEWIS [*That* refers to the sense of the whole clause.]

When used carelessly, broad reference can make writing unclear. Be especially careful with *this* and *that*.

(1) Avoid broad reference to an expressed idea.

VAGUE   When class attendance is compulsory, some students feel that education is being forced on them. This is not true.   [*This* has no antecedent.]

CLEAR   When class attendance is compulsory, some students feel that education is being forced on them. **This feeling** is not true.

(2) Make the antecedent explicit rather than implicit.

VAGUE   Lois said that she would stay in Yuma for at least a year. This suggests that she is happy there.   [*This* has no expressed antecedent.]

CLEAR   Lois said that she would stay in Yuma for at least a year. **This remark** suggests that she is happy there.

VAGUE   My father is a music teacher. It is a profession that requires much patience.   [*It* has no expressed antecedent.]

CLEAR   My father is a music teacher. **The teaching of music** is a profession that requires much patience.

28d

Avoid the awkward use of *it* or *you*.

AWKWARD   It was no use in trying.
REVISED   **There was** no use trying.   OR   **Trying was** useless.

AWKWARD   If people break the law, you may be arrested.   [The pronoun *you* (second person) refers to *people* (third person). See also **27b**.]

REVISED   If **people** break the law, **they** may be arrested. [Both the pronoun *they* and the noun *people* are now in the third person.]

AWKWARD   In the book it says that many mushrooms are edible. [*It* has no expressed antecedent. See also **23d**.]

REVISED   The author of the book says that many mushrooms are edible.

In an informal context, the use of the impersonal, or indefinite, *you* is both natural and acceptable. Notice in the following example that *you* is equivalent in meaning to "people in general" or "the reader."

The study of dreams has become a significant and respectable scientific exploration, one that can directly benefit **you**.

—PATRICIA GARFIELD

Generally, however, *you* is not appropriate in a formal context.

▲ Note: Avoid the awkward placement of *it* near another *it* with a different meaning.

AWKWARD   It would be unwise to buy the new model now, but it is a superior machine.   [The first *it* is an expletive. The second *it* refers to *model.*]

REVISED   Buying the new model now would be unwise, but it is a superior machine.

■ Exercise 2 Revise the following sentences as necessary to make all references clear. Put a check mark after any sentence that needs no revision.

1. Sandra did not buy a season ticket, which turned out to be a mistake.
2. If you are taken to the courthouse, they will fine you.
3. When the termite eggs are hatched, they grow wings and fly around the country in swarms.
4. In the book it says that the author dislikes anteaters.
5. Sherry decided not to go to the movie, which she came to regret.
6. Everyone has trouble writing, but this is not true when you are excited about your subject.

7. Collette told Li that she was a good friend.
8. Marilyn decided not to attend the reunion which was a disappointment for our grandparents.
9. When building railroads, the engineers planned embankments for fear that flooding would cover them and make them useless.
10. The increase in tuition discouraged students which seemed unreasonably high.

29
Emphasis

Construct sentences to emphasize important ideas.

You can emphasize ideas by using exact diction (see chapter **20**), concise language (**21**), and appropriate subordination and coordination (**24**). This chapter presents other ways to gain emphasis.

29a

Place important words at the beginning or end of the sentence—especially at the end.

UNEMPHATIC	A healthy body is just as important as a healthy mind, however, for many reasons.
EMPHATIC	A healthy body, however, for many reasons, is just as important as a healthy mind.
UNEMPHATIC	In his book, Morrow argued against capital punishment, it seemed to me. [An unemphatic prepositional phrase begins the sentence, and an unnecessary qualification ends it.]
EMPHATIC	Morrow argued against capital punishment. [See also chapter **21**.]

Because the semicolon (see also chapter **14**) is a strong punctuation mark when used between main clauses, the words placed immediately before and after a semicolon tend to receive emphasis.

The colon and the dash often precede an emphatic ending. (See also **17d** and **17e**.)

> In short, the freedom that the American writer finds in Europe brings him, full circle, back to himself, with the responsibility for his development where it always was: in his own hands.
> —JAMES BALDWIN

> It was simply this—I went to the movies.   —ISAAC ASIMOV

There is/are constructions can emphasize a topic the writer will address later. (See also **21a**.)

> There is such a thing as the freedom of exhaustion. Some people are so worn down by the yoke of oppression that they give up. . . .   —MARTIN LUTHER KING, JR.

■ **Exercise 1**   Placing important words carefully, revise the following sentences to improve emphasis.

1. Robyn was very successful and was a tireless worker, if we can believe the reports.
2. Rock music affects the brain's alpha waves, so they say.
3. It had never before entered his mind to challenge the decisions Marla made or to offer ideas of his own, however.
4. The expedition cannot possibly fail unless we lose our enthusiasm.
5. A trailer saves hotel expense and can be moved about from place to place readily.

29b

Occasionally use a periodic instead of a cumulative sentence.

In a **cumulative sentence**, the main idea (the independent clause or sentence base) comes first; less important ideas or details follow. In a **periodic sentence**, however, the main idea comes last, just before the period.

CUMULATIVE	History has amply proved that large forces may be defeated by smaller forces who are superior in arms, organization, morale, and spirit.
PERIODIC	That large forces may be defeated by smaller forces who are superior in arms, organization, morale, and spirit has been amply proved by history.
CUMULATIVE	The old Dunkard preacher and his wife came into the county in 1856, their wagon full of what they had imagined in Indiana they would need in the new land. —WILLIAM LEAST HEAT-MOON
PERIODIC	Suffering from malnutrition and neglect and who knows what mental agonies, Phillis Wheatley died. —ALICE WALKER

Both types of sentences can be effective. The cumulative sentence is the more common form. Although the periodic sentence is often the more emphatic, be careful not to overuse it.

29c

Occasionally arrange ideas in an ascending order of climax.

Notice in the following examples that the ideas are arranged in an order that places the writer's most dramatic or important idea last.

Urban life is unhealthy, morally corrupt, and fundamentally inhuman.   —RENÉ DUBOS   [adjectives in the series arranged in climactic order]

They could hear the roar of artillery, the crash of falling timbers, the shrieks of the wounded.   [sentence climax reached with *shrieks of the wounded*]

In the language of screen comedians four of the main grades of laugh are the titter, the yowl, the belly laugh and the boffo. The titter is just a titter. The yowl is a runaway titter. Anyone who has ever had the pleasure knows all about a belly laugh.

The boffo is the laugh that kills. —JAMES AGEE [First, words are placed in climactic order, then sentences.]

▲ Note: Anticlimax—an unexpected shift from the dignified to the trivial or from the serious to the comic—is sometimes used for special effect.

But I still fear it will all end badly, this Protective Syndrome. I see a future in which the government has stripped us of all worldly goods worth having: clothes hangers, toothpaste, Alka-Seltzer, toasters, pencil sharpeners, and maybe even thumb tacks. —S. L. VARNADO

■ **Exercise 2** Arrange the ideas in the following sentences in what you consider to be the order of climax.

1. Rene loved everything on wheels—ATV's, bicycles, roller blades, skateboards.
2. His knowledge of people, his confident manner, and his friendliness made him a natural for the position.
3. Give me death or give me liberty.
4. I gathered together the souvenirs from my trip: my passport, my airplane ticket receipt, and the letter from Erin.
5. Something must be done at once. The commission is faced with a deficit.

29d

Rely on the active voice and forceful verbs.

(1) Use the active voice rather than the passive voice to gain emphasis.

The **active voice** emphasizes the *doer* of the action and presents ideas strongly and directly. The **passive voice** emphasizes the *receiver* of the action, minimizes the role of the doer, and creates wordier sentences.

ACTIVE   The burglar stole the television set and the computer.
[emphasis on the burglar]

PASSIVE   The television set and the computer were stolen by the burglar.   [emphasis on the stolen items]

ACTIVE   All citizens should insist on adequate medical care.

PASSIVE   Adequate medical care should be insisted on by all citizens.

▲ Note: In reporting research or scientific experiments, writers often use the passive voice to preserve objectivity, to emphasize the work being done on a project rather than who is performing the work.

PASSIVE   The experiment was conducted over several months and under several conditions.

Use the active voice, unless you have a strong reason to use the passive voice.

(2) Prefer an action verb or a forceful linking verb to a form of *have* or *be*.

Forms of *have* or *be*, when used without an action verb, rob your writing of energy and forcefulness. The real action often lies in a verbal phrase or in an object or complement.

UNEMPHATIC   Our college is always the winner of the conference.   [The subject complement—*winner*—contains the real action.]

EMPHATIC   Our college always wins the conference.   [The verb *win* presents the real action.]

UNEMPHATIC   The meat has a rotten smell.   [Action is in the direct object—*smell*.]

EMPHATIC   The meat smells rotten.   [The verb *smell* presents the real action.]

UNEMPHATIC   You can be more effective at solving problems by understanding the problem first.   [Objects of prepositions contain the real action—*solving, understanding*.]

EMPHATIC   You can solve problems more effectively if you understand the problem first.   [Verbs present the real action.]

■ **Exercise 3** Make each sentence more emphatic by substituting the active for the passive voice or by substituting a more forceful verb for a form of *have* or *be*. Write five sentences of your own using forceful verbs.

1. The campers are taught good environmental practices by the park naturalist.
2. Every Saturday violence is taught to children through cartoons.
3. Every politician has the desire to be president.
4. It is usually required by the professor that the students have a ten-page paper to write each term.
5. Carla is a manipulator of other people.

29e

Repeat important words to gain emphasis.

> We *shall go on* to the end, *we shall fight* in France, *we shall fight* on the seas and oceans, *we shall fight* with growing confidence and growing strength in the air, *we shall defend* our Island, whatever the cost may be, *we shall fight* on the beaches, *we shall fight* on the landing grounds, *we shall fight* in the fields and in the streets, *we shall fight* in the hills; *we shall never surrender.* —WINSTON CHURCHILL [italics added]

▲ Caution: Repetition of words is not effective if it is used without purpose. See **21**.

■ **Exercise 4** First make each sentence below more emphatic by substituting repetition for the use of synonyms; then write two sentences of your own using repetition for emphasis.

1. She thought about the children, she considered the budget, she reflected on her past experience, and finally she reached a conclusion.

2. He fusses constantly: he gripes about taxes, he complains about the weather, he grumbles about the price of groceries, and criticizes everyone around him.

29f

Invert the word order of a sentence to gain emphasis. See also **30b**.

> At the feet of the tallest and plushiest offices lie the crummiest slums. —E. B. WHITE [Compare "The crummiest slums lie at the feet of the tallest and plushiest offices."]
>
> Basic to all the Greek achievement was freedom.
> —EDITH HAMILTON [Compare "Freedom was basic to all the Greek achievement."]

▲ Caution: This method of gaining emphasis, if overused, will make the style awkward and distinctly artificial.

29g

Use balanced sentence construction to gain emphasis.

A sentence is balanced when grammatically equal structures—usually main clauses with parallel elements—express contrasted (or similar) ideas: see chapter **26**. A balanced sentence emphasizes the contrast (or similarity) between parts of equal length and movement.

> Love is positive; tolerance negative. Love involves passion; tolerance is humdrum and dull. —E. M. FORSTER

■ **Exercise 5** Write emphatic sentences using balanced construction to show the similarities or contrasts between the following.

1. success and failure
2. love and hate
3. city and country
4. spring and fall

29h

Abruptly change sentence length to gain emphasis.

> In the last two decades there has occurred a series of changes in American life, the extent, durability, and significance of which no one has yet measured. No one can. —IRVING HOWE [The short sentence, which abruptly follows a much longer one, is emphatic.]

■ **Exercise 6** Write a short emphatic sentence to follow each long sentence below. Then write another pair of sentences—one long and one short—of your own.

1. According to a number of journalists, not to mention the references in the Condon Report, our astronauts have seen flying objects in outer space, objects that may have been clouds, satellites, or space debris.
2. For at least four hours, Charles worked with my hair; he painstakingly parted each segment, measured and cut each layer, carefully timed the waving lotion and the neutralizer; finally, after applying a dark rinse, setting and resetting each wave, shuttling me under and out from under a dryer, he handed me a mirror.

■ **Exercise 7** Prepare for a class discussion of emphasis on the following passages.

1. Through all the centuries of war and death and cultural and psychic destruction have endured the women who raise the children and tend the fires, who pass along the tales and the traditions, who weep and bury the dead, who are the dead, and who never forget. There are always the women, who make pots and weave baskets, who fashion clothes and cheer their children on at powwow, who make fry bread and piki bread, and corn soup and chili stew, who dance and sing and remember and hold within their hearts the dream of their ancient peoples—that one day the woman who thinks will speak to us again, and everywhere there will be peace.
   —PAULA GUNN ALLEN
2. The April mornings are bright, clear and calm. Not until the afternoon does the wind begin to blow, raising dust and sand in funnel-shaped twisters that spin across the desert briefly, like dancers, and then

collapse—whirlwinds from which issue no voice or word except the forlorn moan of the elements under stress.   —EDWARD ABBEY

3. No one reads anymore—blame television. Families are breaking up—blame television. High culture is being despoiled—blame television. . . . What a splendid all-purpose explanation television has become.

4. In fantasy, the timid can be bold and aggressive, the weak are strong, the clumsy are full of grace, the tongue-tied discover vast verbal resources. In the privacy of the mind, we can all rise up in righteous wrath, and vengeance is ours.   —ADELAIDE BRY

■ **Exercise 8**   Revise each sentence for emphasis. Be prepared to explain why your revision provides appropriate emphasis within a particular context.

1. I gave him the letter, two weeks ago, when he asked me.
2. Make the most of it if this be treason.
3. She saw much to interest her: the Statue of Liberty, the art galleries, the tall buildings, and the crowds on the street.
4. Scouting develops a person morally, mentally, and physically.
5. I met Sheila in Boston, many years ago, in a shop on Tremont Street, late in the fall.
6. It was no fault of hers that the program was a failure.
7. As we approached the house, lights were turned on and faces appeared at the window.
8. Fields of daisies were all around us.
9. The tornado came at the end of a hot and humid day.
10. As the station is reached, the train is seen coming around the bend.

30
Variety

Vary the structure and length of your sentences to maintain the reader's interest.

Seek sentence variety to make your writing livelier. Inexperienced writers tend to rely too heavily—regardless of content or purpose—on a few comfortable, familiar structures.

Compare the two paragraphs below. Both express the same ideas in virtually the same words; both use acceptable sentence patterns. It is the variety in sentence structure and length that makes one livelier and more interesting than the other.

NOT VARIED

This account is *about* television only in part. I don't mean to cast it as an evil appliance. I will be describing phenomena that appear on television often, but they are also on the radio and in magazines and everywhere else. They are parts of modern life. Television covers an extraordinary amount of territory in twenty-four hours. I could find fifty references to any topic.
[six sentences: five simple, one compound; all starting with the subject; three starting with *I*]

VARIED

But only in part is this account *about* television, which I don't mean to cast as an evil appliance. Often I will be describing phenomena that appear on television, but they are also on the

279

radio and in magazines and everywhere else, because they are parts of modern life. The amount of territory that television covers in twenty-four hours is extraordinary—I could find fifty references to any topic that interested me.   [three sentences: one complex, one compound–complex, and one compound; first sentence subject/verb order reversed; four dependent clauses.]   —THE *NEW YORKER*

▲ **Note:** If you have difficulty distinguishing various types of structures, review the fundamentals of the sentence treated in chapter **1**, especially **1b**.

30a

Vary the length of your sentences, avoiding a series of short simple ones. See also **29h**.

To avoid choppiness produced by a series of short simple sentences, lengthen some sentences by showing how the ideas are subordinate or coordinate. (See chapter **24**.)

CHOPPY   The Maine coast and the Oregon coast look very much alike. The houses by the sea, however, are different. It's a matter of architectural style.

EFFECTIVE   Although the Maine coast and the Oregon coast look very much alike, the architectural style of the houses by the sea is different.   [use of subordination to combine sentences]

CHOPPY   Some people simply put coffee in an enamel saucepan. Next, they pour very hot water over it. Then they wait until flavor develops. Finally, they add eggshell or a small amount of cold water. The idea is to get the floating grounds to settle to the bottom.

EFFECTIVE   Some people simply put coffee in an enamel saucepan, pour very hot water over it, wait until flavor develops, and get the floating grounds to settle to the bottom by adding eggshell or a small amount of cold water.   [use of coordination to combine sentences]

Occasionally, as the example below illustrates, a series of brief, subject-first sentences may be used for special effect:

EFFECTIVE   I looked like Li'l Abner. Mason, Michigan, was written all over me. My kinky, reddish hair was cut hick style, and I didn't even use grease in it. My green suit's coat sleeves stopped above my wrists, the pants legs showed three inches of socks.

—MALCOLM X

■ **Exercise 1**   Study and prepare to discuss the following excerpt, giving attention to the variety of sentence lengths.

Marya stared at his swinging foot. He was a satyrish middle-aged man, red-brown tufts of hair in his ears, a paunch straining against his shirt front, a strangely vulnerable smile; a totally mediocre personality in every way—vain, uncertain, vindictive—yet Marya could see why others liked him; he was predictable, safe, probably decent enough. But she hated him. She simply wished him dead.   —JOYCE CAROL OATES

■ **Exercise 2**   Revise the following paragraph by combining some of the short simple sentences. Relate ideas carefully.

¹A salesperson's speech, recently recorded, has an interesting thesis. ²Human beings should solve problems. ³And human beings should create problems to solve. ⁴For instance, a man's car will not start. ⁵He has a problem. ⁶An auto-parts salesperson solves it by selling him a battery. ⁷I think that by nature human beings are solvers of problems. ⁸A teacher baffles his class with problems. ⁹Then he helps the students solve them. ¹⁰A doctor solves the problems of her patients by recommending drugs or surgery. ¹¹And ditch diggers eliminate the drainage problems of a city. ¹²How to spend leisure hours is a problem for many Americans. ¹³Singers, dancers, actors, and writers help solve this problem. ¹⁴Human beings can see problems everywhere. ¹⁵And they do something about them.

30b

Vary the beginnings of your sentences.

Most writers begin about half their sentences with the subject—far more than the number of sentences begun in any other way. But overuse of the subject-first beginning results in monotonous writing.

(1) Begin with an adverb or an adverbial clause.

Suddenly a hissing and clattering came from the heights around us. —DOUGLAS LEE [adverb]

Even though baseball is essentially the same, the strategy of play then and now is different. —JAMES T. FARRELL [adverbial clause]

When you first start writing—and I think it's true for a lot of beginning writers—you're scared to death that if you don't get that sentence right that minute it's never going to show up again. —TONI MORRISON [adverbial clause]

(2) Begin with a prepositional phrase or a verbal phrase.

Out of necessity they stitched all of their secret fears and lingering childhood nightmares into this existence.
—GLORIA NAYLOR [prepositional phrase]

To be really successful, you will have to be trilingual: fluent in English, Spanish, and computer. —JOHN NAISBITT [infinitive phrase]

Looking out of the window high over the state of Kansas, we see a pattern of a single farmhouse surrounded by fields, followed by another single homestead surrounded by fields.
—WILLIAM OUCHI [participial phrase]

(3) Begin with a sentence connective—a coordinating conjunction, a conjunctive adverb, or a transitional expression.

Notice how each sentence connective relates the ideas in each set of sentences. See also **32b(4)**.

For students who have just survived the brutal college-entrance marathon, this competitive atmosphere is all too familiar. **But** others, accustomed to being stars in high school, find themselves feeling lost in a crowd of overachievers. —NANCY R. GIBBS [The coordinating conjunction *but* makes a contrast.]

If any group has options to change and improve its life, it is the American middle class. **And** yet with freedom comes turmoil. —GAIL SHEEHY

Health experts are cautioning that many new oat products are high in saturated fats and calories. **Moreover**, oat enthusiasts are mistaken if they think scarfing down oats allows them to gorge on steak and French fries. —ANASTASIA TOUFEXIS [conjunctive adverb]

If the Soviet care and feeding of athletes at times looks enviable, it is far from perfect. **For one thing**, it can be ruthless.
—WILLIAM A. HENRY III [transitional expression]

(4) Begin with an appositive, an absolute phrase, or an introductory series. (See **24a**.)

A place of refuge, the Mission provides food and shelter for Springfield's homeless. —SHELLEY ALEY [appositive]

His fur bristling, the cat went on the attack. [absolute phrase]

Light, water, temperature, minerals—these affect the health of plants. [introductory series—see **17e(3)**]

Occasionally using a declarative sentence with inverted word order also provides sentence variety (see **29f**).

■ **Exercise 3**   Prepare for a class discussion of the types of sentence beginnings in the following paragraph. For instance, White begins the first sentence with a long prepositional phrase that includes a verbal phrase. See **30b(2)**.

[1]In attempting to recapture this mild spectacle, I am merely acting as recording secretary for one of the oldest of societies—the society of those who, at one time or another, have surrendered, without even a show of resistance, to the bedazzlement of a circus rider.   [2]As a writing man, or secretary, I have always felt charged with the safekeeping of all unexpected items of worldly or unworldly enchantment, as though I might be held personally responsible if even a small one were to be lost.   [3]But it is not easy to communicate anything of this nature.   [4]The

circus comes as close to being the world in microcosm as anything I know; in a way, it puts all the rest of show business in the shade. [5]Its magic is universal and complex. [6]Out of its wild disorder comes order; from its rank smell rises the good aroma of courage and daring; out of its preliminary shabbiness comes the final splendor. [7]And buried in the familiar boasts of its advance agents lies the modesty of most of its people. [8]For me the circus is at its best before it has been put together. [9]It is at its best at certain moments when it comes to a point, as through a burning glass, in the activity and destiny of a single performer out of so many. [10]One ring is always bigger than three. [11]One rider, one aerialist, is always greater than six. [12]In short, a man has to catch the circus unawares to experience its full impact and share its gaudy dream. —E. B. WHITE

■ **Exercise 4** Rewrite each sentence so that it begins with (1) an appositive, (2) an absolute phrase, or (3) an introductory series.

1. A limestone plateau studded with razor-sharp pinnacles stretched ahead of them.
2. The longest-running television series anywhere may be the British science fiction saga, *Dr. Who*.
3. Potential franchise buyers crowded around the booth that displayed small household robots and asked questions about how many tasks the machines could perform.
4. Rita Levi-Montalcini initiated study into the development of the central nervous system using the simplest scientific tools while she was hiding from the Nazis in a farmhouse.
5. A new, smart elevator samples the location, destination, and passenger load of each car, rerouting individual elevators to eliminate long waits in the hall and stops by elevators already too full to admit additional riders.

30c

Avoid loose, stringy compound sentences.

To revise an ineffective compound sentence, try one of the following methods.

(1) Make a compound sentence complex. (See also **24b**.)

COMPOUND   Gazpacho is a cold Spanish soup, and it has a history going back to Roman times, and it is usually

made with bread, tomatoes, green peppers, and
garlic.

COMPLEX   Gazpacho, which is a cold Spanish soup usually
made with bread, tomatoes, green peppers, and
garlic, has a history going back to Roman times.

(2) Use a compound predicate in a simple sentence.

COMPOUND   She caught the bird expertly, and next she held
it so its feet were still, and then she slipped a
numbered yellow band around its left leg.

SIMPLE   She caught the bird expertly, held it so its feet
were still, and slipped a numbered yellow band
around its left leg.

(3) Use an appositive in a simple sentence.

COMPOUND   J. T. Nichols was an old-fashioned naturalist, and
he spent his life studying birds and turtles on
Long Island.

SIMPLE   J. T. Nichols, an old-fashioned naturalist, spent
his life studying birds and turtles on Long Island.

(4) Use a prepositional or verbal phrase in a simple sentence.

COMPOUND   The rain was torrential, and we could not see
where we were going.

SIMPLE   Because of the torrential rain, we could not see
where we were going.

COMPOUND   I checked into the hotel about 4:30, and then I
called the office about my return flight.

SIMPLE   After checking into the hotel about 4:30, I called
the office about my return flight.

COMPOUND   The town was near the Atlantic Ocean, and the
hurricane struck it, and it was practically demolished.

SIMPLE   The town, located near the Atlantic Ocean, was struck by the hurricane and practically demolished.

■ **Exercise 5** Using the methods illustrated in **30c**, revise the stringy compound sentences below.

1. The house is small, and it is easy to keep clean, but it is too cramped.
2. Our friends the Comptons grew tired of the long, cold winters, so they moved to Arizona, but there they had to endure long, hot summers.
3. Plastic can be sliced in thin sheets to form computer disks, and it can be molded into cases for keyboards and monitors, and it can also be removed from one's wallet to purchase equipment one cannot afford.
4. Keith kept asking the library board about the budget, and he asked about increasing the amount spent on books and salaries, but he did not mention the amount spent for maintenance.

30d

Vary the conventional subject-verb sequence by occasionally separating subject and verb with words or phrases.

Each subject and verb below is in boldface.

SUBJECT-VERB   **Water Oaks was** once an ugly charcoal plant, but now **it is** a beautiful natural forest.

VARIED   **Water Oaks**, once an ugly charcoal plant, **is** now a beautiful natural forest.

SUBJECT-VERB   The **crowd applauded** every basket and **cheered** the team to victory.

VARIED   The **crowd**, applauding every basket, **cheered** the team to victory.

An occasional declarative sentence with inverted word order can also contribute to sentence variety. See **29f**.

■ **Exercise 6** Using the methods illustrated in **30d**, vary the conventional subject-verb sequence.

1. The grocery store is across from the high school, and it attracts many students.
2. Her ability to listen is an acquired skill that attracts many friends.
3. Adolpho was hurrying to get home before the storm broke, but he flooded the engine of his car.
4. The manager identified with the employees, so she supported their decision to ask for shorter hours.
5. The crowd sympathized with the visitors and applauded every single play.

30e

Occasionally, instead of the usual declarative sentence, use a question, an exclamation, or a command.

> What was Shakespeare's state of mind, for instance, when he wrote *Lear* and *Antony and Cleopatra*? It was certainly the state of mind most favourable to poetry that there has ever existed. —VIRGINIA WOOLF [Woolf's answer follows the initial question.]

> Now I stare and stare at people, shamelessly. Stare. It's the way to educate your eye. —WALKER EVANS [A one-word imperative sentence provides variety.]

■ **Exercise 7** Prepare for a class discussion of the sentence variety in the following paragraph.

[1]It is too much that with all those pedestrian centuries behind us we should, in a few decades, have learned to fly; it is too heady a thought, too proud a boast. [2]Only the dirt on a mechanic's hands, the straining vise, the splintered bolt of steel underfoot on the hangar floor—only these and such anxiety as the face of a Jock Cameron can hold for a pilot and his plane before a flight, serve to remind us that, not unlike the heather, we too are earthbound. [3]We fly, but we have not "conquered" the air. [4]Nature presides in all her dignity, permitting us the study and the use of such of her forces as we may understand. [5]It is when we presume to intimacy, having been granted only tolerance, that the harsh stick falls across our impudent knuckles and we rub the pain, staring upward, startled by our ignorance. —BERYL MARKHAM

LARGER ELEMENTS

31
Critical Reading and Logical Thinking

To read critically and to think logically is to distinguish between ideas that are credible and those that are less credible. Critical readers and thinkers study language carefully because they have learned that they cannot believe everything they are told. They understand that different writers may reach significantly different conclusions when discussing the same topic and drawing upon the same evidence. Instead of routinely agreeing with the writer who seems to reinforce beliefs that are reassuringly familiar, critical readers are likely to discover that different writers have each revealed a part of what may ultimately prove to be true. The challenge for readers, then, is to identify which ideas make more sense than others and to determine the extent to which those ideas are reliable and useful. Logical thinking helps readers to meet this challenge.

Because critical reading and logical thinking involve making well-reasoned choices, these closely related skills are among the most valuable that you can acquire. You can master them through practice, just as you have mastered other skills. You can practice them when you read paragraphs (**32**), essays (**33**), and other types of writing (**34**, **35**).

Although the focus of this chapter is on acquiring skills that can improve your reading, these skills are equally applicable to writing. Good writers are critical readers of their own work; you should read your own writing critically by imagining that you are one of your own readers (**33g**). Doing so will help you write logically and persuasively.

31a

Distinguish between fact and opinion.

As you acquire information through reading, you may believe that you are acquiring "facts." *Facts* are reliable pieces of information that can be verified through independent sources or procedures. Facts are valued because they are believed to be true. *Opinions* are judgments or inferences that may or may not be based on facts. When these ideas are widely accepted, they may seem to be factual when they are actually only opinion. Accepting opinions unsupported by facts can lead you to faulty conclusions that damage your credibility.

To distinguish between fact and opinion, ask yourself questions about a statement you have read: Can it be proved? Can it be challenged? How often is the same result achieved? (See **31b**.) If a statement can be consistently proved true, then it is a fact. If it can be disputed, then it is an opinion.

FACT   Spinach contains iron.
OPINION   Americans should eat more spinach.

To say that spinach contains iron is to state a well-established fact; it can be verified by consulting published studies or by conducting laboratory testing. But to say that Americans need to eat more spinach is to express an opinion that may or may not be supported by facts. When considering the statement "Americans should eat more spinach," a critical reader might ask, "Do *all* Americans suffer from a deficiency of iron?" If yes, the reader might then ask, "Is spinach the only source of iron?" If the answer to these questions is yes, then the statement is a fact. But the answers are both no, so it is an opinion.

Critical readers and logical thinkers need to remain flexible as they distinguish between fact and opinion because the facts themselves can change. The erroneous belief that the sun revolves around the earth was once considered a fact, and Newtonian physics was once believed indisputably true. Describing what can easily happen in research, a distinguished physician writes that a good scientist must be prepared for the day when his or her life work is suddenly called into question:

> All the old ideas—last week's ideas in some cases—are no longer good ideas. The hard facts have softened, melted away and vanished under the pressure of new hard facts.
>
> —LEWIS THOMAS, "The Art of Teaching Science"

No matter how knowledgeable, a reader who is unwilling to assimilate new information and question old ideas cannot expect to meet the challenges of a rapidly changing world. The collapse of the Soviet Union, for example, necessitated new approaches by other countries to the republics that emerged from that nation. Or, to take another example, researchers working to fight AIDS must maintain their intellectual dexterity to adapt their work as new information becomes available.

■ **Exercise 1**   Determine which of the following statements are fact and which are opinion. Explain your decisions in writing, and be prepared to discuss your choices in class.

1. Willa Cather won the Pulitzer Prize for fiction in 1923.
2. Women often earn less money than men holding the same position.
3. Women are more emotional than men.
4. You cannot write well unless you know how to write correctly.
5. A college diploma is necessary for jobs that pay well.
6. The capital of California is Sacramento.

7. Running is good for your health.
8. The United States won the Second World War.
9. Water freezes at 32 degrees Fahrenheit.
10. John F. Kennedy was assassinated by Lee Harvey Oswald.

31b

Read for evidence.

Critical readers expect writers to support their claims with ample evidence consisting of facts and other data such as personal experience and observation. When you are reading a work that makes a specific point, ask yourself if the writer has provided evidence that is accurate, representative, and sufficient. Critically examine any information that writers present. Information that is accurate should be verifiable. Recognize, however, that a writer may provide you with data that is accurate but unreliable because it is drawn from an exceptional case or a biased sampling. If, for example, you are reading an argument about the death penalty that draws all of its information from material distributed by a police association, the evidence cited is unlikely to represent the full range of data available on this topic.

Similarly, carefully examine polls and other statistics. How recent is the data, and how was it gathered? In 1936 a poll conducted by the *Literary Digest* predicted the election of Alf M. Landon, but Franklin D. Roosevelt won by a landslide. The poll was faulty because it was limited to people who owned cars or had personal telephone service. During one of the worst economic depressions in American history, Americans with cars and personal telephones were among the financially secure citizens most likely to vote against Roosevelt, who advocated increased government spending on domestic programs. Even with representative polls, statistics can be manipulated. Do not accept statistics uncritically.

To decide how much evidence is appropriate, consider the size and originality of the claim. As a general rule, a writer who takes an unusual position on an issue will need to provide more evidence than a writer who has taken a stand that is less controversial. But in either case, a surplus is usually better than a deficit. Be sure, however, to consider the quality and significance of the evidence.

■ **Exercise 2** Study the evidence within the following two excerpts. How accurate and reliable is the evidence in each? Explain your opinion in writing.

The single most talked-about consequence of a global warming is probably the expected rise in sea level as the result of polar melting. For the past several thousand years, sea level has been rising, but so slowly that it has almost been a constant. In consequence, people have extensively developed the coastlines. But a hundred and twenty thousand years ago, during the previous interglacial period, sea level was twenty feet above the current level; at the height of the last ice age, when much of the world's water was frozen at the poles, sea level was three hundred feet below what it is now. Scientists estimate that the world's remaining ice cover contains enough water so that if it should all melt it would raise sea level more than two hundred and fifty feet. —BILL McKIBBEN, "The End of Nature"

Paradoxically, the historical records of temperature change do not jibe with the greenhouse theory. Between 1880 and 1940, temperatures appeared to rise. Yet between 1940 and 1965, a period of much heavier fossil-fuel use and deforestation, temperatures dropped, which seems inconsistent with the greenhouse effect. And a comprehensive study of past global ocean records by researchers from Britain and M.I.T. revealed no significant rising temperature trends between 1856 and 1986. Concludes Richard Lindzen of M.I.T.'s department of Earth, Atmospheric and Planetary Sciences, "The data as we have it does not support a warming."
    —ROBERT J. BIDINOTTO, "What Is the Truth about Global Warming?"

31c

Evaluate for credibility.

Writers gain the confidence of readers by presenting themselves as well informed and fair minded. To determine how credible a writer is, ask yourself the following questions:

Evaluating Credibility

1. Does the writer support claims with evidence?
2. Does the writer reveal how and where evidence was obtained?
3. Does the writer recognize that other points of view may be legitimate?
4. Does the writer use sarcasm or make personal attacks upon opponents?
5. Does the writer reach a conclusion that is in proportion to the amount of evidence provided?

Thoughtful writers consider views that are different from their own. The most common strategy is to anticipate what an opponent might say about a particular issue and then to refute that point by demonstrating why it is questionable. Consider the following example:

> The National Rifle Association is fond of quoting a University of Wisconsin study that says, "gun control laws have no individual or collective effect in reducing the rate of violent crime." . . . Agreed—but what if handguns were not available? What if the manufacture of handguns is severely regulated, and if the guns can be sold only to police officers? True, even if handguns are outlawed, some criminals will manage to get them, but surely fewer petty criminals will have guns. It is simply untrue for the gun lobby to assert that all criminals—since they are by definition lawbreakers—will find ways to get handguns. For the most part, if the sale of handguns is outlawed, guns won't be available, and fewer criminals will have guns. And if fewer criminals have guns, there is every reason to believe that violent crime will decline. —NAN DESUKA, "Why Handguns Must Be Outlawed"

In this excerpt from an argument for gun control, the author begins by recognizing research cited by her opponents. And later in the paragraph, she addresses the opposition argument that criminals will manage to obtain handguns even if their possession is illegal. By showing that she is aware of these arguments, the author demonstrates that she has considered views different from her own. This demonstration helps to establish her credibility. But because she wishes to persuade readers to support a ban on handguns, the author must show why opposing views have not led her to abandon her own position. Although she agrees that existing gun control laws have not reduced violent crime, she then proposes much stricter controls than have been previously adopted. And in the last three sentences of this excerpt she refutes the argument that criminals will always "find ways to get handguns." (In turn, her opponents might question the constitutionality of a handgun ban—another argument which should be responded to in an essay advocating a ban.)

Closely related to this strategy is the willingness to concede that an opponent has a good point—as this author does when she accepts the conclusion of the university study cited by her opponents and later when she concedes, "even if handguns are outlawed, some criminals will manage to get them." In both cases, however, the author is able to move ahead with her own argument. Writers who concede too much are unlikely to be convincing. As you evaluate for credibility, question any writer who seems entirely one-sided, but also question any writer who seems over anxious to please.

■ **Exercise 3**   Read a series of editorials or letters in a newspaper. Select one that is one sided or inadequately supported; select another that is well supported and fair minded. Your choices should be of similar length. Prepare to read them in class and to explain your evaluation of them.

31d

Recognize inductive reasoning.

When writers use **inductive reasoning**, they begin with a number of facts or observations and use them to draw a general conclusion. Inductive reasoning is used commonly in daily life. For example, if you get indigestion several times after eating sauerkraut, you might conclude that eating sauerkraut gives you indigestion. This use of evidence to form a generalization is called an inductive leap, and the leap should be in proportion to the amount of evidence gathered. It is reasonable to stop eating sauerkraut if it consistently makes you ill—especially if you had sampled sauerkraut from more than one source (since different preparations may change the effect). But if you conclude that no one should eat sauerkraut, your conclusion would be too general for the amount of evidence in question.

Because it involves leaping from evidence to the interpretation of evidence, inductive reasoning can help writers to reach probable and believable conclusions but not some absolute truth that will endure forever. Making a small leap from evidence to a conclusion that seems probable is not the same as jumping to a sweeping conclusion that could easily be challenged. Generally, the greater the evidence, the more reliable the conclusion.

Science's use of inductive reasoning is known as the scientific method. For instance, early medical studies equated diets high in fat with coronary disease. The scientific community reserved judgment since the early studies were based on small samplings, but later studies with broader sampling confirmed the early reports. Although all persons with coronary disease cannot be studied, the sampling is now large enough to make the conclusion with confidence.

In writing, inductive reasoning often employs examples. When you cannot cite all the instances that support your well-reasoned generalization, one or a few examples closely related to the point you are making will provide evidence (see **32c**). In the following inductively organized paragraph, a number of examples support the last sentence.

> In Chicago last month, a nine-year-old boy died of an asthma attack while waiting for emergency aid. After their ambulance was pelted by rocks in an earlier incident, city paramedics

wouldn't risk entering the Dearborn Homes project [where the boy lived] without a police escort. In Atlanta, residents of the Bankhead Courts project had their mail service suspended for two days last month after a postman nearly lost his life in the cross fire of a gun battle. Mail carriers wouldn't resume service until police accompanied them on their rounds. This is the day-to-day reality of life now in America's urban ghettos. Their residents, under siege by what are essentially organized drug terrorists, deserve the benefit of an unapologetic assault on drug-driven crime. —"Hot Towns," *Wall Street Journal*

How you organize your inductive reasoning varies with the situation. You may wish to state the conclusion first, in the form of a topic sentence (**32a[2]**) or a thesis statement (**33d**), and then present the supporting examples. Or you may wish to reverse the order by presenting the conclusion or the generalization after the evidence. Still another way is to let the reader draw the conclusion. These last two strategies work well when your conclusion is one your reader may resist.

31e

Recognize deductive reasoning.

When writers use **deductive reasoning**, they begin with generalizations (premises) and apply them to a specific instance to draw a conclusion about that instance. For example, if you know that all soldiers must complete basic training, and that Martha has enlisted in the army, then you could conclude that Martha must complete basic training. This argument can be expressed in a structure called a **syllogism**.

MAJOR PREMISE	All soldiers must complete basic training.
MINOR PREMISE	Martha is a soldier.
CONCLUSION	Martha must complete basic training.

Sometimes premises are not stated.

Martha has enlisted in the army, so she must complete basic training.

In this sentence, the unstated premise is that all soldiers must complete basic training. A syllogism with an unstated premise—or even an unstated conclusion—is called an *enthymeme*. Enthymemes are frequently found in arguments and can be very effective in writing, but they should be examined with care since the omitted statement may be inaccurate. "Samuel is from Louisiana, so he must like Cajun food" contains the unstated major premise that "Everyone from Louisiana likes Cajun food." This premise is unacceptable because there is no reason to assume that everyone from a particular region shares the same taste in food—even if the food in question happens to be a local specialty. As a critical reader, you must accept the truth of a writer's premises in order to agree with the writer's conclusion.

A deductive argument must be both true and valid. A *true* argument is based on generally accepted, well-backed premises. A *valid* argument is based on logical thinking. The conclusion in the following syllogism is valid because the conclusion follows logically from the major and minor premises, but it is not true because the major premise is not generally accepted.

MAJOR PREMISE   All redheads are brilliant.
MINOR PREMISE   Jane is a redhead.
CONCLUSION   Therefore Jane is brilliant.

The following deductively organized paragraph, from an argument on the welfare of children, draws upon the premise stated in the first sentence.

America cannot afford to waste resources by failing to prevent and curb the national human deficit, which cripples our children's welfare today and costs billions in later remedial and custodial dollars. Each dollar we invest in preventive health care for mothers and children saves more than $3 later. Every dollar put into quality preschool education like Head Start saves $4.75 later. It costs more than twice as much to place a child in foster care as to provide family preservation services. The question is not whether we can afford to invest in every child; it is whether we can afford not to. At a time when future demographic trends guarantee a shortage of young adults who will be workers, soldiers, leaders, and parents, America cannot afford to waste a single child. With unprecedented economic competition from abroad and changing patterns of production at home that demand higher basic educational skills, America cannot wait another minute to do whatever is needed to ensure that today's and tomorrow's workers are well prepared rather than useless and alienated—whatever their color.

—MARIAN WRIGHT EDELMAN, *The Measure of Our Success*

According to the reasoning in this paragraph, America must invest more money in programs for the education and welfare of children. This conclusion rests upon the premise "America cannot afford to waste resources." If children are resources for our country's future, and if current programs for children are failing "to ensure that today's and tomorrow's workers are well prepared," then it is logical to conclude that more money should be invested in those programs most likely to yield good results.

■ **Exercise 4** Supply the missing premise in the following statements and determine if the reasoning is valid and true.

1. He must be a nice person. He smiles all the time.
2. She is a good writer. She is easy to understand.
3. It is going to rain tomorrow. There is a circle around the moon.
4. Omtronic Co. must be well managed. Its earnings have grown steadily during the last few years.
5. Dr. Kordoff must be a good teacher. Her classes always fill up quickly.

31f

Learn how to use the Toulmin method.

Another way of viewing the use of logic is through the method devised by Stephen Toulmin in *The Uses of Argument* (New

York: Cambridge UP, 1964). To create a working logic suitable for the needs of writers, Toulmin drew upon deductive reasoning but put less emphasis upon the formal conventions of a syllogism. His approach sees arguments as the progression from accepted facts or evidence (*data*) to a conclusion (*claim*) by way of a statement (*warrant*), which establishes a reasonable relationship between the two. For example, in the argument,

> Since soldiers are required to complete basic training, and since Martha is a soldier, Martha must complete basic training,

the claim is that Martha must complete basic training, and the data is that she is a soldier. The warrant, that soldiers are required to complete basic training, ties the two statements together, making the conclusion follow from the data.

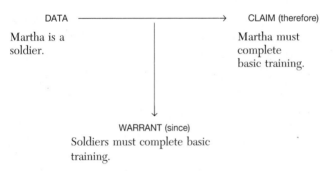

DATA ⟶ CLAIM (therefore)

Martha is a soldier.

Martha must complete basic training.

WARRANT (since)
Soldiers must complete basic training.

The warrant is often implied in arguments and, like the unstated premise in the syllogism, needs careful examination to be acceptable.

Of course, few arguments are as simple as this example. For instance, Martha may have been exempted from basic training because she has a special skill that is in short supply. In such cases, writers can make allowances for exceptions. Qualifiers such as *usually*, *probably*, and *possibly* show the degree of certainty of the conclusion, and rebuttal terms such as *unless* allow writers to anticipate objections.

> **Since** Martha is a soldier, she **probably** passed basic training **unless** an exception was made for her.

Notice that the boldfaced transitional words express logical relationships among ideas in the argument and corresponding elements in the sentence. Like inductive and deductive reasoning, the Toulmin model makes allowances for important elements of probability and rebuttal of readers' objections.

▲ Caution: Too many qualifiers can make an argument seem hesitant and unconvincing.

In the following paragraph, the writer claims that all Americans should learn English. Her data is that English is the language of the government and the primary language of the media. Her warrant is "To be an effective citizen one ought to vote, and to do so intelligently one must be well informed."

> The movement to make English the official language of the United States is in no way a put-down of other languages or cultures. But it is the language used predominantly by the print and electronic media; it is the tongue in which government at every level is conducted. To be an effective citizen one ought to vote, and to do so intelligently one must be well informed. Candidates, of course, present the issues and outline their platforms in English. —YOLANDA DE MOLA, "The Language of Power"

■ **Exercise 5** Analyze the argument in the following excerpt by asking yourself the following questions:

    (a) What is the conclusion or claim?
    (b) What data supports the claim?
    (c) What is the warrant that underlies the argument?

Whether in liquefied form, or used—as many recommend—as a substitute for oil or natural gas to produce electricity, coal is not so simple as it seems. You don't just dig it out of the ground and burn it like waste paper. It is a bulky commodity, and it has more than its share of disadvantages as a fuel.

Railroad facilities and barge canals must be greatly expanded and pipelines constructed to carry the coal in dry or slurry form thousands of miles. Underground mining is hazardous and expensive; open-pit, or strip, mining engenders stiff opposition because it threatens to scar the landscape—in the United States, some particularly beautiful Western landscapes would be an early target. Burned under electric-generating boilers, coal leaves behind vast tonnages of residue, and the gasses it releases upon burning are heavy with contaminants. Getting rid of coal's ashes—usually in the form of a fine powder, because coal must be pulverized before burning for maximum efficiency—is difficult. Expensive scrubbers must be installed in new plants that burn coal with a high sulfur content to prevent the creation of "acid rain." The huge quantities of carbon dioxide that would be released into the air by burning coal on a vastly expanded scale could raise further havoc with the earth's atmosphere.

—ROGER STARR, "The Case for Nuclear Energy"

31g

Recognize logical fallacies.

Fallacies are lapses in logic that may result from misusing or misrepresenting evidence, from relying on faulty premises, or from distorting the issues. They may be the result of poor thinking, but they may also be a deliberate attempt to manipulate—as suggested by the origin of the term *fallacia* which is Latin for "deceit." Fallacies are common, especially in persuasive writing (**33a**). Here are some of the major forms of fallacies. Be alert for them in your reading.

(1) Ad hominem: Attacking the person who presents an issue rather than dealing logically with the issue itself.

FAULTY His arguments might impress us more if he didn't have false teeth. [His false teeth have nothing to do with his arguments.]

(2) Bandwagon: An argument saying, in effect, "Everyone's doing or saying or thinking this, so you should too."

> FAULTY   Everyone else is cheating, so why shouldn't I? [The majority is not always right.]

(3) Begging the question: An assertion that restates the point just made. Such an assertion is circular in that it draws as a conclusion a point stated in the premise.

> FAULTY   He is lazy because he doesn't like to work. [Being lazy and not liking to work mean essentially the same thing.]

(4) Equivocation: An assertion that falsely relies on the use of a term in two different senses.

> FAULTY   Your party platform is right about the economy—as far right as you can get. [*Right* in the first sense implies correct but in the second sense implies a side of the political spectrum.]

(5) False analogy: The assumption that because two things are alike in some ways, they must be alike in other ways.

> FAULTY   Since the books are about the same length and cover the same material, one is probably as good as the other. [The length and coverage of the books cannot predict whether one is as good as the other.]

(6) False authority: The assumption that an expert in one field can be a credible expert in another.

> FAULTY   The defense budget must be cut, as the country's leading pediatrician has shown. [Pediatric medicine is unrelated to economics or political science.]

(7) False cause: The assumption that because one event follows another, the first is the cause of the second.

Sometimes called *post hoc, ergo propter hoc* ("after this, so because of this").

FAULTY The new tax assessor took office last January, and crime in the streets has already increased 25 percent. [The assumption is that having a new tax assessor caused the increase in crime, an assumption unlikely to be true.]

(8) False dilemma: Stating that only two alternatives exist when in fact there are more than two (sometimes called the *either/or* fallacy).

FAULTY We have only two choices: to build more nuclear power plants or to be completely dependent on foreign oil. [In fact, other possibilities exist.]

(9) Guilt by association: An unfair attempt to make someone responsible for the beliefs or actions of others.

FAULTY Senator Barlow must be dishonest because she belongs to the same club as that judge who was recently disbarred. [People can belong to the same club—or live in the same neighborhood—without committing the same crimes.]

(10) Hasty generalization: A generalization based on too little evidence or on exceptional or biased evidence.

FAULTY Teenagers are reckless drivers. [Many teenagers are careful drivers.]

(11) Non sequitur: A statement that does not follow logically from what has just been said—a conclusion that does not follow from the premises.

FAULTY Billy Joe is honest, therefore, he will get a good job. [Many honest people do not get good jobs.]

(12) **Oversimplification:** A statement or argument that leaves out relevant considerations about an issue.

> FAULTY People who pass tests are lucky. [People who pass tests have usually studied and prepared.]

(13) **Red herring:** Dodging the real issue by drawing attention to an irrelevant issue (sometimes called *ignoring the question*).

> FAULTY Why worry about a few terrorists when we ought to be doing something about acid rain? [Acid rain has nothing to do with the actions of terrorists.]

(14) **Slippery slope:** The assumption that if one thing is allowed it will only be the first step in a downward spiral.

> FAULTY Handgun control will lead to a police state. [Handgun control has not led to a police state in England.]

■ **Exercise 6** Identify the fallacies in the following statements. For each statement, write one or two sentences in which you explain the flaw in reasoning.

1. Women will vote for him because he is good-looking.
2. A person who cannot spell should not become a journalist.
3. If you walk self-confidently, you probably won't get mugged.
4. Our jails are full because a lot of people don't have enough money to buy necessities.
5. He is a man, so he must know how to fix cars.
6. Mike missed class twice last week. He must have been sick.
7. Erika is the most popular girl in the class. You should vote for her for president.
8. These razor blades give the smoothest shave; all the baseball players use them.
9. There are only two kinds of politicians: those interested in their own welfare and those interested in the welfare of the people.
10. Why can't I buy a car? All my friends have cars.

■ **Exercise 7** Examine several recent magazine advertisements and study the claims that the ads make. Look specifically for examples of logical fallacies. Choose one ad that seems especially illogical. Bring a copy of it to class, and write a paragraph in which you explain why the ad is unconvincing.

■ **Exercise 8** Read the following paragraph and identify logical fallacies that you find within it. Then, adopting the point of view of someone opposed to animal experimentation, write two or three paragraphs responding to the argument offered here.

As the Oscar-winning director Scavan Kleck has argued, "Animal experimentation saves lives." Isn't the life of a little girl more important than the life of a chimpanzee? We have to choose: we can either experiment upon animals to find cures for life-threatening diseases or we can stand by helplessly while thousands of children die. Experimentation is necessary because research is important. And why should we worry about what happens to animals in laboratories when the real problem is how people treat their pets? Advocates of animal rights are a bunch of sentimental vegetarians who don't care what happens to children, and they will never be satisfied with banning painful experiments on animals. If they succeed in getting legislation passed that restricts experimentation, it's only a question of time before the sale of meat is prohibited. Just look at the trouble they've already caused. The cost of research has soared since people started protesting against animal experimentation.

32

The Paragraph

Write paragraphs that are unified, coherent, and adequately developed.

An essential unit of thought in writing, paragraphs develop the main idea of a paper in the same way that sentences develop the main idea of a paragraph. Sentences and paragraphs rarely stand alone; they are integral parts of the greater units—that is, the paragraphs and the essays—to which they belong. The beginning of a paragraph is indicated by indention to signal the reader that a new idea is being introduced. (Indention is also used in dialogue, as discussed in **16a[2]**.)

Good paragraphs are *unified*, *coherent*, and *well developed*. In paragraph 1, observe how the sentences relate to a single main idea (showing unity), how ideas progress easily from sentence to sentence (showing coherence), and how specific details support the main idea (showing development). (For easy reference, the paragraphs in this section are numbered—except for those in need of revision. The topic sentences of the initial paragraphs are indicated by italics.)

1   But *those Levi's marked more than my move from little-girl clothes to big-brother clothes*. Indeed, they were the only hand-me-downs ever handed down. Instead, those old ratty pants marked my move to freedom, freedom from the conventional girl-stuff my mother had so carefully fostered only one

year earlier. Maybe my mother—who was learning the difference between roofing nails and wood screws, who was learning to mix paint in the vise-gripping shake-machine bolted to the floor in the back room of the hardware store, who would later teach me to cut glass, make keys, and clean Surge milk pumpers—wanted me to know what she was learning about women's work and men's work. I don't know. I just know that those Levi's—old, worn, with a difficult-to-manage button fly—meant the world to me, at least the limited world offered by my neighborhood.   —MARILYN SCHIEL, "Levi's"

Paragraphs have no set length. Typically, they average perhaps 100 words, ranging from 50 to 250 words. Paragraphs in books are usually longer than those written for the narrow columns of newspapers and magazines.

Although occasionally one-sentence paragraphs are used for emphasis (see paragraphs 33–35, page 326), short paragraphs often indicate inadequate development. Long paragraphs, too, can reveal problems in your writing, especially if they exhaust one point or combine too many points.

▲ Note: Introductory, concluding, and transitional paragraphs serve other purposes and are discussed in **32b(6)** and **33f**.

32a

Construct unified paragraphs.

In a unified paragraph, each sentence helps develop the main idea. Stating the main idea in a topic sentence will help you achieve unity.

(1) Make sure every paragraph has a main idea.

Writers usually convey the main idea of a paragraph in a topic sentence, which may appear at any point in the paragraph. Notice how the topic sentence of paragraph 2 (in italics) announces the idea of our reaction to eye behavior. It also suggests the approach of the paragraph by establishing an expectation that the writer will go on to provide an example.

2   *Much of eye behavior is so subtle that we react to it only on the intuitive level.* The next time you have a conversation with someone who makes you feel liked, notice what he does with his eyes. Chances are he looks at you more often than usual with glances a little longer than the normal. You interpret this as a sign—a polite one—that he is interested in you as a person rather than just in the topic of conversation. Probably you also feel that he is both self-confident and sincere.

—FLORA DAVIS,
"Inside Intuition: What We Know about Nonverbal Communication"

Notice in paragraph 3 how the phrase "two flying-squirrel species" in the first sentence suggests the approach the writer will follow.

3   *There are two flying-squirrel species in North America, and their ranges overlap slightly.* The northern species is found throughout Canada, Alaska and the Northern states. In mountains of the East and West, the species extends its range farther south but is restricted to the higher altitudes. The southern flying squirrel inhabits the forests of the Eastern states and southern Ontario, and a few isolated populations have also been found in Mexico and Central America. Fortunately for me, both species occur in Michigan, with their ranges meeting in the upper part of the state.

—NANCY WELLS-GOSLING, "The Little Squirrel That Flies"

The main idea of a paragraph is frequently stated at or near the beginning, as in examples 2 and 3. It is sometimes also restated at the end to emphasize its importance. In paragraph 4, compare "Americans do not achieve this status until" with the final "we often meander through an analogous rite of passage."

4   *In most cultures, adulthood is equated with self-reliance and responsibility, yet often Americans do not achieve this*

*status until we are in our late twenties or early thirties—
virtually the entire average lifespan of a person in a traditional
non-Western society.* We tend to treat prolonged adolescence
as a warm-up for real life, as a wobbly suspension bridge
between childhood and legal maturity. Whereas a nineteenth-
century Cheyenne or Lakota teenager was expected to alter
self-conception in a split-second vision, we often meander
through an analogous rite of passage for more than a decade—
through high school, college, graduate school.

—MICHAEL DORRIS, "Life Stories"

Occasionally, the topic sentence is stated near the end of
the paragraph, especially when the writer progresses from
specific examples to a generalization, as in paragraph 5.

5   In the warmth of the inner Solar System a comet releases
clouds of vapor and dust that form the growing head and then
leak into the tail, which is the cosmic equivalent of an oil slick.
Pieces of the dust later hit the Earth, as meteors. A few
survivors among the comets evolve into menacing lumps of
dirt in tight orbits around the Sun. *For these reasons comets
are, in my opinion, best regarded as a conspicuous form of
sky pollution.*   —NIGEL CALDER, "The Comet Is Coming"

A single topic sentence may serve for a sequence of two
or more paragraphs.

6   *The world has always been divided into two camps: those
who love garlic and onions and those who detest them.* The
first camp would include the Egyptian pharaohs who were
entombed with clay and wood carvings of garlic and onions
to ensure that meals in the afterlife would be well seasoned.
It would include the Jews who wandered for 40 years in the
Sinai wilderness, fondly remembering "the fish which we did
eat in Egypt so freely, and the pumpkins and melons, and the
leeks, onions and garlic." It would include Sydney Smith, the
19th-century essayist, whose "Recipe for Salad" includes this
couplet: "Let onion atoms lurk within the bowl, / And, scarce-
suspected, animate the whole."

7   The camp of the garlic and onion haters would include the
Egyptian priests who, according to Plutarch, "kept themselves

clear of the onion. . . . It is suitable neither for fasting nor festival, because in the one case it causes thirst, and in the other tears for those who partake it." The camp would include the ancient Greeks, who considered the odor of garlic and onions vulgar and prohibited garlic and onion eaters from worshiping at the Temple of Cybele. It would include Bottom, who in *A Midsummer Night's Dream* instructs his troupe of actors to "eat no onions nor garlic, for we are to utter sweet breath." —ERIC BLOCK, "The Chemistry of Garlic and Onions"

Occasionally, a paragraph contains no topic sentence because the details unmistakably imply the main idea. Notice how the idea that perceptions change as people change, although never explicitly stated, is clearly the central idea of the following paragraph.

8 Everything Chuck did that summer was kind, and helped me to grow normally. I would love to meet him now and thank him for all the strength I took from him. Every person probably encounters these "saints" again and again in his lifetime, without understanding their importance or being grateful. If I saw him now, the way he was then, I wonder if I would even appreciate Chuck. He was fresh out of the army, starting college on the GI Bill, had a cautious way of speaking, not much book culture. What hurts in all this is knowing that I probably would have condescended to someone like him at college, barely eight years after looking up to him as everything. —PHILIP LOPATE, "Summer Camps"

■ **Exercise 1** Identify the topic sentences in the following paragraphs. If the main idea is implied, write out the implied topic sentence.

9 Ambivalence as a defining sensibility, widespread and full-blown, is something new. There is virtually nothing today about which thoughtful people—especially thoughtful younger people—do not feel mixed emotions. Every hankering, whether it's for a policy (like national health insurance), or a commodity (like microwave ovens), or a performer (like David Letterman), comes with disclaimers, a special codicil of qualifiers or qualms. —KURT ANDERSEN, "Hot Mood"

10   A TV set stood close to a wall in the small living room crowded with an assortment of chairs and tables. An aquarium crowded the mantelpiece of a fake fireplace. A lighted bulb inside the tank showed many colored fish swimming about in a haze of fish food. Some of it lay scattered on the edge of the shelf. The carpet underneath was sodden black. Old magazines and tabloids lay just about everywhere.

—BIENVENIDO SANTOS, "Immigration Blues"

11   Certainly the [U.S.] political problems, difficult and delicate though they may be, are not insoluble. Some, like the control or the liquidation of monopolies which stand in the way of individual initiative, have a long history in this country. Others, like the struggle to liberate individuals from the degrading fear of unemployment or old age or sickness, are less familiar—at least in the United States. Still others, like the overriding question of the relation between individual freedom and the intervention of the state, have a meaning for our generation which they did not have for generations before. But only a man who did not wish to find an answer to questions such as these would argue that no answer can be found.

—ARCHIBALD MACLEISH, "The Conquest of America"

■ **Exercise 2**   Write a paragraph with a topic sentence at the beginning, another with the topic sentence at the end, and a third with the topic sentence at the beginning and restated at the end. Here are a few possible approaches.

1. A good pizza is . . .
2. The first time that I . . .
3. Two results of . . .
4. Depression can be defined as . . .

(2) Relate each sentence to the main idea of the paragraph.

Unify a paragraph by making each sentence support the main idea. Notice in paragraph 12 how each sentence shows exactly what the writer means by the curious experiences referred to in the topic sentence.

12   *A number of curious experiences occur at the onset of sleep.* A person just about to go to sleep may experience an electric shock, a flash of light, or a crash of thunder—but the most common sensation is that of dropping or falling, which is why "falling asleep" is a scientifically valid description. A nearly universal occurrence at the beginning of sleep (although not everyone recalls it) is a sudden, uncoordinated jerk of the head, the limbs, or even the entire body. Most people tend to think of going to sleep as a slow slippage into oblivion, but the onset of sleep is not gradual at all. It happens in an instant. One moment the individual is awake, the next moment not.

—PETER FARB, "Humankind"

As you check your paragraphs for unity, revise or eliminate any information that does not clearly relate to the main idea. If the relationship between details and the main idea is obvious to you but not to your reader, add a phrase or a sentence to make their relevance clear. If more than one major idea appears in a single paragraph, either refocus your main idea or develop each idea in a separate paragraph.

■ **Exercise 3** Note how each sentence in the following paragraph expresses a different major idea. Select one sentence and develop it into a unified paragraph by using it as a topic sentence and supporting it with specific details and examples. Use your imagination and write in the voice of a 30-year-old man or woman.

People don't always understand how hard it is to go to college while you're trying to support yourself and your kids. After the divorce, I had to get a different kind of job to support my kids, but jobs with the right hours are hard to find if you don't have any real education, so I had to take a job as a cook. My mom keeps the kids during the day while I go to school, but I have to get a sitter to take care of them while I work the dinner shift. I try to study in between when I get home from school and when I have to go to work, but the kids are usually all over me wanting attention. So, what I don't get done then I have to do after I get off work which is pretty late in the evening. Then, I have to be up to get the kids fed before I go to class. It doesn't leave much time for study or for my kids either.

■ **Exercise 4** The following paragraph lacks unity since either the sentences do not relate to the main idea—the similarities between the coasts of Maine and Oregon—or the relationship to the main idea is not clear. Revise by making the connections clear and deleting unrelated sentences.

When I visited the coast of Maine last summer, I noticed that it looked very much like the coast of Oregon. It was very cold and rainy in Maine, and we had to wear coats even though it was late July. In Maine, the coastline is rocky and in many places evergreens march straight to the water. In other places, bluffs lined with evergreens overlook the sea. One day we saw a large sailboat diving hard toward some half-submerged rocks. In Oregon, pine rimmed bluffs usually overlook the ocean, but sometimes the trees extend to a partly submerged rocky ledge or a pebble beach. Small islands, called sea stacks, dot this coastline much as the low, wooded islands lie offshore in Penobscot Bay. Lighthouses can be found here and there along both coastlines.

32b

Make paragraphs coherent by arranging ideas in a clearly understandable order and by providing appropriate transitions.

A paragraph is coherent when the relationship among ideas is clear and the progression from one sentence to the next is easy for the reader to follow. To achieve coherence, arrange ideas in a clearly understandable order. Link them by effective use of pronouns, repetition, conjunctions, transitional phrases, and parallel structure. These transitional devices also ease the transitions between paragraphs.

ARRANGEMENT OF IDEAS

(1) Arrange ideas in a clearly understandable order.

There are many ways to arrange ideas in a paragraph. One of the simplest is **chronological order**.

13   Standing in line at the unemployment office makes you feel very much the same as you did the first time you ever

flunked a class or a test—as if you had a big red "F" for "Failure" printed across your forehead. I fantasize myself standing at the end of the line in a crisp and efficient blue suit, chin up, neat and straight as a corporate executive. As I move down the line I start to come unglued and a half hour later, when I finally reach the desk clerk, I am slouching and sallow in torn jeans, tennis shoes and a jacket from the Salvation Army, carrying my worldly belongings in a shopping bag and unable to speak.

—JAN HALVORSON, "How It Feels to Be Out of Work"

Descriptive passages are often arranged in **spatial order**. Starting from a single point of reference, the description can move from north to south, from near to distant, from left to right, and so on. Note the movement from the top of the plateau to the bottom of the gorge in paragraph 14 and from a broad to a close perspective in 15.

14   The highway, without warning, rolled off the plateau of green pastures and entered a wooded and rocky gorge; down, down, precipitously down to the Kentucky River. Along the north slope, man-high columns of ice clung to the limestone. The road dropped deeper until it crossed the river at Brooklyn Bridge. The gorge, hidden in the tableland and wholly unexpected, was the Palisades. At the bottom lay only enough ground for the river and a narrow strip of willow-rimmed floodplain. —WILLIAM LEAST HEAT MOON, *Blue Highways*

15   Weasel! I'd never seen one wild before. He was ten inches long, thin as a curve, a muscled ribbon, brown as fruit wood, soft-furred, alert. His face was fierce, small and pointed as a lizard's; he would have made a good arrowhead. There was just a dot of chin, maybe two brown hairs' worth, and then the pure white fur began that spread down his underside. He had two black eyes I didn't see, any more than you see a window. —ANNIE DILLARD, "Living with Weasels"

Another useful arrangement is **order of importance** (climactic), from most important to least or from least to most.

(See also **29c**). In paragraph 16 the author focuses on a hierarchy of intelligence, moving from lower to higher forms of life.

16   An ant cannot purposefully try anything new, and any ant that accidentally did so would be murdered by his colleagues. It is the ant colony as a whole that slowly learns over the ages. In contrast, even an earthworm has enough flexibility of brain to enable it to be taught to turn toward the left or right for food. Though rats are not able to reason to any considerable degree, they can solve such problems as separating round objects from triangular ones when these have to do with health or appetite. Cats, with better brains, can be taught somewhat more, and young dogs a great deal. The higher apes can learn by insight as well as by trial and error.
—GEORGE RUSSELL HARRISON, *What Man May Be*

Sometimes the movement within the paragraph is from **general to specific** or from **specific to general**. A paragraph may begin with a general statement or idea, which is then supported by particular details, as in paragraph 15 above, or it may begin with a striking detail or series of details and conclude with a climactic statement as in paragraph 17, or a summarizing statement as in paragraph 18.

17   It was not the only disappointment my mother felt in me. In the years that followed, I failed her so many times, each time asserting my own will, my right to fall short of expectations. I didn't get straight As. I didn't become class president. I didn't get into Stanford. I dropped out of college. —AMY TAN, "Two Kinds"

18   When we watch a person walk away from us, his image shrinks in size. But since we know for a fact that he is not shrinking, we make an unconscious correcting and "see" him as retaining his full stature. Past experience tells us what his true stature is with respect to our own. Any sane and dependable expectation of the future requires that he have the same stature when we next encounter him. Our perception is thus

a prediction; it embraces the past and the future as well as
the present.

—WARREN J. WITTREICH, "Visual Perception and Personality"

One common form of the general-specific pattern is **topic-
restriction-illustration**, in which the writer announces the
topic, restricts it, and illustrates the restricted topic. In paragraph 19, the writer announces the topic—the desire to associate with successful people—restricts it in the third sentence
to the uses of testimonial advertisements and then illustrates
it with examples of testimonials. In addition, this particular
example illustrates a variation of the pattern in which the
topic is restated at the end of the paragraph:

19   Another human desire advertising writers did not invent
(although they liberally exploit it) is to associate with successful
people. All of us tend to admire people who are widely known
for their achievements. We are therefore already primed for
the common advertising device of the testimonial or personality ad. Once we have seen a famous person in an advertisement, we associate the product with the person. "I like
Mr. X. Mr. X likes (endorses) this product. I like this product,
too." The logic is faulty, but we fall for it just the same.
That is how Joe DiMaggio sells Mr. Coffee. Although cartoon
characters are not admired per se, they too are easily recognized; that's why Pac-Man sells vitamins and Bugs Bunny sells
Post Raisin Bran. The people who write testimonial ads did
not create our trust in famous personalities. They merely
recognize our inclinations and exploit them.

—CHARLES A. O'NEILL, "The Language of Advertising"

In the **question-answer** pattern, the first sentence asks a
question that the supporting sentences answer.

20   What's wrong with the student-union book shop? Everything. It's interested in selling sweatshirts and college mugs
rather than good books. Its staff often is incompetent and
uncivil. The manager may not be intelligent enough even to
order a sufficient number of copies of required textbooks for
the beginning of a term. As for more lively books—why, there

are masses of paperbacks, perhaps, that could be procured at any drugstore; there are a few shelves or racks of volumes labeled "Gift Books," usually lavishly illustrated and inordinately costly, intended as presents to fond parents but there are virtually no book books, of the sort that students might like to buy.

—RUSSELL KIRK, "From the Academy: Campus Bookshops"

Another common paragraph arrangement is the **problem-solution** pattern, in which the first sentence or two states the problem and the rest of the paragraph suggests the solution.

21   That many women would be happier not pursuing careers or intellectual adventures is only part of the truth. The whole truth is that many people would be. If society had the clear sight to assure men as well as women that there is no shame in preferring to stay non-competitively and non-aggressively at home, many masculine neuroses and ulcers would be avoided, and many children would enjoy the benefit of being brought up by a father with a talent for the job instead of by a mother with no talent for it but a sense of guilt about the lack.   —BRIGID BROPHY, "Women"

Paragraphs 13 through 21 illustrate eight of the many possible types of arrangement within the paragraph. Any order or combination of orders is satisfactory as long as the sequence of ideas is logical and clear.

■ **Exercise 5**   Prepare for a class discussion of paragraph arrangement by identifying the pattern of each of the following paragraphs (chronological, spatial, climactic, general to specific, specific to general, topic-restriction-illustration, question-answer, problem-solution). Explain in writing how each paragraph follows the pattern you have identified.

22   Perhaps the most mystifying of the habits peculiar to whales is their "singing." Humpback whales are the most renowned for a wide range of tones, and whole herds often join together in "songs" composed of complete sequences, which repeated, can last for hours. Some evenings, we listened to the humpbacks starting to make a few sounds, like musicians

tuning their instruments. Then, one by one, they began to sing. Underwater canyons made the sounds echo, and it seemed as though we were in a cathedral listening to the faithful alternating verses of a psalm.

—JACQUES-YVES COUSTEAU, "Jonah's Complaint"

23 The so-called "Western Code" never really existed. Men bent on killing did so in the most efficient and expeditious way they knew. Jesse James was shot in the back by Bob Ford as he stood on a chair adjusting a picture. Ben Thompson was led into a trap in a theater and shot down with his friend King Fisher. Billy the Kid died as he entered a darkened room. Wild Bill Hickok was shot from behind while he was playing poker. In each case the victim had no chance to defend himself. —JOSEPH G. ROSA, "The Gunfighter"

24 Our unsustainable, unecological agriculture cannot—and should not—continue. The good news, reported by many speakers at the celebration in Salina, is that it doesn't have to. Where ecology and agriculture have gotten together, the partnership works. Quietly, with little help from science or government, thousands of American farmers have been pioneering a new form of modern, high-yield agriculture using industry much less and the nutrient-cycling, pest-controlling principles of nature much more. —DONELLA H. MEADOWS, "Ecology and Agriculture: A Marriage That Must Be Made on Earth"

25 The humorous story is told gravely; the teller does his best to conceal the fact that he even dimly suspects that there is anything funny about it; but the teller of the comic story tells you beforehand that it is one of the funniest things he has ever heard, then tells it with eager delight, and is the first person to laugh when he gets through. And sometimes, if he has had good success, he is so glad and happy that he will repeat the "nub" of it and glance around from face to face, collecting applause, and then repeat it again. It is a pathetic thing to see. —MARK TWAIN, "How to Tell a Story"

26 The next day we took the main street—the highway— out of Chesterville. It was almost autumn, so the air was cool and tart that morning, and a few trees were tinged orange.

When we moved into town, we'd come on the highway, too. I watched out the window as we passed everything we'd passed when we first came: the church, our school, the doughnut shop. I tried to pretend we were going backward in time, to before we came to Chesterville, but then I noticed how the huge brown doughnut, new when we came, was chipped now and weathered.   —CYNTHIA KADOHATA, "Devils"

27   Who is to say, then, if there is any right path to the top, or even to say what the top consists of? Obviously the colleges don't have more than a partial answer—otherwise the young would not be so disaffected with an education that they consider vapid. Obviously business does not have the answer—otherwise the young would not be so scornful of its call to be an organization man.   —WILLIAM ZINSSER, "The Right to Fail"

■ **Exercise 6**   Using paragraphs 13 through 21 as models, write paragraphs following three of the arrangements described in this section (chronological, spatial, climactic, general to specific, specific to general, topic-restriction-illustration, question-answer, problem-solution). Use the following as possible topics: insects, football, desserts, sport shoes, or any other topics your instructor approves.

■ **Exercise 7**   Examine paragraphs from your own writing in other projects and find examples of three of the arrangements described in this section. Make copies of them and be ready to discuss your paragraphs in class.

TRANSITIONS

Many of the same kinds of transitions link sentences within paragraphs and paragraphs within a paper: pronouns, repetition of key words or ideas, conjunctions and other transitional phrases, and parallel structures. (See also chapters **26**, **28**).

(2) Link sentences by using pronouns.

In paragraph 28 the writer links sentences by using the pronouns *their* and *they*. Although these same two pronouns are used repeatedly, their referent, "easy victims," is always clear.

28   Several movements characterize easy victims: their strides were either very long or very short; they moved awkwardly, raising their left legs with their left arms (instead of alternating them); on each step, they tended to lift their whole foot up and then place it down (less muggable sorts took steps in which their feet rocked from heel to toe). Overall, the people rated most muggable walked as if they were in conflict with themselves; they seemed to make each move in the most difficult way possible.

—CARIN RUBENSTEIN, "Body Language That Speaks to Muggers"

(3) Link sentences by repeating words, phrases, or ideas.

In paragraph 29, the repetition of the key word *wave* links the sentences. (The repetition also provides emphasis, see **29e**.)

29   The weekend is over, and we drive down the country road from the cottage to the pier, passing out our last supply of waves. We wave at people walking and wave at people riding. We wave at people we know and wave at people who are strangers.   —ELLEN GOODMAN, "Waving Goodbye to the Country"

(4) Link sentences by using conjunctions and other transitional expressions.

Conjunctions and transitional phrases demonstrate the logical relationship between ideas. Notice the subtle changes in the relationship between two clauses linked by different conjunctions.

He laughed, and she frowned.
He laughed while she frowned.
He laughed because she frowned.
He laughed, so she frowned.
He laughed; later, she frowned.

Here is a list of some frequently used transitional connections arranged according to the kinds of relationships they establish.

a. *Alternative and addition*: or, nor, and, and then, moreover, further, furthermore, besides, likewise, also, too, again, in addition, even more important, next, first, second, third, in the first place, in the second place, finally, last
b. *Comparison*: similarly, likewise, in like manner
c. *Contrast*: but, yet, or, and yet, however, still, nevertheless, on the other hand, on the contrary, conversely, even so, notwithstanding, for all that, in contrast, at the same time, although this may be true, otherwise, nonetheless
d. *Place*: here, beyond, nearby, opposite to, adjacent to, on the opposite side
e. *Purpose*: to this end, for this purpose, with this object
f. *Result, cause*: so, for, hence, therefore, accordingly, consequently, thus, thereupon, as a result, then, because
g. *Summary, repetition, exemplification, intensification*: to sum up, in brief, on the whole, in sum, in short, as I have said, in other words, that is, to be sure, as has been noted, for example, for instance, in fact, indeed, to tell the truth, in any event
h. *Time*: meanwhile, at length, soon, after a few days, in the meantime, afterward, later, now, then, in the past, while

(5) Link sentences by using parallel structures.

Parallelism is the repetition of the sentence pattern or of other grammatical structures. (See also **26**.) In paragraph 30, notice that the first three sentences are structured in the same way:

> When you're three years old . . . , that's expected.
> When you're six . . . , you deserve some credit. . . .
> When you're nine . . . , you should be applauded. . . .

Repeating this pattern emphasizes the close relationship of the ideas.

30   When you're three years old and stick mashed potatoes up your nose, that's expected. When you're six and make your bed but it looks like you're still in it, you deserve some credit for trying. When you're nine and prepare the family meal but the casserole looks worse than the kitchen, you should be applauded for your effort. But somewhere along the line, some responsible adult should say, "You're too old for this nonsense."

—DAN KILEY,
The Peter Pan Syndrome: Men Who Have Never Grown Up

■ **Exercise 8**   Prepare for a class discussion of transitional devices in the following paragraphs by circling the pronouns, underlining repeated words and phrases, bracketing conjunctions, double underlining transitional phrases, and placing parentheses around parallel structures.

31   So far I have been pretty vague about just what the freedom of the androgynous man is. Obviously it varies with the case. In the case I know best, my own, I can be quite specific. It has freed me most as a parent. I am, among other things, a fairly good natural mother. I like the nurturing role. It makes me feel good to see a child eat—and it turns me to mush to see a 4-year-old holding a glass with both small hands, in order to drink. I even enjoyed sewing patches on the knees of my daughter Amy's Dr. Dentons when she was at the crawling stage. All that pleasure I would have lost if I had made myself stick to the notion of the paternal role that I started with.   —NOEL PERRIN, "The Androgynous Male"

32   There are obvious advantages for the writers of allegorical tales like country music's to have a conventionalized geography to reinforce the message. But why does country music use *this* image of America? Why is country music so pleased with the South and so upset with the North? The answer to this question lies not in the actual geography of the United States, but in how country music's audience perceives the geography of the United States. It is not a question of what America is, but of what America means to these people. As a result, the

question has to do with far more than just a style of singing; it has to do with the attitudes of the millions of Americans who listen to country music—attitudes about regional differences in American society, about the role of the media as part of the American power structure, and about the value of progress in general.   —BEN MARSH, "A Rose-Colored Map"

■ **Exercise 9**   Revise the following paragraph so the thought flows smoothly from one sentence to the next. Add pronouns and linking devices, and revise sentences to create parallel structure and to repeat key phrases.

Cable television sounds like a good deal at first. All available local channels can be piped into a television set for a relatively low cost per month. The reception is clear—a real bonus in fringe and rural areas. Several channels for news and local access are in the basic monthly fee. A cable connection to a second or third TV set costs extra. In most places subscribers have to pay as much as fifty dollars a month extra to get the channels like Home Box Office and The Disney Channel. The movies change each month. The pay-TV movie channels run the same films over and over during a month's time. Many of the films offered each month are box office flops or reruns of old movies that can be viewed on regular channels. Cable television isn't really a bargain.

(6) Link paragraphs with clear transitions.

Transitions between paragraphs are as important as transitions between sentences and are achieved by many of the same devices—repetition of words or ideas, conjunctions and other transitional expressions, and parallel structures. Such devices are usually evident in the first sentence of a paragraph. (The italics in each of the following examples were added.)

You can repeat a word or idea from the last paragraph in the first sentence of the new paragraph.

Psychologists call these toys—these furry animals and old, cozy baby blankets—*"transitional objects"*; that is, objects that help the child move back and forth between the exactions of everyday life and the world of wish and dream.

Superstitions have some of the qualities of these *transitional objects*. —MARGARET MEAD, "New Superstitions for Old"

No man was born to anything, except perhaps to a chance to show how far he could rise. Life was competition.

Yet along with *this feeling* had come a deep sense of belonging to an optional community.

—BRUCE CATTON, "Grant and Lee: A Study in Contrasts"

You can use transitional words or phrases to connect paragraphs.

The decision was made to reduce the thickness of the paper and to provide different-sized bags to go with larger or smaller orders.

As a result, the supermarket chain's profits dropped further. —LEONARD SILK, "What Economics Can Do for You"

You can use parallel structures to demonstrate relationships between paragraphs.

33   *I have a dream that one day* on the red hills of Georgia the sons of former slaves and the sons of former slaveowners will be able to sit down together at the table of brotherhood.

34   *I have a dream that one day* even the state of Mississippi, a desert state sweltering with the heat of injustice and oppression, will be transformed into an oasis of freedom and justice.

35   *I have a dream that* my four little children will one day live in a nation where they will not be judged by the color of their skin but by the content of their character.

—MARTIN LUTHER KING, JR., "I Have a Dream" Speech

Sometimes a transitional paragraph serves as a bridge between two paragraphs. Ordinarily, such a paragraph is short (often consisting of only one sentence) because the writer intends it to be merely a signpost.

36   Now you are expecting me to describe how I saw the folly of my ways and came back to the warm nest, where prejudices are so often called loyalties, where pointless actions

are hallowed into custom by repetition, where we are content to say we think when all we do is feel.

37   But you would be wrong. I dropped my hobby and turned professional.

38   If I were to go back to the headmaster's study and find the dusty statuettes still there, I would arrange them differently. I would dust Venus and put her aside, for I have come to love her and know her for the fair thing she is. But I would put the Thinker, sunk in his desperate thought, where there were shadows before him—and at his back, I would put the leopard, crouched and ready to spring.

—WILLIAM GOLDING, "Thinking as a Hobby"

32c

Develop the paragraph with details and examples.

Many short paragraphs are adequately developed and supply enough information within the context of the essay to satisfy the reader. For example, the following paragraph, although only one sentence, contains considerable detail.

39   If environment refers to what's around us, then our environment also includes the awesome coast of Oregon, the sparkling desert nights in southern Arizona, the Everglades glowing red in the summer dawn, the waltzing wheatfields of Kansas, the New York City skyline at dusk, the luxurious cabin of a jet airliner, air-conditioned autos and broad turnpikes and winding parkways, the pretty clothes of American women, and the laughter of children.   —EDWIN A. ROBERTS, JR., "Struggling to Control Growing Trash Heaps"

Sometimes short paragraphs can be combined if they deal with the same idea. More often, however, short paragraphs need to be developed with more specific details or examples.

(1) Develop with specific details.

Notice how the series of details in the following example support the topic sentence (italicized).

40   *Today's pop music is sending several dominant messages.*
Material values are on the ascendant, but idealism is by no
means a spent force. Most pop songs are love songs, as always,
but today's versions try to look at relationships without rose-
colored glasses. Romantic notions are viewed with some suspi-
cion; so are drugs. And important rock artists and rappers,
while no longer anticipating radical change, are addressing
issues, and challenging their listeners to actively confront the
world around them. There have probably been more angry
protest lyrics written and recorded in the last three or four
years than in any comparable period of the 60's.
                        —ROBERT PALMER, "What Pop Lyrics Say to Us"

(2) Develop with examples.

Use appropriate and specific examples to clarify your ideas.
The following definition may be unclear without the italicized
example.

A euphemism is the substitution of a pleasant expression for
an unpleasant one, *such as "passed away" for "died."*

Paragraph 41 uses several closely related examples (as well
as details) to explain why violence is both impractical and
immoral.

41   Violence as a way of achieving racial justice is both impractical and immoral. It is impractical because it is a descend-
ing spiral ending in destruction for all. The old law of an eye
for an eye leaves everybody blind. It is immoral because it
seeks to humiliate the opponent rather than win his understanding; it seeks to annihilate rather than to convert. Violence
is immoral because it thrives on hatred rather than love. It
destroys community and makes brotherhood impossible. It
leaves society in monologue rather than dialogue. Violence
ends by defeating itself. It creates bitterness in the survivors
and brutality in the destroyers. A voice echoes through time
saying to every potential Peter, "Put up your sword." History
is cluttered with the wreckage of nations that failed to follow
this command.   —MARTIN LUTHER KING, JR.,
                                "Three Types of Resistance to Oppression"

You can also use one striking example, as in paragraph 42, to clarify your idea.

42 The letters were trivial in content. They began with criticism of the poem each had sent in the letter before, and proceeded into an endless banter, in which each related the music he had heard, daily episodes in his family, impressions of girls he found beautiful, reports of books he had read, poetic experiences in which worlds would be revealed from single words, and so on. Neither the twenty-year-old youth nor the fifteen-year-old boy tired of this habit.

       —MISHIMA YUKIO, "The Boy Who Wrote Poetry"

43 Still and all, I remember him with great affection and a touch of sadness. I say sadness because eventually Leroy was to suffer the misery of being an outsider in an already outside ghetto. As he grew older, it was apparent that he longed to be a Mexican, that he felt terribly dark and alone. "Sometimes," he would tell me, "I feel like my damn skin's too tight, like I'm gonna bust out of it." One cold February night I found him in the coal shed behind Pacheco's store, desperately scraping his forearm with sandpaper, the hurt tears streaming down his face. "I got to get this off, man. I can't stand all this blackness." We stood there quietly staring at the floor for a long, anguished moment, both of us miserable beyond word or gesture. Finally he drew a deep breath, blew his nose loudly, and mumbled half audibly, "Man, you sure lucky to be a Mexican." —ENRIQUE "HANK" LOPEZ, "Back to Bachimba"

Details and examples clarify and explain your point.

■ **Exercise 10** Develop the following sentences with enough details and/or examples to make an interesting paragraph.

1. Many people wonder how _____ stays in shape.
2. It was the filthiest room that I had ever seen.
3. The class was so boring I decided to cut.
4. I grew up in the friendliest neighborhood in the world.

■ **Exercise 11** Examine your own writing and select a paragraph you think needs additional details or an appropriate example. Rewrite the paragraph.

32d

Use various strategies of paragraph development.

You can learn to write good paragraphs by studying the various techniques professional writers use to develop ideas. All the strategies for developing paragraphs discussed in the following pages are useful for developing whole compositions. (See also chapter **33**.)

The more you read, the more you will find that most paragraphs are developed by a combination of methods. Some good paragraphs almost defy analysis. Because these development strategies reflect ways people think, we tend to use them in combination with each other. For example, the formal definition may be developed through both classification and contrast, or narration may be developed by using descriptive details. The important consideration is not that a specific method is used to develop the paragraph, but that the development is clear, complete, and appropriate. No one method, or no one combination, is better than another. Use the one—or ones—that best suit your purpose. As you study the following illustrations of good paragraphs, notice how each main idea is developed.

(1) Narrate a series of events.

A narrative discusses a sequence of events, normally in the order in which they occur, that develop the point you are making. This form often uses time markers such as *then, later,* or *at a later date.* (Longer narratives often begin in the middle of a sequence of events and contain flashbacks to earlier events.) The narrative must be closely related to your main idea and must develop that idea. Notice how the writer in paragraph 44 uses narrative to develop the main idea stated in the last sentence in the paragraph.

44   The man didn't hear me or had decided, in retaliation for our semantic disagreement, to ignore me for a while. I reached up to knock again, but noticed that my glove had left a greasy smear on the window. Ever my mother's son, I reflexively reached into my pocket for my handkerchief and was about to wipe the grease away when it hit me: at last the oil industry had me where it wanted me—standing in the rain and washing its windshield.   —ANDREW WARD,
"They Also Wait Who Stand and Serve Themselves"

(2) Describe to make a point.

Focus your description according to your purpose. In describing your car you would emphasize certain features to a prospective buyer, others to a mechanic who is going to repair it, and still others to a friend who wants to borrow it.

Present descriptive details in a clear order—from near to far, from general to particular, from right to left, from top to bottom—thus providing an orderly scheme for the reader. In paragraph 45, Thomas Merton uses a near-far perspective, enabling the reader to share his experience of approaching the monastery that was to become his home. Notice also his use of metaphors ("a barrier and a defense against the world"), similes ("as gray as lead"), and personification ("The tires sang"). See figurative language in **20a(4)**.

45   I looked at the rolling country, and at the pale ribbon of road in front of us stretching out as gray as lead in the light of the moon. Then suddenly I saw a steeple that shone like silver in the moonlight, growing into sight from behind a rounded knoll. The tires sang on the empty road and breathless I looked at the monastery that was revealed before me as we came over the rise. At the end of an avenue of trees was a big rectangular block of buildings, all dark, with a church

crowned by a tower and a steeple and a cross: and the steeple was as bright as platinum and the whole place was as quiet as midnight and lost in the all-absorbing silence and solitude of the fields. Behind the monastery was a dark curtain of woods and over to the west was a wooded valley and beyond that a rampart of wooded hills, a barrier and a defense against the world. —THOMAS MERTON, *The Seven Storey Mountain*

Write descriptions that appeal to all of the senses, not just sight. Alice Walker in paragraph 46 makes her description of Mr. Sweet vivid by using the senses of touch, smell, and sound in addition to sight.

46   We never felt anything of Mr. Sweet's age when we played with him. We loved his wrinkles and would draw some on our brows to be like him, and his white hair was my special treasure and he knew it and would never come to visit us just after he had had his hair cut off at the barbershop. Once he came to our house for something, probably to see my father about fertilizer for his crops because although he never paid the slightest attention to his crops, he liked to know what things would be best to use on them if he ever did. Anyhow, he had not come with his hair since he had just had it shaved off at the barbershop. He wore a huge straw hat to keep off the sun and also to keep his head away from me. But as soon as I saw him I ran up and demanded that he take me up and kiss me with his funny beard which smelled so strongly of tobacco. Looking forward to burying my small fingers into his woolly hair I threw away his hat only to find he had done something to his hair, that it was no longer there! I let out a squall which made my mother think that Mr. Sweet had finally dropped me in the well or something and from that day I've been wary of men in hats. However, not long after Mr. Sweet showed up with his hair grown out and just as white and kinky and impenetrable as it ever was.

—ALICE WALKER, "To Hell with Dying"

(3) Explain a process.

Process paragraphs, in explaining how something is done or made, often use both description and narration. You might describe the items used in the process and then narrate the steps chronologically, as in paragraph 47.

47   The best of all scientific tricks with an egg is the well-known one in which air pressure forces a peeled hard-boiled egg into a glass milk bottle and then forces it out again undamaged. The mouth of the bottle must be only slightly smaller than the egg, and so you must be careful not to use too large an egg or too small a bottle. It is impossible to push the egg into the bottle. To get the egg through the mouth you must heat the air in the bottle. That is best done by standing the bottle in boiling water for a few minutes. Put the egg upright on the mouth and take the bottle off the stove. As the air in the bottle cools it contracts, creating a partial vacuum that draws the peeled egg inside. To get the egg out again invert the bottle so that the egg falls into the neck. Place the opening of the bottle against your mouth and blow vigorously. This will compress the air in the bottle. When you stop blowing, the air expands, pushing the egg through the neck of the bottle and into your waiting hands.

—MARTIN GARDNER, "Mathematical Games"

Or your explanation of a process might be phrased as advice, as César Chávez's is in paragraph 48.

48   I also learned to keep away from the established groups and so-called leaders, and to guard against philosophizing. Working with low-income people is very different from working with the professionals, who like to sit around talking about how to play politics. When you're trying to recruit a farmworker, you have to paint a little picture, and then you have to color the picture in. We found out that the harder a guy is to convince, the better leader or member he becomes. When you exert yourself to convince him, you have his confidence and he has good motivation. A lot of people who say OK right away wind up hanging around the office, taking up the workers' time. —CÉSAR CHÁVEZ, "The Organizer's Tale"

(4) Show cause and effect.

A paragraph that explores causes raises the question Why? and must answer that question to the satisfaction of the reader.

(Make sure to avoid the fallacy of assuming that since one event precedes another it is necessarily the cause of that event [see **31c**, False cause].) Paragraph 49 provides several reasons why the dollar became the basis of American currency.

49   Why did the dollar, a Spanish monetary unit, become the basis of American currency rather than the British pound sterling, to which the Americans were accustomed? In part, it was a reaction against all things British. More important, there was more Spanish than British coin circulating in the colonies and states in the late eighteenth century. The British paid in trade goods for the American products they purchased, and they preferred British coin for what they sold to the colonies. Thus pounds tended to flow back to Great Britain. But the colonists had a favorable balance of trade with Spanish America—selling more than they bought—so Spanish coin was comparatively abundant.

—JOSEPH CONLIN, "The American Past"

Paragraphs can also demonstrate effects, as in the following paragraph, which discusses some results of protecting the endangered alligator.

50   The alligator's turnaround since that time has made national news. Protection and strict controls on interstate shipment of gator hides have worked: the animals have come back strong. Every so often, one will eat a poodle or take up residence in the water hazard on the sixteenth hole. Fish-and-game people are then called out to lasso the uncomprehending reptile and move it to an out-of-the-way place. There is even some limited commerce again in the skins. At least one entrepreneur is ranching alligators, just as though they were cattle or mink. Not long ago, someone in Florida was killed by an alligator in what I suspect must have been a well-deserved attack.   —GEOFFREY NORMAN, "Gators"

(5) Compare and contrast to develop an idea.

A *comparison* points out similarities; a *contrast* points out differences. A comparison or contrast may be organized in either of two ways (or a combination of them), the choice depending on the writer's purpose. Writers often use both methods for the sake of variation. Arthur L. Campa uses the *part-by-part method* in paragraph 51, in which he analyzes cultural differences between the Spanish and the English colonizers by looking first at the effects of geography on the English, then on the Spanish, and next at the effects of demographics on first the English and then the Spanish.

51   Cultural differences are implicit in the conceptual content of the languages of these two civilizations, and their value systems stem from a long series of historical circumstances. Therefore, it may be well to consider some of the English and Spanish cultural configurations before these Europeans set foot on American soil. English culture was basically insular, geographically and ideologically; was more integrated on the whole, except for some strong theological differences; and was particularly zealous of its racial purity. Spanish culture was peninsular, a geographical circumstance that made it a catchall of Mediterranean, central European, and north African peoples. The composite nature of the population produced a market regionalism that prevented close integration, except for religion, and led to a strong sense of individualism. These differences were reflected in the colonizing enterprise of the two cultures. The English isolated themselves from the Indians physically and culturally; the Spanish, who had strong notions about *pureza de sangre* [purity of blood] among the nobility, were not collectively averse to adding one more strain to their racial cocktail. Cortés led the way by siring the first *mestizo* in North America, and the rest of the conquistadores followed suit. The ultimate products of these two orientations meet today in the Southwest.

Campa switches in the next paragraph (52) to the *unit-by-unit method*, developing first the Anglo and then the Hispanic values.

52   Anglo-American culture was absolutist at the onset; that is, all the dominant values were considered identical for all,

regardless of time and place. Such values as justice, charity, and honesty were considered the superior social order for all men and were later embodied in the American Constitution. The Spaniard brought with him a relativistic viewpoint and saw fewer moral implications in man's actions. Values were looked upon as the result of social and economic conditions.
—ARTHUR L. CAMPA, "Anglo vs. Chicano: Why?"

Two valuable kinds of comparisons are analogy and metaphor. A *metaphor* is a figure of speech (see **20a[4]**). An *analogy*, often used in argument, makes a point by comparing a complex or unfamiliar concept to a simple or familiar one or by comparing two familiar concepts that are not ordinarily thought to be similar. In paragraph 53, Anthony Lukas draws an analogy between controlling one's own life and controlling the ball in a pinball machine.

53   A player is not powerless to control the ball's wild flight any more than man is powerless to control his own life. He may nudge the machine with hands, arms, or hips, jogging it just enough to change the angle of the ball's descent. And he is armed with "flippers" which can propel the ball back up the playfield, aiming at the targets with the richest pay-offs. But, just as man's boldest strokes and bravest ventures often boomerang, so an ill-timed flip can ricochet the ball straight down "death alley," and a too vigorous nudge will send the machine into "tilt." Winning pinball, like rewarding life, requires delicate touch, fine calibrations, careful discrimination between boldness and folly.   —ANTHONY LUKAS, "Pinball"

Make sure you do not assume that because two things are alike in some ways they are alike in all ways (see **31g[5]**, False analogy).

(6) Use classification and division to develop an idea.

To classify is to categorize things in large groups that share certain common characteristics. *Classification* is a way to understand or explain a large or diverse subject and discover the relationships within it. When you classify chocolate pudding as a dessert, you tell your reader that, like most desserts, it is probably sweet and high in calories. *Division*, in contrast, breaks objects and ideas into parts that are smaller and examines the relationships among them. A store manager might group books according to publisher for her own inventory or according to types—biography, science fiction, mystery, and so forth—for her customers.

Classification and division represent two different perspectives; ideas may be put into groups (classification) or split into subclasses (division) on the basis of a dividing principle. Classification and division most often work together because once you have placed something in a class, the next logical step is to explain the characteristics of that class, which is division. So you may find yourself using both classification and division to approach your subject. They work together to give a view that places the subject in a context and develops it in detail. Notice how Russell Baker first establishes his classifications in paragraph 54 and then explains them in paragraph 55:

54   Inanimate objects are classified scientifically into three major categories—those that break down, those that get lost, and those that don't work.

55   The goal of all inanimate objects is to resist man and ultimately to defeat him, and the three major classifications are based on the method each object uses to achieve its purpose. As a general rule, any object capable of breaking down at the moment when it is most needed will do so. The automobile is typical of the category.

—RUSSELL BAKER, "The Plot Against People"

Analysis is a kind of division that breaks an object or idea into its elements. In paragraph 56, Aaron Copland analyzes three ways to listen to music.

56   We all listen to music according to our separate capacities. But, for the sake of analysis, the whole listening process may

become clearer if we break it up into its component parts, so to speak. In a certain sense we all listen to music on three separate planes. For lack of a better terminology, one might name these: (1) the sensuous plane, (2) the expressive plane, (3) the sheerly musical plane. The only advantage to be gained from mechanically splitting up the listening process into these hypothetical planes is the clearer view to be had of the way in which we listen. —AARON COPLAND, "How We Listen to Music"

(7) Formulate a definition.

Paragraphs of definition explain. Sometimes we define arbitrarily: "They use the term 'pony' to refer to an equine of any size." Or we may define by describing how something works: "A security system is supposed to hinder burglars." The effect of definition is to put a concept, a term, or an object into a class and then differentiate it from other members of the class: "A concerto [the term] is a symphonic piece [the class] performed by one or more solo instruments and orchestra [the difference]." The *difference* distinguishes the *term* from all other members of the *class*. Paragraph 57 defines volcanos by putting them in a class ("landforms") and by distinguishing them ("built of molten material") from other members of that class. The definition is then clarified by examples.

57   Volcanos are landforms built of molten material that has spewed out onto the earth's surface. Such molten rock is called *lava*. Volcanos may be no larger than small hills, or thousands of feet high. All have a characteristic cone shape. Some well-known mountains are actually volcanos. Examples are Mt. Fuji (Japan), Mt. Lassen (California), Mt. Hood (Oregon), Mt. Etna and Mt. Vesuvius (Italy), and Paricutin (Mexico). The Hawaiian Islands are all immense volcanos whose summits rise above the ocean, and these volcanos are still quite active. —JOEL AREM, *Rocks and Minerals*

Definitions may be clarified and extended by details, as in paragraph 57, or by examples, synonyms, or etymology (the history of the word). Synonyms are often only one or two words enclosed in commas immediately following the term.

Sophomores, *second-year students*, derive their name from two Greek words meaning "wise fool."

■ **Exercise 12** Prepare for a class discussion of the following paragraphs by identifying main ideas (**32a**), transitions (**32b**), and methods of development (**32c** and **32d**).

58   Imagine that you have bobbled two fly balls in this rout and now you have just tried to stretch a single into a double and have been easily thrown out sliding into second base, where the base runner ahead of you had stopped. It was the third out and a dumb play, and your opponents smirk at you as they run off the field. You are the goat, a lonely and tragic figure sitting in the dirt. You curse yourself, jerking your head sharply forward. You stand up and kick the base. How miserable! How degrading! Your utter shame, though brief, bears silent testimony to the worthiness of your teammates, whom you have let down, and they appreciate it. They call out to you now as they take the field, and as the second baseman runs to his position he says, "Let's get 'em now," and tosses you your glove. Lowering your head, you trot slowly out to right. There you do some deep knee bends. You pick grass. You find a pebble and fling it into foul territory. As the first batter comes to the plate, you check the sun. You get set in your stance, poised to fly. Feet spread, hands on hips, you bend slightly at the waist and spit the expert spit of a veteran ballplayer—a player who has known the agony of defeat but who always bounces back, a player who has lost a stride on the base paths but can still make the big play.

                 —GARRISON KEILLOR, "Attitude"

59   Sound has shaped the bodies of many beasts. Noise tapped away at the bullfrog until his ears became bigger than his eyes. Now he hears so well that at the slightest sound of danger he quickly plops to safety under a sunken leaf. The rabbit has long ears to hear the quiet "whoosh" of the owl's wings, while the grasshopper's ears are on the base of his

abdomen, the lowest point of his body, where he can detect the tread of a crow's foot or the stealthy approach of a shrew.
—JEAN GEORGE, "That Astounding Creator—Nature"

60   The strain of not relating is what provokes the bloodshed, and some people will kill each other for love, particularly during the holidays when we're supposed to love each other to death. But perhaps the reason it's so hard to relate is because it's so hard to be disappointed, to know that the schizoids, compulsive cleaners, alcoholics, and dullards, all the relatives who come home to roost, are not so different from us.
—PHYLLIS THEROUX, "Fear of Families"

61   For years the measurement of one's IQ figured most significantly in our description of who is and who is not mentally retarded. IQ is a measurement of mental age divided by chronological age; a child of six who has the mental abilities of a six-year-old has an IQ of 100, the American mean. (About 50 percent of Americans are thought to have an IQ between 90 and 110.) An IQ of 70 is two standard deviations below the mean and is, therefore, the cutoff for defining retardation.
—SALLIE TISDALE, "Neither Morons Nor Imbeciles Nor Idiots: In the Company of the Mentally Retarded"

62   Just as I meant "shimmer" literally I mean "grammar" literally. Grammar is a piano I play by ear, since I seem to have been out of school the year the rules were mentioned. All I know about grammar is its infinite power. To shift the structure of a sentence alters the meaning of that sentence, as definitely and inflexibly as the position of a camera alters the meaning of the object photographed. Many people know about camera angles now, but not so many know about sentences. The arrangement of the words matters, and the arrangement you want can be found in the picture in your mind. The picture dictates the arrangement. The picture dictates whether this will be a sentence with or without clauses, a sentence that ends hard or a dying-fall sentence, long or short, active or passive. The picture tells you how to arrange

the words and the arrangement of the words tells me, what's going on in the picture. *Nota bene* [note well].

—JOAN DIDION, "Why I Write"

■ **Exercise 13** Write paragraphs using any of the strategies of development described in **32d**. Start with one of the following topic sentences.

1. A dog is the best friend a person can have.
2. Tying your shoe is more complicated than it looks.
3. High school courses are very different from college courses.
4. There are three different kinds of friends who will help you out in an emergency.

33

The Whole Composition: Planning, Drafting, and Revising

Plan, draft, and revise your writing effectively.

No writing takes place in a vacuum. The rhetorical situation—purpose, audience, and occasion—determines your tone and shapes your writing (**33a**). Whenever you write, you engage in a process of developing an appropriate topic (**33b**) for a certain audience. You will explore and gather information and focus the subject (**33c**), form a thesis (**33d**), and develop an appropriate plan of organization (**33e**). You will probably revise two or more drafts before preparing a final version (**33f–33g**).

As you move through the process, you may need to engage in any of the activities several times. For example, you may need to go back and collect more ideas. Or you may write a draft only to discover that you have strayed from your main idea (or thesis). Such a discovery only contributes to making your writing better. You may need to change your thesis, or even start over with a new one. Whatever repetition of the steps in the process is necessary, the effort will be worthwhile. The process of planning, drafting, and revising is seldom as neat and straightforward as inexperienced writers may suppose, but working out your ideas fully and making them clear to your reader is a rewarding activity. The celebrated novelist Eudora Welty once said that she disliked writing but loved *having written*. The process of writing is one of the best ways of clarifying your own views and gaining new insights.

As you read the following essay, notice how the author arouses your interest by developing his main idea through use of definition, examples, and specific details.

Appetite

Laurie Lee

One of the major pleasures in life is appetite, and one of our major duties should be to preserve it. Appetite is the keenness of living; it is one of the senses that tells you that you are still curious to exist, that you still have an edge on your longings and want to bite into the world and taste its multitudinous flavours and juices. **1**

By appetite, of course, I don't mean just the lust for food, but any condition of unsatisfied desire, any burning in the blood that proves you want more than you've got and that you haven't yet used up your life. Wilde said he felt sorry for those who never got their heart's desire, but sorrier still for those who did. I got mine once only, and it nearly killed me, and I've always preferred wanting to having since. **2**

For appetite, to me, is this state of wanting, which keeps one's expectations alive. I remember learning this lesson long ago as a child, when treats and orgies were few, and when I discovered that the greatest pitch of happiness was not in actually eating a toffee but in gazing at it beforehand. True, the first bite was delicious, but once the toffee was gone one was left with nothing, neither toffee nor lust. Besides, the whole toffeeness of toffees was imperceptibly diminished by the gross **3** act of having eaten it. No, the best was in wanting it, in sitting and looking at it, when one tasted an inexhaustible treasure-house of flavours.

So, for me, one of the keenest pleasures of appetite remains in the wanting, not the satisfaction—in wanting a peach, or a whisky, or a particular texture or sound, or to be with a particular friend. For in this condition, of course, I know that the object of desire is always at its most flawlessly perfect, which is why I would carry the preservation of appetite to the extent of deliberate fasting, simply because I think that appetite is too good to lose, too precious to be bludgeoned into insensibility by satiation and overdoing it.

For that matter, I don't really want three square meals a day—I want one huge, delicious, orgiastic, table-groaning blow-out, say every four days, and then not be too sure where the next one is coming from. A day of fasting is not for me just a puritanical device for denying oneself a pleasure, but rather a way of anticipating a rarer moment of supreme indulgence.

Fasting is an act of homage to the majesty of appetite. So I think we should arrange to give up our pleasures regularly—our food, our friends, our lovers—in order to preserve their intensity and the moment of coming back to them. For this is the moment that renews and refreshes both oneself and the thing one loves. Sailors and travelers enjoyed this once, and so did hunters, I suppose. Part of the weariness of modern life may be that we live too much on top of each other and are entertained and fed too regularly. Once we were separated by hunger both from our food and families, and then we learned to value both. The men went off hunting, and the dogs went with them; the women and children waved goodbye. The cave was empty of men for days on end; nobody ate or knew what to do. The women crouched by the fire, the wet smoke in their eyes; the children wailed; everybody was hungry. Then one night there were shouts and the barking of dogs from the hills, and the men came back loaded with meat. This was the great reunion, and everybody gorged themselves silly, and appetite came into its own; the long-awaited meal became a feast to remember and an almost sacred celebration of life. Now we go off to the office and come home in the evenings to cheap chicken and frozen peas—very nice, but too much of it, too easy and regular, served up without effort or wanting. We eat, we are lucky, our faces are shining with fat, but we don't know the pleasure of being hungry any more.

Too much of anything—too much music, entertainment, 7 happy snacks, or time spent with one's friends—creates a kind of impotence of living by which one can no longer hear, or taste, or see, or love, or remember. Life is short and precious, and appetite is one of its guardians, and loss of appetite is a sort of death. So if we are to enjoy this short life, we should respect the divinity of appetite and keep it eager and not too much blunted.

It is a long time now since I knew that acute moment of bliss 8 that comes from putting parched lips to a cup of cold water. The springs are still there to be enjoyed—all one needs is the original thirst.

Essays like Lee's, so natural and seemingly effortless, are the result of hard work. His carefully chosen metaphor—appetite as something that makes you "want to bite into the world"—tells you immediately that he is talking about appetite, as he says, in the larger sense of "any condition of unsatisfied desire." He supports his thesis that "loss of appetite is a sort of death" by examples and details. Such carefully crafted writing does not come easily. Experienced writers wrestle with the same activities that inexperienced writers do: planning, drafting, and revising. Writing is a process of returning again and again to the various writing tasks, adjusting and fine-tuning until the result is a unified, coherent, and well-developed composition.

33a

Consider your purpose, audience, occasion, and tone.

Purpose, audience, and *occasion* shape your writing in many ways. For example, a letter describing your summer job to a friend will differ from one directed to a prospective employer.

Your subject is the same but your purpose is different. You may be *expressing* your pleasure and satisfaction to your friend, whereas you are *informing* your prospective employer of skills you have gained. In each instance, you have a specific audience in mind. And the occasion is also different. When you write to your friend, the circumstances under which you write are different from those you must consider when you write to a prospective employer. Such circumstances are reflected in your *tone*—the attitude you take toward your subject.

(1) Clarify your purpose.

The clearer your purpose, the better your writing is likely to be. The **purposes** of nonfiction writing may be classified as expressive, expository, and persuasive. These purposes are often combined in an extended piece of writing.

Expressive writing emphasizes the writer's feelings and reactions to the world—to people, objects, events, and ideas. Some examples of expressive writing are journals and diaries, reminiscences, and, frequently, personal letters. The following example is a reminiscence.

> We went fishing the first morning. I felt the same damp moss covering the worms in the bait can, and saw the dragonfly alight on the tip of my rod as it hovered a few inches from the surface of the water. It was the arrival of this fly that convinced me beyond any doubt that everything was as it always had been, that the years were a mirage and there had been no years. The small waves were the same, chucking the rowboat under the chin as we fished at anchor, and the boat was the same boat, the same color green and the ribs broken in the same places, and under the floor-boards the same fresh-water leavings and débris—the dead helgramite, the wisps of moss, the rusty discarded fishhook, the dried blood from yesterday's catch. We stared silently at the tips of our rods, at the dragonflies that came and went. I lowered the tip of mine into the water, tentatively, pensively dislodging the fly, which darted two feet

away, poised, darted two feet back, and came to rest again a little farther up the rod. There had been no years between the ducking of this dragonfly and the other one—the one that was part of memory. I looked at the boy, who was silently watching his fly, and it was my hands that held his rod, my eyes watching. I felt dizzy and didn't know which rod I was at the end of.

—E. B. WHITE, "Once More to the Lake"

Referential, or *expository,* writing focuses the reader's attention upon the objective world—the objects, the events, and the ideas themselves rather than upon the writer's feelings or attitudes about them. Some examples of referential writing are news accounts, encyclopedia articles, laboratory and scientific reports, textbooks, and articles in professional journals and other publications directed to specialized audiences. Most of your writing in college will be referential. In the following referential paragraph, the writer discusses how our culture came to be concerned with age.

This preoccupation with age came about because modern technological society radically changed the conditions of growing up and the entire human life cycle. As modern societies developed age-graded institutions, age came to matter in new ways: our birthdates came to determine when we must go to school and when we can leave school, when we can vote, or work full time, drive, marry, buy liquor, enter into contracts, run for public office, retire, and receive Social Security.

—ARLENE SKOLNICK, *The Psychology of Human Development*

Persuasive writing is intended to influence the reader's attitudes and actions. Most writing is to some extent persuasive; even something as apparently straightforward as a résumé may be persuasive through the choice and arrangement of material. However, writing is usually called persuasive if it is clearly arguing for or against a position.

When you write persuasively, you need many of the critical reading and logical thinking skills that you were introduced to in chapter **31**. Persuasion depends on both rational and emotional appeals. The reader's perception of a writer's honesty, fairmindedness, and goodwill is as crucial as the writer's presentation of evidence and rational arguments. (See **31b**.) In turn, the writer needs to respond to a reader's concerns and doubts. In the following opening paragraph of his "Letter from Birmingham Jail," notice how Martin Luther King, Jr., establishes his own patience and good sense while confirming that his readers are persons "of genuine good will."

> MY DEAR FELLOW CLERGYMEN:
> While confined here in Birmingham city jail, I came across your recent statement calling my present activities "unwise and untimely." Seldom do I pause to answer criticism of my work and ideas. If I sought to answer all the criticisms that cross my desk, my secretaries would have little time for anything other than such correspondence in the course of the day, and I would have no time for constructive work. But since I feel that you are men of genuine good will and that your criticisms are sincerely set forth, I want to try to answer your statement in what I hope will be patient and reasonable terms.
> —MARTIN LUTHER KING, JR., "Letter from Birmingham Jail"

A fourth kind of writing, *literary* writing, focuses on the imaginative use of language—the drive to create something new through the medium of language. This is one source of fiction, poetry, and drama (see **35a**). Humor often uses literary writing for expressive or persuasive purposes. Consider the following passage:

> As a general rule, any object capable of breaking down at the moment when it is most needed will do so. The automobile is typical of the category.
> With the cunning peculiar to its breed, the automobile never breaks down while entering a filling station which has a large staff of idle mechanics. It waits until it reaches a downtown intersection in the middle of the rush hour, or until it is fully loaded with family and luggage on the Ohio Turnpike. Thus it

creates maximum inconvenience, frustration, and irritability, thereby reducing its owner's lifespan.

—RUSSELL BAKER, "The Plot Against People"

Most writing combines all of the purposes, but usually one predominates. You might write one essay expressing your personal encounter with poverty, another exposing the effects of poverty, a third persuading readers to accept certain measures to eliminate poverty, and a fourth using a literary device to develop an example of poverty. You could also draw all of these together; for example, the persuasive paper might be more effective if it included a discussion of the effects of poverty together with your personal experience, and imaginative use of language will increase the impact of your discussion.

■ **Exercise 1** Select two of the following subjects and write paragraphs detailing how you could treat each subject (a) as expressive writing, (b) as expository writing, (c) as persuasive writing, and (d) as literary writing.

a. word processors   b. nutrition   c. athletics   d. job hunting

(2) Clearly identify your audience.

Always be aware of your **audience**—that is, who will read your writing. Your understanding of your audience will determine your choice of words (diction), examples, and details. Audiences vary considerably.

Specialized audiences

A *specialized audience* has considerable knowledge of the subject you are writing about and a keen interest in it. For example, if your subject is a new skiing technique, a group of ski instructors would obviously constitute a specialized audience. So would readers of *Ski* magazine, though in writing for this audience you would allow for a greater variation in knowledge and interest of the reader. A specialized audience for one subject would be a general audience for another; the ski instructor, unless also a gifted chef, would probably constitute a general audience for an essay on cooking with a wok since using a wok requires a fair amount of skill.

It is often easier to write for specialized audiences because you have a specific idea of how much and what kinds of information, as well as what methods of presentation, are called for. You can adjust your tone and the kind of language you use as you tailor your presentation to their expertise and attitudes (see **19g**). The general reader would probably find the following example impenetrable, but it is written for a specialized audience of experts who understand linguistics and are familiar with the terminology.

> The notions of illocutionary force and different illocutionary acts involve really several quite different principles of distinction. . . . So we must not suppose what the metaphor of "force" suggests, that the different illocutionary verbs mark off points on a single continuum. Rather, there are several different continua of "illocutionary force," and the fact that the illocutionary verbs of English stop at certain points on these various continua and not at others is, in a sense, accidental. For example, we might have had an illocutionary verb "rubrify," meaning to call something "red." Thus, "I hereby rubrify it" would just mean "It's red." Analogously, we happen to have an obsolete verb "macarize," meaning to call someone happy.
>
> —J. R. SEARLE, "Speech Acts: An Essay in the Philosophy of Language"

General audiences

A *general audience* consists of a reader or readers not expert on your topic but presumably willing to read what you have to say about it. It is possible to identify certain characteristics even in a general audience so you can shape your presentation accordingly. For example, the audience which your instructor usually wishes you to write for is one made up of educated adults, intellectually alert and receptive to ideas, but with many different special interests of their own. This assumed audience is not very different from the one which the articles in a general encyclopedia or a textbook are written for. Consider the following description from an introductory linguistics textbook.

> The study of how we do things with sentences is the study of **speech acts**. In studying speech acts, we are acutely aware of the importance of the *context of the utterance*. In some circumstances *There is a sheepdog in the closet* is a warning, but the same sentence may be a promise or even a mere statement of fact, depending on circumstances. We call this purpose—a warning, a promise, a threat, or whatever—the **illocutionary force** of a speech act.
>
> —VICTORIA FROMKIN and ROBERT RODMAN,
> *An Introduction to Language*

General audiences may be of quite different kinds and may require some adjustment of subject matter and diction. For example, an upper division textbook in linguistics presents a somewhat more complete approach to speech acts than the introductory text:

> Every speech act has two principal components: the utterance itself and the intention of the speaker in making it. First, every utterance is represented by a sentence with a grammatical structure and a meaning; this is variously called the **locution** or the utterance act. Second, speakers have some intention in making an utterance, something they intend to accomplish; that intention is called an **illocution**, and every utterance consists of performing one or more illocutionary acts.
>
> —EDWARD FINEGAN and NIKO BESNIER,
> *Language: Its Structure and Use*

When you are writing for a general audience, a useful technique is to imagine one specific reader whose background and expectations are typical; then adjust your choice of details and your tone accordingly. Sometimes you may know little about a general audience. You can usually assume an audience of educated adults, but be careful when making assumptions about their sex, religion, politics, or special interests.

Multiple audiences

In academic settings you will often write for *multiple audiences.* The most common example is submitting a paper in which you detail information that the instructor already knows. In work-related situations you will often write a single document—such as an application or a proposal—for a group of readers with different interests. In reading a proposal for a new city parking garage, for instance, the city treasurer is primarily concerned with cost, the ecologist with the environment, the general public with convenience, and the police department with safety. The writer of such a proposal must think critically and consider a variety of attitudes and positions (see **31**).

■ **Exercise 2** Choose a recent class or party and write a letter describing it (a) to a close friend, (b) to a former teacher, and (c) to a member of your family.

(3) Understand the occasion.

The rhetorical situation involves not only audience and purpose but also the occasion for which you are writing. **Occasion** is the context that the writing occurs in—what a dramatist might call the setting. In the sentence below, the writer does more than set forth his purpose and his audience; he makes the occasion clear—the time, the place, the circumstances under which the writing occurred.

> In the twenty-second month of the war against Nazism we meet here in this old Palace of St. James's, itself not unscarred by the fire of the enemy, in order to proclaim the high purposes

and resolves of the lawful constitutional Governments of Europe whose countries have been overrun; and we meet here also to cheer the hopes of free men and free peoples throughout the world. —WINSTON CHURCHILL, "Until Victory Is Won"

(4) Set the appropriate tone.

Tone is a reflection of your attitude toward your subject and must be appropriate to your purpose, audience, and occasion, whether for a personal essay or a lab report. Although humor might well be suitable in a letter to a friend telling her of trouble with your new car, it would be inappropriate in a letter of complaint to the manufacturer. Notice how the tone of a Nez Percé chief's speech, delivered in 1877, reflects the defeat and despair that he feels as his tribe loses the struggle to keep its lands and surrenders to the U.S. Cavalry.

I am tired of fighting. Our chiefs are killed. Looking Glass is dead. Toohulsote is dead. The old men are all dead. It is the young men who say no and yes. He who led the young men is dead. It is cold and we have no blankets. The little children are freezing to death. My people, some of them, have run away to the hills and have no blankets, no food. No one knows where they are—perhaps they are freezing to death. I want to have time to look for my children and see how many of them I can find. Maybe I shall find them among the dead. Hear me, my chiefs, I am tired. My heart is sad and sick. From where the sun stands I will fight no more forever.

—CHIEF JOSEPH, "I Am Tired of Fighting"

■ **Exercise 3** Write a letter to three different audiences about a college or university problem: a humorous letter to a friend, a serious letter to a family member, and a letter of complaint to the administration.

33b

Find an appropriate subject.

Finding a subject frequently unnerves inexperienced writers. If you are assigned a subject to write about or if your situation clearly dictates a subject—as in most business writing, for example—you can move directly to a consideration of your audience (pages 349–52), of the particular aspect of the subject you will emphasize (**33c–33d**), and of the ways you might organize your discussion (**33e**). However, when you must choose your own subject, remember to consider your purpose, audience, occasion, and tone.

When you are free to choose a subject, you can write an appealing paper on almost anything that interests you. Often the best subject is one drawn from your own experience— your personal knowledge, interests, and beliefs. Keeping a journal of ideas for writing and your responses to the world around you is one proven way to find a subject. Do you play a musical instrument? Climb mountains? Like to travel? Do you have a job? What classes are you taking? Can you think of a particular place that is important to you? An interesting character you have met? Something unusual about your family? What ambitions do you have for yourself? What strong convictions do you hold? Note your responses and feelings about things you care about in your journal. The trick, of course, is to make what interests you interesting to readers. Whether your purpose is to express, inform, or persuade, take this opportunity to share something that is important to you so that others will recognize its value.

In your courses other than English, often the instructor will assign a paper but will not otherwise restrict your choice of subject. This subject will almost certainly be outside your own experience. For instance, if you have to write a term paper for a microbiology course, you may be free to write on any aspect of that discipline that interests you, but the instructor making the assignment wants a referential paper demonstrating your command of information, not your personal feelings about or experiences with microbes. Just as with writing about personal experience, however, you should make an effort to find an aspect of microbiology that interests you.

Look in your textbook, particularly in the sections listing suggestions for further reading and study. Go through your lecture notes, examine books and articles in the library, look through the subject catalog, or refer to encyclopedias.

In all cases when choosing a subject, don't neglect to talk to your instructor and to other students. Such collaboration is almost always fruitful.

■ **Exercise 4**

1. Choose a personal experience that might be an appropriate subject to write about. If you keep a journal, consult it to jog your memory about how the experience was meaningful to you. What reasons can you think of for sharing this experience with others?
2. Select a controversial subject that interests you. What are the issues involved?
3. Write a short composition on any of the subjects that you selected.

33c

Explore and focus the subject.

When you have a subject in mind—whether it is one assigned by an instructor, one dictated by some other writing situation, or one you have chosen for yourself—you will need to explore all the possible ways to develop it. You will also need to follow certain leads while eliminating others as you direct and focus your ideas.

(1) Explore your subject.

Writers use many different methods to explore a subject. If you are having a hard time getting started, try *freewriting*—writing nonstop for a brief period of time about any aspect of your subject that occurs to you—and then examine your writing for productive approaches. Some other useful methods are *listing*, *questioning*, and *applying different perspectives*. Use whatever methods that seem productive for you. Different methods may work best for different subjects; if you run out of ideas using one method, switch to another. Sometimes, especially for an assigned subject remote from your own interests and knowledge, you may need to try several methods.

Freewriting Some writers use freewriting to find a subject, but it is particularly helpful in exploring a subject you already have decided to write on. Aaron Webb knew he wanted to write about Heavy Metal music, but at the outset he had little idea of what he wanted to do with the subject. Freewriting got him started.

> I really like Heavy Metal but what can I say it's cool, exciting, crazy? Yeah, crazy. The dudes in the BMWs get really torqued when you have your boom box on loud. But the guys in the old beatup Firebirds wave and head bang right along. And I guess it doesn't help that most metalheads have long hair—just puts the old folks right off. They start thinking we're sociopaths or something—crazy, maybe. Or drugged out. And we wear a lot of black which they see as sorta Satanic. But most headbangers I know are responsible folks, just enjoying the sounds. Just listen to what the songs say and you can tell Heavy Metal isn't what people think. Jeez, I even had to show my Mom that only one or two bands are anti-feminist before she would let me play it in the house. Now she listens too. . . .

Freewriting gave Aaron several profitable directions: Who listens to Heavy Metal? What is it about? Why does it have a bad reputation?

Listing One way to gather ideas about your writing topic is to make an informal list. The advantage to listing is that, like an outline, it lets you see individual items at a glance rather than having to pick them out of a block of writing. It also encourages establishing relationships. Jot down any ideas that come to you while you are thinking about your subject. Don't worry if the ideas come without any kind of order, and don't worry about the form in which you write them down; grammar, spelling, and diction are not concerns at this stage. Devote as much time to making your list as necessary—perhaps five minutes, perhaps an entire evening. The point is to collect as many ideas as you can.

Aaron made the following list in about ten minutes after he had some idea of where he was going with his subject. His list helped him refine his thoughts.

What does Heavy Metal sound like?
Who listens to it?
Who are some of the people who play it?
What does it stand for?
Why do people listen to it? Why do I?
Where do the bands stand on the issues?
Does Heavy Metal corrupt the listener?
What is the purpose of Heavy Metal?
Is Heavy Metal accepted in society?
Should Heavy Metal be accepted in society?
What is the general stereotype of the Heavy Metal listener?
Is this stereotype true?
Stress relief
Having fun
Develop opinions about social issues
What are they?
    Abortion
    Anti-war
    Justice System
    Euthanasia
    Inner city violence
    Drugs
    Censorship
Characteristics of Heavy Metal
    Thunderous, loud
    Hard to hear lyrics
What do others feel about Heavy Metal?
    Disturbing
    Noise

This list may appear chaotic, but earlier items suggest later ones, and a review of the whole list may suggest ones that need to be added. As you look through the list you will find some ideas that are closely related and might be grouped together. For instance, items concerning attitudes about Heavy Metal and its value group together readily. Late in his listing Aaron began to establish some relationships by developing subgroups of certain items. Out of this seeming chaos, order and direction will begin to emerge.

Questioning Explore a subject by asking yourself questions. There are two structured questioning strategies you might use—journalists' questions and a similar approach known as the pentad that encourages seeing relationships. The *journalists' questions* ask *Who? What? When? Where? Why?* and *How?*; they are easy to use and can help you discover ideas about any subject. Using journalists' questions to explore the subject of Heavy Metal music could lead you to think about *who* listens to it or *who* performs it, *what* it is, *when* and *why* it was developed, *where* it is performed, played, recorded or listened to, *why* people listen to it or perform it, *how* the music affects people, and so on.

The *pentad* considers the five dramatic aspects of a subject: the *act*, what happens; the *actor*, who does it; the *scene*, the time, place, and conditions under which the event occurred; the *agency*, the method or circumstances facilitating the event; and the *purpose*, the intent or the reasons surrounding the act. This method differs from journalists' questions by suggesting relationships among the various aspects of the subject. For instance, what relationships can be explored between the playing of Heavy Metal music (the act) and those who perform it (the actors)? or between its performance and the time, place, and conditions of performance?

Applying perspectives Sometimes it is helpful to consider a subject in three quite different ways—as static, dynamic, and relative. A *static* perspective would focus your attention on what Heavy Metal music is. You might define it, describe its characteristics, analyze its parts or its main uses, or refer to specific examples of Heavy Metal music.

The *dynamic* perspective focuses on action and change. Thus you might examine the history or development of Heavy Metal music, its workings or the processes involved in presenting or composing it, and changes of all sorts involved in its development.

The *relative* perspective focuses on relationships, on systems. You might examine relationships of Heavy Metal music to other things and people. You can view the music as a system in itself or as a part of a larger system of musical presentation. You can also analyze it in relation to other kinds of music, such as soft rock, country-western, or classical.

(2) Limit and focus your subject.

Exploring the subject will suggest not only productive strategies for development but also a direction and focus for your writing. Some ideas will seem worth pursuing; others will seem inappropriate for your purpose, audience, or occasion. You will find yourself discarding ideas even as you develop new ones. A simple analogy will help explain. When you want a picture of a landscape, you cannot photograph all that your eye can take in. You must focus on just part of that landscape. Then as you aim your camera, you look through the viewfinder to make sure the subject is correctly framed and in focus. At this point you may wish to move in closer and focus on one part of the scene or to change your angle, using light and shadow to emphasize some features of the landscape over others. You can think of your writing in the same way—focusing and directing your ideas just as you focus and direct the lens of your camera—moving from a general subject to a more specific one.

For example, rock music is too large and general a subject to make a good writing topic. However, some of the items that appear on the list about Heavy Metal music (page 357) can be grouped to form a writing topic that might be manageable. The list has already revealed some possible ways to limit the paper. Aaron grouped items concerning attitudes about Heavy Metal and concerning the value of Heavy Metal. And he began drawing relationships right away by establishing some subgroups. These indicate profitable ways to focus the subject. Conceivably, an essay focusing on any one of these groups—eliminating all the other, irrelevant items—might be both workable and interesting.

However, chances are that still more focusing will be required. A sizeable book could be written on the topic of the value of Heavy Metal music, and even the topic of attitudes about Heavy Mertal could produce a sizeable article. For a short paper Aaron would do better to focus on, for example, ways that Heavy Metal music is misunderstood.

Strategies for development, which are more fully discussed in **32d** as ways to develop paragraphs, are natural thinking processes that are especially useful for shaping ideas about a subject. Remember that purpose, audience, and occasion, as well as the subject, must be considered when selecting a guiding strategy. Often the strategy emerges as you brainstorm or draft; do not impose an inappropriate strategy. Refer to the explanations and examples in **32d** as you work through the various strategies. Here are some questions that you might ask yourself.

    a. *Narration*   Have you had a significant experience with Heavy Metal music? When did you first learn about it?

    b. *Process*   How does Heavy Metal work? How do you understand Heavy Metal?

    c. *Cause and Effect*   Why was Heavy Metal developed? Why do you like it? What effect does it have on different audiences? What effects does it have on you?

d. *Description*   What does Heavy Metal sound like? How can you tell if you are listening to Heavy Metal?

e. *Definition*   What is Heavy Metal? What are some of its common characteristics? Can you define them?

f. *Classification and Division*   What class does Heavy Metal music belong to? Performance? Protest music? How can you divide Heavy Metal music into subclasses? Music where groups are dominant? Music where individual performers are?

g. *Example*   What does Heavy Metal music mean to you? Give an example. Give an example to show how you can tell it from other kinds of popular music.

h. *Comparison and Contrast*   How is Heavy Metal music similar to classic rock? How are they different?

The following introductory sentence suggests a focus on comparison and contrast:

> Several similarities between Heavy Metal music and rap suggest that the two might be profitably combined.

This sentence suggests classification and division:

> As I see it, Heavy Metal music divides into two main categories, the music performed by groups and the music performed by individuals.

Frequently compositions combine several of these strategies to achieve yet another strategy. Yi-Fu Tuan narrates, describes, and defines in the process of comparing Chinese place and American space.

> Americans have a sense of space, not of place. Go to an American home in exurbia, and almost the first thing you do is drift toward the picture window. How curious that the first compliment you pay your host inside the house is to say how lovely it is outside his house! He is pleased that you should admire his vistas. The distant horizon is not merely a line separating earth from sky, it is a symbol of the future. The American is not rooted in his place, however lovely; his eyes are drawn

> by the expanding space to a point on the horizon which is his
> future.   —YI-FU TUAN, "American Space, Chinese Place"

In the following introduction, Desmond Morris suggests the
overall organization of a classification-division essay, but in
the essay itself he uses definition, narration, and description
to develop his discussion of the three kinds of territory he
names in the opening.

> A territory is a defended space. In the broadest sense, there
> are three kinds of human territory: tribal, family, and personal.
>   —DESMOND MORRIS, "Territorial Behavior"

The exact focus you finally choose will be determined by your
purpose, your audience, and the time and space available.

■ **Exercise 5** Explore one of the subjects from Exercise 4 by writing
down your answers to the journalists' questions (who? what? when?
where? why? and how?). Next use the three perspectives to explore
by writing answers to the questions What is it? How does it change?
What is it related to (part of, different from, or like)? Finally, explore the
subject by writing questions appropriate to the various development
strategies. How would you limit your subject? What would you focus on?

33d

Establish a thesis.

If you have limited and focused your subject, you have worked
a long way toward developing an idea that controls the content
you include and the approach you take. Your controlling idea,
or thesis, insures that decisions you have made about purpose,
audience, occasion, and tone fit together.

(1) Writing with a thesis statement

In academic and many other kinds of writing you will be
expected to state your main idea succinctly. This **thesis statement** contains a single idea, clearly focused and specifically

stated, which grows out of your exploration of a subject. A thesis statement can be thought of as a central idea phrased in the form of an assertion. It is basically a claim statement (see **31b**)—that is, it indicates what you claim to be true, interesting, or valuable about your subject.

An explicitly stated thesis statement helps you keep your writing on target. It identifies what you are writing about, what approach you are taking, and in some cases the plan of development you are using. Note how the thesis statements below do all of these:

> The effects of drugs on the individual involved are disastrous, but the social, economic, and personal effects on that person's close associates can be equally serious.

The following thesis statement for an expository essay divides "discipline" into three kinds.

> A child, in growing up, may meet and learn from three different kinds of disciplines.   —JOHN HOLT, "Kinds of Discipline"

The main idea in a persuasive essay usually carries a strong point of view—an argumentative edge.

> Nothing better illustrates the low regard that the NCAA has often had for the rights of student-athletes than its random drug-testing policy.
> —ALLEN L. SACK, "Random Tests Abuse Dignity"

You will probably try out several thesis statements as you explore your subject. Rather than starting with a preconceived thesis that you must then rationalize, let it develop out of your thinking and discovery process (see **33c**). However, your goal should be a claim that is neither self-evident nor too broad or too specific to interest your reader.

A clear, precise thesis statement will help unify your paper; it will guide many decisions about what details to keep and what to toss out. You can also use the thesis to guide your search for additional information that you may need to strengthen your point. But it is important to allow your composition to remain flexible in the early stages. If you have information about your subject that is interesting but does not really help you make your point, including it in your early drafts may lead you to a better essay because it may indicate a more profitable focus. As you write, check your thesis statement frequently to see if you have drifted away from it. Do not hesitate to change your thesis, however, if you find a more productive path, one you would rather pursue. Make whatever adjustments you need to insure a unified essay. When you revise, test everything you retain in your essay against the thesis you have finally decided on—your original or a new version you have developed—and scrupulously discard any information that does not contribute.

In some cases a thesis may be stated in more than one sentence, but it is more often stated in a declarative sentence with a single main clause (**1e**)—that is, in either a simple or a complex sentence. If your thesis statement announces two or more coordinate ideas, as a compound sentence does, be sure you are not in danger of having your paper lose direction and focus. If you wish to sharpen the thesis statement by adding information that qualifies or supports it, subordinate such material to the main idea.

Beware of vague qualifiers such as *interesting, important,* and *unusual.* Often such words signal that you have chosen a subject that does not interest you much; you would do better to rethink your subject to come up with something you care about. In a thesis statement such as "My education has been very unusual" the vague word *unusual* may indicate that the idea itself is trivial and unproductive and that the writer needs to find a more congenial subject. On the other hand, this kind of vague thesis may disguise an idea of real interest that simply needs to be made specific: "Unlike most people, I received my high school education from my parents on a boat." Sometimes thesis statements containing vague words can be made more effective by simply replacing the bland words with other, more meaningful ones. The following examples show ways to focus, clarify, and sharpen vague thesis statements.

VAGUE   I have trouble making decisions.
BETTER Making decisions is difficult for me, especially when money is involved and most of all when such decisions affect other people.

VAGUE   Summer is an interesting season.
BETTER Summer is the best season for losing weight.

Thesis statements appear most often in the introductory paragraph, although you may put them anywhere that suits your purpose—occasionally even in the conclusion. The advantage, however, of putting the thesis statement in the first paragraph is that your reader knows from the beginning what you are writing about and where the essay is going. Especially appropriate in academic writing, this technique helps readers who are searching for specific information to develop the essay. If the thesis statement begins the introductory paragraph, the rest of the sentences in the paragraph usually support or clarify it with more specific information.

> Clutter is the disease of American writing. We are a society strangling in unnecessary words, circular constructions, pompous frills and meaningless jargon.
> —WILLIAM ZINSSER, *On Writing Well*

> In many ways a pool is the best place to do real swimming. Free water tends to be too tempestuous, while in a pool it is tamed and imprisoned; the challenge has been filtered out of it along with the bacteria. —JOHN KNOWLES, "Everybody's Sport"

(2) Writing without a thesis statement

Some kinds of writing do not require a formulated thesis statement, but they do contain a main, or controlling, idea. A memoir, for example, or a journal—such as the record you might keep of a camping trip—is a focused piece of writing preserving your reflections and observations. In the example below, notice how Edward Abbey uses the quality of light and air in Death Valley as a controlling idea for focusing the reader's attention.

> The glare is stunning. Yet also exciting, even exhilarating—a world of light. The air seems not clear like glass but colored, a transparent, tinted medium, golden toward the sun, smoke-blue in the shadows. The colors come, it appears, not simply from the background, but are actually present in the air itself—a vigintillion microscopic particles of dust reflecting the sky, the sand, the iron hills.   —EDWARD ABBEY, *The Journey Home*

Exploratory writing is generally characterized by a spirit of inquiry in which the writer plays with possibilities without necessarily coming to a conclusion or making a specific point. Rather than approaching his topic as a definition, Joseph Epstein establishes his essay as an inquiry, inviting the reader to consider the subject from various angles.

> What's vulgar? Some people might say that the contraction of the words *what* and *is* itself is vulgar. On the other hand, I remember being called a stuffed shirt by a reviewer of a book of mine because I used almost no contractions. I have forgotten the reviewer's name but I have remembered the criticism. Not being of that category of writers who never forget a compliment, I also remember being called a racist by another reviewer by observing that failure to insist on table manners in children was to risk dining with Apaches. The larger criticisms I forget, but, oddly, these goofy little criticisms stick in the teeth like sesame seeds. Yet that last trope—is it, too, vulgar? Ought I really to be picking my teeth in public, even metaphorically?
> —JOSEPH EPSTEIN, "What is Vulgar?"

Writing without a thesis statement is especially common when the main thrust of the development is narrative or descriptive. And reports of information, whether research papers (**34**) or business documents (**35c**), frequently require no thesis. Sometimes, even in persuasive writing the thesis may be implicit rather than explicit. Yet, even when your thesis is implied, your readers should be able to sense a clear direction and focus in your paper. You can make sure that they will by articulating your main idea for yourself and then checking that idea frequently as you move along. What is important is that your writing be clear and well focused.

■ **Exercise 6**   Write a focused thesis statement for one of the subjects you listed in Exercise 4.

33e
Choose an appropriate method or combination of methods to arrange ideas.

Many writers need a working plan to direct their ideas and to keep their writing on course. Some follow a formal arrangement pattern (see classical arrangement, pages 370–71); others use informal written lists or formal topic or sentence outlines. Such plans are especially helpful for full-length papers and for writing under pressure (**35b**). Whatever method you choose for planning your writing, remember that you can always change your plan to suit any new direction your writing takes. The point is to have a goal that you direct your effort toward.

▲ **Note:** If you enjoy freewriting, you may benefit from doing it before you make any plan.

Informal working plans   An informal working plan need be little more than an ordered list that grows out of a collection of ideas like those used to explore subjects (see **33c**) and suggests a way of organizing your information. Look at the list on page 357 that Aaron Webb made as he prepared to write on Heavy Metal music.

When he was ready to actually write, Aaron examined the list and noticed a large number of entries concerning attitudes toward Heavy Metal music and how those attitudes are misinformed. He had already grouped and subordinated some ideas toward the end of his list (page 357). So he focused these groups on attitudes and the value of Heavy Metal music and wound up with the following thesis statement and informal list:

Thesis: Most Heavy Metal music is about social problems.

1. People who are against Heavy Metal music
2. Their feeling that it is just crazy noise
3. What issues Heavy Metal really deals with
4. Why Heavy Metal can be valuable to the society

When you make a list such as this, ideas often overlap. Some are general; some are specific. They appear in no particular order. But you have the beginning of a plan. Examine your list carefully to see if any items are repeated and if any particular plan suggests itself.

Working from the original list he developed to explore his subject, Aaron opened his essay with a discussion of who criticizes Heavy Metal music. Looking at his list, he proposed to develop the point that critics think of this music as "crazy noise," a point he later found he did not really want to develop fully. Looking at his list again, he realized that several of the items fit into a category that he would make his next point— a discussion of the real issues that Heavy Metal addresses. His final point grew out of this discussion of the issues. Notice that as Aaron narrowed and focused his topic he abandoned a number of items on his expository list.

An informal working plan can help writers not only organize but also think of new ideas. After he decided to focus on the issues that Heavy Metal music deals with, Aaron realized the next logical development would be to show why Heavy Metal is valuable to society—a subtopic only hinted at in his exploratory list.

Outlines   Outlines often grow out of working plan lists, and they can be changed at any point in the writing process. Some writers prefer to construct a formal outline before beginning to draft. Almost any writer will find a formal outline helpful in analyzing a draft to be sure ideas are effectively organized. For instance, if an outline shows only one subgroup under a heading, that section of the draft probably needs rethinking.

A structured outline uses indention and numbers to indicate various levels of subordination. Thus it is a kind of graphic scheme of the logic of your paper. The main points form the major headings, and the supporting ideas for each point form the subheadings. An outline of Aaron's paper might begin as follows:

Thesis: Most Heavy Metal music is about social problems:
  I. People's attitudes about Heavy Metal music
     A. Characteristics of people who dislike Heavy Metal
        1. Man in a Honda
           a. Hot, going home from work
           b. Lots of traffic, red lights
        2. Man's response to hearing Heavy Metal
           a. Noise
           b. Frustration
     B. Characteristics of people who play Heavy Metal
        1. Teenager
        2. Long hair, peculiar dress
        3. Old, beatup car
  II. Heavy Metal and social consciousness

A decimal system is also commonly used.

Thesis: Most Heavy Metal music is about social problems.
1. People's attitudes about Heavy Metal music
  1.1. Characteristics of people who dislike Heavy Metal
  1.2. Characteristics of people who play Heavy Metal
2. Heavy Metal and social consciousness
  2.1. Encourage change
  2.2. Continue attitudes of sixties

The types of outlines most commonly used are the topic outline and the sentence outline. The headings in a *topic outline* are expressed in grammatically parallel phrases, and a *sentence outline* presents headings in complete and usually parallel sentences. A topic outline has the advantage of brevity and highlights the logical flow of your paper; a sentence outline forces you to think through your ideas more thoroughly. The major headings in the sentence outline can serve as topic sentences. Regardless of what type of outline you choose, you will need enough major headings to develop your subject fully within the boundaries established by your thesis.

Even if you do not use an outline as a planning aid, you may use it profitably in revision. A topic outline, for example, could have highlighted a problem with the first draft of the paper on Heavy Metal music—the digression about the effects of the music on the listener (pages 384–85). If you have difficulty outlining your draft, it may have organizational problems.

Also use outlines to summarize main ideas of lectures and reading materials and to communicate ideas to other persons in a brief and readily accessible form.

Classical arrangement You may follow a classical arrangement, especially when your primary purpose is expository or persuasive.

Introduction   Announce the subject, set the tone, and gain the reader's attention and interest.

Background   Provide any background information that the reader may need.

Definition of Terms and Issues   Define technical terms. Stipulate meanings for ambiguous terms. Make clear the particular meaning that will be used throughout the composition.

Development or Proof   Develop thesis. This is the body of your paper containing well-developed paragraphs that support the thesis.

Refutation   After you have presented your own ideas, try to predict and answer the disagreements or questions that your reader might have. (See chapter **31**.)

Conclusion   Summarize the main points of your paper, leaving your reader well-disposed toward what you have said. You may repeat the thesis, setting it in a wider context, or urge your reader to action or reconsideration of an accepted viewpoint.

Classical arrangement encourages you to put your readers first by providing information necessary for them to understand your point. It also encourages your readers to think of you as a thorough, fair-minded person because you anticipate (and answer) your readers' questions and disagreements. Depending upon the rhetorical situation, you may choose to emphasize certain of these parts more than others. For instance, an expository composition might emphasize background and definition, whereas a persuasive paper would probably focus on the proof and refutation.

33f

Write the first draft.

Put your ideas on paper quickly. In the first draft matters such as spelling, punctuation, and usage are not as important as they are in the final draft. You will probably not show these first efforts to anyone else. Sometimes called a *zero* draft, it may be sloppy, tentative, and impossible for anyone else to read, but don't worry about legibility until you revise. Save all of your early work in case you need to refer to it during revision. Keep your plan in mind as you draft. If you find you stray from it, stop drafting and reread what you have written. You may need to revise your plan, or you may need only to reorient yourself. If you are stuck and don't know what to write next, referring to your plan can help.

You may prefer to write chunks or blocks of your essay without worrying about the final order of those chunks. Many writers do. For example, if you have trouble writing the introduction, start with a supporting idea you feel sure of, and write until you reach a stopping point. When you actually are writing, you will probably think more efficiently. You can then move on to another part that will be easy to write next—another supporting idea paragraph, even the introduction or conclusion. What is important is to begin writing and to write as quickly as you can. You may find that using a computer makes moving, adding, and deleting text easier. Print out a copy or make a separate computer file for each of your versions. One word of caution: if you write in chunks or if you use a computer, make sure you use clear transitions and smoothly integrate new or moved material.

(1) Write effective introductions.

An effective introduction arouses the reader's interest and indicates the subject and tone of the composition (see **33a**). The introduction usually contains the thesis statement (see **33d**). Introductions have no set length; they can be as brief as a couple of sentences or as long as a couple of paragraphs or more. Although introductions appear first in the essay, experienced writers may compose them at any time during the writing process—even after they have drafted the rest of the paper. Notice how the author of the following introduction indicates his subject (gluttony) and his tone (humorous).

> How do things stand with you and the seven deadly sins? Here is my scorecard: Sloth I fight—to a draw. I surrendered to Pride long ago. Anger I tend to give in to so often that it makes me angry. Lust I'd rather not discuss. I haven't thus far done well enough in the world to claim Avarice as anything more than a theoretical sin. I appear to be making some headway against Envy, though I realize that it's touch and go. Of the seven deadly sins, the only one that has a continuing interest for me is Gluttony. But "continuing interest" is a euphemism; by it I mean that Gluttony is the last deadly sin that excites me in a big way—so much so that, though I am prepared to admit that Gluttony can be deadly, I am not all that prepared to say it is a sin. As soon as I pop this chocolate-chip cookie in my mouth, I shall attempt to explain what I mean.
>
> —ARISTIDES, "A Fat Man Struggles to Get Out"

You can arouse your reader's interest by writing your introduction in a number of ways:

1. Start with an interesting fact or unusual detail that catches the reader's attention.

    > Twenty-eight percent of the occupations that will be available to children born in 1976 were not in existence when those children were born.

2. Use an arresting statement to lure the reader into continuing.

    > During the Gold Rush of 1849 and the years that followed, San Francisco attracted more than any city's fair share of eccentrics. But among all the deluded and affected that spilled through the Golden Gate in those early days, one man rose to become perhaps the most successful eccentric in American history: Norton I, Emperor of the United States and Protector of Mexico. —JOAN PARKER, "Emperor Norton I"

3. Engage the reader's attention with an anecdote.

> It was during the thirteenth inning, with it all tied up at
> 3–3, that I found myself hanging over the partition inside a
> Checker cab, my back end in the back seat, my front end
> in the front, twisting the dials of the radio to find the playoff
> game between the Mets and the Astros.
>
> —ANNA QUINDLEN, "A Baseball Wimp"

4. Begin with a question that the composition will answer.

> What do they do at the computer at all hours of the day
> or night? They design and play complex games; they delve
> into the computer's memory bank for obscure tidbits of
> information; like ham radio operators, they communicate
> with hackers in other areas who are plugged into the same
> system. They even do their everyday chores by computer,
> typing term papers and getting neat printouts. One hacker
> takes his terminal home with him every school vacation so
> he can keep in touch with other hackers. And at Stanford
> University, even the candy machine is hooked up to a com-
> puter, programmed by the students to dispense candy on
> credit to those who know the password.
>
> —DINA INGBER, "Computer Addicts"

5. Start with an appropriate quotation.

> "All students study for the revolution, not just for grades,"
> declared Liu Shu-min in a quiet yet firm voice. "They usually
> do not think about how high their grades are but just about
> what their real knowledge is—for without real knowledge
> one cannot join the construction of the motherland!" Liu
> Shu-min, a lively girl of seventeen, with eyes at once smiling
> and serious and long dark pigtails which swing just below
> her shoulders, is the third oldest of the five Liu children.
>
> —RUTH SIDEL, "The Liu Family"

6. Open with an illustration.

> Almost all housework is hard and dangerous, involving
> the insides of ovens and toilets and the cracks between

bathroom tiles, where plague germs fester. The only housework that is easy and satisfying is the kind where you spray chemicals on wooden furniture and smear them around until the wood looks shiny. This is the kind of housework they show on television commercials: A professional actress, posing as the Cheerful Housewife (IQ 43), dances around her house, smearing and shining, smearing and shining, until before she knows it her housework is done and she is free to spend the rest of the afternoon reading the bust-development ads in *Cosmopolitan* magazine. She never cleans her toilets. When they get dirty, she just gets another house. Lord knows they pay her enough.

—DAVE BARRY, "A Solution to Housework"

7. Simply begin with general information as background about the subject and then focus specifically upon the thesis.

In a world riven by hate, greed, and envy, everyone loves tomatoes. I have never met anyone who didn't eat tomatoes with enthusiasm. Like ice cream, the whole, perfect, vine-ripened tomato is a universal favorite.

—RAYMOND SOKOLOV, "The Dark Side of Tomatoes"

8. Simply state your thesis.

Even today, when the American landscape is becoming more and more homogeneous, there is really no such thing as an all-American style of dress. A shopping center in Maine may superficially resemble one in Georgia or California, but the shoppers in it will look different, because the diverse histories of these states have left their mark on costume.

—ALISON LURIE, "American Regional Costume"

Avoid beginning with a dictionary definition such as "Webster's defines *hate* as. . . ." Where possible, use your introduction to present yourself positively by explaining your experience or knowledge of your subject. Establish your credibility and goodwill.

(2) Write effective conclusions.

The conclusion often summarizes the main points and may also encourage the reader to action or further thought on the subject. A composition should not merely stop; it should finish. Some suggestions follow:

1. You might conclude with a rephrasing of the thesis.

> Such considerations make it clear that it's time for schools to choose between real amateurism and real professionalism. They can't have a little of both. From now on, in college sports, it's got to be poetry or pros.
> —LOUIS BARBASH, "Clean Up or Pay Up"

2. Direct the reader's attention to larger issues.

> That night I thought hard and long. Could not this simple gambit of Joad's be extended to include other aspects of the game—to include all games? For me, it was the birth of gamesmanship. —STEPHEN POTTER, "Gamesmanship"

3. Encourage your readers to change their attitudes or to alter their actions, as in the following example.

> Consuming less, conserving more, they (the poor) are the good citizens of this country, but not by their own choice. They are patriots by necessity, because the expensive choices have already been made, and those of us still naive to the power of their witness would be well—would do mortally well—to fear their rebuke.
> —BARBARA BROWN, "All the Poor Patriots"

4. Conclude with a summary of the main points covered.

> All our giving carries with it messages about ourselves, our feelings about those to whom we give, how we see them as people and how we phrase the ties of relationship. Christmas giving, in which love and hope and trust play such an intrinsic part, can be an annual way of telling our children

that we think of each of them as a person, as we also hope
they will come to think of us.
—MARGARET MEAD and RHODA METRAUX,
"The Gift of Autonomy"

5. Clinch or stress the importance of the central idea by
   referring in some way to the introduction.

INTRODUCTION   I read *The National Enquirer* when I want
to feel exhilarated about life's possibilities. It
tells me of a world where miracles still occur.
In the world of *The National Enquirer,* UFOs
flash over the Bermuda Triangle, cancer cures
are imminent, ancient film stars at last find
love that is for keeps. Reached on The Other
Side by spiritualists, Clark Gable urges
America to keep its chin up. Of all possible
worlds, I like the world of *The National Enquirer* best. . . .

CONCLUSION   So I whoop with glee when a new edition
of *The National Enquirer* hits the newsstands
and step into the world where Gable can
cheer me up from The Other Side.
—RUSSELL BAKER, "Magazine Rack"

Whatever strategy you choose, bear in mind that readers may
be wondering, "So what?" Your conclusion should respond to
that concern, even if only in a sentence or two.

(3) Choose an appropriate title.

The title is the reader's first impression and, like the introduction, fits the subject and tone of the paper. Sometimes the
title announces the subject simply and directly: "Grant and
Lee" or "Civil Disobedience." Often a title uses alliteration
to reflect the writer's humorous approach, as in "A Pepsi
Person in the Perrier Generation," or a twisted cliché, as in
"The Right Wrong Stuff." A good title may also arouse the

reader's curiosity by asking a question, as does "Who Killed the Bog Men of Denmark? And Why?"

A good way to begin developing a title is to try condensing your thesis statement without becoming too vague or general. Reread your introduction and conclusion, and examine key words and phrases for possible titles. Try to work in some indication of what your attitude and approach are.

■ **Exercise 7**   First, select two of the example introductions in this section and write possible conclusions. Next, select two of the conclusions and write possible introductions. Finally, write a comment explaining what the titles of the essays from which the example paragraphs are taken suggest about the tone of the essay.

33g
Revise, edit, and proofread your composition.

In one way or another you revise throughout the writing process. For example, even in the earliest planning stages, as you consider a possible subject and then discard it in favor of another, you are revising. Similarly, after choosing a subject, if you decide to change your focus to emphasize some new aspect of it, you are revising. And of course you are revising when you realize that a sentence or a paragraph you have just written does not belong where it is, so you pause to strike it out or move it elsewhere. Once you have finished a draft, set it aside for a time, at least overnight, so you will be able to see it freshly and objectively. Then revise it carefully and systematically as a whole. In scheduling your work, allow plenty of time for multiple drafts and revising or for peer editing if your instructor encourages it.

(1) Revising

Revise means "to see again," and this activity implies that you take a fresh look at your draft and rethink what you have written. Review your draft *as a whole* to be sure ideas are clearly expressed in language your audience understands. Does the point of your essay come early? Unintentionally delaying the point to the end and revising only minimally, even with heavy editing, are characteristics of novice writers. Add and delete ideas where appropriate. Be sure everything in your paper relates to the subject, contributes to your purpose, and supports your thesis.

The truly challenging task in revision is to look for what you might have left out that your audience expects to see. Ideas do not always occur in order of their importance. A late idea may be the most important one and may govern the need to cut things that have become unnecessary. If you see problems, rewrite to fix them.

When you have rehaped your writing overall, examine paragraphs to be sure they are unified, coherent, and well developed. Ensure that sentences in a paragraph all relate to the topic sentence and are placed in the most effective order. Check for effective transitions between sentences and paragraphs. (See the following checklist.)

Revising Checklist

The essay as a whole

1. Is the purpose of the work clear (**33a[1]**)? Does the work stick to its purpose?
2. Does the work address the appropriate audience (**33a[2]**)?
3. Is the tone appropriate and consistent (**33a[4]**)?
4. Is the subject focused (**33b**)?
5. Is the thesis sharply conceived (**33d**)? Does your thesis statement (if one is appropriate) clearly suggest the position and approach that you take? Do the ideas expressed in the work show clear relationships to the thesis?

6. Are the paragraphs arranged in a logical, effective order (**33e**)?
7. Does the work follow an effecive method or combination of methods of development (**33e**)?
8. Is the reasoning sound in the writing as a whole and in individual paragraphs and sentences (**31**)?
9. Will the introduction arouse the reader's interest (**33f[1]**)? Does it indicate what the work is about?
10. Does the work come to a satisfying close (**33f[2]**)?

Paragraphs

1. Are all paragraphs unified (**32a**)? Are there ideas in any paragraph that do not belong?
2. Is each paragraph coherent (**32b**)? Are sentences within each paragraph arranged in a natural and deliberate order? Are the sentences connected with effective transitions?
3. Are the paragraphs linked effectively with easy and natural transitions (**32b[6]**)?
4. Is each paragraph purposefully and effectively developed (**32c–32d**)?

(2) Editing

After you are satisfied with the revised structure of your paper and the content of your paragraphs, the next step is to edit the individual sentences. Edit sentences for clarity, effectiveness, and variety (see chapters **19–30**). Consider combining choppy or unconnected sentences and rework long, overly complicated ones. If you overuse some structures, say introductory prepositional phrases, try to rework some of those into other patterns. Eliminate any needless shifts in grammatical structures, tone, style, or point of view.

Examine your diction. Check that your choice of words is appropriate for the rhetorical situation and that you have defined technical and unfamiliar words. Avoid vague words, such as *area, interesting,* and *unusual,* where more precise words would be more effective. Watch for clauses and sentences in the passive voice. The active voice usually, though by no means always, makes your writing more direct and forceful. Cut any nonessential words, phrases, and sentences to make your writing tighter and more emphatic. Make sure sentences are grammatically correct. The following checklist will help you edit your paper.

Editing Checklist

Sentences and diction

1. Are ideas related effectively through subordination and coordination (**24**)?
2. Are all sentences unified (**23**)?
3. Do any sentences contain misplaced parts or dangling modifiers (**25**)?
4. Is there any faulty parallelism (**26**)?
5. Are there any needless shifts in grammatical structures, in tone or style, or in viewpoint (**27**)?
6. Does each pronoun refer clearly to its antecedent (**28**)?
7. Are ideas given appropriate emphasis within each sentence (**29**)?
8. Are the sentences varied in length and in type (**30**)?
9. Are there any fragments (**2**)? Are there any comma splices or fused sentences (**3**)?
10. Do all verbs agree with their subjects (**6a**)? Do all pronouns agree with their antecedents (**6b**)?
11. Are all verbs in their appropriate forms (**7**)?
12. Are any words overused, imprecise, or vague (**20a**)? Are all words idiomatic (**20b**)?

13. Have all *unnecessary* words and phrases been eliminated (**21**)? Have any *necessary* words been left out by mistake (**22**)?
14. Is the vocabulary appropriate for the audience, purpose, and occasion (**19, 33a**)?
15. Have all technical words that are unfamiliar to the audience been eliminated or defined (**19g**)?

(3) Proofreading

Once you have revised and edited your paper, carefully format and proofread your final draft. A clean, neat paper makes your ideas more credible: showing that you care about presentation indicates that you care about your argument as well. Before you prepare your final version, consult your instructor and follow the guidelines in chapter **8** for manuscript form. (If your paper is to be in MLA style, see **34g–34h**; for APA style, see **34i–34k**.) Use the Proofreading Checklist in section **8c**, pages 101–102, to check your layout, spelling, punctuation, and mechanics. Enlist a friend to help you proofread; two pairs of eyes are better than one.

33h

An essay undergoing revision

Following are two drafts of an essay by Aaron Webb: his original first draft with handwritten early revisions and his final draft. Aaron made a number of changes in his working drafts. The final version is more effective than his first one because he pays attention to focus and development. Aaron made many of his revisions in response to suggestions from his instructor, but a number of them resulted from his own rethinking of his ideas.

FIRST DRAFT

Draft 1

You move down the street in your gray Honda.
It is a hot summer day, the ~~a/c~~ *air conditioning* is out *of freon* and you have
the windows rolled down to maintain a slight sense
of comfort. You ~~reach~~ *ease to a stop at* the last ~~stop~~light *traffic* of a long
hard working day. Just as you stop, a green *ten-year-old* ~~'82~~
*B*uick rolls up beside you. A teenager, hidden
behind long hair,*/and* sunglasses and *wearing* a Metallica T-shirt
glances at you/ *and* produces a *M*emorex tape from the
depths of the *B*uick. Slowly and gracefully he
pushes it into the casse*t*e player on his dashboard.
The light is still red. Sudden*l*y, as if from B-17
bombers, the teenager's car erupts into a bastion of
noise. Manmade thunder ~~with incomprehensible~~ *accompanied by* incomprehensible lyrics
take*s* the air, violently, ~~showing no mercy~~. *mercilessly* You
think to yourself "What is this noise!" You
consider rolling up the windows, ~~no~~ *but it is* too hot. ~~It is~~ *The noise*
too loud to ~~put it out of your head~~. *ignore.* You are
helpless. "Why must they listen to this noise?" you
ask yourself.
~~This is why. First of all I think that~~ *There are reasons. Teens listen to* Heavy
Metal (also Speed, Trash and Death) *as a form of rebellion* ~~is really cool~~.
But there is also another *more acceptable* reason. Most Heavy Metal

is ~~scocially~~ *socially* active. ~~Yes active.~~ Megadeth is pro-
choice, anti-nuke, anti-war. Metallica attacks the
failing Justice system and supports euthanasia.
Iron Maiden: the problem in the inner cities and
Anthrax: Anti-censorship. Heavy Metal is fates
warning for our society. The bands that play this
music are not out to corrupt kids but to tell them
that the problems in our society should not be
there. They encourage young people to push for
change but not to stop enjoying themselves.
You may think that the era of social protest passed
~~The reader might not agree with me and say that~~
away with the sixties, but the   *is still alive*
~~time is gone.~~ ~~The~~ truth is that it never left.
This is because the problems that the
counter-culture tried to tackle in the sixties have
not been removed, but have gotten worse. Like a
tumor in the heart of society, Heavy Metal is not
about killing parents and burning babies while
tearing down the government. It is about changing
the world ~~to where the~~ *so that those* babies ~~will~~ *can* grow up with
something to live for and ~~the~~ parents can raise
their children without worrying every time their
children go to school or go out with friends. ~~Its~~
Heavy Metal is
not about worshiping the devil, but *it is about the fact* that satan is
more present in our society than ever *before,* and that

watching out might be a good idea. ⌃People who hunt

the⌃ (se) witches eventually become evil when they censor

nurs⌃ey (n) r⌃ymes (h) and ⌃the old ~~childrens~~ stor⌃ys (ie) that have

been told ⌃+children for generations. ~~and enjoyed by billions.~~ Not only does censorship

rob us of some important parts of our culture, but

~~In todays world the heavy metal listener has about~~ it also silences powerful voices for change.

~~⌃as much potential for suicide as the man who runs~~ Many young people who listen to Heavy Metal

~~the local hardware store or the strait A student.~~ feel as I do:

~~It⌃ doesn't depend on what you listen to. It depends~~

~~on what happens in your life. I know that I for~~

~~sure am not about ready to go curl up and die on my~~

~~own accord. But one thing is for sure,~~ I am ready

to make sacrifices and take chances to change what

is wrong⌃ in our world. ~~It is about~~ E⌃veryone ⌃is working together to

change the bad to good. Everyone doing their little

part no matter how small will make a change. ~~It is~~

~~about saying~~ Heavy Metal says that prisons and cen⌃sor ship will only

make things worse. and the push for change doesn't only ~~It is not just metal; it is rap~~ come from Heavy Metal bands. It comes from rap,

⌃new rock, and even a little bit of country⌃ too. It is

for this ⌃message that I listen to ⌃metal. (M)

Furthermore, prohibiting Heavy Metal music is a form of censorship. Those who want to censor the critical elements in our society are like the people who hunted the witches of Salem. They are frightened and ignorant.

Instructor's comments

I rather like the zest of your introduction, though some readers may think it is not quite unified with the rest of your essay. You'll have to decide what to do about that, but you do need to strengthen your focus. You could do that by combining your short second paragraph with your third paragraph, but you should state your point early in the revised paragraph. Consider revising at that point to emphasize the social appeal to younger listeners, and then support your point with specific details.

You've revised nicely by deleting the information following "fate warning for our society" and have also revised well to ease your transition to the discussion of censorship. I'm glad you took out the material on suicide. I agree that it doesn't belong and it could have diluted the impact of your conclusion.

When you rework your paper, be careful to fill out sentences so that you don't have unacceptable fragments. Watch out for careless errors. Be consistent with mechanics. Proofread. This could be quite a powerful paper if you take care.

FINAL DRAFT

The final draft that Aaron submitted follows. Although it could still benefit from more revising and editing, particularly for style, Aaron has greatly amplified his material on Heavy Metal bands, explaining why he thinks they comment on social problems, and he has also strengthened his focus.

Why Listen to Heavy Metal?

You move down the congested street in your gray Honda. It is rush hour on a hot summer day, the air conditioning is out of freon, and you have the windows rolled down to maintain a slight sense of comfort. You ease to a stop at the last traffic light of a long hard working day. Just as you stop,

a ten-year-old green Buick rolls up beside you. A
teenager, hidden behind long hair and sunglasses,
and wearing a Metallica T-shirt, glances at you, and
produces a Memorex tape from the depths of the
Buick. He pushes it into the cassette player on his
dashboard. The light is still red. Suddenly, as if
from B-17 bombers, a barrage of noise erupts from
the teenager's car. Man-made thunder accompanied by
incomprehensible lyrics attacks the air, violently,
mercilessly. You consider rolling up the windows to
get relief from the din, but you realize you would
roast. You are helpless. "Why must they listen to
this noise?" you ask yourself.

There are reasons. Teens listen to Heavy Metal
(also called Speed, Trash, or Death) as a form of
rebellion. But there is also another, more
acceptable, reason. Much of Heavy Metal music
carries a message that appeals directly to the
younger generation. Most Heavy Metal is socially
active. The bands that play this music are not out
to corrupt kids but to alert them to problems in our
society. They encourage young people to push for
change but not to stop enjoying themselves.

For instance, the lead singer of Megadeth has
stated that he is pro-choice, and the group also
attacks the use of nuclear weapons in "Set the World
Afire" and "Rust in Peace . . . Polaris" and
condemns the invocation of jihad in "Holy Wars."
Metallica attacks the failing justice system and
supports euthanasia in such songs as "And Justice
for All" and "One." Iron Maiden attacks the problem

of the inner cities with "Public Enema #1" which also criticizes drug use and corrupt politicians. "Holy Smoke" slams greedy televangelists who prey upon the poor and ignorant. Anthrax campaigns against censorship with the satirical song "Starting Up a Posse." Heavy Metal warns young people about what is going wrong in our society.

You may think that the era of social protest died with the sixties, but the truth is that it is still alive. This is because the problems that the counter-culture tried to tackle in the sixties have not been removed, but, like a tumor in the heart of society, have grown larger, more ominous. The controversy surrounding Heavy Metal music itself reflects one of the worst ills that society suffers from--the belief that views different from one's own have no right to be aired and that these different views are inspired by evil and should therefore be prohibited.

Some people believe that Heavy Metal music is Satanic, and they think that it should be prohibited. Heavy Metal is not about killing parents and burning babies while tearing down the government. It is about changing the world so that those babies can grow up with something to live for, and so that parents can raise their children without worrying about their safety every time those children go to school or out with friends. Heavy Metal is not about worshipping the devil; it is about the fact that Satan--that is, evil, cruelty, and lack of compassion--is more present in our society than ever before and that watching out might be a good idea.

Furthermore, prohibiting Heavy Metal music is a form of censorship. Those who want to censor the critical elements in our society are like the people who hunted the witches of Salem. They are frightened and ignorant. People who hunt these modern-day, so-called witches eventually become evil themselves when they censor nursery rhymes and folk tales that have been told to children for generations. Not only does such censorship rob us of some important parts of our culture, but it also silences powerful voices for change. Heavy Metal says that prisons, repression, and censorship will only make things worse. And the push for change doesn't only come from Heavy Metal bands. It comes from other elements of the popular music scene: rap, new rock, and even country. Many young people who listen to Heavy Metal feel as I do: I am ready to make sacrifices and take chances to change what is wrong in our world.

But real change requires cooperation, not fear and repression. Change works best when everyone works together. Everyone doing their little part, no matter how small, can and must make a change. It is for this message of change that I listen to Metal.

Instructor's comments

You've made many improvements in this draft, Aaron. I am glad to see that you have modified the tone of your introductory paragraph somewhat. It makes a strong bid for the reader's interest, but I think it still needs to be more tightly integrated with your whole paper. The other changes you have made are a great improvement. I am glad to see you have developed some of the ideas more fully; however, the paragraph about how some think Heavy Metal is Satanic seems to be misplaced— or at least the transition is rather creaky. You might consider shifting that information to a point earlier in the essay so that you can go directly from the information about tolerating views different from one's own to the discussion of censorship. Still, the essay is a strong statement of your beliefs and helps the reader who finds Heavy Metal unsavory to understand some of its positive elements.

■ Exercise 8

1. Rewrite the above composition taking the opposite viewpoint.
2. Rewrite the above composition as a humorous essay. Start by redefining "Heavy Metal."

34
Writing from Research

Learn how to acquire information and how to write a paper that uses your research.

Although writing from research usually takes more time than writing essays based on information already familiar to you, the process involves many of the same skills. The distinctive feature of a research assignment is that it requires you to develop a subject by drawing upon outside resources and acknowledging those resources properly. Improving your ability to work with sources may subsequently help you with other writing assignments as well, since you may need to obtain information from sources even when you are not specifically required to do research.

Rather than considering the research paper as a special assignment that is unrelated to other kinds of writing, you should recognize that almost anything you write requires you to acquire and use information. On some occasions, you may discover that you have sufficient information from your own experience or observations. On other occasions, you may need to explore the resources of a library to discover the work of other writers or researchers who can help you. In either case, remember that you are a writer, not simply a compiler of data. No matter how many sources you may use, you are the most important presence in a paper that has your name on it. Think of the paper as a *researched* paper—that is, written from research that you have evaluated and then used to advance a *thesis* (**33d**).

You may begin a researched paper with a subject that interests you, with a question that you want to answer, or even with a tentative thesis. If you begin with a thesis, be prepared to revise it if your research findings do not support it (see also **31b**). However you choose to begin, you will need to decide whether the *purpose* (**33a[1]**) of your paper will be chiefly expository (to report, analyze, or explain) or persuasive (to prove a point). Your *audience* (**33a[2]**) may or may not be an expert on your subject, but you should usually envision a reader who is intelligent, fair-minded, and interested in what you have to say. Similarly, you should present yourself as a writer who is thoughtful, fair-minded, and responsive to the views of others, because any sign of bias can undermine your credibility (**31c**) as a researcher.

A few words of advice: scheduling your time is especially important because researched papers are usually assigned several weeks before they are due, and the temptation to procrastinate may be strong. Make sure to allow enough time for the long process of choosing a subject (**34a**), preparing a preliminary bibliography (**34b**), reading extensively, taking notes (**34c**), outlining (**33e**), drafting (**33f**), and revising (**33g**). Begin early and keep your schedule flexible. As you write your paper, you may need to return to a part of the research process that you thought you had already completed. For example, when drafting your essay, you may discover that you need additional information—you may need to conduct a personal interview or to return to the library for further research.

34a

Choose a subject for a researched paper and limit it appropriately.

Occasionally, you may be assigned a specific topic. If so, you are ready to begin your search for sources (**34b**). Often, however, choosing a subject will be up to you. An inquiring mind is the best equipment you can bring to this task: choose a subject that interests you and is appropriate for your audience. If you are stuck for an idea, consider some of the methods mentioned in **33b**. You might also try scanning the subjects covered in the *Library of Congress Subject Headings* (see page 398) or an index like the *Reader's Guide* (see pages 398–400), keeping alert for headings that interest you.

Once you have a subject in mind, the exploration methods discussed in **33c**—freewriting, listing, questioning, considering perspectives—will almost certainly help you find an interesting focus. Limiting the topic is especially important with a researched paper, since one of your main objectives is to show your ability to treat a subject in some depth within the constraints of time and (usually) a specified length. One basic test of any subject you may have in mind is the amount of pertinent material in the library. If you find dozens of relevant sources, you should probably narrow the subject to one with a more manageable scope. On the other hand, if you have difficulty finding sources, chances are that your subject is too narrow and needs to be made more inclusive. Because the best researched papers usually draw upon different kinds of material, you should also reconsider any topic that would force you to rely exclusively upon one type of source. A paper based only on newspaper articles, for example, could easily lack depth, and research drawn exclusively from books might overlook the most current information in the field.

■ **Exercise 1** Evaluate the following subjects for a ten-page researched paper. If any seem too broad, suggest a narrower topic—for example, "The Second World War" can be narrowed to the "Bombing of Pearl Harbor." If any seem too narrow, suggest a broader subject—for example, "Raising Wheat in Brazil" could be expanded to "The Variety of Crops in Brazilian Agriculture." Eliminate any subject that you would be unable to find reliable sources for.

censorship	capital punishment
Fidel Castro	AIDS in Mozambique
Japanese television advertising	drug abuse
animal experimentation	puns in Shakespeare

34b

Learn to find the sources you need and to prepare a working bibliography.

College and university libraries are organized to make research as efficient as possible. Most provide a map or diagram—either printed for handing out or posted on the wall—to show you where various kinds of materials are located. Reference books, encyclopedias, and indexes—materials that cannot usually be checked out of the library—are located in the *reference collection*. Other books are located in the *stacks* or at the *reserve desk* and may be checked out for a specified length of time. If your library has a closed-stack policy, you request the books you need by call number from the *circulation desk*. You can find the call number in the *main catalog*. If the stacks are open, however, you may find it useful to browse among the books shelved near those you have located through the catalog. *Periodicals* (magazines, journals, newspapers) are usually stored in a special section of the library. Bear in mind that many colleges participate in interlibrary loan programs, which are arrangements among local or regional college libraries for the exchange of books. You may also be entitled to use the facilities of other college libraries in your area. If you have difficulty locating or using any research materials, do not hesitate to ask a *reference librarian* for help.

Remember also that your search does not need to be limited to a library unless an instructor has asked you to confine yourself to published information. As you gather information for your paper, you may benefit from conducting interviews with experts on your topic and drawing upon observations that you have acquired through personal experience. Much of the research that people do in their daily lives involves more than one approach to the issue in question. If you plan to buy a new car, for example, you may read reviews published in various magazines available in your library, interview people who are familiar with the cars that interest you, and take a test drive or two. A similar strategy may be appropriate for research assignments in school or at work: read, interview, and observe.

(1) Learn to find books and periodicals.

BOOKS

The first place to look is usually the *main catalog,* which may take the form of cards or computer files. The main catalog lists all books owned by the college or university and shows whether a book is in the general library or elsewhere in a special collection.

A *card catalog* consists of cards arranged alphabetically in drawers. For each book, cards are filed alphabetically in three ways: by author, by title, and by subject or subjects.

Many libraries have now computerized their catalogs to save space and to make research more efficient. By pressing a few keys at reference terminals (located in the library and often elsewhere on campus), users have instant access to the same information previously available in a card catalog. Like a card catalog, a *computerized catalog* is designed to identify books by author, title, or subject. Some programs also allow researchers to locate sources by supplying the computer with other information, such as a book's call number or a key word that may appear in the title.

Visually, there may be a slight difference between the format of a catalog card and its equivalent on a computer screen. (See the following illustrations.) But whether you use a card catalog or a computer catalog, you will be provided with essentially the same information: author, title, place of publication, publisher, date of publication, the length and size of the book, and any special features such as a bibliography. You will also be given the book's call number, which tells you exactly where the book is located in the library.

If your library provides you with access to both a card catalog and a computer catalog, check with a librarian to see which is more current. Libraries that have computerized their catalogs may have stopped including new acquisitions in their card catalogs, and libraries that have only recently computerized their catalogs may not yet have their entire collection on-line.

A catalog card

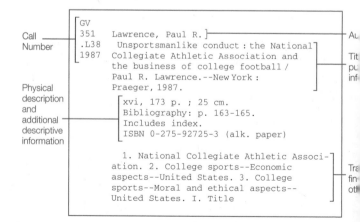

Call Number

Physical description and additional descriptive information

GV
351
.L38
1987

Lawrence, Paul R.
  Unsportsmanlike conduct : the National
Collegiate Athletic Association and
the business of college football /
Paul R. Lawrence.--New York :
Praeger, 1987.
  xvi, 173 p. ; 25 cm.
  Bibliography: p. 163-165.
  Includes index.
  ISBN 0-275-92725-3 (alk. paper)

    1. National Collegiate Athletic Associ-
ation. 2. College sports--Economic
aspects--United States. 3. College
sports--Moral and ethical aspects--
United States. I. Title

Au

Tit
pu
inf

Tra
fin
ot

This example is an author card. Cards filed by title and by subject will have the same information under different headings.

An entry from a computer catalog

```
AUTHOR          Lawrence, Paul R.
TITLE           Unsportsmanlike conduct :
                the National Collegiate
                Athletic Association
                and the business of
                college football / Paul
                R. Lawrence.
PUBLICATION     New York : Praeger, 1987.
DESCRIPTION     xvi, 173 p. ; 25 cm.
NOTES           Includes index.
                Bibliography: p. 163-165.
SUBJECTS        1. National Collegiate
                Athletic Association. 2.
                College sports--Economic
                aspects--United States.
                3. College sports--Moral
                and ethical aspects--
                United States.

LOCATION   CALL NUMBER         STATUS
STACKS      GV351 .L38 1987     Available
```

In addition to providing all the data found on the printed card, a computerized catalog entry often reveals the location and status of the book—information that can save a reseacher time when looking for a book that has been moved to a special collection or checked out by someone else. Libraries use a number of different systems for computerizing catalogs, so expect to encounter variations on this example.

Library of Congress subject headings If your library uses Library of Congress numbers for cataloging books, you can quickly find what books your library has in your subject area. First, look for your subject in the *Library of Congress Subject Headings.* If your subject is indexed by that catalog, you will find a specific catalog number for books on your subject as well as cross-references to related subject areas that may help you sharpen your focus. If you find a number indexed, write it down; then find that number in your library's own *shelf list,* which lists all the books in the library by call number. The first part of a call number indicates the subject of a book (for example, the GV in GV351 stands for Physical Education). Therefore, when you look up the call number of only one book, you should find adjacent to it the call numbers of other books the library owns on that subject.

PERIODICALS

Since periodicals (magazines, journals, newspapers) are published frequently, they often contain the most recent information on your subject. A variety of the periodical indexes (usually located in the reference section of the library) do for articles what the main catalog does for books. You may need to consult a number of indexes to find the information you need, since each index includes many publications not listed in the others.

Indexes for general interest periodicals If articles on your subject may have appeared in popular or general interest magazines or in newspapers, you might want to consult the *Readers' Guide to Periodical Literature,* published from 1900 to the present, and a newspaper index, the best known of which is the *New York Times Index,* published since 1913.

COLLEGE ATHLETICS

Cross-references

See also
Athletic directors
Baseball, College
Basketball, College
Fencing
Football, College
Gymnasiums
Hockey, College
Lacrosse, College
National Collegiate Athletic Association
Rowing
Soccer, College
Swimming
Tennis
Track and field athletics
Volleyball, College
Women athletic directors
Wrestling, College

Subtopics arranged in alphabetical order

Cheerleading
See Cheerleading

Economic aspects
The myth of the student-athlete. S. Brownlee. il *U.S. News & World Report* 108:50–2 Ja 8 '90

Ethical aspects

Articles on topic

The battle of Dallas [reform measures passed at NCAA convention] R. Sullivan. il *Sports Illustrated* 72:7 Ja 22 '90

Clean up or pay up [cover story] L. Barbash. *The Washington Monthly* 22:38–41 Jl/Ag '90

College Sports Inc.: the athletic department vs. the university [excerpt] M. Sperber. il *Phi Delta Kappan* 72:K1–K12 O '90

Curb campus corruption. W. M. Barrett. il *USA Today (Periodical)* 118:93 My '90

The *Readers' Guide* excerpt above (from the search Calvin Beale conducted for his paper on the exploitation of college athletes, reprinted on pages 443–63 shows that *The Washington Monthly* published a cover story on the ethical aspects of college sports. The author's name is L. Barbash, and the article can be found in volume 22, pages 38–41, of the July/August 1990 issue. If you need help reading an entry during your own research, you can find a sample entry as well as a key to abbreviations in the front pages of each issue of the *Readers' Guide.*

Many college and university libraries now provide access to the *Readers' Guide* on a CD-ROM computer disk. This disk, which is updated regularly, covers several years' worth of information otherwise found in a number of separate, bound volumes.

Like the *Readers' Guide*, the *New York Times Index* arranges its articles' authors and subjects in alphabetical order. Entries include a brief summary of the contents and an abbreviation that reveals the article's length.

Article summary

{ Article on special programs being created by school districts around nation to encourage involvement of parents in their children's education; photo; drawing (special section, Education Life) (L), N 9,XII,18:2

A long article   November 9 issue (in year of volume consulted)   Section, page, and column numbers

The *New York Times Index* is widely available in bound volumes published annually. Depending upon the resources of your library, you may also be able to search for information in the *New York Times* (and in other newspapers like the *Christian Science Monitor* and the *Wall Street Journal*) with a CD-ROM disk or through an on-line database search.

For older articles of general interest, you can consult *Poole's Index,* 1802–1907, or *Nineteenth Century Readers' Guide,* 1890–99.

Indexes for special interest periodicals Virtually, every specialized field has its own periodicals, which usually provide much more detailed information than can be found in magazines or newspapers designed for the general public. When conducting research in college, you should be familiar with the indexes that cover periodicals within various professions. Some of the most useful ones are listed below.

> *Applied Science and Technology Index.* 1958–.
> *Art Index.* 1929–.
> *Biological and Agricultural Index.* 1946–.
> *Business Periodicals Index.* 1958–.
> *Education Index.* 1929–.
> *General Science Index.* 1978–.
> *Humanities Index.* 1974–.
> *Index to Legal Periodicals.* 1908–.
> *Music Index.* 1949–.
> *Public Affairs Information Service* (Bulletin). 1915–.
> *Social Sciences Index.* 1974–.

These indexes are organized like the *Reader's Guide.* (Consult the front of any volume for a key to the abbreviations used in individual entries.) A similar format is also used by the *MLA Bibliography,* which is essential for doing research in literature (see **35a**). The *MLA Bibliography* includes books as well as periodicals, and each volume is divided into separate sections covering research on the literature of different languages and time periods. Like most indexes to special interest periodicals, the *MLA Bibliography* can be consulted in printed volumes, through an on-line database search, or through access to a CD-ROM disk covering several years.

Abstracting services In addition to providing bibliographical information necessary for locating sources, an abstracting service provides short summaries of the articles and books it indexes. Your library may have CD-ROM disks for such abstracts as *Academic Abstracts, Biology Abstracts, Chemical*

Abstracts, and *Psychological Abstracts* (all of which are also published in bound volumes). It may also subscribe to databases such as ERIC (for research in education) and Psych-INFO (for research in psychology). When using one of these services, you can quickly scan the short summaries and decide which seem likely to be the most useful. You may also be able to print out a list of citations, a list of citations with abstracts, and even the full text of some of the articles you discover. Here is a citation and abstract from *Academic Abstracts,* a service that covers many widely available periodicals.

Computerized abstract

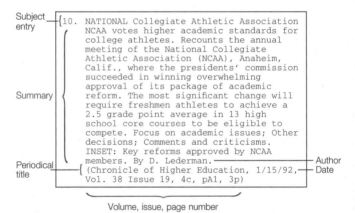

Volume, issue, page number

REFERENCE BOOKS

When doing research, you may need to consult a variety of reference works. A general encyclopedia, such as *Encyclopedia Americana* or *Encyclopaedia Britannica,* can provide useful information, especially at an early stage in your research. And you will almost certainly need to consult a dictionary (see **19a**). For a detailed list of reference books and a short description of each, consult *Guide to Reference Books* by Eugene P. Sheehy, and *American Reference Books Annual* (*ARBA*) edited by Boydan S. Wynar. For a list of reference books useful when writing about literature, see pages 497–98. A few of the most widely used reference books are listed here with abbreviated bibliographical information. Note that these are sources for *reference:* refer to them for help, but do not rely upon any of them as a principal source for a college paper.

Special dictionaries and encyclopedias

> Adams, James T. *Dictionary of American History.* Rev. ed. 8 vols. 1983.
> *Encyclopedia of American Foreign Policy.* Ed. Alexander DeConde. 3 vols. 1978.
> *Encyclopedia of Philosophy.* Ed. Paul Edwards. 4 vols. 1973.
> *Encyclopedia of Psychology.* Ed. Raymond J. Corsini. 4 vols. 1984.
> *Encyclopedia of Religion.* Ed. Mircea Eliade. 16 vols. 1986.
> *Encyclopedia of World Art.* 15 vols. 1959–68. Supp. 1983, 1987.
> *International Encyclopedia of Higher Education.* Ed. Asa S. Knowles. 10 vols. 1977.
> *International Encyclopedia of the Social Sciences.* Ed. D. E. Sills. 8 vols. 1977. Supplements.
> *McGraw-Hill Encyclopedia of Science and Technology.* 15 vols. 6th ed. 1987. Yearbooks.
> *The New Grove Dictionary of Music and Musicians.* Ed. Stanley Sadie. 20 vols. 1980.

Biography

> *Biography Index.* 15 vols. 1946–88.
> *Current Biography Cumulated Index, 1940–1985.* 1986. Annual supplements.
> *Dictionary of American Biography.* 17 vols. and index. 1927–81. Supplements.
> *Dictionary of National Biography* (British). 22 vols. 1882–1953. Rpt. 1981. Supplements.

Dictionary of Scientific Biography. 8 vols. 1970–80.
Notable American Women: 1607–1950. 3 vols. 1972. Supplements.
Notable Black American Women. 1990.
Webster's New Biographical Dictionary. 1983.
Who's Who in America. 1899–. (See also Marquis's *Who's Who Publications: Index to All Books,* revised annually.)

Almanacs and yearbooks

American Annual. 1924–.
Britannnica Book of the Year. 1938–.
Broadcasting Yearbook. 1982–.
Facts on File. 1940–.
New International Yearbook. 1907–.
Official Associated Press Almanac. 1969–.
Statesman's Year-Book. 1863–.
Statistical Abstract of the United States. 1878–.
World Almanac and Book of Facts. 1868–.

(2) Learn to use nonprint sources.

Depending upon your topic, you may want to supplement your reading with other types of research. The most common alternative to library research is to conduct an *interview.* The faculty members of your college, business and professional people, and even relatives and friends may make appropriate subjects for an interview if they have relevant firsthand experience with the subject you are researching. Schedule the interview in advance and ask permission to use a tape recorder if you plan to use one. For the interview itself, prepare a list of questions, avoiding any that could be answered with a simple yes or no. Begin with questions that are broad enough to give people room to reveal their own special interests; then follow up with more specific questions. Be prepared to depart from your list of planned questions whenever your subject says something of particular interest that would be useful to pursue. Since well-informed interviewers usually ask the best questions, you should consider an interview only after you have done some reading on your subject. After the interview, send a letter to thank the interviewee. A courtesy of this sort is especially appropriate when someone has made time for you in a busy schedule or has been genuinely helpful in the interview itself.

In addition to interviewing, you may also have occasion to draw directly upon your own experience or observations. In the paper reprinted on pages 443–63, for example, Calvin Beale incorporated his own experience as an athlete with the material he located through a library search. This strategy was appropriate for his topic: the exploitation of college athletes. But check with your instructor to make sure that personal experience is appropriate for your own research project.

(3) Evaluate your sources.

When you are doing research, one important consideration always is the reliability of your sources (see **31c**). Ask the following questions about the sources you discover:

Source Evaluation Checklist

a. What are the author's credentials?
b. Do others speak of the writer as an authority?
c. Does the work contain evidence indicating that the author is well informed?
d. Does the work contain evidence that the author is prejudiced in any way?
e. Is the work recent enough to provide up-to-date information?
f. Is the work published by a reputable company?
g. Does the work provide documentation to support important points?
h. Does the work include a bibliography that could help you to identify other sources?

The *Book Review Digest,* which contains convenient summaries of critical opinion on a book, may help you decide which books are most dependable. The *Literary Marketplace* will provide basic information about publishers. You can usually assume that university presses demand a high standard of scholarship. As for periodicals, an article published in an academic journal (as opposed to a popular magazine) has usually been reviewed by experts before publication. Be alert for bias that may be built into a source, even if it is not obvious when you are reading. For example, an article on malpractice suits in the *Journal of the American Medical Association* is likely to be sympathetic to physicians.

As you read your sources, learn how to find and evaluate useful passages with a minimum of time and effort. Seldom will a whole book, or even a whole article, be of use for any given researched paper. You will usually find that you must turn to many books and articles, rejecting some altogether and using others only in part. You cannot always take the time to read each book completely. Use the table of contents and the index of a book, and learn to skim the pages until you find the passages you need. When you find them, read critically (see **31**). Ask yourself if you agree with what you are reading and if the material raises any unanswered questions.

(4) Prepare a working bibliography.

A working, or preliminary, bibliography contains information (titles, authors, dates, and so on) about the materials you think you might use. Write down the most promising sources you can find. Often the books you consult will have helpful bibliographies. Draw upon them, but do not use them exclusively; otherwise the research will no longer be your own, and you will miss other sources. Put each on a separate index card (preferably 3 × 5 inches) so you can readily drop or add a card and can arrange the list alphabetically without recopying it. Follow consistently the bibliographical form you are instructed to use. Using the specified style from the start will save you valuable time later, when you must compile a formal list of works cited to appear at the end of your paper. Be sure to note the call number for books in case you need to recheck a book after you have returned it or want to see if there are similar books shelved near it.

The style illustrated by the sample bibliography cards below follows the guidelines of the Modern Language Association (MLA). See pages 419–40 for examples of entries you are likely to need for a bibliography in MLA style.

■ **Exercise 2** Select a subject that you would like to become more knowledgeable about. Consult the main catalog in your library and at least one periodical index. Propose two different ways of narrowing the subject. Write a paragraph in which you (a) report these two possibilities, (b) explain which of the two you have selected for further research, and (c) determine the number and quality of the sources that seem available. Then prepare at least four bibliography cards for your instructor.

Bibliography cards

> Barbash, Louis. "Clean Up or Pay Up." *The Washington Monthly* July–Aug. 1990: 38–41.

> Lawrence, Paul R. *Unsportsmanlike Conduct: The National Collegiate Athletic Association and the Business of College Football.* New York: Praeger, 1987.
>
> GV
> 351
> .L38
> 1987

■ **Exercise 3** Do preliminary reading on your research subject. Iden-tify one source that seems reliable and another that seems biased. Write a two-paragraph-long evaluation in which you compare the credibility of these two sources.

34c

Take notes on your sources.

As you take notes, use a system that will help you organize them. One of the best ways to take notes is on cards of uniform size, preferably 4 × 6 inches. (Many researchers use larger cards for notes than for bibliographical references because notes often require more room than references. Different sizes of cards also help a writer keep the cards' functions sep-arate.)

Each card must show the author's name (and title if your bibliography contains more than one work by that author), including the exact page(s) from which the information is drawn. (See the sample note card on page 409.) Put no more than a single note, however brief, on each card. Then put a heading of two or three key words on the top of each card. Filling out your note cards this way will allow you to arrange your cards easily as you prepare to write your paper.

Be careful to write down accurate bibliographic information about every source from which you take notes. Scrupulous care now can prevent a multitude of problems later on—such as being forced to abandon important information because you lost track of exactly where it came from. When you discover a useful passage that you think you may later quote, take it down verbatim—that is, copy every word, every capital letter, and every mark of punctuation exactly as it is in the original. Be especially careful to put quotation marks around any words you take directly from a source; failure to do so on a note card may lead to unintended plagiarism when you draft your paper. See **34e**.

Note card

Measuring Test Anxiety
(Davies '53)

Traditional means of measuring TA
may not be accurate. People may
exaggerate or be influenced by other
factors like time of day. "Clearly,
the tests are inadequate...."

Source (from Davies, page 53)

The accuracy of the above tests, as with all self-report measures, is generally influenced by such factors as honesty and the desire to create a favourable impression or to be seen in a "good light." Even when people try to be honest, however, the answers they give may not be objectively true. Neurotic people, for example, have a tendency to exaggerate their defects. They complain about aches and pains and about sleep problems to an objectively excessive degree. Generally, they tend to be more self-deprecative than people of a calmer and more stable disposition. Scores on self-report measures are also influenced by such factors as the personality of the tester, the time of day, experience of previous tests and temporary moodswings. In a review of self-report instruments to assess trait anxiety, Tryon (1980) . . . concludes by saying that the tests are easily "fakeable." Clearly, the tests are inadequate by themselves except when used for research purposes with large groups of people. (Don Davies, *Maximizing Examination Performance,* New York: Nichols, 1986.)

Another way to take notes is to use photocopies of short excerpts from materials you think you may quote directly. On a photocopy you can mark quotable material and jot down your own ideas as you study the source. Make sure you document the source on the photocopy.

Photocopied source with notes   (from "Clean Up or Pay Up" by Louis Barbash, page 201)

[handwritten margin note, left:] meaning?

[handwritten margin note, left:] Iowa? Ohio. Is this problem to limited to the Midwest?

[handwritten margin note, left:] How much could they see when they played 10 games within 14 days?

Not only are these at<u>hletes being cheated out of a promised education</u>, but they and their universities are forced to erect elaborate, <u>meretricious</u> curricula to satisfy the <u>student-athlete requirement</u>, so of those who *do* get degrees, <u>many receive diplomas that are barely worth the parchment they're printed on</u>. Running back Ronnie Harmon majored in computer science at the University of <u>Iowa</u>, but took only one computer course in his three years of college. Another Iowa football player also majored in computer science, but in his senior year took only courses in billiards, bowling, and football; he followed up by getting a D in a summer school watercolor class. Transcripts of the members of the basketball team at <u>Ohio</u> University list credit for something called "International Studies 69B"—a course composed of a 14-day/10-game trip to Europe.

[handwritten margin notes, right:] reference; How typical are these examples.

34d

Make a working plan or outline.

After completing a working bibliography and taking notes on your subject, make a working plan for your paper. (See **33e.**) Do not feel that you must adhere rigidly to this plan, though. No plan or outline should be regarded as complete until the paper has been finished. As you write, you will probably revise your original plan frequently, adding points, changing points, and perhaps dropping points you had originally intended to cover.

It is sometimes useful, especially if your paper is long or complicated, to have a detailed outline before you actually begin to write. If you work best with a formal outline, decide whether to use a topic outline or a sentence outline. A topic outline presents information in parallel phrases or single words. A sentence outline presents the same ideas in declarative statements. (See pages 369–70.) If your instructor has asked you to submit a formal outline of your paper before you begin to draft, prepare a topic or sentence outline as you are directed.

When you have finished drafting your paper, a good way to check your organization is to correlate the ideas in your text with those in an outline and to make any needed revisions. Working directly from the paper you have drafted, prepare a new outline. Compare this outline with your working plan. Ask yourself if you need to revise your thesis or make any changes in your organization.

34e

Use sources responsibly.

When you write a paper, you have several options for including material from other writers. You can quote their exact words, paraphrase them, or summarize them. Whatever option you choose, make sure that you use sources responsibly. *Words or ideas borrowed from other writers should not be distorted in any way, and credit should be given whenever appropriate.*

▲ Note: The documentation style of the Modern Language Association is used in the following examples of quotation, paraphrase, and summary. For additional information on documentation, see **34g**, **34i**, and **34j**.

(1) Plagiarism

You must acknowledge all material quoted, paraphrased, or summarized from any published or unpublished work. Failing to cite a source, deliberately or accidentally, is **plagiarism**— presenting as your own work the words or ideas of another. As the *MLA Handbook* (New York: MLA, 1988) states,

> The most blatant form of plagiarism is to repeat as your own someone else's sentences, more or less verbatim. . . .
>
> Other forms of plagiarism include repeating someone else's . . . apt phrase without appropriate acknowledgment, paraphrasing another person's argument as your own, and presenting another's line of thinking as though it were your own. (22–23)

After you have read a good deal about a given subject, you will be able to distinguish between common knowledge in that field and the distinctive ideas or interpretations of specific writers. When you use the ideas or information that these writers provide, be sure to cite your source.

Source (from *Agents of Opportunity* by Kenneth Shropshire, page 110)

> Even if affirmative steps are taken, collegiate athletics may never return to a time of raccoon coats, tailgate parties, and fight songs. But some action will remove the constant association of college sports with the scandalous headlines of the 1980's. Collegiate athletics must now be recognized as big, profit-making entertainment, and reforms must be made that recognize the changing nature of the enterprise.

NOT: Collegiate athletics must now be recognized as big, profit-making entertainment, and reforms must be made that recognize the changing nature of the enterprise.
[undocumented copying]

BUT: According to Kenneth Shropshire, who teaches Legal Studies at the University of Pennsylvania, "Collegiate athletics must now be recognized as big, profit-making entertainment, and reforms must be made that recognize the changing nature of the enterprise" (110).   [Quotation marks enclose copied words, and the number in parentheses refers the reader to the exact page in the source. In this case, the author is identified in the sentence that includes the quotation. An alternative is to provide the author's name within the parenthetical reference: (Shropshire 110).]

If you are in doubt about whether you need to cite a source, the best policy is to cite it.

▲ Caution: Plagiarism is a serious offense. Penalties can range from failing a paper to failing a course. In some cases, plagiarism can also lead to being expelled from school or fired from a job.

(2) Direct quotations

A quotation should contribute an idea to your paper. Select quotations only if (a) you want to retain the beauty or clarity of someone else's words or (b) you plan to discuss the implications of the words in question. Keep quotations as short as possible and make them an integral part of your text. (For examples of ways this can be done, see pages 443, 483, and 525.)

Quote *accurately*. Enclose every quoted passage in quotation marks. Any quotation of another person's words (except for well-known or proverbial passages) should be placed in quotation marks or, if longer than four lines, set off as an indented block (see **16a[4]**). Exact sources should be cited. If a source may be unfamiliar to your audience, identify the author to establish his or her authority in your first reference to this source:

> Don Davies, a British psychologist, argues that traditional methods of measuring test anxiety are "inadequate . . . except when used for research purposes with large groups of people" (53).

When you write from research, keep a few guidelines in mind: direct quotations must be accurate in all details. Pay close attention to form, punctuation, and spacing: see **16a**. Use ellipsis points appropriately to indicate omissions: see **17i**. But do not use ellipsis points before quotations that are clearly only parts of sentences. Use brackets (**17g**) to surround any word or phrase that you add within a quotation to clarify its meaning.

▲ Caution: Too many quotations in a paper can convey the impression that you have little to say for yourself.

(3) Paraphrase

A **paraphrase** is a restatement of a source in about the same number of words. Paraphrasing enables you to demonstrate that you have understood your reading; it also enables you to help your audience understand the results of your reading. Paraphrase when you can (a) clarify poor writing in your source or (b) restate difficult material more simply.

Your restatement of someone else's words should honor two imporant principles: your version should be almost entirely in your own words, and your words should accurately convey the content of the original passage. If you simply change a few words in a passage, you have not adequately restated it. As you compare the source below with the paraphrase that follows, notice differences in sentence structure as well as word choice.

Source (from *Agents of Opportunity* by Kenneth Shropshire, page 106)

> Athletes must be able to receive more income as students. The logical entities to provide these increased funds are, first, the member institutions and, if that is not financially feasible, then the NCAA. At a minimum the additional amount the student

athlete receives should be equal to the amount that brings the spending money available to the student athlete up to the university's average student. This amount may be enough to prevent substantial cheating.

Indequate paraphrase

```
Student athletes deserve more income.  They should
be paid by their schools or by the NCAA.  Pay should
be set at a level so that student athletes have at
least as much spending money as the average student
on campus.  Paying students this amount could
eliminate cheating (Shropshire 106).
```

Although this passage ends with a parenthetical reference to the original sources, the reference does not reveal the size of the debt. The author could be giving credit to Shropshire for the whole passage or only the last sentence—it is hard to tell. And when you compare this "paraphrase" to the original source, you will find that the author has followed the same structure. Although the wording has changed, the paraphrase in this case is so close to the original that it could be considered plagiarism.

Adequate paraphrase

```
Kenneth Shropshire has argued that corruption in
college sports could be reduced if college athletes
received stipends from the schools that they play
for or, if necessary, from the NCAA.  Athletes
should have at least as much spending money as their
fellow students do (106).
```

In this example, the page reference establishes where the paraphrase ends; the introductory "Kenneth Shropshire has argued" establishes where it begins. When you paraphrase, make sure that your audience will be able to tell whether you are paraphrasing a single sentence or more. As a general rule, begin paraphrases with a phrase that indicates that you are about to restate another writer's words.

▲ Caution: If you simply change a few words in a passage, you have not adequately restated it. You may be charged with plagiarism if the wording of your version follows the original too closely, even if you provide a page reference to the source you used. A page reference after an inadequate paraphrase would acknowledge the source of your idea but not the extent of your debt to another writer's language.

(4) Summary

A summary is a concise restatement (shorter than the original source). An essential skill for writing researched papers, summarizing enables writers to report the work of others without getting bogged down in unnecessary detail. Paraphrase when you want to restate a passage so that it is easier to understand or fits more smoothly into your paper; summarize whenever you can save space by condensing a passage (or, in some cases, an entire work).

Source (from *Maximizing Examination Performance* by Davies, page 27)

> Competition during study and practice sessions can be an incentive and a useful motivational technique provided it is used wisely and is closely related to the needs of individuals. Moderate competition between students provides interest and enjoyment, but it can be disastrous and destroy morale if too much importance is attached to the results. Motivation will also be weakened if an individual is either being continuously outclassed or is surpassing the other students with ease. Competition between low-skilled people tends to disrupt performance but for highly skilled people performance tends to be enhanced.

Summary

According to Don Davies, competition can hurt
students if the results are emphasized too much.
But moderate competition can help improve both the
motivation and performance of highly skilled
students who are evenly matched (27).

▲ Note: When you are summarizing, you may find it useful
to retain a key phrase from your source; but if you do so, put
quotation marks around the words in question.

■ **Exercise 4** Carefully read paragraphs 2 (page 310), 12 (page 314),
and 21 (page 319) in chapter **32**. First paraphrase one of these paragraphs; then write a one-sentence summary of the same paragraph.
Unless you are quoting directly, avoid using the same sentence patterns
as the source. To convey the source's ideas exactly, choose your words
carefully.

34f
Use the documentation style appropriate for the discipline.

Different disciplines usually employ different documentation
styles, so there is no single way to document or to prepare a
bibliography that can be used in every department of a college
or university. Use the style your instructor specifies. The manuals listed below discuss documentation form in detail. If you
are asked to use one of these manuals, look for it in the
reference collection of your library. Study it carefully and
make sure your notes and bibliography correspond exactly to
the examples it provides.

STYLE BOOKS AND MANUALS

American Chemical Society. *American Chemical Society Style
Guide and Handbook*. Washington: American Chemical Soc.,
1985.

American Institute of Physics. Publications Board. *Style Manual for Guidance in the Preparation of Papers.* 3rd ed. New York: American Inst. of Physics, 1978.

American Mathematical Society. *A Manual for Authors of Mathematical Papers.* 7th ed. Providence: American Mathematical Soc., 1980.

American Psychological Association. *Publication Manual of the American Psychological Association.* 3rd ed. Washington: American Psychological Assn., 1983.

Associated Press. *The Associated Press Stylebook and Libel Manual.* Reading: Addison, 1987.

The Chicago Manual of Style. 13th ed. Chicago: U of Chicago P, 1982.

Council of Biology Editors. Style Manual Committee. *CBE Style Manual: A Guide for Authors, Editors, and Publishers in the Biological Sciences.* 5th ed. Bethesda: Council of Biology Editors, 1983.

Gibaldi, Joseph, and Walter S. Achtert. *MLA Handbook for Writers of Research Papers.* 3rd ed. New York: Modern Language Assn., 1988.

Harvard Law Review. *A Uniform System of Citation.* 13th ed. Cambridge: Harvard Law Review, 1981.

Turabian, Kate L. *A Manual for Writers of Term Papers, Theses, and Dissertations.* 5th ed. Chicago: U of Chicago P, 1987.

United States Government Printing Office. *Style Manual.* Rev. ed. Washington: GPO, 1973.

If your instructor does not require a specific documentation style, follow the style set forth by the discipline of your paper. When you are unsure what type of documentation is appropriate, go to the periodical room of your library and model your documentation upon the style you find used in one of the journals in your field.

To provide you with further help, the rest of this chapter discusses the two documentation styles that are the most widely used in college writing: MLA style, which is appropriate for papers in English and often for other courses in the humanities (**34g–h**); and APA style, which is appropriate for papers in psychology and other courses in the social sciences (**34j–k**). Some disciplines prefer to use the footnote or endnote system of documentation, so samples of this style are provided in **34i**.

34g
Draft and revise a researched paper with MLA style documentation.

As you draft a researched paper, remember that it is *your* paper. Using the headings on your note cards (see page 409), arrange your notes in the order of your working plan or outline, and then use the notes as the basis of your paper. Make sure to write the paper in your own words and your own style. Integrate your source material—paraphrases, summaries, quotations—with your own statements rather than making the paper a patchwork of other people's comments.

(1) Parenthetical citations

Give proper credit by citing your sources. Traditionally, such citations took the form of notes numbered consecutively throughout the paper and placed either at the bottoms of the appropriate pages (footnotes) or all together at the end of the paper (endnotes). Although some disciplines still use a note system (see **34i**), the Modern Language Association (MLA) recommends placing citations directly in the text, in parentheses. These parenthetical citations refer the reader to a list of works cited at the end of the paper. The advantage of this sytem is that it is easy for both writers and readers to use. The MLA suggests reserving the numbered note system for cases in which the writer needs to make supplementary or explanatory comments about given references. (The numbers are inserted in the appropriate places in the text, and the notes are gathered at the end of the paper [see page 461].)

The basic elements of the parenthetical citation are the author's last name and the page number of the material used in the source. However, it is not necessary to repeat any information that is already clearly provided. In other words, omit the author's name from the parenthetical citation if you have identified it in the text of the paper, shortly before the material being cited. As you study the following examples, observe that common sense determines the information that must be included in a parenthetical citation and that this system is easy to use. (The first example is taken from the researched paper on pages 443–63 so you can see how a citation refers readers to a source listed alphabetically in the list of works cited at the end of the paper.) See also the details of punctuation and mechanics on pages 425–27.

A work by one author

By emphasizing the distinction between college sports and professional sports, the NCAA has helped to create "a perversion of the entire educational process and system" (Lawrence 144).

In this citation, the author's name is included within the parentheses because it is not mentioned in the text. Since there is only one work by Lawrence in the list of works cited (on page 463), there is no need to use a title in the parentheses. However, a page number is included because the reference is to a specific passage. Notice how the citation changes if the text includes more information about the source:

According to Paul Lawrence, the NCAA has helped to create "a perversion of the entire educational process and system" (144).

A work by two or three authors

```
During the 1960s, economic failure was widely blamed
for social alienation and political extremism
(Aiken, Ferman, and Sheppard 114—16).
```

Provide the last name of each author, punctuating as you would for items in a series. Commas are not necessary in a citation involving only two authors, for example: (Brownlee and Linnon 52). (See page 463 for the corresponding bibliographic entry for this example.)

A work by more than three authors

If you are citing a source by more than three authors, supply the name of the first author and follow the name with "et al." (the Latin abbreviation for "et alii," meaning "and others"). Do not italicize or underline the Latin phrase.

```
In one important study, women graduates complained
more frequently about "excessive control than about
lack of structure" (Belenky et al. 205).
```

A multivolume work

When you cite material from a multivolume work, include the volume number (followed by a colon and a space) before the page number.

```
As Katherine Raine has argued, "true poetry begins
where human personality ends" (2: 247).
```

If your list of works cited includes only one volume of a multivolume work, then you do not need to include the volume number within the parenthetical citation.

More than one work by the same author

When your list of works cited includes more than one work by the same author, your parenthetical citations should include a shortened title revealing which of the author's works is being cited in a particular instance. Separate with a comma the author's name from the shortened title when both are provided in parentheses.

```
According to John Kenneth Galbraith, 17% of the
American work force was unemployed as late as 1939
(Uncertainty 221).  Many historians have argued that
the Depression was ended by the Second World War.
But after the war, "it would be a deliberate purpose
of government to . . . ensure full employment"
(Galbraith, Economics 251).
```

This passage cites two different books by John Kenneth Galbraith, *The Age of Uncertainty* and *Economics in Perspective*. The author's name is not necessary in the first citation since it is mentioned in the text; it is included in the second citation because Galbraith's name is not mentioned in this sentence or the preceding sentence.

You can often avoid cumbersome references by including information in the text that might otherwise have to appear parenthetically:

```
In Economics in Perspective, John Kenneth Galbraith
argues that government interest in ensuring full
employment began after the Second World War (251).
```

Works by different authors with the same last name

Occasionally your list of works cited will contain sources by two authors with the same last name—for example, K. Patricia Cross and Wilbur Cross. In such cases, you must use the first name as well as the last.

Educator Wilbur Cross has suggested that the
situation of the mature student has excited
considerable interest in academic circles (8-9).
Other commentators explore the ways that academe can
serve these students (K. Patricia Cross 32, 41).

▲ **Note:** In these references to more than one page, "8–9"
identifies continuous pages and "32, 41" indicates that the
reference is to two separate pages. (See page 425.)

An indirect source

Although you should try to consult original sources whenever
possible, you may want to include a quotation that one of
your sources quoted from a work you have not read. In this
situation, use the following form:

The critic Susan Hardy Aikens has argued on behalf
of what she calls "canonical multiplicity" (qtd. in
Mayers 677).

A reader turning to the list of works cited should find a
bibliographic entry for Mayers (which was the source consulted) but not for Aikens (because the quotation was obtained secondhand).

Poetry, drama, and the Bible

When you refer to poetry, drama, and the Bible, you must
often give numbers of lines, acts, and scenes, or of chapters
and verses, rather than page numbers. This practice enables
a reader to consult an edition other than the one you are
using. Nonetheless, your list of works cited should still identify
your edition.

Act, scene, and line numbers (all Arabic) are separated by periods with no space before or after them. MLA suggests that biblical chapters and verses be treated similarly, although some writers prefer to use colons instead of periods in scriptural references. In all cases, the progression is from larger to smaller units.

The following example illustrates a typical citation of lines of poetry.

```
Emily Dickinson concludes "I'm Nobody! Who Are You?"
with a characteristically bittersweet stanza:
          How dreary to be somebody!
          How public, like a frog
          To tell your name the livelong June
          To an admiring bog! (5-8)
```

The following citation shows that Hamlet's "To be, or not to be" soliloquy appears in act 3, scene 1, lines 56–89 of *Hamlet*.

```
In Hamlet Shakespeare presents the most famous
soliloquy in the history of the theater: "To be, or
not to be . . ." (3.1.56-89).
```

For additional examples, see chapter **35**. The following reference to the Bible indicates that the account of creation in Genesis extends from chapter 1, verse 1, through chapter 2, verse 22.

```
The Old Testament creation story (Gen. 1.1-2.22),
told with remarkable economy, culminates in the
arrival of Eve.
```

▲ **Note:** Names of books of the Bible are neither italicized (underlined) nor enclosed in quotation marks, and abbreviation is desirable.

PUNCTUATION AND MECHANICS

Punctuation and numbers Commas separate the authors' names from the titles (Galbraith, *Economics*) and indicate interruptions in a sequence of pages or lines (44, 47). Hyphens indicate continuous sequences of pages (44–47) and lines (1–4). Colons separate volume and page numbers (Raine 2: 247); a space follows the colon. Periods separate acts, scenes, and lines in drama (3.1.56–89). Periods (or colons) distinguish chapters from verses in biblical citations (Gen. 1.1 or Gen. 1:1)—see **17d**.

Ellipsis points (**17i**) indicate omissions within a quotation: "They lived in an age of increasing complexity and great hope; we in an age of . . . growing despair" (Krutch 2). Brackets (**17g**) indicate interpolations within quotations: "The publication of this novel [*Beloved*] establishes Morrison as one of the most important writers of our time" (Boyle 17).

When a quotation ends with a question mark (**17b**), include the question mark before the closing quotation mark; then add a period after the parenthetical citation: Paulo Freire asks, "How can the oppressed, as divided, unauthentic beings, participate in developing the pedagogy of their liberation?" (33).

The MLA favors Arabic numbers throughout, except when citing pages that are identified by Roman numerals within the source itself (such as the frontmatter of a book: page vi).

Placement of citations Wherever possible, citations should appear just before punctuation in the text of the paper.

Wilbur Cross speaks of adult learners who "range in age from the mid-twenties to the upper sixties, and vary in background from nurses, teachers, business people and government employees to truck drivers, police officers and 'just ordinary people'" (116), whereas K. Patricia Cross views adult learners as a

```
class of students disproportionately young, white,
and affluent (45).
```

Wilbur Cross's citation falls just before a comma; K. Patricia Cross's just before a period. However, in a sentence such as the following, the citations should follow the authors' names to keep the references separate.

```
Wilbur Cross (116) and K. Patricia Cross (45) speak
of different kinds of adult learners.
```

Lengthy quotations When a quotation is more than four lines long, set it off from the text by indenting ten spaces from the left margin (**16a[4]**). The citation in this case follows the final punctuation, to avoid making it seem part of the quotation:

```
In a study of black athletes, Richard E. Lapchick
concludes:

          Colleges and universities are supposed to
          be, along with parents and religious
          organizations, the guardians of our
          nation's moral values.  When
          discrimination is part of the hiring
          system, when exploitation is part of the
          recruiting process, when athletes do not
          get an education, our nation's
          institutions of higher education have
          forfeited that guardianship.  (69)
```

▲ **Note:** When quoting more than one paragraph, indent by three additional spaces the first line of each paragraph. Do not indent if you are quoting only one paragraph (or if the first sentence quoted is not the first sentence in a paragraph).

(2) List of works cited

The list of works cited is the reference list for MLA papers. (Other documentation styles differ from MLA in how they arrange and name their reference lists—see, for example, **34f** and **34j**.)

When you are ready to make the final draft of your paper, eliminate from your working bibliography the cards for the works that you have not cited. Arrange the remaining bibliography cards in alphabetical order by the authors' last names. You are now ready to prepare the list of works cited that will conclude your paper. As you make your final revision, check your citations against this list to ensure that they are complete and correct.

Arrange the list of works cited alphabetically by author. If a source has more than one author, alphabetize by the first author's last name. Type the first line of each entry flush with the left margin; indent subsequent lines five spaces. Double-space throughout.

As you study the following MLA style entries, which cover most of the types of sources you are likely to list, observe both the arrangement of information and the punctuation. See also pages 438–40 for a list of abbreviations that are used in works cited, notes, and tables.

BOOKS

Most book entries consist of only three units, which are separated by periods:

1. *Author.* Give the last name first, followed by a comma and the author's first name.

2. *Title.* Italicize (underline) the title of the book, and capitalize all major words (see **9c**). Always include the book's subtitle. Make the underlining continuous, not separate under each word.

3. *Publication data.* Provide the city of publication, the brief name of the publisher, and the latest copyright date shown on the copyright page. Type a colon after the city and a comma after the publisher. To shorten the name of the publisher, use the principal name: Alfred A. Knopf becomes Knopf; Harcourt Brace becomes Harcourt; Harvard University Press becomes Harvard UP; University of Michigan Press becomes U of Michigan P.

One author

Reynolds, David. <u>Beneath the American Renaissance:
   The Subversive Imagination in the Age of
   Emerson and Melville</u>. New York: Knopf, 1988.

Note that a colon separates the main title from the subtitle.

More than one work by the same author

Cisneros, Sandra. <u>The House on Mango Street</u>.
      Houston: Arte Publica, 1983.
---. <u>Woman Hollering Creek</u>. New York, Random, 1991.

If you use more than one work by the same author, alphabetize the works by the first *major* word in each title. Give the author's name with the first title, but substitute three hyphens for the name in subsequent entries.

Two authors

Barlett, Donald L., and James B. Steele.
    Forevermore: Nuclear Waste in America. New
    York: Norton, 1985.

Invert only the first author's name. Make sure to follow the first author's name with a comma.

Three authors

Aiken, Michael, Lewis A. Ferman, and Harold L.
    Sheppard. Economic Failure, Alienation, and
    Extremism. Ann Arbor: U of Michigan P, 1968.

Note that abbreviations (without periods) are used for "university" and "press" for books published by universities.

More than three authors

Quirk, Randolph, et al. A Comprehensive Grammar of
    the English Language. London: Longman, 1985.
or
Belenky, Mary Field, Blythe McVicker Clinchy, Nancy
    Rule Goldberger, and Jill Mattuck Tarule.
    Women's Ways of Knowing: The Development of
    Self, Voice, and Mind. New York: Basic, 1986.

Corporate author

Institute of Medicine. Confronting AIDS: Directions
    for Public Health, Health Care, and Research.
    Washington: National Academy P, 1986.

Anonymous author

Guide to the Laboratory Diagnosis of Trachoma.
    Geneva: World Health, 1975.

Begin the entry with the title. Do not use "Anonymous" or "Anon."

Editor as author

Zigler, Edward F., and Meryl Frank, eds. The
    Parental Leave Crisis. New Haven: Yale UP,
    1988.

Edition after the first

Strike, Kenneth A., and James F. Soltis. The Ethics
    of Teaching. 2nd ed. New York: Teacher's
    College P, 1992.

Work from an anthology

Hollander, John. "Wordsworth and the Music of
    Sound." New Perspectives on Coleridge and
    Wordsworth. Ed. Geoffrey H. Hartman. New
    York: Columbia UP, 1972. 41-84.

Use this form for an article or essay that was first published in an anthology; use it also for a story, poem, or play reprinted in an anthology. For an article or essay that was published elsewhere before being included in an anthology, use the following form:

```
Welty, Eudora. "The Eye of the Story." Yale Review
     55 (1966): 265-74. Rpt. in Katherine Anne
     Porter: A Collection of Critical Essays. Ed.
     Robert Penn Warren. Englewood Cliffs:
     Prentice, 1979. 72-80.
```

Report where the essay first appeared and then show where you read it. Use the abbreviation "Rpt." for "reprinted."

▲ Note: Both forms require you to cite the pages where the material can be found. In the second example it is necessary to cite both the pages of the original publication and the pages of the anthologized version.

Translation

```
Irani, Manuchehr. King of the Benighted. Trans.
     Abbas Milani. Washington: Mage, 1990.
```

Reprint

```
Massie, Robert K. Peter the Great: His Life and
     World. 1980. New York: Ballantine, 1986.
```

The original hardcover edition was published six years earlier than this paperback version. Use this form for books that have been reissued in a new format. (For reprinted articles, see "Work from an anthology.")

A multivolume work

```
Odell, George C. D. Annals of the New York Stage.
     15 vols. New York: Columbia UP, 1927-49.
```

This multivolume work was published over a period of years.

▲ Note: Cite the total number of volumes in a work when you have used more than one volume. If you use only one volume, include that volume number (preceded by the abbreviation *Vol.*) after the title and include the number of volumes in the complete work at the end of the entry:

```
Unger, Irwin. These United States: The Questions of
     Our Past. 5th ed. Vol. 2. Englewood Cliffs:
     Prentice, 1992. 2 vols.
```

Encyclopedias and almanacs

```
Hopkinson, Ralph G. "Electric Lighting."
     Encyclopedia Americana. 1985 ed.
Hile, Kenneth S. "Rudolfo Anaya." Contemporary
     Authors. New Revised Series, 1991.
```

Full publication information is not necessary for a well-known reference work organized alphabetically. For sources that are more unusual, you should reveal more about the source:

```
Dreyer, Edward L. "Inner Mongolia." Encyclopedia of
     Asian History. Ed. Ainslee T. Embree.
     4 vols. New York: Scribner's, 1988.
```

When an author's name is indicated only by initials, check the table of contents for a list of contributors. When an article is anonymous, begin your entry with the article title and alphabetize according to the first important word in the title.

A book in a series

Reilley, Edward J. <u>Approaches to Teaching</u> Gulliver's
      Travels. Approaches to Teaching World
      Literature 18. New York: MLA, 1988.

When citing a book that is part of a series, provide the name
of the series and the number designating the work's place in
the series.

▲ **Note:** When citing a book title that contains another book
title within it—that is, a title that would normally be underlined—do not underline the internal title. If the title within
the title would normally appear within quotation marks, retain
the quotation marks and underline the complete title.

An introduction, foreword, or afterword

Grumbach, Doris. Foreword. <u>My Antonia</u>. By Willa
      Cather. Boston: Houghton, 1988. vii-xxix.

Pamphlets and bulletins

<u>Safety Data Sheet: Kitchen Machines</u>. Pamphlet 690.
      Chicago: Natl. Restaurant Assn., 1970.

Titles of pamphlets are italicized (underlined).

Government publication

United States. Dept. of Transportation. <u>National
      Transportation Statistics</u>. Washington: GPO,
      1990.

When citing a government publication, identify the government (e.g., "United States," "Minnesota," "Great Britain," "United Nations") followed by the agency that issued the work. Underline the title of a book or pamphlet. Federal publications are usually printed by the Government Printing Office (GPO), but be alert for exceptions.

ARTICLES

The documentation format for articles differs slightly from that for books. The three units are the same, and they are still separated by periods, but note the differences in treatment for titles and publication information.

1. *Author.* Give the last name first, followed by a comma and the author's first name.
2. *Article title.* Type the article title in regular (Roman) face, and put it in quotation marks. Capitalize all major words in the title (see **9c**). Place the period within the final quotation marks.
3. *Publication data.* The exact kind of information differs according to type of periodical, but all references provide the periodical title, the date of publication, and the page numbers on which the article appeared. Continuously underline (italicize) the periodical title, and capitalize all major words in the title (see **9c**). Note that no punctuation follows the periodical title and that a colon introduces the inclusive page numbers. If the periodical provides both a volume number and a date, put the date in parentheses.

Weekly magazine or newspaper

Stresser, Stan. "Report from Cambodia." <u>The New Yorker</u> 18 May 1992: 43-75.

```
Wyatt, Edward A. "The Missing Link." Barrons 30
     Mar. 1992: 40-41.
```

▲ **Note:** MLA style abbreviates the names of months (except May, June, and July). Volume numbers are unnecessary because specific dates are given. (To compare with APA style, see page 472).

Daily newspaper

```
Ibata, David. "Information Highway to the Future."
     Chicago Tribune 17 Nov. 1992, final ed., sec.
     1: 8.
```

When it is not part of the newspaper's name, the city's name should be given in brackets after the title: *Star Tribune* [Minneapolis]. If a specific edition is not named on the masthead, put a colon after the date and then provide the page reference. Specify the section by inserting the section number immediately before the page number. If the section is lettered, simply include the section letter next to the page number as it appears in the newspaper: A7 or 7A.

Editorial

```
Lewis, Anthony. "Black and White." Editorial. New
     York Times 18 June 1992, natl. ed., A19.
```

Begin the citation with the title if the editorial is not signed.

Monthly magazine   A *journal* is a scholarly publication written for a specific profession, whereas a *magazine* is written for the general public.

```
Barlow, John Perry. "Is There a There in
    Cyberspace?" Utne Reader March-April, 1995: 53-
    56.
```

▲ **Note:** Magazine articles are often interrupted by other articles. If the first part appears on pages 45–47 and the last on pages 213–221, give only the first page number followed by a plus sign: 45+.

Journal: Continuous pagination

```
Himmelfarb, Gertrude. "Manners into Morals: What
    the Victorians Knew." American Scholar 57
    (1988): 223-32.
```

Citing a specific issue (e.g., Fall 1988) is not necessary when a journal's pages are numbered continuously throughout the year.

Journal: Separate pagination

```
Leroux, Neil. "Frederick Douglass and the Attention
    Shift." Rhetoric Society Quarterly 21.2 (1991):
    36-46.
```

When an issue is paged separately (each issue begins with page 1), put a period after the volume number and add the issue number.

NONPRINT SOURCES
Motion picture

```
The Crying Game. Dir. Neil Jordan.  Miramax, 1992.
```

Radio or television program

```
At Your Service. Writ. and prod. Jim White. KMOX,
    St. Louis. 24 May 1985.
```

Leavitt, David. <u>The Lost Language of Cranes</u>. Prod.
     Ruth Caleb. Dir. Nigel Finch. Great
     Performances. PBS, WNET, New York. 24 June
     1992.

Play

<u>A Streetcar Named Desire</u>. By Tennessee Williams.
     Dir. Gregory Mosher. Barrymore Theater, New
     York. 9 Aug. 1992.

Recording

Clapton, Eric. <u>Journeyman</u>. Compact Disc. Reprise,
     813581-2, 1989.

Specify the type of recording immediately after the title. Include the manufacturer, the catalog number, and the date of issue.

Electronic Media

Schipper, William. "Quirk and Wrenn Grammar." <u>AnSax-
     L</u>. (Feb. 22, 1995): n. pag. <u>Online</u>. Available;
     Gopher (ANSAXDAT cwis.ucs.mun.ca) or WWW
     (http://www.georgetown.edu/labyrinth)).
<u>THE CIA World Factbook</u>. CD-ROM. 1992.

Provide author and title of document, title of journal (conference, database, CD-Rom) underlined, number of volume (issue, file), publication date (in parentheses), number of pages (paragraphs, or n. pag.) publication medium, name of network, data of access.

<u>Norton Utilities</u>. Vers. 6.01. Computer software.
     Symantec, 1991. PC-DOS 2.0 or higher, 512k,
     disk.

Provide title, version number, descriptive label, distributor, and copyright date. Add other pertinent information at the end of the entry, including the operating system and units of memory necessary for running the program. When a program is attributed to an author, insert the author's name (last name first) immediately before the title.

Lecture

```
Piorkowski, Joan. Class lecture. English 364.
     University of St. Thomas, St. Paul, MN.
     16 Mar. 1993.
```

Provide a descriptive label for an untitled lecture, use the title if available, and give the location and date.

Interview

```
Dorgan, Ruth. Personal interview. 14 Aug. 1993.
```

For samples of citations of other nonprint sources—such as games, filmstrips, microscope slides, and transparencies—consult Eugene B. Fleischer's *A Style Manual for Citing Microform and Nonprint Media* (Chicago: American Library Association, 1978).

COMMON ABBREVIATIONS

Below is a list of abbreviations commonly used in documenting research papers.

abr.	abridged, abridgment
Acad.	Academy
anon.	anonymous
app.	appendix
Apr.	April
Assn.	Association
Aug.	August
biog.	biography, biographer, biographical
bk., bks.	book, books
bull.	bulletin

c.	*circa,* "about" (for example, "c. 1960")
cf.	compare
ch., chs.	chapter, chapters
col., cols.	column, columns
Coll.	College
comp.	compiled by, compiler
Cong. Rec.	*Congressional Record*
cont.	contents OR continued
DAB	*Dictionary of American Biography*
Dec.	December
dept.	department
dir.	directed by, director
diss.	dissertation
div.	division
DNB	*Dictionary of National Biography*
ed., eds.	edition(s) OR editor(s)
enl.	enlarged (as in "rev. and enl. ed.")
et al.	et alii, ("and others")
Feb.	February
fig.	figure
fwd.	foreword, foreword by
gen. ed.	general editor
govt.	government
GPO	Government Printing Office
HR	House of Representatives
illus.	illustrated by, illustrator, illustration
inc.	incorporated OR including
Inst.	Institute, Institution
intl.	international
introd.	[author of] introduction, introduced by
Jan.	January
jour.	journal
l., ll.	line, lines (omitted before line numbers unless reference would be unclear)
mag.	magazine
Mar.	March
ms., mss.	manuscript, manuscripts
n, nn	note, notes (used immediately after page number: 6n3)
natl.	national

n.d.	no date [of publication]
no., nos.	number [of issue], numbers
Nov.	November
n.p.	no place [of publication] OR no publisher
n. pag.	no pagination
Oct.	October
P	Press (used in documentation; see "UP")
p., pp.	page, pages (omitted before page numbers unless reference would be unclear)
pref.	preface, preface by
pseud.	pseudonym
pt., pts.	part, parts
rept.	reported by, report
rev.	revision, revised, revised by OR review, reviewed by
rpt.	reprinted, reprint
sec., secs.	section, sections
Sept.	September
ser.	series
sic	thus, so
Soc.	Society
supp.	supplement
trans.	translated by, translator, translation
U	University (used in documentation; see "UP")
UP	University Press (used in documentation; Wesleyan UP)
vol., vols.	volume, volumes (omitted before volume numbers unless reference would be unclear)

(3) Final revising, editing, and proofreading

After writing and carefully documenting the first draft of your paper, make needed revisions. Check your outline to make sure the organization is logical and unified (**34d**). Revise each paragraph to make its purpose clear, and edit each sentence to support its paragraph. Refer to **33g** as needed, particularly the Revising, Editing, and Proofreading Checklists. As you revise, make sure you continue to use your sources carefully

and responsibly (**34e**). If you have questions about final manuscript form, refer to chapter **8** and to the sample research
papers in **34h** and **34k**.

Some instructors ask their students to submit outlines,
notes, and drafts along with the final paper. Other instructors
require a title page and a final outline along with the text of
the paper. A title page usually gives the title of the paper,
the author, the name of the course and its section number,
the instructor's name, and the date—all attractively centered
on the page. The MLA recommends using no title page and
giving the identification on the first page before the title of
the paper: see page 443.

When submitted with the text of a research paper, the final
outline serves as a table of contents. In this case, a title page
is advisable. (For a sample title page that can be modified for
an MLA style paper, see page 475 and the comment on
page 474.)

34h

Sample MLA research paper

A sample researched paper follows that illustrates an MLA
style paper. The left-hand pages contain note cards, excerpts
from earlier drafts, and comments on content and form. (For
an MLA style researched paper about literature, see pages
520–27.)

■ **Exercise 5**   Read the following paper and create an outline for it
(review **33e** if necessary). Your instructor will indicate whether you
should create a sentence outline or a topic outline.

■ **Exercise 6**   Write a 200-word response to the following questions
about the MLA paper: (a) Does the paper have a clear thesis? (b) Where
is it first introduced? (c) How well is the paper organized? (d) Could it
be organized in another way? (e) How well has the source material been
included? (f) How well does the author include ideas of his own?

COMMENTS

1. The identification, double-spaced, begins one inch from the top of the page and flush with the left margin. A double-spaced line precedes the centered title of the paper. A margin of one inch is provided at the left, right, and bottom.

2. Double-space between the title and the first line of the text. (A title consisting of two or more lines is double-spaced, and each line is centered.)

3. All pages (including the first page) are numbered with Arabic numerals in the upper right-hand corner, one-half inch from the top. The page number is preceded by the author's last name. Notice that no period follows the page numbers.

4. The quotation in paragraph 1 comes from a source by two authors, but the authors in question did not write these words. The abbreviation "qtd. in" indicates that Brownlee and Linnon used the quotation from Frederick Jackson Turner and that Beale obtained the quotation from them rather than directly from Turner. (See page 423.)

5. To make sure that readers understand what "NCAA" stands for, Beale writes out the organization's name in full in this first reference to it. He then provides the abbreviation he will use when making subsequent references to this organization. (See page 116.)

6. The first citation in paragraph 2 includes a shortened version of the title because the works cited list includes more than one work by this author. (See page 463.)

Calvin Beale

English 200, Section 3

Professor Larson

May 10, 1993

       The Exploitation of College Athletes

     Speaking at the University of Wisconsin in 1906, the historian Frederick Jackson Turner declared that football "has become a business, carried on too often by professionals, bringing in vast gate receipts, demoralizing student ethics and confusing the ideals of sport, manliness and decency" (qtd. in Brownlee and Linnon 52). Times have not changed: college sports are still in trouble. Although the National Collegiate Athletic Association (NCAA) was formed to resolve the crisis in college football, many people now believe that the NCAA has failed in its mission. As a football player who is working hard to get a college education, I want to draw attention to a serious problem: the exploitation of college athletes. If there is a problem in college football today, the problem should not be blamed on players but upon the system that makes use of us.

     The first contact many athletes have with the college sports system is the coach who visits them in high school, urging them to attend his or her school. Recruitment can be honest and straightforward, including discussion of "graduation rates that are sport, race, and gender specific" (Lapchick, "Future" 32), but it too often involves

COMMENTS

1. The long citation from Sperber in paragraph 2 is set off as a block because it is more than four typed lines. Note that the period comes *before* the parenthetical reference in indented quotations although in text quotations it is placed after the parenthetical reference. (See page 426.)

2. Because Beale wants to support his claim that "at some schools the situation is much worse" but does not want to give disproportionate attention to this point within the paper itself, he adds a note providing additional information. (See page 461.) Although the MLA favors parenthetical documentation to reveal sources, it recommends the use of footnotes or endnotes when authors have supplementary material that cannot be incorporated directly in the text of the paper but that is nevertheless too useful to omit altogether.

3. Study the following note card, and consider why Beale decided the Barbash citation he used was more appropriate than this Brownlee and Linnon citation he could have chosen.

<u>Playing in the Pros</u>

"But for every athlete who makes it to the big time there, are hundreds more who neglect their studies in the mistaken belief that they too can cash in.... In reality, the road to the pros, where salaries in the NFL average $256,000 and in the NBA $650,000 is long and narrow. More than 17,600 young men play Division I-A basketball and football, and each year only 150 of them will reach the big leagues; even fewer will last more than a year or so.

(Brownlee and Linnon 52)

Beale 2

unrealistic promises that exploit the dreams of high
school athletes. According to one successful
basketball coach,

> Every kid I recruited for college felt
> that he had an opportunity to play in the
> NBA (National Basketball Association), and
> I liked them to have those expectations.
> So they give themselves--their trust--to
> you from day one, hoping to reach that
> goal. (qtd. in Sperber K3)

Unfortunately, that trust is naive. The odds   3
against playing pro ball are as much as 400-1 for
college athletes (Barbash 40). That means that only
one in four hundred college football players will
make it to the National Football League (NFL). And
what happens to the others? Some may go on to
successful careers in other fields, but many never
graduate. According to NCAA statistics, only four
out of ten football players on athletic scholarships
actually graduate from college (Barbash 40). And at
some schools the situation is much worse.[1]

The number of athletes who fail to graduate   4
from college should surprise no one. Here in
Division 1-A, football players are expected to spend
up to sixty hours a week on the game during the
season. That doesn't leave much time left for
studying, especially when you come back to the dorm
exhausted and often in pain. Ironically, work-study
students are allowed to spend a maximum of twenty
hours per week on their jobs because the government
believes that more than twenty hours cuts into the

COMMENTS

1. Paragraph 5 begins with a concession recognizing that some college athletes need extra help. But having made this concession, Beale effectively moves his own argument forward by pointing out that the same can be said for many other students.

2. In paragraph 5, Beale defends the intelligence of athletes by drawing upon personal observations of his teammates. Writers frequently cite personal experience or observation to support their views. The risk, in this case, is that a reader might ask, "How credible is your observation? How many people do you know?"

Beale 3

time necessary for being a full-time student. So who
made the exception for football players? Isn't
football a kind of work-study? If I don't play
football, I lose my athletic scholarship; and if I
lose my scholarship, I cannot afford to stay in
school. Football, in my case, is the work that pays
for my study. Allowing athletes to work three times
as many hours a week as work-study students seems
like a double standard. If college administrators
are genuinely concerned about the quality of
education that athletes receive, they should impose
stricter limits on the number of hours that can be
devoted to practice. Otherwise, coaches will work
players overtime. Their job is to produce winning
teams, and it is natural for them to believe that
practice makes perfect. But who is protecting
student athletes from hyperactive coaches?

    Although it is true that some athletes are   5
unprepared for college, many non-athletes are also
unprepared. But regular students can devote extra
hours to studying and consulting professors, whereas
student athletes have much less control over their
own schedules. The stereotype of the dumb jock comes
from seeing athletes fail in the classroom.
Athletes are not dumb; my teammates include some of
the smartest people I know. But many are
overcommitted to playing the sport for which they
were recruited. In a sense, athletes end up getting
blamed for doing what they were hired to do.

    Ironically, many students are convinced that   6
athletes get all sorts of special deals. The truth

COMMENTS

1. Paragraphs 7–8 incorporate personal experience and observations directly related to the topic, demonstrating that the author has found his reading to be personally relevant and not simply an academic exercise. Although writers are seldom obliged to incorporate personal experience (and are, at times, prohibited from doing so), it is always important to make what you read your own by considering how it affects you. When doing so, however, remember that writers have an obligation to think clearly and not allow experience to blind them to new information.

2. In paragraph 8, Beale twice cites an article by Richard E. Lapchick. He identifies Lapchick because his readers might not recognize this name and identification enhances the credibility of the source. Because the list of works cited includes two works by Lapchick, both parenthetical references include a shortened version of the title in question. The first reference does not include the author's name because the name is already revealed in the text of the paper. The second reference includes the author's name because it does not follow immediately after the first reference.

is that athletes are frequently getting a raw deal
rather than a special deal. The athletic department
is allowed to impose demands that prevent players
from giving adequate time to their studies; then
fellow students either look down on us for flunking,
or they resent us for succeeding--believing that we
managed to get a good grade as the result of
favoritism. Athletes who genuinely want to learn
need to overcome what amounts to a type of
prejudice. If athletes are doing too well to be
considered "dumb jocks," they can find themselves
labeled "the jocks who are getting special
privileges."

    Professors may also be prejudiced against 7
athletes. When I was a freshman, I wrote a ten-page
paper on The Great Gatsby. It was returned to me a
week later with only one comment: "Please come see
me in my office." The point of the conference turned
out to be getting me to prove that I had written the
paper. It was a good paper, and my teacher found it
hard to believe that it was written by someone on
the football team.

    The prejudice, in this case, may have more than 8
one source. My teacher was white and may have been
especially suspicious that a black athlete had
written an "A" paper. Racism is a serious problem on
college campuses, and black athletes are often
singled out for particular abuse. The common
assumption seems to be that students who are both
black and athletic have been admitted to play sports

COMMENTS

1. Paragraph 9 includes paraphrases of material by Myers and Sperber. Study the note cards reprinted below, and evaluate the extent to which the paraphrasing accurately reflects the original sources.

Proposals for Reform

"Even if the money to pay college athletes could be found, though, a larger question must be answered—namely, why should a system of professional athletics be affiliated with universities at all? For the truth is that the requirements of athletics and academics operate at cross-purposes, and the attempt to play both games at once serves only to reduce the level of performance of each....

And this is why it is to be marveled at that universities continue to have anything to do with sports."

(Myers 50-51)

Alumni Support

"Concomitant with other myths concerning alumni support is the following one: schools that dare to drop or de-emphasize a sports team will be hit by the wrath—emotional and financial—of their alumni. Only anecdotal evidence exists to refute this assertion, but it is important nonetheless. According to the *Chronicle of Higher Education*, 'Donations to Tulane University rose by $5 million in 1986, the year after the institution dropped basketball; annual giving at Wichita State University nearly doubled the year after officials suspended its debt-ridden football program.'"

(Sperber kg)

and don't care about their studies. This prejudice
may be reinforced by the number of black athletes
who have academic difficulties, but it can also be
responsible for those difficulties in the first
place. According to Richard Lapchick, director of
the Center for the Study of Sport in Society at
Northeastern University, 95 percent of college teams
are coached by whites ("Race" 64). These coaches may
encourage black athletes to take undemanding
courses, or they may simply ignore what is happening
in the classroom as long as their athletes remain
eligible for play. A 1989 NCAA study reported that
"only 31% of black athletes felt their coaches
encouraged them academically" (Lapchick, "Race" 66).

Problems such as these, together with widely   9
publicized incidents in which college athletes get
in trouble with the law,[2] have led some critics to
call for ending collegiate athletics (Myers 50-51).
Such critics also cite evidence that ending sports
can benefit schools. For example, as Sperber notes,
when Tulane University dropped basketball, alumni
donations increased by $5 million the following
year, and when Wichita State University dropped
football, donations almost doubled the following
year (K9). It is clear that college sports need to
be reformed or they will wind up being eliminated.

That reform must come from the NCAA. Nearly a   10
thousand institutions belong to this association,
which sponsors national championships in 21 sports

COMMENTS

1. Paragraph 10 includes a reference to an anonymous source—in this case, an article from an encyclopedia. When citing an anonymous source, use a shortened version of the title. This particular example does not include a page reference because there is no page reference in the corresponding bibliographical entry on page 463, in keeping with the MLA guideline defined on page 432.

2. Paragraph 11 includes a parenthetical reference to multiple sources. Note that the semicolon separates one source from another and that the sources are listed alphabetically.

3. Consider the reasoning in the last sentence of paragraph 11. Does it reflect logical thinking (**31**)?

4. Paragraphs 12 and 13 each begin with recognizing the views of opponents and then move on to refuting them. This strategy, essential to effective argumentation, demonstrates that Beale has considered his topic from more than one side. See pages 294–96.

("National Collegiate"). I believe that the NCAA must redefine what it means to be a student athlete and must give greater protection to the students that college sports cannot exist without.

The single step that would do the most to end   11
the exploitation of student athletes would be to pay us for our work. Under current NCAA guidelines, athletes cannot be paid for playing sports, and they cannot earn money from other jobs. As a result, corruption is widespread. Many athletes are receiving payment "under the table," and this increases the contempt of critics who think college sports are out of control. If schools had to pay athletes for the hours we devote to our sports, illegal payments would decrease, and athletes would be treated more fairly (Barbash 41; Lawrence 144; Shropshire 71).

Opponents of this proposal claim that schools   12
cannot afford to pay athletes. According to one recent study, less than twenty athletic programs make a consistent profit, and only another twenty to thirty break even in any given year. Most lose money, often a lot of money (Sperber K7). Critics also emphasize that "big-time football programs not only do not earn money for their schools, they routinely siphon off funds that might otherwise go to academic activities" (Goodman 17). But the argument that schools cannot afford to pay athletes reminds me of those that once justified slavery as an economic necessity. Injustice cannot be

COMMENTS

1. The reference to 1906 links paragraph 13 to paragraph 1, helping to make the paper unified and coherent.

2. Study this excerpt from an earlier draft of Beale's paper. Evaluate the changes that he made to paragraphs 12 and 13.

Opponents of this proposal argue that schools can't afford to pay athletes. Kenneth Sperber, a critic of current practices in college sports, says athletic programs already lose money:

> If profit is defined according to ordinary business practices, . . . only 10 to 20 athletic programs make a consistent (albeit small) profit. In any given year, another 20 to 30 break even or do a little better. All the rest--more than 2,300 institutions--lose anywhere from a few dollars to millions of dollars annually on college sports. (K7)

But does poor business management justify taking advantage of college athletes? I think lack of money is no excuse for exploiting people.

Defenders of the status quo also emphasize that paying college athletes would mean that college players would no longer be amateurs. What I don't understand is why it's so important to be an amateur. I can see how that makes sense for the Olympics, but let's face it, there's nothing amateur about a good college team. It's time to reconsider what it means to be an amateur. Making a big deal out of not paying athletes could end up hurting poor students. If poor students are hurt more than rich students, then schools are practicing discrimination.

justified on the grounds that it would be expensive
to correct.

Another common argument against paying college   **13**
athletes is that we are supposed to be "amateurs"
rather than "professionals." Amateurs are expected
to play simply out of the joy of competition, but it
is hard to see what is amateur about sports that
have become big businesses. And what is so valuable
about being an amateur in the first place? Founded
in 1906, the NCAA was built upon values that belong
to the previous century: amateurs are considered
more noble than professionals, just as "gentlemen"
were once believed to be nobler than people who have
to work for a living. Consider the first definition
of "amateur" published by a sports organization:

> Any gentleman who has never competed in an
> open competition, or for public money, or
> for admission money, or with professionals
> for a prize, public money or admission
> money, and who has never at any period of
> his life taught or assisted in the pursuit
> of athletic exercises as a means of
> livelihood; nor is a mechanic, artisan, or
> labourer. (qtd. in Shropshire 57-58)

Look at how many people get left out by this 1866
definition! Women cannot be amateur athletes, nor
can working class men, or anyone who has coached a
sport. The prohibition against payment is simply one
of several conditions designed to make sports
socially exclusive.

COMMENTS

1. Beale chose to identify the president in a note, rather than in the text of the paper itself, in order to emphasize the name of the university rather than the individual who had gone to school there.

2. The last sentence in paragraph 14 contains an example of parallelism (**26**). Compare this sentence with the sentence as it appeared in the first draft of this paper:

```
Many athletes are black and have money problems, and
must play at schools more typical than Harvard or
Yale.
```

3. The conclusion makes a specific recommendation that addresses concerns raised throughout the paper, but especially in paragraphs 3, 11, and 12. And by recommending that athletes be paid no more than work-study students, Beale responds to the issue of special privileges discussed in paragraph 6.

This kind of thinking may have made more sense   14
at the beginning of this century, when Yale
dominated college football and the NCAA was created
in response to the demand of a president who had
graduated from Harvard.[3] But we are not living in
1906 anymore. Emphasis on amateur status
discriminates against students like me, who come
from families that have to struggle to pay their
bills. Out-of-date values are being used to exploit
today's college athletes, many of whom are black,
many of whom are poor, and few of whom are playing
for Harvard or Yale.

In conclusion, I believe that the best way to   15
end the exploitation of college athletes is to lift
the NCAA restriction against financial compensation.
But to avoid bidding wars in which the richest
schools would always get the best athletes, the NCAA
should insist that payments be geared to wages
earned by other students rather than wages earned by
professionals. If a student working in the library
is getting paid $4 per hour, then a student working
on the football field should be paid $4 per hour.
The NCAA should also restrict the number of hours a
student athlete can practice each week to no more
than thirty hours during the season, and no more
than ten out of season (for an average of twenty
hours, which is the limit for work-study). This
restriction would help to protect athletes from
demands that interfere with study time, and it would

COMMENTS

1. Study the following excerpt from the first draft of this paper and evaluate the changes Beale made.

(margin note: move to sep. ¶)

~~Colleges and universities must~~ *If schools cannot* find the money ~~somehow~~ to pay wages to athletes, ~~Because athletes work harder than~~ *like* students that work in the cafeteria or library, ~~they~~ *student athletes* should be paid *at least as much* ~~more.~~ ~~Paying athletes well would stop the exploitation problem.~~ Exploiting athletes is wrong because schools ~~should not exploit students. Going to college is so expensive that students should be treated fairly. Let's not forget that athletes are students. We should be protected not taken advantage of.~~ Schools should ~~encourage~~ *embody* good values, and they ~~are~~ *should* not ~~doing~~ *exploit* ~~that when it comes to the treatment of college athletes. If they can't treat us better, then we should stop playing for them.~~

Athletes are students and no student should be exploited by his or her school.

(margin note: they should get out of the business.)

also make it easier for schools to pay the wages for
which they would now be responsible.

　　If schools cannot find the money to pay this　　**16**
minimum wage, they should get out of the business
that college sports has become. Institutions of
higher education should embody the best of our
country's values, and they should not be in the
business of exploiting students.

COMMENTS

1. Three endnotes provide supplementary information that might be of interest to readers.
2. The first note includes a bracketed editorial interpolation clarifying that the emphasis is Sperber's, not Beale's. (See pages 158 and 173.)
3. The third note refers readers to a source by Constance Johnson identified in the list of works cited. Because Johnson's article is only one page long, a specific page reference is not necessary within the citation.

Notes

[1]The situation is especially bad for black
athletes. "From 1972-73 through 1985, Memphis State
University . . . did not graduate a single black
player, [emphasis in original]" (Sperber K6), even
though the men's basketball team was predominantly
black during these years. And the situation at the
University of Georgia was almost as bad.

[2]The University of Oklahoma received much
negative publicity in 1989 when "a young woman was
gang-raped in the athletic dormitory, one football
player shot another, and the star quarterback (who
had appeared in anti-drug announcements) was
arrested for selling cocaine" (Myers 49).

[3]The NCAA was created in response to pressure
from President Theodore Roosevelt prompted by an
unusually violent football season in 1905.
According to Constance Johnson, 18 college players
were killed that season, and nearly 160 had serious
injuries.

COMMENTS

1. All (and only) works cited as sources in the paper should be included in the list of works cited.

2. Alphabetization: Alphabetize entries according to author's last name. Works with more than one author are alphabetized under the name of whichever writer is listed first in the source itself.

3. Punctuation: Observe the use and placement of periods and commas, especially in relation to parentheses and quotation marks. A colon separates a title from a subtitle and the place of publication from the publisher's name. A colon also precedes page numbers of articles from periodicals.

4. The entries for Barbash and Goodman reveal that these two articles were published in magazines issued bimonthly. In this case, the form follows that of a magazine issued monthly (see pages 435–36), but both months appearing on the issue are cited, separated by a slash.

5. The first entry for Lapchick reveals that the source is a scholarly journal in which each issue is paginated anew, hence the issue number included after the volume number. See page 436.

6. An anonymous source (such as "National Collegiate Athletic Association") is alphabetized under the first important word in the title.

7. When listing two or more works by the same author (see the Lapchick entries), type three hyphens in the space where you would repeat the author's name and insert the period that regularly follows the name. List multiple works by the same author in alphabetical order determined by the first important word in the title.

Works Cited

Barbash, Louis. "Clean Up or Pay Up." The Washington
      Monthly July-Aug. 1990: 38-41.

Brownlee, Shannon, and Nancy S. Linnon. "The Myth of
      the Student-Athlete." U.S. News & World Report
      8 Jan. 1990: 50-52.

Goodman, Matthew. "Universities: The Real Losers in
      College Football." Utne Reader Nov.-Dec. 1991:
      17-18.

Johnson, Constance. "Defense Against the NCAA."
      U.S. News & World Report 13 Jan. 1992: 25.

Lapchick, Richard E. "Future of the Black Student
      Athlete." Educational Record 70.1 (1989): 32-
      35.

---. "Race on the College Campus." The Rules of the
      Game: Ethics in College Sport. Ed. Richard E.
      Lapchick and John B. Slaughter. New York:
      Macmillan, 1989. 55-70.

Lawrence, Paul R. Unsportsmanlike Conduct: The
      National Collegiate Athletic Association and
      the Business of College Football. New York:
      Praeger, 1987.

Myers, D. G. "Why College Sports?" Commentary Dec.
      1990: 49-51.

"National Collegiate Athletic Association."
      Encyclopedia Americana. 1987 ed.

Shropshire, Kenneth. Agents of Opportunity: Sports
      Agents and Corruption in Collegiate Sports.
      Philadelphia: U of Pennsylvania P, 1990.

Sperber, Murray. "College Sports Inc.: The Athletic
      Department vs. the University." Phi Delta
      Kappan Oct. 1990: K1-K12.

34i

The note style of documentation

Although parenthetical documentation has been recommended by the Modern Language Association since 1984 (and by the influential *Chicago Manual of Style,* since 1982), some disciplines in the humanities still use either footnotes or endnotes for documentation. We provide the information here in case you are instructed to follow a note style of documentation.

Both footnotes and endnotes require that a superscript (raised) number be placed wherever documentation is necessary. The number should be as near as possible to whatever it refers to, following the punctuation (such as quotation marks, a comma, or a period) that appears at the end of the direct or indirect quotation.

Footnotes should be single-spaced four lines below the last line of text on the same page where the documentation is necessary. (Double-space between footnotes if more than one appears on any one page.) *Endnotes* should be double-spaced on a separate page headed *Notes.*

The following notes use the same sources as those used for "List of works cited" on pages 427–36. By comparing the model footnote with its corresponding works cited entry, you will see differences between the two forms. (These numbered notes are arranged in a pattern for your convenience. They are numbered sequentially, as your notes would be for documentation. But your notes would not necessarily begin with "a book by one author" followed by "a book by more than one author" etc.).

A book by one author

[1] David Reynolds, <u>Beneath the American Renaissance: The Subversive Imagination in the Age of Emerson and Melville</u> (New York: Knopf, 1988) 123.

Indent five spaces, then give the note number (without punctuation) followed by a space. Additional lines in a note should be flush with the left margin. Note that an abbreviation for "page" is not used before the page number at the end of the note.

A book by more than one author

2 Donald L. Barlett and James B. Steele,

Forevermore: Nuclear Waste in America (New York:

Norton, 1985) 46.

If the book has more than two authors, use commas to separate the authors' names.

A multivolume work

3 George C. D. Odell, Annals of the New York

Stage, vol. 15 (New York: Columbia UP, 1949) 243.

An edited book

4 Edward F. Zigler and Meryl Frank, eds., The

Parental Leave Crisis (New Haven: Yale UP, 1988)

xii.

A work in an anthology

5 John Hollander, "Wordsworth and the Music of

Sound," New Perspectives on Coleridge and

Wordsworth, ed. Geoffrey H. Hartman (New York:

Columbia UP, 1972) 56.

An introduction, preface, foreword, or afterword

⁶ Doris Grumbach, foreword, <u>My Antonia</u>, by Willa Cather (Boston: Houghton, 1988) xvi.

An article from a newspaper

⁷ David Ibata, "Information Highway to the Future," <u>Chicago Tribune</u> 17 Nov. 1992, final ed., sec. 1: 8.

An article from a magazine

⁸ Stan Stresser, "Report from Cambodia," <u>The New Yorker</u> 18 May 1992: 63.

An article from a journal with continuous pagination

⁹ Gertrude Himmelfarb, "Manners into Morals: What the Victorians Knew," <u>American Scholar</u> 57 (1988): 228.

34j

Draft and revise a research paper using APA style documentation.

(1) Parenthetical citations

The documentation style recommended by the American Psychological Association (APA) is widely used for writing in the social sciences. In APA style, the basic elements of a parenthetical citation in the text are the author's last name, the year of publication, and the page number if the reference is to a specific passage in the source. If the author's name is mentioned in the text of the paper, give the date alone or the date and the page number within the parentheses. In the following examples, note the details of punctuation and the treatment of the page number.

A work by one author

```
One writer has stated, "Prisons can be divided into
specific social groups organized by type of crime"
(Liptz, 1979, p. 235).
```

OR

```
Liptz has stated, "Prisons can be divided into
specific social groups organized by type of crime"
(1979, p. 235).
```

OR

```
Liptz (1979) has stated, "Prisons can be divided
into specific social groups organized by type of
crime" (p. 235).
```

▲ Note: APA style, unlike MLA style, requires the abbreviation *p.* (or *pp.* for "pages") before the page reference. Use commas to separate the author's name from the date and the date from the page reference.

A work by two authors

```
There is evidence that students in second and third
grade respond favorably to guidance from elementary
school students in higher grades (Bowman & Myrick,
1987).
```

▲ Note: Use the ampersand (&) to separate the authors' names.

A work by more than two authors

```
One recent study has shown that people who fear
failure are not susceptible to hypnosis (Manganello,
Carlson, Zarillo, & Teeven, 1985).
```

For works with *three to five authors,* cite all the authors in the first reference, but in subsequent references give only the last name of the first author followed by "et al." ("Manganello et al." in this case). For works with *more than six authors,* provide only the last name of the first author followed by "et al.," even in the first citation.

Anonymous works

Use a shortened version of the title to identify an anonymous work:

```
Chronic insomnia usually requires medical
intervention ("Sleep," 1993).
```

In this case, the author has cited a short article identified in the bibliography as "Sleep disorders: What can be done about them."

Two or more works within the same parentheses

```
Much animal experimentation may be both unnecessary
and cruel (Mayo, 1983; Singer, 1975).
```

Use a semicolon to separate different studies, and arrange the studies in alphabetical order.

(2) References list

Format the "References" (alphabetical list of works cited) in the APA style your instructor specifies. For **final** manuscript style, indent the second and subsequent lines of each entry three spaces. For **copy** style, indent only the first line one-half inch. The reference entries below follow the final style of the 1994 edition of the *APA Publication Manual*. Observe all details of indention, spacing, and mechanics.

BOOKS

Most book entries consist of four units, which are separated by periods:

1. *Author.* Give the author's last name and use initials for first and middle names. For entries that contain more than one author, invert all names and put an ampersand (&) before the last author. (If two authors have the same last name and initials, spell out their first names and list the references in the alphabetical order of their first names.)

2. *Date.* Put the date in parentheses after the author's name. By including the date near the beginning of the entry, APA style draws attention to the importance of when the material was published.

3. *Title.* Capitalize only the first word in titles and subtitles. Do not capitalize other words (except for proper names that would be capitalized in other contexts). Separate the title and subtitle with a colon.

4. *Publication data.* Give only enough of the publisher's name so that it can be identified clearly.

Book by one author

Liptz, A. (1979). <u>Prisons as social structures</u>.
    Los Angeles: Scholarly Press.

More than one work by the same author

If you use more than one work by the same author, list the works in order of the publication date, earliest first. Repeat the author's name for each work.

```
Giroux, H. (1988). Schooling and the struggle for
    public life. Minneapolis: University of
    Minnesota.
Giroux, H. (1992). Border crossings. New York:
    Routledge.
```

Book by two or more authors

```
Klein, D. F., & Wender, P. H. (1981). Mind, mood,
    and medicine: A guide to the new biological
    psychiatry. New York: Farrar.
```

Contrast APA style with MLA style, which inverts only the first author in a multi-author work (see page 429).

An edition after the first

```
Kelly, D. H. (1989). Deviant behavior: A text-
    reader in the sociology of deviance (3rd ed.).
    New York: St. Martin's.
```

Translation

```
Freud, S. (1960). Jokes and their relationship to
    the unconscious (J. Strachey, Trans.). New York:
    Norton. (Original work published 1905).
```

Cite the date of the translation. Include date of original publication at the end of the entry. In text, use the following form: (Freud, 1905/1960).

A government document

```
Department of energy. (1987). Energy security
    (DOE/S-0057). Washington, DC: U.S. Government
    Printing Office.
```

Treat the issuing agency as the author when no author is specified. Include a document or contract number (but not a library's call number) if either number is printed on or in the document.

ARTICLES

Capitalize only the first word and any proper nouns in article titles, and do not put quotation marks around the title. (If the article has a subtitle, put a colon after the title, and capitalize the first word in the subtitle.) For an article in an edited book, provide both the title of the article and the title of the book in which it appears. Identify who edited the book and give the complete pages of the article. For an anonymous article, place the article title where the author's name would normally appear, and alphabetize by the first important word in the title.

▲ **Note:** The titles of journals are capitalized differently from article or book titles. Underline the volume number and the commas preceding and following it so it will be distinct from the page reference (which is not preceded by an abbreviation).

Journal: Continuous pagination

Faulstitch, M. E. (1984). Effects upon social
    perceptions of the insanity plea. Psychological
    Reports, 55, 183-187.

Journal: Separate pagination

Kolakowski, L. (1992). Amidst moving ruins.
    Daedalus, 121(2), 43-56.

Insert the issue number within parentheses immediately after the volume number.

Monthly or weekly magazine

Levy, D. H. (1992, June). A sky watcher discovers
    comets and immortality. <u>Smithsonian</u>, pp. 75-82.

▲ Note: For a monthly magazine, give the year first, followed
by a comma and the full spelling of the month. For a weekly
magazine, provide the exact date of issue: (1993, February 18).

Newspaper

Ingersoll, B. (1988, December 2). FDA asked to ban
    sales of quinine over the counter. <u>Wall Street</u>
    <u>Journal</u>, p. A12.

Work in an anthology

Chlad, F. L. (1991). Chemical storage for industrial
    laboratories. In D. A. Pipitone (Ed.), <u>Safe</u>
    <u>storage of laboratory chemicals</u> (pp. 175-191).
    New York: Wiley.

Book review

Becker, J. G. (1992). The dilemma of choice [Review
    of <u>Psychiatric aspects of abortion</u>].
    <u>Contemporary Psychology, 37,</u> 457-458.

When a review is titled, insert the subject of the review within
brackets after the review title. When a review is untitled, use
the material within brackets as the title, retaining the brackets
to show that this "title" is a description.

NONPRINT SOURCES

Film

Redford, R., & Markey, P. (Producers), & Redford, R.
    (Director). (1992). <u>A river runs through it</u>.
    [Film]. New York: Columbia Pictures.

Recording

Fellows, W. (Speaker). (1993). <u>Nutritional needs for
    women with AIDS</u> (Cassette Recording No. 8294).
    Madison, WI: Nutritionworks.

Computer Program

O'Reilley, R. (1993). Prostyle [Computer program].
    Bloomington, MN: Wordcorp. (OTR-71148).

Electronic media—on-line

Form for references to electronic media:
Author, I. (Year, Month). Title of article [00 lines or para-
graphs]. <u>Name of Periodical</u> [on-line or other medium], <u>vol-
ume and issue</u>. Available: specify path (no final period). Cite
e-mail, newsgroup, or bulletin board messages in the text but
do not list them in References.

Crump, E. (1995, February). RhetNet, a cyberjournal
    for rhetoric and writing [30 lines]. <u>ACW
    Connections</u> [on-line serial]. Available: acw-
    mem@unicorn.acs.ttu.edu (e-mail) or (WWW) http://
    prairie_island.ttu. edu/acw/acw.html

34k

Sample APA research paper

For additional examples of APA style documentation, see the
following student essay and the commentary on it printed on
the left-hand pages.

COMMENT

1. The title page should include the title, the author's full name, the course in which the paper is being submitted, the name of the instructor who is teaching the course, and the date the essay is submitted. The *APA Publication Manual* requires that a shortened version of the title, identified as "Running Head" appear centered near the bottom of the title page. This heading is then used in the upper right-hand corner of every page, including the title page—which is counted as page 1. This format allows a reader to remove the title page and evaluate the paper without being influenced by prior knowledge of the author. (If you use this model for an MLA paper, do not number the title page and do not include a running head.)

Test Anxiety

1

Treatment for Test Anxiety

Sharon Johnson

Psychology 101, Section 7

Professor Marquez

May 4, 1990

Running head: TEST ANXIETY

COMMENTS

1. An abstract is a short summary of a paper. The APA requires that an abstract be supplied on the second page of any essay that is to be submitted for publication. Check with your instructor to see if an abstract is required for your own assignment.

2. Although Sharon Johnson draws upon personal experience in her opening paragraph to catch the interest of her audience, she introduces her topic by the end of that paragraph.

3. Paragraph 2 (report page 4) includes a citation to a specific page, a citation to an entire work, and a citation to several studies that reached the same conclusion. The data reported in this paragraph establish the purpose for the paper by demonstrating that test anxiety is a widespread problem.

4. Paragraph 3 (report page 5) defines "test anxiety" by showing how it differs from nervousness.

5. Paragraph 4 (report pages 5–6) surveys early research in this field and offers an explanation for disappointing results.

Abstract

The cause-and-effect relationship between test anxiety and poor academic performance now seems well established. Although some researchers question whether reducing test anxiety will necessarily lead to higher grades, the most recent research in this field suggests that the grades of test-anxious students are raised when such students are provided with therapy that combines relaxation training and tutoring to improve study skills.

Treatment for Test Anxiety

Although my younger sister is very smart, she   1
had trouble in school for many years. She would carefully do her homework and usually seem to have mastered her assignments when my parents or I helped her to review. Unfortunately, whenever Stacey had to take a test, she would freeze up and seem to forget everything she knew. Since her grades were based mostly upon her tests, she usually received low grades that did not reflect how much she really knew. Everyone in the family could see that Stacey was nervous about taking tests, and we kept telling her to try to relax. What we did not realize was that Stacey was suffering from a condition called

"test anxiety," a psychological syndrome that has been the subject of much research since the early 1950s when an important study on college students was conducted at Yale University (Mandler & Sarason, 1952).

Research reveals that my sister's problem is not unusual. It has been estimated that "4-5 million children in elementary and secondary schools experience strong debilitating evaluation anxiety" and that another 5 million experience "significant anxiety" (Hill & Wigfield, 1984, p. 110); moreover, as much as 25% of college students may suffer from this condition (McGrath, 1985; Wilson & Rotter, 1986). Although there is evidence that females may be more vulnerable than males to test anxiety (Couch, Garber, & Turner, 1983; Furst, Tennenbaum, & Weingarten, 1985; Hembree, 1988), the problem is widespread within both sexes, and it can be found at all levels of intelligence. One recent study suggests that students of Asian background may be especially likely to suffer from test anxiety because they come from cultures that emphasize the importance of scholastic excellence (Dion & Toner, 1988), but most research reports that test anxiety is not limited to students of any particular race or culture.

Test anxiety should not be confused with simple   3
nervousness. A student may be nervous before a test
but then be able to successfully concentrate on
taking the test once it is under way; this same
student may be relaxed before another exam in a
subject he or she enjoys. In some cases, a little
anxiety can even be helpful, since some students are
motivated to excel when they are concerned about
performance. In other cases, anxiety may be
appropriate if a student has neglected assignments
and has no real hope of passing an examination on
material that has gone unread. A student with test
anxiety, on the other hand, is likely to be
dominated by negative feelings (including anger,
guilt, and frustration) before almost *any* exam, and
these feelings will subsequently interfere with
performance once the test has begun. Students
suffering from test anxiety thus lose the ability to
concentrate on problem solving. Instead of
concentrating on the exam before them, they are
usually distracted by other concerns such as how
poorly they are doing and what other people will
think of them if they fail.

Early research in this field demonstrated that   4
students who scored high in tests designed to
measure test anxiety consistently did poorly in test
situations (Mandler & Sarason, 1952). But the

COMMENTS

1. Paragraph 5 includes evidence that will support John-son's argument. Note that she was careful to avoid relying too heavily on Zitzow (which, as the reference list reveals, is a short article). When introducing the Hembree study, Johnson was careful to include back-ground information that would enable her audience to recognize the value of this source.

2. Paragraph 6 (report page 7) includes a second citation to a source with more than two authors.

3. Paragraphs 7–10 (report pages 8–10) include recom-mendations for treatment. Note how paragraphs 9 and 10 begin with concessions likely to reassure a skepti-cal audience.

4. Note that the long quotation—a quotation of more than 40 words—in paragraph 8 (report page 9) is in-dented five spaces only, per APA style. (See **16a[4]**.)

tests used to measure student anxiety may not be
entirely accurate. Some students may exaggerate
their defects (Davies, 1986), and the tests
themselves may be biased (Couch et al., 1983).
Faulty methods of measuring test anxiety may account
for the disappointing results of much research in
this field: many researchers have reported
successful reduction of student anxiety levels
without noting a corresponding improvement in
academic achievement (Lent, Lopez, & Romano, 1983;
Ricketts & Galloway, 1984).

     Evidence suggests, however, that there is hope
for students who suffer from test anxiety. In one
study, "grade improvements were noted for over 70%
of participants in identified courses . . ."
(Zitzow, 1983, p. 565). Although a single study is
insufficient to prove anything conclusively, a
recent, exhaustive study is highly persuasive.
Reviewing the results of 562 separate studies on
test anxiety (including 369 journal articles and 148
doctoral dissertations) and subjecting them to
statistical analysis, a mathematician has concluded,
"Contrary to prior perceptions, improved test
performance and grade point average (GPA)
consistently accompany TA reduction" (Hembree, 1988,
p. 47). According to this study, early researchers
failed to detect significant academic

improvement because many of them based their observations on sample groups that were too small. Drawing the results of many studies together reveals that treatment for test anxiety improves students' test scores by an average of 6 points on a 100-point scale (p. 73). This may seem like a small improvement for a student who is failing a course, but a 6-point improvement can be significant in some cases. More importantly, even a 6-point improvement helps to prove that there is a cause-and-effect relationship between test anxiety and academic performance. If this is the case, then improved methods of treatment may produce greater academic improvement in the future.

For treatment to be effective, counselors need to realize that test anxiety is a complex state involving two factors: "worry," which involves thinking about negative possibilities; and "emotionality," which describes the perception of such physiological phenomena as accelerated heart beat and sweating (Furst et al., 1985). Irwin G. Sarason, one of this country's foremost experts on test anxiety, has concluded that "worry" has an especially significant impact upon academic performance (1985). Taking this research into account, it would seem that therapy that does not address the problem of worry is unlikely to help students do better on tests. A test-anxious student needs something more than soft music and deep-breathing exercises.

The best results seem to be achieved by counseling programs that provide students with more than one type of help. Many test-anxious students devote insufficient time to studying because they spend so much time worrying (Davies, 1986) or because they have given up in frustration. Such students often need specific help in learning good study habits in addition to receiving therapy to reduce anxiety. Several experts recommend that treatment for test anxiety be accompanied by a tutoring program in study skills (Lent et al., 1983; Wilson & Rotter, 1986; Zitzow, 1983). Tutoring alone, however, is not likely to provide much help for someone suffering from test anxiety: "Study skills training is . . . not effective unless another treatment style is also present" (Hembree, 1988, p. 73).

One problem in the treatment of test anxiety is that individual students respond very differently to the same situation: "The same test that seems to maximize the performance of low anxious examinees results in relatively poor performance by moderately anxious examinees" (Rocklin & Thompson, 1985, p. 371). A possible solution to this problem would be to devise different tests for students with different degrees of anxiety. Another possibility would be to put students into testing groups determined by anxiety levels. According to I. G. Sarason,

> A highly test-anxious college student might simply become more tense before, during, and after tests by virtue of contacts with completely confident, effective, and seemingly worry-free models. On the other hand, opportunity to observe and perhaps interact with other students who are mildly fearful of tests but who are not immobilized by them . . . might have decidely therapeutic results.
> (1972, p. 396)

Reorganizing classes to group together students of similar anxiety levels may not be feasible, however, since this would require elaborate organization and registration procedures. (This method might be considered, however, when planning for special tests, like the SATs, that are of particular importance and are independent of course work.) Within a classroom situation, teachers can help reduce anxiety levels by providing students in advance with clear instructions regarding the nature of upcoming tests and how to prepare for them (Davies, 1986). Teachers should also realize that anxiety levels in general increase when students are undergoing a stressful life event such as the transition from junior to senior high school or from high school to college. Additional support for students during these times has been shown to be beneficial (Bloom, 1985). One type of support that should be considered is to reduce test time pressure by allowing students sufficient time to complete tests (Hill & Wigfield, 1984).

It would be a mistake, however, to assume that the responsibility for treating test anxiety rests within the schools. Many schools do not have the resources to undertake any new special programs, and many teachers are so overworked that it would be unrealistic to expect them to give troubled students the individualized attention they may need. Parents should be alert to the problem of test anxiety and take the initiative in seeking therapeutic help for any child who seems regularly immobilized by tests. And college students should be prepared to seek such help for themselves if they are certain that anxiety--rather than lack of preparation--causes them to do poorly on tests.

I now know that simply telling someone with test anxiety to "try to relax"--as my parents and I

COMMENTS

1. The conclusion, with its reference to "my sister," establishes a link with the introduction.
2. The reference list is organized alphabetically and begins on a new page. The last name is always given first, and initials are provided for first and middle names. The date of publication is always given parenthetically, immediately after the author's name. See pages 468–73.
3. Observe the use of periods and commas, the style of capitalization for book and article titles, and the different capitalization style for journal titles. Underline book titles, journal titles, and volume numbers for periodicals. If citing material from more than one work by the same author, repeat the author's name (as in the Sarason, I. G., entry) before each work.
4. APA distinguishes between a **copy** style for manuscripts from which a book or journal article will be typeset and a **final** style, for those not intended for typesetting, such as most college writing. The sample paper shows a reference list prepared for a final manuscript. A copy manuscript version appears below. Ask your instructor which version to use.

Bloom, B. L. (1985). <u>Stressful life event theory and research: Implications for primary prevention</u> (DHHS Publication No. ADM 85-1385). Rockville, MD: National Institute of Mental Health.

used to tell my sister--is about as useful as telling someone with severe depression to "try to cheer up." Whatever the cause that triggers it, someone suffering from anxiety needs trained, professional help. Students with test anxiety are no exception, and they need to know that help is available. Although the evidence is not conclusive, and more research needs to be done, what we know about test anxiety suggests that it can be treated effectively: treatment that combines therapy with tutoring is likely to improve students' self-concepts and lead to higher scores on tests.

References

Bloom, B. L. (1985). Stressful life event theory and research: Implications for primary prevention (DHHS Publication No. ADM 85-1385). Rockville, MD: National Institute of Mental Health.

Couch, J. V., Garber, T. B., & Turner, W. E. (1983). Facilitating and debilitating test anxiety and academic achievement. Psychological Record, 33, 237-244.

Davies, D. (1986). Maximizing examination
performance. New York: Nichols.

Dion, K. L., & Toner, B. B. (1988). Ethnic
differences in test anxiety. Journal of Social
Psychology, 128, 165-172.

Furst, D., Tennenbaum, G., & Weingarten G. (1985).
Test anxiety, sex, and exam type. Psychological
Reports, 56, 663-668.

Hembree, R. (1988). Correlates, causes, effects,
and treatment of test anxiety. Review of
Educational Research, 58, 47-77.

Hill, K. T., & Wigfield, A. (1984). Test anxiety: A
major educational problem and what can be done
about it. Elementary School Journal, 85,
105-126.

Lent, R. W., Lopez, F. G., & Romano, J. L. (1983).
A program for reducing test anxiety with
academically underprepared students. Journal of
College Student Personnel, 24, 265-266.

Mandler, G., & Sarason, S. (1952). Some correlates
of test anxiety. Journal of Abnormal and Social
Psychology, 47, 561-565.

McGrath, A. (1985, November 4). Mettle testing.
Forbes, pp. 236-239.

Ricketts, M. S., & Galloway, R. E. (1984). Effects
of three different one-hour single-session

treatments for test anxiety. Psychological
Reports, 54, 115-120.

Rocklin, T., & Thompson, J. M. (1985). Interactive
effects of test anxiety, test difficulty, and
feedback. Journal of Educational Psychology, 77,
368-372.

Sarason, I. G. (1972). Experimental approaches to
test anxiety: Attention and the uses of
information. In C. D. Spielberger (Ed.), Anxiety:
Current trends in theory and research (Vol. 2,
pp. 381-403). New York: Academic.

Sarason, I. G. (1985). Cognitive processes, anxiety
and the treatment of anxiety disorders. In A. H.
Tuma & J. Maser (Eds.), Anxiety and anxiety
disorders (pp. 87-107). Hillsdale, NJ: Erlbaum.

Wilson, N., & Rotter J. C. (1986). Anxiety
management training and study skills counseling
for students on self-esteem and test anxiety and
performance. School Counselor, 34, 18-31.

Zitzow, D. (1983). Test anxiety: A trimodal
strategy. Journal of College Student Personnel,
24, 564-565.

■ **Exercise 7**　Rewrite the opening and concluding paragraphs of this paper, omitting personal experience and making the tone more objective.

■ **Exercise 8**　Drawing upon the bibliographical information on page 463, change the following MLA style citations to APA style:

(Brownlee and Linnon 52)
(Sperber K3)
(Lapchick, "Race" 66)
("National Collegiate")
(Barbash 40, Lawrence 144; Shropshire 71)

35

Writing for Special Purposes

Write effective papers about literature; essay exams; and letters, résumés, and memos.

When you write for special purposes, you will benefit from the information and advice conveyed throughout this handbook. But you may need to adapt these lessons to make them useful in situations that limit the time you have for writing or that require you to employ conventions that determine the form and length of what you write.

You may be asked to read a work of literature and to write a paper about it. Doing so can enlarge your world by helping you understand your own experience as well that of others. Writing about literature is the focus of **35a**.

You will need to accelerate your writing process when you are required to write an essay within a single class period— or several short essays during an exam. There are several strategies that can help you to write well when your time is brief. Writing effective essays in class is the focus of **35b**.

Business writing is the focus of **35c**. Whether it takes the form of a letter, résumé, or memo, business writing generally combines informative and persuasive aims (see **33a**). A business writer selects and presents information to win a favorable response from the reader. Additionally, such documents often become important records, so they should be accurate and clear.

35a

Learn to read literature and write effective papers about fiction, drama, and poetry.

Like all writing in specialized fields, literature has its own vocabulary. When you learn this vocabulary, you are not just learning a list of terms and definitions. You are grasping concepts that will help you to read and understand literature and to write about it effectively. This section introduces these concepts and basic guidelines for writing about literature. Your instructor can give you further help in reading and writing about literature.

Writing about literature involves using the principles of all good writing. Consider the rhetorical situation, mainly your audience and your purpose (**33a**). Explore, limit, and focus your subject (**33c**) as you read and write. Work toward formulating a thesis statement (**33d**) that can be supported from the work itself. And plan how to organize your thoughts so that your essay will have sound structure.

(1) Explore your personal response to literature.

As you read, take notes and jot down ideas. Trust your own reactions. What characters do you admire? Did the work remind you of any experience of your own? Did it introduce you to a world that is different from your own? Were you amused, moved, or confused? These first impressions can provide the seeds from which strong essays will grow. You may find that you need to modify your initial impressions as you study the work more closely or as writing takes you in a direction that you did not originally anticipate. But writing about literature begins with active, personal engagement with what you read.

You can facilitate this engagement by freewriting (see **33c**) or by keeping a journal in which you record your reactions and questions. These methods of exploring a subject can help you discover what you think or what you want to understand. In addition to generating topics for writing, they provide a useful method for identifying questions you could raise in class. Here is a piece of freewriting on "Lullaby," a short story discussed in the paper that begins on page 504. The author quickly wrote whatever came to mind, confident that doing so would help him discover a topic for an essay.

> I felt really sad when I finished this story. Looks like the characters are about to die. A form of suicide? What would Chato have said if he was alert? Ayah must be very unhappy. Doesn't seem to have anything left to live for. One thing I didn't understand though is why she laughs when she sees the shoes her husband is wearing. Does she think it's funny? She seems peaceful watching the sky though I think nature calms her down. At other times she seems angry.

After briefly noting how the story made him feel, the author of this excerpt then moves on to ask three questions, each of which could lead to an essay through the exploration of possible answers. Another essay could explore Ayah's relationship with nature: Is it true that "nature calms her down," and if so, why does it have this effect? Note also that this excerpt does not consist entirely of grammatically correct sentences. When you freewrite about literature, write whatever comes to mind without worrying about whether or not you are correct. You are thinking on paper, not editing an essay.

(2) Read and reread with care.

Experienced readers understand that a literary work can provoke different responses from different readers, and you can have a significantly different response when rereading a work—even a work that you think you understand already. Whenever possible, reread any work that you are planning to write about. If the length of the work makes doing so unfeasible, at least reread those chapters or scenes that impressed you as especially important or problematic.

If you have a tentative thesis, rereading a work will help you find the evidence you need for its support. You are likely to find evidence that you did not notice on your first reading. You may also find evidence that will require you to modify your thesis. Use evidence that is appropriate for your purpose (see **31b**), and present it fairly, establishing yourself as a credible source (**31c**).

A good way to note evidence, ideas, and concerns, is to annotate as you read. Because they are actively engaged with their reading, experienced readers often keep a pen or pencil at hand so they can mark passages that they may wish to study or to draw upon when writing.

(3) Analyze, interpret, explicate, and evaluate.

Although you may have occasion to write papers in which you simply explore your personal response to a work of literature and relate it to your own life, writing papers about a literary work usually requires you to focus on the work itself. Your personal response may help you discover a direction you want to explore. But as you explore you will often need to look at a work by analyzing it, interpreting it, or evaluating it. A short paper may do only one of these; a long paper may do all three.

Analyze (see **32d[6]**) a work of literature by breaking it into its parts and examining how such parts as setting, characters, and plot combine to form a whole. How do the parts interact? How does one part contribute to the overall meaning of the work? For example, in her paper on *King Lear* (beginning on page 511), Susan Ferk demonstrates how the characters in the subplot comment on and intensify the main plot and theme.

Interpret a work by asking what it means, bearing in mind that a work may have more than one meaning. Support your interpretation by referring to elements in the work itself. For example, in his paper on "Lullaby" (beginning on page 504), Tom Villalta cites evidence to support his belief that the story shows how Native American culture has been violated. Closely related to analysis, interpretation allows writers to draw freely upon any part of a work that can be used to explain its meaning.

An interpretation that attempts to explain every element within a work is called an *explication*, which is usually limited to poetry. When explicating William Wordsworth's "A Slumber Did My Spirit Seal," a writer might note that the "s" sound reinforces the hushed feeling of sleep and death in the poem. But it would also be necessary to consider the meaning of "slumber," "spirit," and "seal" as well as why the words in this line are arranged as they are (as opposed to "A Slumber Sealed My Spirit" or "My Spirit Was Sealed By My Slumber").

Evaluate a work by asking how successful the author is in communicating meaning to readers. Like interpretation, evaluation is a type of argument in which a writer cites evidence to persuade readers to accept a clearly formulated thesis. In her paper on Galway Kinnell (beginning on page 520), Susan Schubring argues that "The Milk Bottle" successfully conveys "the division in humans between mind and body." Evaluation of a literary work should consider both strengths and weaknesses if there is evidence of both.

▲ Caution: Although summarizing a literary work can be a useful way to make sure that you understand it, do not confuse summary with analysis, interpretation, or evaluation. An audience that has read the literary work is unlikely to benefit from reading a summary of it. Do not submit a summary unless your instructor has asked for one.

(4) Choose a subject and develop it.

If your instructor asks you to choose your own subject, your first step should be to reflect upon your personal response (**35a[1]**). Reviewing your responses to the work may enable you not only to choose a subject but also to formulate a tentative thesis. The purpose of your paper in this case would be to persuade readers to agree with your view. Also try some of the methods suggested in **33c** to explore the work in question. If you generate more than one possible topic, decide which seems the most original.

Choose a topic that would be interesting both to write and read about. Readers are usually interested in learning what *you* think. If you choose an easy topic, you may find yourself repeating what many other writers have already said. As a rule, try to avoid writing what is obvious. On the other hand, do not let the quest for originality lead you to choose a topic that would be too hard to develop adequately.

Apply strategies of development (**32d**). You might *define* why you consider a character heroic, *classify* a play as a comedy of manners, or *describe* a setting that contributes to a work's meaning. Perhaps you could *compare and contrast* two poems on a similar subject or explore *cause-and-effect* relationships in a novel. Why, for example, does an important character marry the wrong man?

(5) Do research when appropriate.

Both writers and readers often favor papers that are focused on an individual's personal response, analysis, interpretation, or evaluation. But by reading criticism that reveals what other readers think of a given literary work, you can engage in dialogue about that work. When you draw upon the ideas of other people, remember that you must use those sources responsibly (**34e**). And when you incorporate these ideas, you must still advance a position that is clearly your own. Few readers enjoy papers that offer little more than a collection of quotations.

When you read criticism, remember that a work of literature rarely has a single meaning. Three different critics may offer three radically different interpretations. Your responsibility is not to determine who is right but to determine the extent to which you agree or disagree with the differing views you encounter. Read critically (**31**) and formulate your own thesis (**33d**).

Chapter **34** explains how to do research. To locate material on a specific writer or work, consult your library's main catalog (**34b**) and the *MLA Bibliography*, an index of books and articles about literature. Like most indexes to special interest periodicals (p. 401), the *MLA Bibliography* can be consulted in printed volumes, through an on-line database search, or through access to a CD-ROM disk covering several years.

You may also locate useful information in the following reference books:

> Benét, William Rose, *The Reader's Encyclopedia*. 3rd ed. 1987.
>
> Drabble, Margaret. *The Oxford Companion to English Literature*. 5th ed. 1987.
>
> *Cambridge History of English Literature*. 15 vols. 1907–33.
>
> Elliott, Emory, et al. *Columbia Literary History of the United States*. 1988.
>
> Evory, Ann, et al. *Contemporary Authors*. New Revision Series. 1981–.
>
> Hart, James D. *The Oxford Companion to American Literature*. 5th ed. 1983.

Harvey, Sir Paul. *The Oxford Companion to Classical Literature*. 2nd ed. 1937. Rpt. 1986.

Hazen, Edith P., and Deborah J. Fryer. *The Columbia Granger's Index to Poetry*. 9th ed. 1990.

Holman, C. Hugh, and William Harmon. *Handbook to Literature*. 5th ed. 1986.

Klein, Leonard. *Encyclopedia of World Literature in the 20th Century*. 2nd ed. 5 vols. 1981–84.

New Cambridge Bibliography of English Literature. 5 vols. 1969–77.

For an example of a paper that incorporates research about literature, see the essay by Susan Schubring (beginning on page 520).

▲ Caution: Research is not appropriate for all assignments. Your instructor may want to learn only your own response or interpretation. If your instructor has not assigned a researched paper, ask if one would be acceptable.

(6) Writing about fiction.

Although the events have not happened and the characters may never have existed, serious fiction expresses truth about the human condition through such components as setting, character, and plot. In "Lullaby" (1979), Leslie Silko tells the story of a Navajo family headed by an old woman named Ayah and her crippled husband, Chato. Moving between the present and the past, Silko reveals that this couple has lost their three children. The oldest, Jimmie, died in a helicopter crash while serving in the army; the younger two, Danny and Ella, have been taken away by the state. At the end of the story, Ayah decides to freeze to death with her husband after they have been walking home from town, where

Chato has been drinking. Here is an excerpt from the conclusion:

> He was walking along the pavement when she found him.
> He did not stop or turn around when he heard her behind him.
> She walked beside him and she noticed how slowly he moved
> now. He smelled strong of woodsmoke and urine. Lately he
> had been forgetting. Sometimes he called her by his sister's
> name and she had been gone for a long time. Once she had
> found him wandering on the road to the white man's ranch,
> and she asked him why he was going that way; he laughed at
> her and said, "You know they can't run that ranch without me,"
> and he walked on determined, limping on the leg that had been
> crushed many years before. Now he looked at her curiously, as
> if for the first time, but he kept shuffling along, moving slowly
> along the side of the highway. His gray hair had grown long
> and spread out on the shoulders of the long overcoat. He wore
> the old felt hat pulled down over his ears. His boots were worn
> out at the toes and he had stuffed pieces of an old red shirt in
> the holes. The rags made his feet look like little animals up to
> their ears in snow. She laughed at his feet; the snow muffled
> the sound of her laugh. He stopped and looked at her again.
> The wind had quit blowing and the snow was falling straight
> down; the southeast sky was beginning to clear and Ayah could
> see a star.
>
> "Let's rest awhile," she said to him. They walked away from
> the road and up the slope to the giant boulders that had tumbled
> down from the red sandrock mesa throughout the centuries of
> rainstorms and earth tremors. In a place where the boulders
> shut out the wind, they sat down with their backs against the
> rock. She offered half of the blanket to him and they sat
> wrapped together.
>
> The storm passed swiftly. The clouds moved east. They were
> massive and full, crowding together across the sky. She watched
> them with the feeling of horses—steely blue-gray horses startled
> across the sky. The powerful haunches pushed into the distances
> and the tail hairs streamed white mist behind them. The sky
> cleared. Ayah saw that there was nothing between her and the
> stars. The light was crystalline. There was no shimmer, no

distortion through earth haze. She breathed the clarity of the night sky; she smelled the purity of the half moon and the stars. He was lying on his side with his knees pulled up near his belly for warmth. His eyes were closed now, and in the light from the stars and the moon, he looked young again.

She could see it descend out of the night sky: an icy stillness from the edge of the thin moon. She recognized the freezing. It came gradually, sinking snowflake by snowflake until the crust was heavy and deep. It had the strength of the stars in Orion, and its journey was endless. Ayah knew that with the wind he would sleep. He would not feel it. She tucked the blanket around him, remembering how it was when Ella had been with her; and she felt the rush so big inside her heart for the babies. And she sang the only song she knew to sing for babies. She could not remember if she had ever sung it to her children, but she knew that her grandmother had sung it and her mother had sung it.

Setting   *Setting* involves time—not only historical time, but also the length of time covered by the action. It also involves place—not only the physical setting but also the atmosphere created by the author. The time sequence in "Lullaby" is in one sense brief: the story begins and ends on the same day. But within this day, Ayah remembers experiences that she had throughout her life, ultimately making the time sequence several decades. The physical setting is the countryside near Cebolleta, a small town in the American Southwest. The contrast between the town and the open countryside complements the conflict of cultures within the story.

Plot   The sequence of events that make up the story is the *plot*. Unlike a narrative, which simply reports events, a plot establishes how events relate to one another. Narrative asks "What comes next?"; plot asks "Why?" For example:

NARRATIVE	The king died, and the queen died.
PLOT	The queen died because the king died.

A work of fiction may have a complicated plot or almost no plot at all, depending upon the author's purpose. The plot of "Lullaby" is fairly simple. After years of loss, drought, and racism, a Navajo woman and her husband freeze to death. This plot reveals the conflict between cultures that the story is designed to convey.

Characters The *characters* carry the plot forward and usually include a main character, called a *protagonist*, who is in conflict with another character, with an institution, or with herself. In "Lullaby," Ayah is the protagonist. She is in conflict to a degree with her husband. But more importantly, she is in conflict with the Anglo culture into which her husband has unsuccessfully tried to integrate. By examining a character's conflict, you can often discover a story's *theme*.

Point of view The position from which the action is observed—the person through whose eyes the events are seen— is the *point of view*. The point of view may be that of a single character within the story or of a narrator who tells the story. Many works of fiction are told from a single point of view, but some shift the point of view from one character to another. "Lullaby" is told from Ayah's point of view. We know her thoughts throughout the story but not those of other characters. In this case, the narrator is *partially omniscient*—that is partially all-knowing. A narrator who knows the thoughts of all characters is *omniscient*. A story told by a character who refers to herself or himself as "I" employs the *first-person* point of view. (Do not confuse this character with the author.) When the narrator does not reveal the thoughts of any character, the story is being told from the *dramatic* or *objective* point of view.

Tone Conveyed by point of view, *tone* is the narrator's attitude toward the events and characters in the story or even, in some circumstances, toward the readers. The tone of the narrator in "Lullaby" is somber and respectful, helping to establish sympathy for Ayah and her husband. Another story could have a tone that is ironic, humorous, wry, or bitter. By determining the nature of a work's tone, and the impact it has upon you as a reader, you can gain insight into the author's purpose.

Symbolism A common characteristic of fiction, symbolism is also used in drama and poetry. A *symbol* is an object, usually concrete, that stands for something else, usually abstract. On one level, it is what it is; on another level, it is more than what it is. In writing about a particular symbol, first note the context in which it appears. Then think about what it could mean. When you have an idea, trace the incidents in the story that reinforce that idea. According to the paper by Tom Villalta, Jimmie's blanket in "Lullaby" symbolizes "how little Western aid benefits Native Americans." It could also be said to symbolize the love Ayah had for the son who had used this blanket.

Theme The central or main idea of a literary work is its *theme*. Depending upon how they interpret a work, different readers may identify different themes. To test whether the idea you have identified is central to the work in question, check to see if it is supported by the *setting, plot, characterization, tone,* and *symbols.* If you can relate these components to the idea you are exploring, then that idea can be considered the work's theme. In his paper on "Lullaby," Tom Villalta argues that the story's theme is that Native American culture has been damaged by the American government.

As you read and write, ask yourself the following questions:

Analyzing Literature

1. What is the theme?
2. How does the author use setting, plot, characters, and symbolism to support the meaning?

3. Who is telling the story?
4. What is the tone of the narrator?
5. Who is the protagonist? How is his or her character developed?
6. With whom or what is the protagonist in conflict?
7. How does one character compare with another?
8. What symbols does the author use?

Sample student paper about fiction

In the following paper, a student interprets "Lullaby," identifying what he believes the theme to be and arguing on behalf of his interpretation. His assignment was as follows:

Reread "Lullaby" and look for conflicts within the story. Decide which of these conflicts is, in your opinion, the most important. Write an essay of approximately four pages in which you (a) describe that conflict, (b) determine if the story leads you to sympathize with either side of that conflict, and (c) explore why this conflict is worth reading about. Be sure to support your interpretation with evidence from the story.

Tom Villalta
English 195, Section 1
Prof. Miller
April 21, 1993

Killing with Kindness

Leslie Marmon Silko's short story "Lullaby"   1
explores the loss of Native American culture as a
majority culture halfheartedly tries to compensate
Native Americans for the injustice they have
suffered in the past. If we examine the losses
Native Americans experience and compare them to
the "benefits" Ayah and her family receive, be
they medical, financial, or educational, we find
that Native Americans are still being exploited.

We are introduced to Ayah's losses in the   2
very beginning of the story when we first glimpse
the deep scar that her son's death has made on
her. We learn that "she did not want to think
about Jimmie. So she thought about the weaving and
the way her mother had done it" (43). This passage
suggests that the thought of her son still hurts
her. It also suggests that the culture she turns
to for comfort has already been supplanted:
traditional weaving is something to be remembered
from the past rather than practiced in the
present. Ayah is left with Jimmie's old army
blanket to keep her warm; she no longer has a
family to comfort her or the skill to weave new
blankets.

Like the loss of Jimmie in a foreign war, 3
Ayah's other losses are either directly or
indirectly associated with the American
government. For many years, government policies
were shaped by the belief that the melting of
minority cultures into the majority culture was of
benefit to minority cultures. Access to the
majority culture's medicine, money, and language
was expected to benefit minorities. But Ayah is a
victim of such aid.

We get a clear indication of this 4
victimization when Ayah's children are taken away
from her. While it would seem that the doctors
came with good intentions, their methods of
treatment conflict with Native American customs.
Ayah states, "I want a medicine man first" (46).
But she does not get a medicine man; she gets
white doctors who come with their own kind of aid,
using their own kind of means. It is also
significant that the children's symptoms indicate
that they have tuberculosis, an ailment Europeans
brought to America. When the children are allowed
home for a brief visit, Danny has lost the ability
to speak Navajo easily, and Ella no longer
remembers her mother.

Ayah is thinking about her lost children at 5
the end of the story as she is preparing for her
own death, the ultimate loss she will experience.
Silko writes that Ayah "felt the rush so big

Villalta 3

inside her heart for the babies" (51). This memory
signifies the importance they had in her life and
reinforces the dramatic effect the white man's
actions had on her. Trying to help according to
their own values, the white doctors had, in
effect, stolen Ayah's children.

Welfare subsidies also illustrate how   6
attempts at compensation have contributed to the
Native American's plight. Ayah's apparent desire
to distance herself from government aid is an
indication that she prefers to live within her own
culture, untouched by the potentially addictive
compensation society gives to Native Americans.
The story made me feel that contact with money,
the most basic and versatile of American gifts,
hurts Native Americans rather than helps them.
Welfare money buys material goods, and it is these
goods that are destroying Ayah's husband and the
culture to which he belongs. Conveying Ayah's point
of view, the narrator notes, "if the money and the
wine were gone, she would be relieved because
then they could go home again" (49). Ayah is not
angry with her husband for spending the money; she
just wants to be through with it. It means
nothing to her. Ayah's attitude when accepting the
money reinforces her apparent disdain for
financial compensation. She does not tell us that
the family needs the money every month, but that
they went to get the money "because it was time to

do this" (50). In this statement, she cites habit
as the compelling force in getting the money
rather than need or desire for it.

Chato, Ayah's husband, exemplifies what trust 7
in the dominant society can do to Native
Americans. Chato has tried to integrate himself
within American society by becoming educated in
both English and Spanish. But the story shows that
learning the language of a majority culture can be
dangerous. Chato teaches his wife how to sign her
name, and Ayah's signature leads directly to the
loss of her children. Ayah reflects that "it was
like the old ones always told her about learning
their language or any of their ways: it
endangered you" (47). She notes that Chato is "a
stranger"; he has tried too hard to melt into a
society that is unwilling to accept him. His
reward is the loss of a leg, the loss of his job,
the loss of his dignity, and eventually the loss
of his life.

In the end, when Ayah "tucked the blanket 8
around him [Chato]," (50) it was clear to me that
both Ayah and her husband would die: "Ayah knew
that with the wine he would sleep. He would not
feel it" (51). The blanket, a symbol of how
little government aid benefits Native Americans,
will not save them from freezing to death. The
medical, financial, and educational benefits all
seem, in Ayah's case, to be equally useless. They

are misdirected and incorrectly prescribed
solutions to problems created over many centuries.
Just like Jimmie's blanket, they cover serious
problems with unwanted material goods. The result
within "Lullaby" is death--the death of three
Native Americans, and, perhaps, the culture they
represent.

Villalta 5

Work Cited

Silko, Leslie. "Lullaby." Storyteller. New
York: Seaver, 1981. 43-51.

In this paper, Tom Villalta argues that the theme of
"Lullaby" is that Native Americans have been exploited and
their culture threatened. This thesis is first introduced at the
end of paragraph 1 and is restated in the second half of
paragraph 8. The second sentence of the opening paragraph,
with its references to losses and benefits, establishes the basic
structure of the essay: a discussion of losses leads to a discussion of benefits. The reference in paragraph 1 to medical,
financial, and educational benefits prepares readers for a discussion of each, and this expectation is fulfilled in paragraphs
4–7. And at the end of paragraph 7, Villalta returns to the
idea of loss, as he prepares for a conclusion that links loss to
benefits on the grounds that benefits have contributed to loss.

■ **Exercise 1** Write an outline for this paper. Compare your outline
with the assignment given on page 503. Write a comment of approximately one hundred words in which you evaluate how successfully the
paper fulfills the assignment. Imagine that the author of this paper will
read your comment. Try to be specific and helpful.

■ **Exercise 2** In consultation with your instructor, choose a short
story other than "Lullaby" and complete the assignment on page 503.

(7) Writing about drama

Although it is written to be filmed or performed on a stage, drama can also be read, which is probably the way that you will encounter it in your course work. In a performance, the director and the actors imprint the play with their own interpretations; in a book or script, you have only the printed word and the imagination you bring to it. Drama has many of the same elements as fiction, but they are presented differently.

Dialogue *Dialogue* is the principal medium through which we see action and characterization when reading a play. Examine dialogue to discover motives, internal conflicts, and relationships among characters.

Characters Often identified briefly in a list at the beginning of the play, the *characters* are developed largely through what they say and what is said about them and to them. In Ibsen's *A Doll's House,* for example, Nora's growth from a child to a mature woman can be traced through her gestures and her speech. The play opens with her reciting lines like "Me? Oh, pooh, I don't want anything." It concludes with her deciding to leave her husband and declaring, "I must educate myself." In writing about drama, you might compare characters or analyze their development and the significance of that development through their dialogue and their actions.

Plot *Plot* in drama is similar to plot in fiction and is marked by climax and conflict. Although there may be time lapses between scenes, the story line must be developed within the place constraints of the play. Subplots similar to the one outlined in the sample student paper that follows may reinforce the theme of the main plot.

In a paper you might examine how dialogue, characterizations, setting, and stage directions for gesture and movement further the action.

As you read and write ask yourself the following questions:

Analyzing Drama

1. How are the characters depicted through dialogue?
2. What is the primary conflict within the play?
3. What motivates the characters to act as they do?
4. Are there any parallels between different characters?
5. Does setting contribute to the play's action?
6. What theme can you identify in the play?

Sample student paper about drama

The following student paper discusses the significance of the subplot in *King Lear*. The writer chose to respond to the following question:

Does the conflict between Edmund and Gloucester contribute to the meaning you find in *King Lear*, or is this conflict an unnecessary distraction from the main action of the play?

Susan K. Ferk

Professor Dorgan

English 211

15 March 1993

The Subplot as Commentary in King Lear

To a careless eye, the subplot involving   1
Gloucester, Edgar, and Edmund in Shakespeare's
King Lear may appear to be trivial, unnecessary,
and a simple restatement of the theme of the main
story. After close examination, however, it is
clear that Shakespeare has skillfully introduced a
second set of characters whose actions comment on
and intensify the main plot and theme.

The first scene of King Lear sets up   2
comparison and contrast between Lear and
Gloucester. Gloucester jokes about his bastard
son while Lear angrily banishes his favorite
daughter. By the end of the second scene, we
realize how important their children are to both
men and yet how little they really know them.
Both are easily deceived: Lear by Goneril and
Regan, who convince him of their love with flowery
words, and Gloucester, who is convinced by very
little evidence of Edgar's plot against his life.
The audience is set up to accept Lear and
Gloucester as old fools. Neither man takes
responsibility for what has happened. Gloucester
says "these late eclipses" (1.2.96) have brought
about these changes, and Lear blames Cordelia for

Ferk 2

her losses. Neither realizes or acknowledges that his own foolishness has brought about these events.

Gloucester, however, does comment on Lear's 3 actions in scene 2. He is amazed that the king has limited his power so suddenly. When Edmund suggests that "sons at perfect age, and fathers declined, the father / should be as ward to the son, and the son manage his / revenue" (1.2.68-70), Gloucester is enraged by what he thinks are Edgar's words. He calls Edgar unnatural, and since this is exactly the action taken by Lear with his daughters, we can assume that he thinks Lear's act was unnatural also.

At Goneril's palace Lear foreshadows 4 Gloucester's fate when he says "Old fond eyes, / beweep this cause again, I'll pluck ye out" (1.4.278-79). In the same way that Lear fears for his eyes because of Goneril, so does Gloucester lose his eyes because of Edmund. At the end of act 1, Lear foreshadows his own destiny, "Oh, let me not be mad, not mad, sweet heaven!" (1.5.38).

Shakespeare brings together the two plots in 5 act 2 scene 2 when Regan, Cornwall, Gloucester, and Edmund meet at Gloucester's castle. Cornwall's offer of employment to Edmund made on the pretense of his royal service seems logical to the audience who knows the similarities of their

true natures. It is interesting to note that
Gloucester calls Edmund his "loyal and natural
boy" (2.1.85), while Lear names Goneril a
"degenerate bastard" (1.4.230).

Lear arrives at the castle and is outraged 6
when Cornwall and Regan do not meet him. However,
Lear decides that perhaps Cornwall is ill and
unable to come. Likewise, throughout the remainder
of act 2 Lear tries to imagine that Regan and
Cornwall love and respect him, and he makes
excuses for them when their actions do not conform
to his expectations. Lear has more at stake here
than Regan's love. If she proves as evil as
Goneril (and she proves even more so), then Lear
cannot deny that he was wrong in supposing these
two daughters more loving than his banished
Cordelia. Lear soon acknowledges that the disease
of his daughters is in his own blood. The
realization of his errors and his loss of power
and Cordelia drive him to the madness seen in
act 3.

Gloucester and Lear meet in scene 4 of act 3 in 7
the midst of a raging storm, Lear's madness, and
Gloucester's despair. Gloucester has not suffered
the worst, but his words begin to echo those of
Lear in earlier scenes. He says "Thou sayest the
King grows mad: I'll tell thee, friend, / I am
almost mad myself" (152-53). Gloucester helps the
king into the hovel and cares for him like a

child, similar to the way Edgar later helps Gloucester after his eyes are plucked out.

Death begins in act 3 scene 7. A servent dies **8** defending Gloucester, and Cornwall is fatally wounded. In the confusion, Gloucester realizes his mistakes and his former blindness. After losing his sight, he can now see. When he is turned out, his wanderings in the country remind us of Lear in the storm. Lear likewise in his despair now has learned to see.

Gloucester and Lear share many similarities **9** at this point. Both men at the height of their afflictions desire the company of Tom o'Bedlam, who represents wisdom. They also acquire a sense of justice and care for less fortunate men. Lear looks after his fool in the storm, and Gloucester calls for clothes for Tom. Their similarities intensify the pain and change in each man. Also, Shakespeare's use of a king and a nobleman both suffering from their foolishness emphasizes the universality of man's suffering. On the other hand, they do not suffer in the same way. Gloucester does not lose his mind, and Lear does not try suicide.

In the end, the story comes full circle. **10** Edgar tells Gloucester his identity and asks his father's forgiveness, thus causing Gloucester's heart to break "Twixt two extremes of passion, joy and grief" (5.3.202). Lear also dies, with

Cordelia in his arms, trying so hard to believe
her alive that it strains his heart as well. These
men have learned much, but as in real life, wisdom
in old age and recognizing one's children for what
they are do not always bring peace and happiness.
The dismal final scenes of this play in which
almost everyone dies serve to emphasize
Shakespeare's intent to show two unfortunate
characters who suffer from foolishness and
Fortune's wheel.

Work Cited

Shakespeare, William. The Tragedy of King
    Lear: The HBJ Anthology of Drama. Ed. W. B.
    Worthen. Ft. Worth: Harcourt, 1993. 174–214.

Susan Ferk supports her thesis by comparing and con-
trasting the characters of Lear and Gloucester as they move
through the play. In act 1, the plots are separate, but she
points out how in act 2 they move together and proceed
along parallel lines, crossing only occasionally. She traces this
progression throughout the play, following the characters'
actions and dialogue while emphasizing the significance of
each plot in reinforcing and intensifying the other.

■ **Exercise 3** Select a recent film or television dramatization. Write
a short essay in which you identify the theme and show how the actions
of the characters reveal that theme.

(8) Writing about poetry

Poetry shares many of the components of fiction and drama. It too may contain a narrator with a point of view, and dramatic monologues and narrative poems may have plot, setting, and characters. Like all literature, poetry uses symbols. But poetry is primarily characterized by voice and tone and its concentrated use of connotative diction, figures of speech, imagery, symbols, sound, and rhythm. Before starting to write a paper about a poem, try to capture the literal meaning of the poem in a sentence or two; then analyze how the poet transfers that meaning to the reader through the use of the following devices.

Voice   The speaker in the poem—the persona—is referred to as the *voice*. The first-person *I* in the poem is not necessarily the poet. Listen to the tone of the voice in a poem just as you do in conversation. Is it angry, joyful, melancholy, or fearful? What elements in the poem reinforce that impression?

Diction   The term *diction* means "choice of words," and the words in poetry connote meanings beyond the obvious denotative ones (see **20a[2]**). As you read, check definitions and derivations of key words in your dictionary to find meanings beyond the obvious ones. How do such definitions and derivations reinforce the meaning of the poem?

Imagery   The *imagery* in a poem is a word or phrase describing a sensory experience. Notice the images in the following lines from the poem "Meeting at Night" by Robert Browning about a lover journeying to meet his sweetheart.

> Then a mile of warm sea-scented beach;
> Three fields to cross till a farm appears;

A tap at the pane, the quick sharp scratch
And a blue spurt of a lighted match,
And a voice less loud, through its joys and fears,
Than the two hearts beating each to each!

The feeling, the smell, and the sound of the beach; the sounds of the tap at the window, the scratch of a match being lighted, the whispers, and the hearts beating; and the sight of the two lovers in the match light, embracing—all are images conveying the excitement and anticipation of lovers meeting in secret.

Figures of speech   The words or phrases that depart from the expected thought or word arrangement, to emphasize a point or to gain the reader's attention, are known as *figures of speech*. Metaphor, simile, and personification are common in poetry (see **20a**). The richness of such figures, although fully felt, is often subtle and difficult to identify. Sir Walter Raleigh uses metaphor and simile in this tightly woven couplet (a pair of rhyming or rhythmic lines):

Our graves that hid us from the searching sun
Are like drawn curtains when the play is done.

The above metaphor equates life with the sun and death with darkness, closure, endings, and separation, while the simile equates graves with curtains, suggesting that life is like a drama. All of this is suggested in just two lines. As you read a poem, identify the figures of speech and then consider how they enrich the meaning by what they suggest.

Sound   *Sound* is an important element of poetry. *Alliteration* is the repetition of initial consonants, *assonance* is the repetition of vowel sounds in a succession of words, and *rhyme* is the repetition of similar sounds either at the end of lines or within a line (internal rhyme). When you encounter such repetitions, examine and analyze their connection to each other and to the meaning of a line or a stanza or a poem. For instance, notice how the repetition of the *w* and the *s* sounds in the following lines from Elinor Wylie's "Velvet Shoes" sound like the soft whisper of walking in a snowstorm.

> Let us walk in the white snow
>   In a soundless space;

Whenever possible, read poetry aloud so that you can hear the sound of it.

Rhythm   The regular occurrence of accent or stress that we hear in poetry is known as *rhythm*, and the rhythm is commonly arranged in patterns called *meters*. Such meters depend on the recurrence of stressed and unstressed syllables in units commonly called *feet*. The most common metrical foot in English is the *iambic*, which consists of an unstressed syllable followed by a stressed one (prŏceéd). A second common foot is the *trochaic*, a stressed foot followed by an unstressed one (fíftў). Less common are the three-syllable *anapestic* (ŏvĕrcome) and the *dactylic* (páragrăph). A series of feet make up a line to form a regular rhythm, as exemplified in the following lines from Coleridge's "Frost at Midnight."

> Thĕ Frost pĕrforms ĭts secrĕt ministrў,
> Unhelpĕd bў anў wind. Thĕ owlet's cry
> Cămĕ loud—and hark, ăgain! loud as before.

Note the changes in rhythm and their significance—the ways in which rhythm conveys meaning. The second line contains a pause (caesura), which is marked by the ending of the sentence and which adds special emphasis to the intrusion of the owlet's cry.

When you study a poem, ask yourself the following questions:

Analyzing Poetry

1. What words have strong connotations?
2. What words have multiple meanings?
3. What images can you identify?
4. What figures of speech does the poet use?
5. How does the poet use sound, rhythm, and rhyme?
6. What does the poem mean to you?
7. How do the various elements of the poem combine to convey meaning?

An essay about poetry need not necessarily explore all of these questions, but by considering them you should begin to understand what the poet has accomplished—important preparation for whatever the focus of your essay will be.

Sample student paper about poetry

The following is a student essay about "The Milk Bottle," a poem by Galway Kinnell. The assignment was as follows:

Choose one of the poets we have discussed this semester; then go to the library and locate at least three articles about this poet. Write an essay of six to eight pages in which you analyze one of this poet's works and determine how your response fits within current critical views of the poet's work. Use MLA style documentation.

Susan Schubring
Professor Miller
English 103, Section 3
31 March 1993

The Thrill of Change

 Galway Kinnell's poem "The Milk Bottle" is 1
about the division in humans between mind and
body, a division which pulls us in two directions
at once. The body desires change and is happiest
when it is flowing, unconsciously, with the
universe. But the conscious mind fights change,
knowing that change ultimately brings us closer to
death, "Kinnell's principal theme for more than
two decades" (Dickstein 12). Tragically, in this
tug-of-war between desire and fear, the tug of
fear is often stronger, producing a life-long
resistance to change that can only bring
unhappiness.

 The entire poem takes place near a tide pool, 2
where the speaker is closely observing the many
creatures of the sea. One, a snail holding up its
spiral shell, is moving slowly. Another, possibly
a clam, is not moving at all, but "clamps / itself
down to the stone" (4-5). A third creature, a sea
anemone, is sucking at the speaker's finger, doing
what it likes to do best: "eat / and flow" (8-9).
As the speaker watches these sea creatures, he
starts to see connections between them and humans.

According to Richard Calhoun, Kinnell often   3
uses animals in his poetry to reveal "an
unsuspected kinship" and suggest "a mythology of
the common fate of living things" (18). Kinnell
himself has argued that

> The best poems are those in which you
> are not this or that person, but anyone,
> just a person. If you could go farther,
> you would no longer be a person but an
> animal. If you went farther still you
> would be the grass, eventually a stone.
> (Walking 23)

Stones seem so far removed from humans, and   4
yet in this poem the sea creatures "half made of
stone" (10) tell our story. The speaker notes that
we are like the creatures in that we both
"thrill / to altered existences" (10-11)--we
thrive on change. The similarity between us and
them is further emphasized in a metaphor in which
the human moving forward through life is like the
snail moving through the tide pool. Caesura helps
to re-create the hesitant movement of the snail:
"we ourselves, / who advance so far, then stop,
then creep / a little, stop again . . ." (11-13).

The connection between the snail and the   5
human actually began back in the first lines of
the poem when the speaker described the snail's
shell as a "fortress foretelling / our tragedies"
(3-4). Then in lines 13 through 17 the reader

Schubring 3

begins to understand what our tragedy is. Every
breath we take is "the bright shell / of our life-
wish encasing us" (14-15). What is our life-
wish?--to be a part of the changing universe, to
move forward, experiencing all that the world has
to offer. This is the body's unconscious desire,
just as breathing is an unconscious act. But--and
here's the tragedy--like the snail that hides
under its shell when it sees danger, our conscious
minds suddenly take over, we see how scary change
can be, and we "gasp / it all back in" (15-16).
Unlike the body, the mind is aware of time--the
past and the future--and can see that "any time /
would be OK / to go" (16-18). This phrase can be
taken two ways. First, we are aware that each
breath brings us closer to death and that we can
die at any time. Second, it means that we have a
concept of "future": there is plenty of time
ahead, so why bother changing now? The result of
this awareness of time is tragic: we stop moving,
we resist change, we stop flowing with the
universe--and in the process we stop being happy.
Ironically, efforts to avoid death produce a
stagnancy and a vague dissociation from nature
that is a kind of living death.

The solution the speaker sees to this dilemma 6
is to somehow "separate out / time from happiness"
(23-24). Lovers seem to be able to do it. Most of
the time lovers are unconsciously flowing with

the wonderful feeling of being in love, but then
they "wake up at night and see / they both are
crying" (19-20). These words recall what critic
Gary Blank has described as a "fitful wakening to
mortality's finite character" (583): the lovers
are suddenly aware that time changes everything--
someday their love will end, through death or
change of heart. But quickly they realize that it
doesn't matter because "already / we will have
lived forever" (21-22). They have separated out
time from happiness. Their happiness now is so
overwhelming, that time means nothing.

In lines 25-28, the speaker wonders whether
it's possible to do what the lovers have done, to
somehow get rid of

> the molecules scattered throughout our
> flesh that remember, skim them off,
> throw them at non-conscious things, who
> may even crave them. . . . (25-28)

In this metaphor, memory is simply molecules on
the surface of our bodies, easily scraped off and
thrown away. Sounds simple enough--but is it
possible?

In the very next line, we see that the answer
is probably no. Ironically, even as the speaker is
wishing we could get rid of our memory and our
consciousness of time, he finds himself caught up
in his own memory--a memory of "one certain /
quart of milk" (29-30). He remembers back to his

childhood in 1932, when the milkman set a bottle
of milk on the doorstep, and he, just a child,
brought it in the house. On one level, this is
just a simple, sweet memory about the olden days,
back when the milkman made daily deliveries and
milk came in bottles. But there are clues that
something more is going on here. Why, for
instance, was the milk bottle brought in and "not
ever set down" (37)? Certainly, if the milk bottle
were simply a milk bottle, it would have been set
down by now, after 30, 40, maybe 50 years have
passed! Perhaps the "certain quart of milk" is a
metaphor for a particular memory, clinking against
other milk bottle memories in his mind. He's
carried this memory in his mind for years like a
milk bottle which was never set down.

But the milk bottle takes on another meaning   9
as the poem continues. In lines 38-50, as the
speaker stands by the tide pool, a sea eagle
flying overhead "rings its glass voice" (39) and
the reader is reminded again of the glass milk
bottle. And then when the speaker talks of first
dreams rising and flowing in waves, it is as if
the dreams are milk flowing from that bottle after
all these years. Milk, so pure and white, is a
wonderful metaphor for dreams. It brings to mind
mother's milk, a source of nourishment. But where
are the dreams flowing?--"out there where there is
nothing" (44). "Out there" is the future, and the

future doesn't exist except in the mind. The
speaker concludes that what is real is "the
meantime" (50)--not the past or the future, but
now. The meantime overflows with the abundance
that life has to offer; it "streams and sparkles
over everything" (52).

In the last lines the emphasis is again on
change and on the continuous flow of the universe.
It's interesting to note that the entire poem
replicates the idea of the continuity of life.
There are no stanza breaks; the poem just runs on
and on without any stops--just as there's no
stopping the flow of time and the changes it
brings: the sea eagle will eventually "cry itself
back down into the sea" (47) and die, as will the
sea creatures, and we ourselves. The powerful love
the young lovers feel will fade with time, or die.
The milk of dreams stored in a bottle will spoil
over time, and the old glass bottle will
eventually "shatter . . . / in the decay of its
music" (45-46). The cry of the eagle and the
decaying music of the bottle create a mournful
tone, a note of sadness, which one critic suggests
comes from "our inability to do much but hold on
for an instant and experience the passing"
(Marusiak 357).

If humans are to escape the tragedy of
letting the fears of our conscious minds take over
and "gasp" at change, then we must become more

like the non-conscious creatures of the sea. In
many ways, when we were babies, before time wove
all of its tangles in our minds, we were like the
sea anemone in the beginning of the poem. As
infants, Kinnell has said, we were "not yet
divided into mind and body" and so we "felt joyous
connection with the things around us" (Poetry
230). Unaware of the concept of past and future,
babies are able to experience the fullness of "the
meantime." They find complete happiness in sucking
on a finger or drinking milk from mother's breast.
Like the sea anemone, a baby's primary concern is
"to eat / and flow."

Kinnell challenges us, in "The Milk Bottle," **12**
to come to grips with the inevitability of change,
the certainty of death--and then allow ourselves
to flow, becoming part of the continuous life/
death cycle of the planet. The division between
mind and body, the pull between desire and fear,
still exists. But we must make a choice: we can
fight change every step of the way; we can be
afraid of it and hide under our shells. Or we can
"thrill" to change, swim in the overflowing
sparkle of the meantime.

Works Cited

Blank, Gary. Rev. of Mortal Acts, Mortal Words by
      Galway Kinnell. Magill's Literary Annual:

Books of 1980. Ed. Frank N. Magill. Englewood
Cliffs: Salem P, 1981. 582-86.

Calhoun, Richard K. Galway Kinnell. New York:
Twayne, 1992.

Dickstein, Morris. "Intact and Triumphant." Rev. of
Selected Poems by Galway Kinnell. The New York
Times Book Review 19 Sept. 1982. 12+.

Kinnell, Galway. "The Milk Bottle." Mortal Acts,
Mortal Words. Boston: Houghton, 1980. 67-68.

---. "Poetry, Personality, and Death." Field 4
(1971): 56-75. Rpt. in Claims for Poetry. Ed.
Donald Hall. Ann Arbor: U of Michigan P, 1982.
219-37.

--- Walking Down the Stairs: Selections from
Interviews. Ann Arbor: U of Michigan P, 1978.

Marusiak, Joe. "Where We Might Meet Each Other: An
Appreciation of Galway Kinnell and William
Everson." The Literary Review 24 (1981): 355-
70.

■ **Exercise 4** In a single sentence, state the literal meaning of the following poem. Find three images that the poet uses to convey that meaning. Identify at least one question that you would like to raise in class.

Sonnet 73

That time of year thou mayst in me behold
When yellow leaves, or none, or few, do hang
Upon those boughs which shake against the cold,
Bare ruined choirs, where late the sweet birds sang.
In me thou see'st the twilight of such day
As after sunset fadeth in the west;

Which by and by black night doth take away,
Death's second self, that seals up all in rest.
In me thou see'st the glowing of such fire,
That on the ashes of his youth doth lie,
As the deathbed whereon it must expire,
Consumed with that which it was nourished by.
This thou perceiv'st which makes thy love more strong,
To love that well which thou must leave ere long.

William Shakespeare

■ **Exercise 5** Go to the library and locate two different discussions of this poem. Summarize these discussions and then explain how they compare or contrast.

(9) Use proper form in writing about literature.

Writing about literature follows certain special conventions.

Tense Use the present tense when discussing literature, since the author is communicating to a present reader in the present time.

Sherwood Anderson lets the boy speak for himself.

Documentation Check with your instructor about the reference format he or she prefers. Ordinarily, you will be writing about a work from a book used in the course. In such cases you usually do not need to give the source and publication information of the book. However, you should indicate if you are using another edition or anthology. One way of doing so is to use the MLA form for works cited, as explained in section **34g**, although in this case your bibliography might consist of only a single work. See the examples on pages 508, and 515.

An alternative way of providing this information is by acknowledging the first quotation in an explanatory note at the end of the paper and then giving all subsequent references to the work in the body of the paper.

[1] Yukio Mishima, "Patriotism," Fictions, ed. Joseph F. Trimmer and C. Wade Jennings, 2nd ed. (San Diego: Harcourt, 1989) 873. All subsequent references to this work will be by page number within the text.

If you use this note form, you may not need a works cited list to repeat the bibliographical information.

Whichever format you use, recall from **34g** that references to short stories and novels are by page number; references to poetry are by line number; and references to plays are usually by act, scene, and line numbers. The information in parentheses should be placed in the text directly after the quotation, and the period or comma follows the quotation marks and the parentheses (see **16e**).

Poetry   For *poems and verse plays*, type quotations of three lines or less within your text and insert a slash with a space on each side to separate the lines.

> "Does the road wind uphill all the way?" / "Yes, to the very end"—Christina Rosetti opens her poem "Uphill" with this two-line question and answer.

Quotations of more than three lines should be indented ten spaces from the left margin with double-spacing between lines (see pages 160 and 521).

Author references   Use the full name in your first reference to the author of a work and only the last name in all subsequent references. Treat male and female authors the same: Dickens and Cather, not Dickens and Miss Cather.

35b

Write well-organized answers to essay tests; write effective in-class essays.

Frequently in college you will be required to write clearly and correctly in a brief time and under pressure—for example, when you write compositions in class and when you take essay examinations.

(1) Write clear, concise, well-organized answers on essay tests.

When you write an answer to an essay question, you are conveying information, but you also are proving to your audience—the examiner—that you have mastered the information and can work with it. In other words, your purpose is both informative and persuasive. You can do several things to prepare for an essay examination.

Prepare ahead of time. Perhaps the best way to get ready for an essay examination is to prepare yourself from the first day of class. Try to decide what is most important about the material you have been learning and pay attention to indications that your instructor considers certain material especially important. As you assimilate facts and concepts, attempt to work out questions that your instructor is likely to ask. Then plan how to answer such questions.

Read instructions and questions carefully. First read the whole examination and underline specific directions (i.e., "Answer either A or B"). Then read the question that you are answering. If there are alternatives, choose wisely and stick to your choice. Most questions are carefully worded and contain specific instructions about *how* as well as *what* you are to answer. Always answer exactly the question asked without digressing. Furthermore, if you are asked to define or identify, do not evaluate. Instead, give clear, concise, and accurate definitions or identifications. If you are asked to explain, you must demonstrate that you have a depth of understanding about the subject. If you are asked to evaluate, you must decide what is important and then measure what you plan to say against that yardstick. If you are asked to compare and contrast, you will need to have a thorough knowledge of at least two subjects, and you will need to show efficiently how they are similar and/or different.

Plan your time. Although you will be working under pressure, take a few minutes to make a time schedule based on the value assigned to each question, or divide the time that you have by the number of questions. Allow some time to revise and proofread. If you are running out of time, outline the answers that you do not have time to write completely.

Plan your answer. Jot down the main points you intend to make as you think through how you plan to respond. This list of main points can serve as a working plan to help you stay on target.

State main points clearly. Make your main points stand out from the rest of the essay by identifying them in some way. For instance, you can use transitional expressions such as *first*, *second*, *third*; you can underline each main point; or you can create headings to guide the reader.

Support generalizations. Be sure you support any generalizations that you make with specific details, examples, and illustrations. Write to convince the instructor that you have a thorough knowledge of the subject. Make sure your answers are complete; do not write one- or two-sentence answers unless it is clearly specified that you should. Do not, however, pad your answers to make the instructor think you know more than you do. A clearly stated, concise, emphatic, and complete answer, though somewhat brief, will impress a reader much more than a fuzzy, shotgun-style answer that is much longer.

Stick to the question.   Sometimes you may know more about a related question than you do about the question asked. Do not wander from the question asked to answer a question you think you could handle better. Similarly, make sure that you follow your thesis as you answer the question; do not include material that is irrelevant.

Revise and proofread.   Finally, save a few minutes to reread your answer. Make whatever corrections and revisions you think are necessary. It is much better to cross out a paragraph that is irrelevant (and to replace it with a relevant one if time permits) than to allow it to stand. Similarly, consider whether your sentences are clear and correct. Check sentence structure, spelling, and punctuation; clarify any illegible scribbles.

(2) Write well-organized, clear in-class essays.

Writing an in-class essay is much like writing any other essay except that you are usually given the topic and required to produce the finished essay during one class period. Consequently, make the best possible use of your time. Take a few minutes at the beginning to consider your main idea or thesis, and jot down a short working outline or make a mental plan. Write on every other line so you have room to make revisions or changes. Be sure to reserve a few minutes at the end for revision and proofreading.

As you draft the essay, keeping your plan in mind will help you stay on track. Pace yourself so you can cover all your major points. Don't forget transitions. It is just as important to support your generalizations and to stick to the point in an in-class essay as in an essay test or in an essay you write at home.

In the time you have saved for revision and proofreading, check your essay for unity and coherence (see **32**). Strike out any unrelated matter and make any needed insertions. Unless you are instructed to do so, it is best not to use your revising time to make a clean copy of the essay. Make your revisions as neatly and clearly as possible. Proofread carefully.

■ **Exercise 6** Revise one of the in-class compositions that you wrote in this class or one of the answers that you wrote for an essay examination in another course.

35c

Write effective letters, résumés, and memos.

(1) Write effective, well-formatted letters and résumés.

Business letters Business letters use only one side of white, unlined, $8\frac{1}{2} \times 11$ inch paper. Standard business envelopes measure about $3\frac{1}{2} \times 6\frac{1}{2}$ inches or 4×10 inches. (Letter-head stationery and envelopes vary in both size and color.)

Check to see if your company or organization has a policy about letter format. The three main formats for business letters—full block, modified block, and indented—can be used for any kind of business letter. Most companies use either full block or modified block for regular correspondence, though an indented format is often used for personal business correspondence such as thank-you notes, congratulations, and the like.

A business letter has six parts: (a) heading; (b) inside address; (c) salutation; (d) body; (e) closing, which consists of the complimentary close and signature; and (f) added notations.

The *heading* gives the writer's full address and the date. Depending on your format, type the date flush left, flush right, or centered just below the letterhead. On plain stationery, type the date below your address. Arrange the letter so that it will be attractively centered on the page—flush with the left- or right-hand margin, as in the letter on page 536. Notice that the heading has no end punctuation.

The *inside address*, typed two to six lines below the heading, gives the name and full address of the recipient. Use the postal abbreviation for the state name.

Type the *salutation* (or greeting) flush with the left margin, two spaces below the inside address, and follow it with a colon. When you know the surname of the addressee, use it in the salutation of a business letter, as in the following examples.

> Dear Dr. Davis: Dear Mayor Rodriguez:
> Dear Ms. Joseph: Dear Mrs. Greissman:

▲ Note: Use *Miss* or *Mrs.* if the woman you are addressing has indicated a preference. Otherwise, use *Ms.*, which is always appropriate and which most women accept.

In letters to organizations, or to persons whose name and sex you do not know, current styles recommend omitting the salutation or addressing the office or company name:

> Dear Mobil Oil:
> Dear Registrar:

For the appropriate forms of salutations and addresses in letters to government officials, military personnel, and so on, check an etiquette book or the front or back of your college dictionary.

In the *body* of the letter, single-space within the paragraphs and double-space between them. If you use the full block or modified block format, do not indent the first line of each paragraph. If you use the indented format, indent the first line of each paragraph five to ten spaces.

Follow the principles of good writing. Organize information so the reader can grasp immediately what you want. Be clear and direct; do not use stilted or abbreviated phrasing:

NOT	The aforementioned letter	BUT	Your letter
NOT	Please send it to me ASAP.	BUT	Please send it to me as soon as possible.

The *closing* appears double-spaced below the body. If your letter is in full-block style, type it flush with the left margin; if it is in modified-block or indented style, align it with the heading. Use one of the complementary closes common to business letters, such as the following:

FORMAL	LESS FORMAL
Very truly yours,	Sincerely,
Sincerely yours,	Cordially,

Type your full name four lines below the closing and, if you are writing on company or organization business, your title on the next line.

Notations, typed flush with the left margin two lines below your title, indicate any materials you have enclosed with or attached to the letter (*enclosure* or *enc.*, *attachment* or *att.*), who will receive copies of the letter (*cc: AAW, PTN or c: AAW, PTN*), and the initials of the sender and the typist (*DM/cll*).

Model business letter

MIRACLE MILE COMMUNITY LEAGUE

LETTERH
CONTAIN
RETURN
ADDRESS

1992 South Cochran Avenue   Los Angeles, CA 90036

February 1, 1993

Dr. Nathan T. Swift
Community Health Center   **INSIDE ADDRESS**
1101 Figueroa Street
Los Angeles, CA 90027

Dear Dr. Swift: **} SALUTATION**

We have completed our study of the nutrition
education program being conducted by the Community
Health Center. The findings are encouraging.
However, we believe that awareness training for
the staff, a few schedule changes, and greater
involvement of the parents could significantly
improve the program.

– BOD

Our final report, available by March 1, will
explain these recommendations more fully. Angel
Chavez, our Vice President for Management
Development, will be happy to work with you if you
would like his assistance.

We look forward to hearing from you soon.

Sincerely,   **Complimentary close**

Dorothy Muir
                              Signature   **CLOSING**

Dorothy Muir   **Typed name**
Director   **Title**

DM/ewl **} NOTATION**

Business envelopes   The address that appears on the envelope is identical to the inside address of the letter. The return address regularly gives the full name and address of the writer.

Model addressed envelope

```
Diane Bellows
1830 Lexington Avenue
Louisville, KY 40227


                    Mr. Aaron Navik
                    Personnel Manager
                    Echo Electronics
                    627 East 3rd Street
                    Louisville, KY 40223
```

(2) Write effective application letters and résumés.

Application letters and résumés are essential parts of applying for a job. In both documents, your main concern is to emphasize your strong points, to present yourself in the best light so a prospective employer will grant you an interview. Usually written to draw the reader's attention to the résumé, the letter of application should indicate the job you want and state your qualifications briefly. In the last paragraph you should say when you are available for an interview. The résumé (page 541) that accompanies the letter of application gives more information about you than your letter can. Ordinarily, your letter should be no longer than one typed page, nor (unless you have worked for a long time and have held many positions) should your résumé.

Model application letter

1830 Lexington Avenue
Louisville, KY 40227
April 10, 1993

Mr. Aaron Navik
Personnel Manager
Echo Electronics
627 East 3rd Street
Louisville, KY 40223

Dear Mr. Navik:

Please consider me for the position of Assistant Director of Employee Benefits in the Personnel Division of Echo Electronics.

As you can see from my résumé, my major was Business Administration with an emphasis in personnel management. Whenever possible, I have found jobs and campus activities that would give me experience in dealing with people. As an assistant in the Admissions Office, I dealt with students, parents, alumni, and faculty. The position required both a knowledge of university regulations and an understanding of people.

As an administrative intern with Echo last summer, I learned about the management of a company at first hand and gained a firmer grasp of the contribution personnel management makes to the overall objectives of the company. Participants in the intern program were required to write a paper analyzing the company where we were placed. If you are interested, I will be happy to send you a copy of my paper.

I would very much like to put my interests and my training to work for Echo Electronics, and I am available for an interview at your convenience.

Sincerely,

Diane Bellows

Diane Bellows

enc.

A résumé is a list of a person's qualifications for a job and is enclosed with a letter of application. It is made up of four categories of information:

1. Personal data: name, mailing address, telephone number
2. Educational background
3. Work experience
4. References

Most businesses appreciate résumés that highlight your experience and abilities. (The traditional academic *curriculum vitae* highlights your education.)

Make your résumé look professional. Like the letter of application, the résumé is a form of persuasion designed to emphasize your qualifications for a job and get you an interview. Since there is usually more than one applicant for every job, your résumé should make the most of your qualifications. Consider devising a résumé especially tailored to each job you apply for so you can present your qualifications in the strongest light. After reading all the letters and résumés received, a potential employer usually decides to interview only the best-qualified candidates.

Writing a résumé requires the same planning and attention to detail that writing a paper does. First, make a list of the jobs you have had, the activities and clubs you have been part of, and the offices you have held. Amplify these items by adding dates, job titles and responsibilities, and a brief statement about what you learned from each of them. Arrange these items with the most recent first. Activities that may not seem relevant to the job you want can often be explained to show that you learned important things from them. See the following tips on writing a résumé and the sample résumé on page 541.

Tips on Résumé Writing

1. Make sure to include your name, address, and telephone number; unless relevant to the job, leave out personal data such as age and marital status.
2. Mention your degree, college or university, and pertinent areas of special training.
3. Think about career goals, but generally reserve mention of them for the application letter or interview (and even then make sure they enhance your appeal as a candidate). Your interest should be to match your qualifications to the employer's goals.
4. Even if an advertisement asks you to state a salary requirement, any mention of salary should usually be deferred until the interview.
5. Whenever possible, make evident any relationship between jobs you have had and the job you are seeking.
6. Use a clean, clear format and make sure the résumé is neat, orderly, and correct to show that you are an efficient, well-organized, thoughtful person.

You may find it helpful to consult one of the following books for further information on application letters, résumés, and interviews:

Angel, Juvenal L. *The Complete Resume Book and Job Getter's Guide*. 3rd ed. New York: Pocket, 1990.

Bolles, Richard N. *What Color Is Your Parachute? A Practical Manual for Job-Hunters and Career-Changers*. Berkeley: Ten Speed, annual.

Petras, Kathryn, and Ross Petras. *The Only Job Hunting Guide You'll Ever Need*. New York: Poseidon, 1989.

Smith, Michael H. *The Resume Writer's Handbook*. 2nd ed. New York: Harper & Row, 1987.

Model résumé

                              Diane Bellows
                              1830 Lexington Avenue
                              Louisville, KY 40227
                              (502) 555-3137

EDUCATION   University of Louisville, B.A., 1993
             Major: Business Administration with
                    emphasis in personnel management
             Minor: Economics with emphasis in
                    corporate finance

EXPERIENCE

   College   <u>Orientation Leader</u>, University Admissions
             Office, 1990-93. Met with prospective
             students and their parents, conducted
             tours of campus, answered questions, wrote
             reports for each orientation meeting.

             <u>Academic Committee</u>, Alpha Phi Sorority,
             1990-92. Organized study halls and
             tutoring services for disadvantaged
             students.

             <u>Advertising Manager</u>, university yearbook,
             1991. Secured advertising that made the
             yearbook self-supporting; wrote monthly
             progress report.

   Summers   <u>Intern</u>, <u>Echo Electronics</u>, June 1991.
             Learned about pension plans, health care
             benefits, employee associations, and work
             regulations as they affect employee
             relations and personnel management.

             <u>Volunteer</u>, Arthur Schneider's School Board
             re-election campaign, 1990. Wrote press
             releases, campaign brochures, direct
             mailings; did research on teacher
             competence.

REFERENCES   Placement Office
             University of Louisville
             Louisville, KY 40222
             (502) 555-3219   541

(3) Write effective memos.

Generally, memos are used for communicating a variety of information within an organization—directives on policy or procedures, requests and responses to requests for information, trip reports and monthly action summaries, and informal reports such as field reports or lab reports. While the length of the memo varies according to its purpose, the basic format is relatively standardized, though companies often have specially printed forms for the first page. Usually, memos identify the person or persons to whom the memo is addressed in the first line, the person who wrote the memo in the second line, the date in the third line, and the subject of the memo in the fourth line.

> To: J. Karl Meyer, Senior Engineer
> From: Lee Dawson, Project Director
> Date: September 20, 1993
> Subject: 4.5 oz. Dacron Load Test Results.

If the memo is long, it sometimes begins with a *statement of the purpose*, and then gives a *summary* of the discussion. This summary helps a manager or executive, who may receive thirty or forty or more memos a day, decide which ones to read carefully and which to skim. The *discussion* is the main part of the memo. If it is more than a page long, it may benefit from the use of headings to highlight the main parts. If appropriate, the memo closes with *recommendations* for action to be taken. Clearly state in this part of the memo who is to do what and when it is to be done.

The tone of a memo can be friendly and casual, informal, or formal depending on its purpose and audience. Naturally, if you are a trainee, you would probably use a relatively formal tone in a memo addressed to your supervisor, but memos you address to co-workers you know well can often be casual. Whatever the tone, however, the memo should be clear, concise, and correct. Notice the format and the tone of the sample memo. It was sent by an executive to the people she supervises. The tone is formal but not stilted, and it is clear and concise.

Model memo

MEMORANDUM

To: All Field Personnel

From: Michelle Rodriguez
           Vice President, Field Operations

Date: October 6, 1993

Subject: PICCOLO 386/486 SOFTWARE DIRECTORY

The latest issue of the PICCOLO 386/486 SOFTWARE
DIRECTORY is attached. It lists Windows-based
software products that are on the market now for
people with 80386 and 80486 microcomputer systems
such as the Piccolo 386 or 486.

We are trying to list only those products that we
have seen demonstrated on the 386 or that a vendor,
dealer, or distributor claims will run on the 386,
but we make no guarantees.

Please note: Inclusion in the directory does not
imply that Piccolo endorses the products or
suppliers or recommends them in preference to others
not listed. Further, Piccolo does not warrant that
these products are compatible with Piccolo systems.
The buyer is solely responsible for determining
application and suitability.

Although this directory can be copied for
distribution to others, it is a temporary listing
intended primarily for your own use. In late
November it will be revised and published in booklet
form as a stock item.

Approximately 250 vendors have already been
contacted for information on software products that
might be appropriate in the directory. A Software
Vendor Listing Form is included in the back of the
directory for additional vendors to whom you may
wish to give copies.

MR/jh

■ **Exercise 7**   Choose one of the following:

1. Write a letter to a former teacher to express appreciation for recommending you for a summer job.
2. In a letter, call the attention of your representative in city government to repairs needed on neighborhood streets.
3. Write a letter to a national record company complaining about the technical quality of a tape you ordered from them.
4. Prepare a résumé, and then write a letter of application for a position you are qualified to fill.
5. Write a memo to the president of the university requesting that the library hours not be cut back.

GLOSSARY OF USAGE

The following short glossary covers the most common usage problems. It also distinguishes between written and spoken English and formal and informal styles. An expression that may be acceptable in spoken English or in a letter to a friend is labelled *informal* and is usually not acceptable in academic or business writing. The formal written style is sometimes referred to as edited American English. The following are labels used in this glossary.

FORMAL   Words or phrases listed in dictionaries without special usage labels, appropriate in college writing.

INFORMAL   Words or phrases that dictionaries label *informal, slang,* or *colloquial,* although often acceptable in spoken language, are not generally appropriate in college writing.

UNACCEPTABLE   Words or phrases labeled in dictionaries as *archaic, illiterate, nonstandard, obsolete, substandard* are generally not accepted in formal or informal writing.

You may also wish to consult **18b** for a list of words whose spelling leads to confusing usages.

a, an, the   Use *a* before the sound of a consonant: **a** yard, **a** U-turn, **a** one-base hit. Use *an* before a vowel sound: **an** empty can, **an** M.D., **an** ax, **an** X-ray. Use *a* or *an* with a singular count noun when generalizing: A dog makes **a** good companion. Use *the* when referring to a specific thing: Did you walk **the** dog? See **count, noncount nouns** in the **Glossary of Terms**.

accept, except   *Accept* means "to receive"; *except* means "to exclude": I **accept** your apology. All **except** Joe will go.

accidently   A misspelling of *accidentally.*

adapt, adopt *Adapt* means "to change for a purpose"; *adopt* means "to take possession": You must **adapt** to extreme cold. The company will **adopt** a new policy.

adverse, averse *Adverse* means "antagonistic" or "unfavorable." *Averse* means "opposed to": We would have gone had it not been for **adverse** weather conditions. After seeing the weather broadcast, I was **averse** to going on the trip.

advice, advise *Advice* is a noun; *advise* is a verb: I accept your **advice.** Please **advise** me of the situation.

affect, effect The verb *affect* means "to influence, attack" or "to touch the emotions." The noun *effect* means "result of an action or antecedent": Smoking **affects** the heart; his tears **affected** her deeply. Drugs have side **effects**; The **effect** on sales was good. When used as a verb, *effect* means "to produce an effect": The medicine **effected** a complete cure.

aggravate Widely used for *annoy* or *irritate*. Many writers, however, restrict the meaning of *aggravate* to "intensify, make worse": Noises **aggravate** a headache.

ain't Unacceptable in writing unless used in dialogue or for humorous effect.

allusion, illusion An *allusion* is a casual or indirect reference. An *illusion* is a false idea or an unreal image: The **allusion** was to Shakespeare. His idea of college is an **illusion.**

alot A misspelling of the overused and nonspecific phrase *a lot*.

already, all ready *Already* means "before or by the time specified." *All ready* means "completely prepared."

alright Not yet a generally accepted spelling of *all right*.

altogether, all together *Altogether* means "wholly, thoroughly." *All together* means "in a group": That book is **altogether** too difficult, unless the class reads it **all together.**

a.m., p.m. (OR **A.M., P.M.)** Use only with figures: The show will begin at 7:00 **p.m.** [OR at seven in the evening]; NOT at seven in the *p.m.*

among, between Prepositions with plural objects (including collective nouns). As a rule, use *among* with objects denoting three or more (a group), and use *between* with those denoting only two (or twos): danced **among** the flowers, whispering **among** themselves; reading **between** the lines, just **between** you and me.

amount of, number of *Amount of* is followed by singular nouns; *number of,* by plural nouns: an **amount of** jewelry, money, work, postage [singular]; a **number of** necklaces, bills, cups, books. [plural]

and etc. *Etc.* is an abbreviation of the Latin *et* ("and") *cetera* ("other things"). Omit the redundant *and.* See also **etc.**

anyone, any one; everyone, every one Distinguish between each one-word and two-word compound. *Anyone* means "any person at all"; *any one* refers to one of a group. Similarly, *everyone* means "all," and *every one* refers to each one in a group.

Was **anyone** hurt? Was **any one** of you hurt?
Everyone should attend. **Every one** of them should attend.

anyways, anywheres Unacceptable for *anyway, anywhere.*

as 1. As a conjunction, use *as* to express sameness of degree, quantity, or manner: Do **as** I do. As a preposition, use *as* to express equivalence: I think of Tom **as** my brother [Tom = brother]. Use *like* to express similarity: Tom is **like** a brother.
  2. Use *if, that,* or *whether* instead of *as* after such verbs as *feel, know, say,* or *see:* I do not know **if** [NOT as] my adviser is right.
  3. In subordinate clauses, prefer *because* to introduce a causal relationship or *while* to introduce a time relationship: **Because** [NOT as] it was raining, we watched TV. OR **While** [NOT as] it was raining, we watched TV.

assure, ensure, insure *Assure* means "to state with confidence." *Ensure* and *insure* are used interchangeably to mean "make certain." *Insure* has the further meaning of "to protect against loss": Marlon **assured** me that he would vote for my ticket. I **insured** (or **ensured**) that Vincent had his tickets before I left home. Bing **insured** her car against theft.

as to Imprecise; use the clearer *about:* He wasn't certain **about** [NOT as to] the time.

awful Unacceptable for the often overused adverb *awfully:* She is **awfully** [NOT awful] intelligent.

awhile, a while *Awhile,* an adverb, is not used as the object of a preposition: We rested **awhile.** [Compare: We rested for **a while.**]

bad Unacceptable as an adverb: Bill danced **badly** [NOT bad]. Acceptable as a subject complement after sense verbs such as *feel, look, smell.* See **4b.**

because Unacceptable in the expression *is because,* since the *to be* signifies equality between the subject and what follows. See **23e**.

being as, being that Wordy and imprecise; use *since, because.*

beside, besides Always a preposition, *beside* usually means "next to," sometimes "apart from": The chair was **beside** the table. As a preposition, *besides* means "in addition to" or "other than": She has many books **besides** those on the table. As an adverb, *besides* means "also" or "moreover": The library has a fine collection of books; **besides** it has a number of valuable manuscripts.

better State the verb; use *had better:* We **had better** [NOT better] run the spellcheck.

between See **among, between.**

bring, take Both words describe the same action but from different standpoints. Someone *brings* something *to* the location of the speaker, while someone else *takes* something *away* from the location of the speaker: **Bring** your book when you come here. I **take** my notes home with my book.

but what, but that Informal after expressions of doubt such as "no doubt" or "did not know." Use *that:* I do not doubt **that** [NOT but what] they are correct.

can, may *Can* refers to ability and *may* refers to permission: I **can** [am able to] drive fifty miles an hour, but I **may** not [am not permitted to] exceed the speed limit.

can't hardly, can't scarcely Use *can hardly, can scarcely.*

capital, capitol A *capital* is a governing city; it also means "funds." As a modifier, *capital* means "chief" or "principal." A *capitol* is a statehouse; the *Capitol* is the U.S. Congressional building in Washington, DC.

censor, censure *Censor* (verb) means "to remove or suppress because of moral or otherwise objectionable ideas"; a *censor* (noun) is a person who suppresses those ideas. *Censure* (verb) means "to blame or criticize"; a *censure* (noun) is an expression of disapproval or blame.

center around Informal for "to be focused on" or for "to center on."

chairman, chairperson, chair *Chairman* is misused as a generic term. *Chairperson* or *chair* is generally preferred as the generic term.

cite, site, sight *Cite* means "to mention." *Site* is a locale. *Sight* is a view or the ability to see: Be sure to **cite** your sources in your paper. The president visited the disaster **site.** What a beautiful **sight!**

compare to, compare with   *Compare to* means "regard as similar" and *compare with* means "examine to discover similarities or differences": The instructor **compared** the diagram **to** [NOT with] a map. The student **compared** the first draft **with** [NOT to] the second draft.

complement, compliment   *Complement* means "to complete" or "to supply needs." *Compliment* means "to express praise." *Complimentary* means "given free," as in "**complimentary** tickets": Their personalities **complement** each other. Betsy **complimented** Jim on his performance.

different than, different from   Both are widely used, although *different from* is generally preferred in formal writing.

disinterested, uninterested   *Disinterested* means "impartial" or "lacking prejudice": a **disinterested** referee. *Uninterested* means "indifferent, lacking in interest."

don't   Unacceptable when used for *doesn't:* My father **doesn't** [NOT don't] dance.

due to   Usually avoided in formal writing when used as a preposition in place of *because* or *on account of:* **Because of** [NOT due to] holiday traffic, we arrived an hour late.

effect   See **affect, effect.**

e.g.   Means "for example." Replace with English equivalent *for example* or *for instance.* Do not confuse with **i.e.**

elicit, illicit   *Elicit* means "to draw forth." *Illicit* means "unlawful": It is **illicit** to **elicit** public funds for your private use.

emigrate from, immigrate to   The prefix *e-* (a variant of *ex-*) means "out of." To *emigrate* is to go out of one's own country to settle in another. The prefix *im-* (a variant of *in-*) means "into." To *immigrate* is to come into a different country to settle. The corresponding adjective or noun forms are *emigrant* and *immigrant:* The Ulster Scots **emigrated from** Scotland to Ireland and then **immigrated to** the southern United States. (Compare export, import.)

eminent, imminent.   *Eminent* means "distinguished"; *imminent* means "about to happen": Linda Hughes is an **eminent** scholar. The storm is **imminent.**

ensure   See **assure, ensure, insure.**

enthused   Informal usage, not accepted in formal writing. Use *enthusiastic.*

especially, specially *Especially* means "outstandingly"; *specially* means "for a particular purpose, specifically": This is an **especially** nice party. I bought this tape **specially** for this occasion.

-ess A female suffix now considered sexist, therefore unacceptable. Use *poet, author, actor,* and *waiter* or *server* instead of *poetess, authoress, actress,* and *waitress.*

etc. In formal writing substitute *and so on* or *and so forth.* Since *etc.* means "and other things," *and etc.* is redundant.

everyone, every one See **anyone, any one.**

except See **accept, except.**

explicit, implicit *Explicit* means "expressed directly or precisely." *Implicit* means "implied or expressed indirectly": The instructions were **explicit.** There was an **implicit** suggestion in her lecture.

farther, further Generally, *farther* refers to geographic distance: six miles **farther.** *Further* is used as a synonym for *additional* in more abstract references: **further** delay, **further** proof.

fewer, less *Fewer* refers to people or objects that can be counted; *less* refers to amounts that can be observed or to abstract nouns: **fewer** pencils, **less** milk, **less** support.

figure Informal for *believe, think, conclude,* or *predict,* all of which are more precise.

former, latter *Former* refers to the first of two; *latter* to the second of two. If three or more items are mentioned, use *first* and *last:* Sean and Ian are both British; the **former** is from Ireland, and the **latter** is from Scotland.

genus Singular form for *genera.* Takes singular verb: The genus **is**. . .

go, goes Inappropriate in written language for *say, says:* **I say** [NOT go] "Hello there!" Then he **says** [NOT goes] "Glad to see you!"

good, well *Good* is an adjective frequently misused as an adverb; *well* is an adverb: He dances **well** [NOT good]. He had a **good** time. *Well* in the sense of "in good health" may be used as a subject complement interchangeably with *good* in such expressions as "Pedro doesn't feel **well** (or **good**)."

great Overworked for more precise words such as *skillful, good, clever, enthusiastic,* or *very well.*

half a, a half, a half a Use *half of a, half a,* or *a half.*

hanged, hung   *Hanged* refers specifically to "put to death by hanging." *Hung* is the usual past participle.

he   Used inappropriately as a generic term that possibly could refer to a woman. See **6b, 19j**.

hisself   Use *himself*.

hopefully   Means "with hope." Used inappropriately for *I hope* or *it is hoped*.

i.e.   Abbreviation for the Latin *id est*. Use instead the English "that is." Do not confuse *i.e.* with **e.g.**

if, whether   Use *if* in a state of condition; use *whether* as condition: I can't go **if** you drive; **whether** or not I go depends upon who is driving.

illusion   See **allusion, illusion**.

imminent   See **eminent, imminent**.

implicit   See **explicit, implicit**.

imply, infer   *Imply* means "suggest without actually stating," and *infer* means "draw a conclusion based on evidence": He **implied** that he was angry, but I **inferred** that he was satisfied.

incidently   A misspelling of *incidentally*.

ingenious, ingenuous   *Ingenious* means "creative or shrewd." *Ingenuous* means "innocent or unworldly": Terry's **ingenious** plan worked without complication. The criminal's **ingenuous** smile was misleading.

irregardless   Use *regardless*.

its, it's   *Its* is a possessive pronoun, as in "The dog buried **its** bone." *It's* is a contraction of *it is*, as in "**It's** a beautiful day."

kind, sort   Used interchangeably. Singular forms are modified by *this* or *that*, plural forms by *these* or *those*: **This kind (sort)** of argument is unacceptable. **These kinds (sorts)** of arguments are unacceptable.

kind of a, sort of a   Use *kind of* and *sort of*: This **kind** of   [NOT kind of a] book. . . .

lay, lie   Use *lay (laid, laying)* in the sense of "put or place." Use *lie (lay, lain, lying)* in the sense of "to rest or recline." *Lay* takes an object (to **lay** something), while *lie* does not. See also **7a(2)**.

> LIE   He had **laid**   [NOT lain] the book on the table.
> The man was **laying**   [NOT lying] the carpet.

> LAY   He had **lain**   [NOT laid] down to take a nap.
> The woman was **lying**   [NOT laying] in the bed.

learn   Unacceptable for *teach, instruct, inform:* He **taught** me   [NOT learned me] bowling.

leave   Unacceptable for *let* in the sense of allowing: **Let**   [NOT leave] him have the hammer.

less   See **fewer, less.**

liable, likely   *Liable* usually means "exposed" or "responsible" in an undesirable sense. *Likely* means "probably," "destined," or "susceptible": If you wreck the car, you are **liable** for damages. With her brains, she is **likely** to succeed.

like   Although widely used as a conjunction in spoken English, *as, as if,* and *as though* are preferred for written English.

lose, loose   *Lose* is a verb: did **lose,** will **lose.** *Loose* is chiefly an adjective: a **loose** belt.

lots   Informal for *many, much.*

mankind   Considered offensive because it excludes women. Use *humanity, human race.*

many, much   *Many,* used with plural nouns, refers to numbers: **many** stores, too **many** cats, *much,* used with singular nouns, refers to amount: **much** courage.

may be, maybe   *May be* is a verb phrase; *maybe* is an adverb: The rumor **may be** true. **Maybe** the rumor is true.

may, can   See **can, may.**

media, medium   *Media* is plural; *medium* is singular.

morale, moral   *Morale* (a noun) refers to a mood or spirit: The **morale** was high. *Moral* (an adjective) refers to correct conduct or ethical character: a **moral** decision. *Moral* (as a noun) refers to the principle of a story: the **moral** of the story.

most   Use *almost* in expressions such as "almost everyone," "almost all." Use *most* only as a superlative: **most** writers.

much   See **many, much.**

myself   Use only when preceded by the antecedent in the same sentence: Chin and **I**   [NOT myself] went swimming.   BUT **I** made **myself** go swimming.

nauseous, nauseated   Frequently confused. *Nauseous* means "producing nausea"; *nauseated* means "enduring nausea": I felt **nauseated** when I smelled the **nauseous** spoiled meat.

nowhere near Informal. Use *not nearly:* I had **not nearly** [NOT nowhere near] enough money.

nowheres Unacceptable for *nowhere.*

number As subjects, *a number* is generally plural and *the number* is singular. Make sure that the verb agrees with the subject: **A number** of possibilities **are** open. **The number** of possibilities **is** limited. See also **amount of, number of.**

of Often mistaken for the sound of the unstressed *have:* "They must **have** [OR would **have,** could **have,** might **have,** ought to **have,** may **have**—NOT must of] gone home.

off of Use *off* in phrases such as "walked **off** [NOT off of] the field."

OK, O.K., okay Informal usage. All three are acceptable spellings. It is often better to replace *OK* with a more specific word.

on account of Use the less wordy *because:* I went home **because** [NOT on account of] I was tired.

plus Acceptable as a preposition. Weak when used instead of the coordinating conjunction *and.*

p.m. See **a.m., p.m.**

precede, proceed To *precede* is to "go ahead of"; to *proceed* is to "go forward": His song will **precede** the fight scene. The song will **proceed** without hesitation.

principal, principle The adjective or noun *principal* means "chief" or "chief official." The noun *principle* means "fundamental truth": A **principal** factor in the salary decision was his belief in the **principle** of sexual equality.

raise, rise *Raise (raised, raising)* means "to lift or cause to move upward, to bring up or increase." *Rise (rose, risen, rising)* means "to get up, to move or extend upward, ascend." *Raise* (a transitive verb) takes an object; *rise* (an intransitive verb) does not: Retailers **raised** prices. Retail prices **rose** sharply.

rarely ever Use either *rarely* alone or *hardly ever:* He **rarely** (or **hardly ever**) [NOT rarely ever] goes to the library.

real, really Use *real* as an adjective, *really* as an adverb. *Real* is often misused in the following expression where it is an adverb modifying the adjective *beautiful:* It is a **really** [NOT real] beautiful day.

regard, regarding, regards Use *in regard to, with regard to,* or *regarding.*

sensuous, sensual *Sensuous* refers to gratification of the senses in response to art, music, nature, and so on; *sensual* refers to gratification **shall, will** of the physical senses.

sit, set Use *sit* in the sense of "be seated" and *set* in the sense of "to place something": Jonathon **sat** under the tree. Maria **set** the cookies on the table. See **7a(2)**.

so Overused as an intensifier; use a more precise modifier: She was **intensely** [NOT so] focused.

some Informal and vague when used as a substitute for such words as *remarkable, memorable:* She was a **remarkable** [NOT some] athlete.

someone, some one Distinguish between each one-word and two-word compound. See **anyone, any one.**

sometime, sometimes, some time *Sometime* is an adverb meaning "at an unspecified time"; *sometimes* is an adverb meaning "at times"; *some time* is an adjective–noun pair meaning "a span of time": Let's go to the movie **sometime. Sometimes** we go to the movies. They agreed to allow **some time** to pass before going to the movies together again.

somewheres Unacceptable for *somewhere.*

sort, sort of See **kind; kind of a.**

specially See **especially, specially.**

stationary, stationery *Stationary* means "in a fixed position"; *stationery* means "writing paper and envelopes."

sure Informal when used as an adverb, as in "I **sure** like your new hat." Use *certainly* or *undoubtedly.*

take See **bring, take.**

that, which Use *that* with a restrictive clause: The cup **that** is on the table is full (distinguishes a specific cup that is full). Use *which* with a nonrestrictive clause: The cup, **which** is on the table, is full. ("which is on the table" gives nonessential information). Read the two example sentences aloud to notice the different intonation patterns. See **12d**.

their, there, they're *Their* is the possessive form of *they; there* is ordinarily an adverb or an expletive; *they're* is a contraction of *they are:* **There** is no explanation for **their** behavior. **They're** making trouble **there** on the ball field.

theirself, theirselves Use *themselves.*

them   Unacceptable when used as an adjective: **those** apples OR **these** apples   [NOT them apples].

then   Sometimes incorrectly used for *than*. Unlike *then*, *than* does not relate to time.

this here, that there, these here, them there   Redundant; use *this, that, these, those*.

thusly   Use *thus*.

to, too   Distinguish the preposition *to* from the adverb *too*: When the weather is **too** hot to play ball, they go **to** the movies.

toward, towards   Both acceptable. *Toward* is preferred as the American usage.

try and   Informal for *try to*: I will **try to**   [NOT try and] see him today.

unique   Because it means "one of a kind," it is illogical to use *unique* with a comparative, as in *very unique*. Do not confuse with *unusual*.

utilize   Often pretentious; use *use*.

ways   Unacceptable for *way* when referring to distance: It's a long **way**   [NOT ways] from home.

where   Informal as a substitute for *that*: I saw on TV **that**   [NOT where] she had been elected.

where . . . at, where . . . to   Omit the superfluous *at, to*: **Where** is the library   [OMIT at]? **Where** are you moving   [OMIT to]?

which   When referring to persons, use *who* or *that*. See **that, which.**

whose, who's   *Whose* indicates possession: **Whose** book is this? *Who's* is the contraction of *who is*: **Who's** going to the movie?

with regards to   See **regard, regarding, regards.**

your, you're   *Your* is the possessive of *you*: in **your** house. *You're* is a contraction of *you are*: **You're** gaining strength. See also **its, it's.**

GLOSSARY OF TERMS

This glossary presents brief explanations of frequently used terms. Consult the index for references to further discussion of most of the terms and for a number of terms not listed.

absolute phrase   A grammatically unconnected part of a sentence—generally a noun or pronoun followed by a participle (and sometimes modifiers): We will have a cookout, **weather permitting** [noun + present participle]; **The national anthem sung for the last time,** the old stadium was closed   [noun + past participle with modifier]. Some absolute phrases have the meaning (but not the structure) of an adverb clause. See **1d(3)**, **24a**, and **30b(4)**. See also **phrase** and **sentence modifier.**

abstract noun   A noun that expresses qualities, concepts, and emotions that cannot be perceived through the senses: truth, justice, fear, future. See **20a(3)**.

accusative case   See **case.**

acronym   A word formed by combining the initial letters of a series of words: LASER—Light Amplification by Stimulated Emission of Radiation.

active voice   The form of a transitive verb indicating that its subject performs the action the verb denotes: Emily *sliced* the ham. See **7**, **29d**. See also **passive voice**, **verb**, and **voice.**

adjective   The part of speech modifying a noun or a pronoun. *Limiting adjectives* restrict the meaning of the words they modify: *that* pie, *its* leaves. *Descriptive adjectives* name a quality of a noun, including degrees of comparison: *red* shirt, *bigger* planes. *Proper adjectives* are derived from proper nouns: *Spanish* rice. See **9a**. Two or more adjectives separated by a comma, instead of by coordinating conjunctions, are referred to as *coordinate adjectives:* A *brisk, cold* walk. See **12c(2)**. *Interrogative adjectives* are used to ask questions: *Whose book is it?* See also **comparative, comparison,** and **predicate adjective.**

adjective clause   A subordinate clause used as an adjective: people *who bite their fingernails.* An adjective clause may be restrictive. See **1e(2)**, **12d(1)**, and **25a**. See also **clause.**

adjective phrase   A phrase used as an adjective: The woman *carrying the large notebook* is my sister. See **1d(2)**. See also **phrase.**

adverb   The part of speech modifying a verb, an adjective, or another adverb: *rapidly* approached, *too* bitter, *very* graciously accepted. An adverb may also modify a verbal, a phrase or clause, or the rest of the sentence: *Usually,* an artist does her best work when she is focusing *entirely* on the task at hand.

adverb clause   A subordinate clause used as an adverb. An adverb clause may indicate time, place, cause, condition, concession, comparison, purpose, or result: *Although he is usually quiet* [concession], *everyone listens to him when he speaks* [time], *because he makes good suggestions* [cause]. See **1e(2)**, **12b** and **30b(1)**. See also **clause** and **conditional clause.**

adverbial conjunction   See **conjunctive adverb.**

adverb phrase   A phrase used as an adverb. An adverb phrase may indicate time, place, cause, condition, concession, comparison, purpose, or result. See **1d(2)** and **24a(2)**. See also **adverb clause.**

agreement   The correspondence in number and person of a subject and verb (*the dog barks, dogs bark*) or in number and gender of a pronoun and its antecedent (the *team* boarded *its* bus, the *members* carrying *their* bags). See **6**.

allusion   A brief, unexplained reference to a work or to a person, place, event, or thing that the writer expects the reader to be familiar with. See also **20a(4)**.

ambiguity   The capability of being understood in two or more different ways: "Reading alone comforts me" could mean *"Reading by myself* comforts me" or *"Only reading* comforts me."

analogy   A rhetorical device using the features of something familiar (and often concrete) to explain something unfamiliar (and often abstract), or similarities between things that are not usually associated.

analysis   A separation of a whole into its constituent parts.

analytical reading   A reader's active engagement by the writer's ideas and how the ideas are expressed; paying attention to content and form.

antecedent A word or a word group that a pronoun refers to. The antecedent may follow (but usually precedes) the pronoun: *Pets can be polite or rude, like their trainers.* See **6b** and **28**.

antonym A word that means the opposite of another: *follow* is the antonym for *lead*.

APA American Psychological Association. See **34j–k**.

appeal The means of persuasion in argumentative writing; appeal relies upon reason, authority, and/or emotion.

appositive A noun or noun phrase placed next to or very near another noun or noun phrase to identify, explain, or supplement its meaning. Appositives may be restrictive. See **12d(1)**, **24a**, **30b(4)**, and **30c(3)**.

appropriate Writing suitable for the audience, purpose, and occasion.

argument A kind of writing that uses various rhetorical strategies and appeals to convince the reader of the truth or falsity of a given proposition or thesis. See **appeal** and **thesis.**

article *The, a,* or *an* used as adjectives before nouns: *the* cups, *a* cup, *an* extra cup. *The* is a definite article. *A* (used before consonant sounds) and *an* (used before vowel sounds) are indefinite articles. See **9f**.

audience The person or persons whom the writing is intended for. See **33a**. A *specific audience* has considerable knowledge of the subject. A *general audience* does not have expertise on the subject but is willing to read about it.

auxiliary A form of *be, have,* or *will* that combines with a verb to indicate voice, tense, or mood: *was* going, *had* gone, *will* go. See **7** and **22b**.

balanced sentence A sentence with grammatically equal structures. See **29g**.

bibliography A list of books, articles, essays, or other material, usually on a given subject.

brainstorming A method of generating ideas about a subject, involves listing ideas as they occur in a session of intensive thinking about that subject. See **33c**.

cardinal number See **number.**

case The form or position of a noun or pronoun that shows its use or relationship to other words in a sentence. The three cases in English are the *subjective* (or nominative), which usually is the subject of a finite verb; the *possessive* (or genitive), which indicates ownership; and the *objective* (or accusative), which functions as the object or the subject of a verb or preposition. See **5** and **15a**.

cause and effect A rhetorical strategy by which a writer seeks to explain why something happened or what the results of a particular event or condition were or will be. See **32d(4)**.

CD-ROM Computer Disk Read Only Memory. See **memory.**

citation Notation (usually parenthetical) in a paper that refers to a given source. See **34g(1)** and **34j(1)**.

chronological order The arrangement of events in a time sequence (usually the order in which they occurred).

claim A conclusion that a writer expects readers to accept. Should be supported by source material that is accurate and representative. See **31**.

classification and division A rhetorical strategy in which a writer sorts elements into categories (*classification*) or breaks down a topic into its constituent parts, showing how they are related (*division*). See **32d(6)**.

clause A sequence of related words within a sentence. A clause has both a subject and a predicate and functions either as an independent unit (*independent clause*) or as a dependent unit (*subordinate clause,* used as an adverb, an adjective, or a noun). See **1e** and **24**. See also **sentence.**

> I saw the moon. It was glowing brightly. [sentences]
> **I saw the moon,** for **it was glowing brightly.** [independent clauses connected by a coordinating conjunction]
> I saw the moon, **which was glowing brightly.** [adjective clause]
> I saw the moon **because it was glowing brightly.** [adverb clause]
> **I saw that the moon was glowing brightly.** [noun clause—direct object]

cliché An expression that may once have been fresh and effective but that has become trite and worn out with overuse. See **20c**.

coherence The principle that all the parts of a piece of writing should stick together, one sentence leading to the next, each idea evolving from the previous one. See **25** and **32b**.

collaborative writing A method of writing involving cooperative effort between two or more persons.

collective noun A noun singular in form that denotes a group: *flock, jury, band, public, committee.* See **6a(8)**.

colloquialism A word or phrase characteristic of informal speech. "He's *grumpy*" is a colloquial expression describing an irritable person.

comma splice, comma fault A punctuation error in which two independent clauses are joined by a comma with no coordinating conjunction. See **3**.

> COMMA SPLICE Patricia went to the game, her brother stayed home.
> REVISED Patricia went to the game, **and** her brother stayed home.

common gender A term applied to words that can refer to either sex (*parent, instructor, salesperson, people, anyone*). See **6b(1)**.

common noun A noun referring to any or all members of a class or group (*woman, city, apple, holidays*) rather than to a specific member (*Susan Anthony, Las Vegas, Winesap, New Year's Day*). See **proper noun.**

comparative degree. See **degree.**

comparison and contrast A rhetorical strategy in which the writer examines similarities and/or differences between two ideas or objects. See **32d(5)**.

complement A word or words used to complete the sense of a verb. Although the term may refer to a direct or an indirect object, it usually refers to a subject complement, an object complement, or the complement of a verbal like *be*. See **1b**.

complete predicate A simple predicate (a verb or verb phrase) with any objects, complements, or modifiers: We *ate the fresh homemade pie before the salad.* See **predicate.**

complete subject A simple subject (a noun or noun clause) with any modifiers: *Everyone at the picnic* liked the pie. See **1b**. See also **subject.**

complex sentence A sentence containing one independent clause and at least one subordinate clause: My neighbor noticed a stranger [independent clause] who looked suspicious [subordinate clause]. See **1c**, **24**, and **30c(1)**. See also **clause.**

compound–complex sentence A sentence containing at least two main clauses and one or more subordinate clauses: When the lights went out [subordinate clause], there was no flashlight at hand [independent clause], so we sat outside and gazed at the stars [independent clause]. See **1e**. See also **clause.**

compound predicate   Two or more predicates having the same subject: Clara Barton *nursed the injured during the Civil War* and *founded the American Red Cross later.* See **2a** and **30c(2).** See also **predicate.**

compound sentence   A sentence containing at least two independent clauses and no subordinate clause: The water supply was dwindling [independent clause], so rationing became mandatory [independent clause]. See **1f, 12a,** and **14a.** See also **clause.**

compound subject   Two or more subjects of the same verb: *Women, men,* and *children* call the crisis center.

conclusion   A sentence, paragraph, or group of paragraphs that bring a piece of writing to a satisfying close, usually by summarizing, restating, evaluating, asking a question, or encouraging the reader to continue thinking about the topic. See **33f(2).**

concrete, concrete noun   Concrete words refer to things that can be experienced through the senses: *cologne, sunset, onions, thorns.* Concrete words make writing clear, vivid, and lively. Compare **abstract noun.**

conditional clause   An adverb clause (beginning with such conjunctions as *if, unless, whether, provided*) expressing a real, imagined, or nonfactual condition: *If she does a good job,* then I will pay her. See **7c.** See **clause.**

conjugation   A set or table of the inflected forms of a verb that indicate tense, person, number, voice, and mood. See **7.**

conjunction   A part of speech (such as *and* or *although*) used to connect words, phrases, clauses, or sentences. *Coordinating conjunctions* (*and, but, or, nor, for, so, yet*) connect and relate words and word groups of equal grammatical rank: Color-blind people can usually see blue, *but* they may confuse red with green *or* with yellow. See **1c(7), 26.** See also **correlatives.**

   Subordinating conjunctions (such as *although, if, when*—see list on page 23) mark a dependent clause and connect it with a main clause: *When* Frank sulks, he acts *as if* he were deaf. See **24.**

conjunctive adverb   A word (*however, therefore, nevertheless*) that serves not only as an adverb but also as a connective. See **3b, 14a,** and **32b(4).**

connective   A word or phrase that links and relates words, phrases, clauses, or sentences (*and, although, otherwise, finally, on the contrary, which, not only . . . but also*). Conjunctions, conjunctive adverbs, transitional expressions, relative pronouns, and correlatives function as connectives. See **32b(4).**

connotation   The suggested or implied meaning of a word through the associations it evokes in the reader's mind. See **20a(2)**. See also **denotation.**

context   The surrounding information that helps to give a particular word, sentence, or paragraph its meaning: *cabinet* means "a group of leaders" in a political context, "a place for storage" in a building context. Context also refers to circumstances surrounding the composition of a piece of writing—the occasion, the purpose, the audience, and what the writer and reader already understand about the topic. See **33a**.

contraction   Condensing two words to one by adding an apostrophe to replace the omitted letter or letters: *aren't, don't*. Contractions are used primarily in spoken or informal written language.

contrast   See **comparison and contrast.**

controlling idea   The central idea of a paragraph or essay, often expressed in the paragraph's *topic sentence* or the essay's *thesis statement.* See **32a**.

conventional   Language that complies with the accepted rules of formal written English, generally termed *correct.*

coordinating adjective   See **adjective.**

coordinating conjunction   One of seven connectives: *and, but, for, or, nor, so, yet.* See **1c**, **12a**, **24**, and **26**. See also **conjunction.**

coordination   The use of grammatically equivalent constructions to link ideas, usually (but not always) those of equal weight. See **12c**, **24b**, and **26**.

correlatives   One of five pairs of linked connectives: *both ... and; either ... or; neither ... nor; not only ... but also; whether ... or.* Correlatives link equivalent constructions: *both* Jane *and* Fred; *not only* in Peru *but also* in Mexico. See **26c**.

count, noncount nouns   Count nouns are individual, countable entities and cannot be viewed as a mass (*word, finger, remark*). Noncount nouns are a mass or a continuum (*grass, humor, winter*).

credibility   The reliability of a person or evidence. See **31c**.

critical thinking/reading/writing   The ability to analyze and synthesize ideas: to distinguish between fact and opinion, to recognize the importance of evidence and logic, to evaluate for credibility, and to avoid common fallacies. See **31**.

cumulative sentence A sentence in which the subject and predicate come first, followed by modifiers. (Also called a loose sentence.) See **29b**.

dangling modifier A word or phrase that does not clearly refer to another word or word group in the sentence. See **25b**. See also **absolute phrase.**

declension A set or table of inflected forms of nouns or pronouns. See the examples on page 55.

deduction A form of logical reasoning that begins with a generalization (*premise*), relates a specific fact to that generalization, and forms a conclusion that fits both. See **31e**. Compare **induction.**

definition A brief explanation of the meaning of a word, as in a dictionary. Also, an extended piece of writing, employing a variety of rhetorical strategies, to explain what something is or means. See **32d(7)**.

degree The form of an adverb or adjective that indicates relative quality, quantity, or manner. The three degrees are as follows: *positive,* (*good/well, bad, fast, rapidly*); *comparative,* between two elements (*better, worse, faster/less fast, more/less rapidly*); and *superlative,* among three or more elements (*best/least good, worst/least worse, fastest/least fast, most/least rapidly*). See **4c**.

demonstratives Four words that point out (*this, that, these, those*): **Those** are as good as **these.** [pronouns] **Those** curtains have never been cleaned. [adjective]

denotation The literal meaning of a word as commonly defined. See **20a(1)**. See also **connotation.**

dependent clause A subordinate clause. See **clause.**

description A rhetorical strategy using details perceivable by the senses to portray a scene, object, performance, and so on. See **32d(2)**.

details Specific information such as facts, sensory data, or examples that clarifies and explains.

determiner A word (such as *a, an, the, my, their*) that signals the approach of a noun: **the** newly mown *hay.*

development The elaboration of an idea through organized discussion filled with examples, details, and other information. See **32c**.

dialect A variety of language characteristic of a region or culture. Dialects are distinguished by vocabulary, pronunciation, and/or syntax: British English, Low German, and Cantonese. See **19d**.

dialogue   A reproduction in writing of conversation by two or more people, real or fictional. See **9e**, **16a**, **19b**.

diction   The writer's choice of exact, idiomatic, and fresh words, as well as appropriate levels of usage. See **19a** and **20**.

direct address   A name or descriptive term (set off by commas) designating the one or ones spoken to: Play it again, *Sam*.

direct object   A noun (or noun clause) naming *whom* or *what* after a transitive active verb: Emily sliced the *ham*. See **1b**. See also **object.**

direct quotation   A repetition of the exact spoken or written words of others: "*Where an opinion is general,*" writes Jane Austen, "*it is usually correct.*" See **16a** and **34e**.

documentation   The citing of sources in a researched paper that conforms to a given style, such as MLA or APA. See **34**.

double negative   The nonstandard combination of two negatives, which has a negative meaning: We ca*n't* do *nothing* about the weather. See **4e**.

draft, drafting   A working version of a piece of writing. The process of setting ideas down in writing so they may be revised and edited. See **33f–g**.

edited American English   The term adopted by the National Council of Teachers of English for the formal style expected in most college writing. EAE observes conventional rules of spelling, punctuation, mechanics, grammar, and sentence structure.

editing   Reworking sentences for clarity, sense, and conformity to conventional rules of spelling, punctuation, mechanics, grammar, and sentence structure.

ellipsis   Three or four spaced periods which indicate material omitted from a quotation. See **17i**.

elliptical construction   The omission of words while retaining the meaning: Cats are cleaner than pigs [are].

emphasis   Special weight or importance given to a word, sentence, or paragraph by any of a variety of techniques. It may also mean stress applied to one or more syllables in a word. See **29**.

essay   A brief piece of nonfiction writing on a single topic in which a writer typically states the thesis in the introduction, develops several points in support of that thesis, and concludes.

etymology The origin and historical development of a word, its derivation.

euphemism An indirect or "nice" expression used instead of a more direct one: *Correctional facility* instead of *jail*. See **20**.

evaluation The process of finding and judging useful passages from source material. See **31b**, **34b(3)**, and **34c**.

evidence Facts, statistics, examples, testimony, sensory details, and so on that support generalizations.

example Any fact, anecdote, reference, or the like used to illustrate an idea. See **32c**.

expletive A signal of a transformation in the structure of a sentence that occurs without changing the meaning. The expletive *there* shifts the order of subject and verb in a sentence: *There* were over four thousand runners in the marathon.   [Compare: Over four thousand runners were in the marathon.] The expletive *it* transforms the main clause into a subordinate clause: It is apparent that the plane is late. [Compare: Apparently, the plane is late.] See **6a(5)**.

expository writing See **referential writing.**

expressive writing Writing that emphasizes the writer's own feelings and reactions to a topic. See **33a**.

fact Any piece of information that can be verified through more than one independent source or procedure. See **31a**.

fallacy A false argument or incorrect reasoning. See **31g**.

faulty predication The use of a predicate that does not logically belong with a given subject: One superstition is a black cat.   [The verb should be *involves*.]

figurative language The use of words in an imaginative rather than a literal sense. See **20a(4)**.

finite verb A verb form that can function as the only verb in the predicate of a sentence: They *ate* a can of pork and beans. Verb forms classified as gerunds, infinitives, or participles cannot. See **predicate;** contrast **verbal.**

first person See **person.**

focus The narrowing of a subject to a manageable size; also the sharpening of the writer's view of the subject. See **33c** and **33d**.

formal/informal writing style Consider the rhetorical situation (your audience, purpose, and occasion) to determine if you need to use a formal or informal style. You should master a formal style for most college and business writing, employing edited American English, but you should also master an informal style for use in personal letters and other kinds of self-expression. See **19b** and **19i**.

fragment   A group of words beginning with a capital letter and ending with a period that form only part of a sentence. See **2**.

freewriting   A method of finding a writing topic by composing for a specified length of time without stopping to reflect, reread, or correct errors.

function words   Words (such as prepositions, conjunctions, auxiliaries, and articles) that indicate the functions of other words in a sentence and the grammatical relationships between them.

fused sentence   Two or more sentences run together, with no punctuation or conjunctions to separate them. Also called run-on sentence. Unacceptable in formal writing. See **3**.

gender   The grammatical distinction that labels nouns or pronouns as masculine, feminine, or neuter. In English, grammatical gender usually corresponds with natural gender.

general/specific, generalization   *General* words are all-embracing, indefinite, sweeping in scope: *food.* *Specific* words are precise, explicit, limited in scope: *spaghetti carbonara.* The same is true of *general* and *specific* ideas. A *generalization* is vague and may be untrue.

genitive case   See **case.**

gerund   A verbal (nonfinite verb) that ends in *-ing* and functions as a noun. Gerunds may take objects, complements, or modifiers: *Riding* bikes is good exercise. [The gerund phrase—*riding* and its object, *bikes*—serves as the subject of the sentence.] A noun or pronoun serving as the subject of the gerund takes the possessive case: *His* [or *Jim's*] *bicycle riding* is good exercise.

grammar   The system of rules by which words are pronounced and arranged into the structures meaningful in a language.

hardware   In computer terminology, consists of the tangible components of the computer system such as the keyboard, the monitor, and the computer itself.

helping verb   A verb that combines with another verb to indicate voice, tense, or mood. See **auxiliary** and **modal.**

historical present   A tense used to describe events in literature or history that are permanently preserved in the present: The tragedy *is* that Iago *deceives* Othello. See **7b, 35a.**

homonyms   Words that have the same sound and sometimes the same spelling but differ in meaning (*their, there, they're*). See **18b.**

hyperbole   An intentional overstatement made for rhetorical effect. See **20a(4).** Compare **understatement.**

idiom   A fixed expression (within a language) whose meaning cannot be deduced from its elements: *put up a fight; to mean well.* See **20b.**

illustration   In writing, the use of specific details to give substance and interest to a subject. See **32c.**

imperative mood   See **mood.**

indefinites   The article *a* or *an* (*a* banana, *an* insect) as well as pronouns (*anyone, everybody*) and adjectives (*any* car, *few* problems, *several* questions) that do not specify distinct limits. See **6a(1)** and **6b(1).**

independent clause   See **clause.**

indicative mood   See **mood.**

indirect object   A word (or words) naming the one (or ones) indirectly affected by the action of the verb: Emily sliced *me* some ham. See **object.**

indirect question   A question phrased as a statement, usually a subordinate clause: We can ask *whether Milton's blindness was the result of glaucoma,* but we cannot be sure. See **27c.**

indirect quotation   A report of the written or spoken words of another without using the exact words of the speaker or writer: The registrar said *that the bank returned my check for my tuition.* Compare **direct quotation.**

induction   A form of logical reasoning that begins with evidence and interprets it to form a conclusion. See **31d.** Compare **deduction.**

infinitive   A verbal (nonfinite verb) used chiefly as a noun, less frequently as an adjective or adverb. The infinitive is usually made up of the word *to* plus the present form of a verb (called the *stem* of the infinitive). Infinitives may have subjects, objects, complements, or modifiers: Lashanda wanted *to continue* the debate. [*Debate* is the object of the infinitive *to continue; to continue the debate* is the object of the verb *wanted.*]

infinitive phrase   A phrase that employs the nonfinite form of the verb: *to go* to the store, *to run* the race. See **phrase.**

inflection   A change in the form of a word to show a specific meaning or grammatical function:

VERB   *talk, talks, talked*
NOUN   *dog, dogs, dog's, dogs'*
PRONOUN   *he, him, his, they, them, their, theirs*
ADJECTIVE   *thin, thinner, thinnest*
ADVERB   *rapidly, more rapidly, most rapidly*

informal   See **formal/informal.**

informative writing   See **referential writing.**

intensifier   A modifier used for emphasis: *very* excited, *certainly* pleased. See **qualifier.**

intensive/reflexive pronoun   The *-self* pronouns (such as *myself, himself, themselves*). The *intensive* is used for emphasis: The teenagers *themselves* had the best idea. The *reflexive* is used as an object of a verb, verbal, or preposition: He blames *himself;* she bought a present for *herself.* An intensive or reflexive pronoun always refers to another noun or pronoun in the same sentence that denotes the same individual or individuals.

interjection   A word (one of the eight parts of speech) expressing a simple exclamation: *Hey! Oops!* When used in sentences, mild interjections are set off by commas. See **17c**.

interpretation   Use inductive reasoning to help interpret facts in order to reach probable and believable conclusions, avoiding sweeping conclusions that can be easily challenged. See **31d**.

interrogative   A word like *which, whose,* or *why* used to ask a question: *Which* is the more expensive?   [pronoun] *Whose* lights are on?   [adjective] *Why* are treasury bills a good investment?   [adverb]

interrogative adjective   See **adjective.**

intransitive verb   A verb (such as *appear* or *belong*) that does not take an object. See **7**. See also **verb** and **transitive.**

introduction   The beginning of an essay, often a single paragraph, that engages the reader's interest and indicates, usually by stating the thesis, what the essay is about. See **33f(1)**.

invention   The process of using strategies to generate ideas for writing. See **32d** and **33b–c.**

inversion   A change in the usual word order of a sentence: Into the valley of death rode the five hundred. See **29f**.

irony A deliberate inconsistency between what is stated and what is meant. Irony may be verbal or situational. See **20a(4)**.

irregular verb A verb that is not inflected in the usual way—that is, by the addition of *-d* or *-ed* to the present form to form the past tense and past participle. There are five common types of irregular verbs classified according to how they indicate past tense and past participle: vowel changes (*begin, began, begun*); *-en* added (*beat, beat, beaten*); vowel shortens (*spin, spun, spun*); *-d* changes to *-t* (*lend, lent, lent*); no change (*put, put, put*).

jargon Technical slang, appropriate as a shortcut to communication when the audience is knowledgeable of the topic and the terms; it should be avoided in writing that is intended for a more general audience. See **19g**.

journal A special-interest periodical (*Rhetoric Review, Environmental Legislation*).

linking verb A verb that relates the subject complement to the subject. Words commonly used as linking verbs are *become, seen, appear, feel, look, taste, smell, sound,* and forms of the verb *be:* She *is* a writer. The bread *looks* burned. See **1a**, **4b**, and **5f**.

logic The presentation of ideas that shows a clear, predictable, and structured relationship among those ideas. See **23** and **31**.

loose sentence See **cumulative sentence.**

main clause See **clause.**

main idea The part of the paragraph or paper to which all the other ideas relate. See **topic sentence** or **theme sentence.**

mechanics The form of words and letters, such as capitals, italics, abbreviations, acronyms, and numbers.

memory In computer terminology, the amount of data that the computer can hold. ROM (read only memory) is memory whose contents remain intact even when the system is turned off. RAM (random access memory) is memory that is lost, and thus must be stored on disk, when the machine is turned off.

metaphor An imaginative comparison between dissimilar things without using *like* or *as*. See **20a(4)**.

misplaced modifier A modifier placed in an awkward position, usually far away from what it modifies: I read that there was a big fire *in* *yesterday's newspaper.* [Place the modifier after the verb *read*.] Sometimes a misplaced modifier confuses the reader because it could qualify either of two words: To do one's best *sometimes* is not enough. *Sometimes* to do one's best is not enough. [Place the adverb closer to the verb.] See **25a**.

mixed construction A garbled sentence that is the result of an unintentional shift from one grammatical pattern to another. See **23c**.

mixed metaphor A metaphor that confuses two or more metaphors: Playing with fire will drown you. See **23c**.

MLA Modern Language Association. See **34g–h**.

modal A helping verb (not conjugated) that shows ability (*can, could*); permission or possibility (*may, might*); determination, promise, or intention (*shall, should; will, would*); obligation (*ought*); or necessity (*must*).

modifier A word or word group that describes, limits, or qualifies another: a *true* statement, walked *slowly,* yards *filled with rocks,* the horse *that jumped the fence.* See **4** and **25**.

mood The way a speaker or writer regards an assertion—that is, as a declarative statement or a question (*indicative* mood); as a command or request (*imperative*); or as a supposition, hypothesis, recommendation, or condition contrary to fact (*subjunctive*). Verb forms indicate mood. See **1f** and **7c**

narration A rhetorical strategy that recounts a sequence of events, usually in chronological order. See **32d(1)**.

nominalization The practice of using nouns instead of active verbs: She *made a list* of the schedule changes. Compare: She *listed* the schedule changes. Excessive nominalization produces a wordy style.

nominative case See **case.**

nonfinite verb A verb form (verbal) used as a noun, adjective, or an adverb. A nonfinite verb cannot stand as the only verb in a sentence. See **1c** and **2a**. See also **verbal.**

nonrestrictive Nonessential to the identification of the word or words referred to. A word or word group is nonrestrictive (parenthetical) when it is not necessary to the meaning of the sentence and can be omitted: My best friend, *Pauline,* understands me. See **12d**.

nonstandard Speech forms that are common in informal writing but that should be avoided in formal writing. See **19d**.

noun   A part of speech that names a person, place, thing, idea, animal, quality, or action: *Mary, America, apples, justice, goose, strength, departure.* A noun usually changes form to indicate the plural and the possessive case, as in *man, men; man's, men's.* See **1c(2)**.

TYPES OF NOUNS

COMMON	a **woman,** the **street,** some **dogs** [general classes]
PROPER	**Ms. Wentworth,** in **Dallas,** the **White House** [capitalized, specific names—**9a**]
COLLECTIVE	a **team,** the **committee,** my **class** [groups]
CONCRETE	a **truck,** the **cup,** my **foot,** two **fish** [tangibles]
ABSTRACT	**love, justice, fear** [ideas, qualities]
COUNT	two **cents,** sixteen **bytes,** an **assignment,** many **revisions** [singular or plural—often preceded by adjectivals telling how many]
NONCOUNT	much **concern,** more **consideration,** less **revenue** [singular in meaning—often preceded by adjectivals telling how much]

noun clause   A subordinate clause used as a noun. See **1e**. See also **clause.**

number   The inflectional form of a word that identifies (one) or plural (more than one): *river–rivers, this–those, he sees–they see.* See **6** and **18d.** *Cardinal numbers* express quantity: *two* (2), *thirty-five* (35). *Ordinal numbers* indicate order or rank: *second* (2nd), *thirty-fifth* (35th).

object   A noun or noun substitute governed by a transitive active verb, by a nonfinite verb, or by a preposition. See **1b(2–3)**, **1c(6)**.

A *direct object,* or the *object of a finite verb,* is any noun or noun substitute that answers the question *what?* or *whom?* after a transitive active verb. A direct object frequently receives, or is in some way affected by, the action of the verb: Bill hit the *ball. What* did he hit? A direct object may be converted into a subject with a passive verb. See **voice.**

An *object of a nonfinite verb* is any noun or its equivalent that follows and completes the meaning of a participle, a gerund, or an infinitive: Building a *house* takes time. She likes to grow *flowers.*

An *indirect object* is any noun or noun substitute that states *to whom* or *for whom* (or *to what* or *for what*) something is done. An indirect object ordinarily precedes a direct object: She gave *him* the keys. I gave the *floor* a good mopping. It is usually possible to substitute a prepositional phrase beginning with *to* or *for* for the indirect object: She gave the keys *to* him.

An *object of a preposition* is any noun or noun substitute that a preposition relates to another word or word group: They play ball in the *park*. [*Park* is the object of the preposition *in*.]

object complement A word that helps to complete the meaning of such verbs as *make, paint, elect, name*. An object complement refers to or modifies the direct object: They painted the cellar door *blue*. See **1b, 4b**. See also **complement**.

objective case See **case**.

opinion Ideas that may or may not be based upon fact. See **31a**.

ordinal number See **number**.

overgeneralization Lacking specificity. See **general/specific**.

paradox A seemingly contradictory statement that may actually be true. See **20a(4)**.

paragraph Usually a group of related sentences unified by a single idea or purpose but occasionally as brief as a single sentence (or even a single word or phrase). The central, or controlling, idea of a paragraph is often explicitly stated in a *topic sentence*. A paragraph is physically defined by the indention of its first line.

parallelism The use of corresponding grammatically equal elements in sentences and paragraphs. It aids the flow of a sentence, making it read smoothly, and also emphasizes the relationship of the ideas in the parallel elements. See **26**.

paraphrase A sentence-by-sentence restatement of the ideas in a passage, using different words. See **34e**.

parenthetical documentation See **documentation**.

parenthetical element Nonessential words, phrases, clauses, or sentences (such as an aside or interpolation) usually set off by commas but often by dashes or parentheses to mark pauses and intonation: *In fact,* the class, *a hardworking group of students,* finished the test quickly. See **12d, 17e**, and **17f**.

participle A verb form that may function as a part of verb phrase (was *thinking*, had *determined*) or as a modifier (a *determined* effort; the couple, *thinking* about their past).

The *present participle* ends in *-ing* (the form also used for verbal nouns: see **gerund**). The past participle of regular verbs ends in *-d* or *-ed;* for past-participle forms of irregular verbs, see **7**. See also **irregular verb**.

Functioning as modifiers in *participial phrases*, participles may take objects, complements, and modifiers: The bellhop *carrying the largest suitcase* fell over the threshold.   [The participle *carrying* takes the object *suitcase;* the whole participial phrase modifies *bellhop*.] See **25b(1)**.

particle   A word like *across, away, down, for, in, off, out, up, with* combined with a verb to form idiomatic usages where the combination has the force of a single-word verb: The authorities refused to *put up* with him.

parts of speech   The classes into which words may be grouped according to their form changes and their grammatical relationships. The traditional parts of speech are *verbs, nouns, pronouns, adjectives, adverbs, prepositions, conjunctions,* and *interjections.* Each of these is discussed separately in this glossary. See also **1c**.

passive voice   The form of the verb which shows that its subject is not the agent performing the action to which the verb refers but rather receives that action: The ham *was sliced* by Emily. See **7** and **29d**. See also **active voice.**

perfect tenses   The tenses formed by the addition of a form of *have* and showing complex time relationships in completing the action of the verb (the present perfect—*have/has eaten; the past perfect—had eaten;* and the future perfect—*will have eaten*).

periodic sentence   A sentence in which the main idea comes last. See **29b**. Compare **cumulative sentence.**

person   The form of pronouns and verbs denoting or indicating whether one is speaking (*I am*—first person), is spoken to (*you are*—second person), or spoken about (*he is*—third person). In the present tense, a verb changes its form to agree grammatically with a third-person singular subject (*I watch, she watches*). See **6a** and **27b**.

personal pronoun   Any one of a group of pronouns—*I, you, he, she, it,* and their inflected forms—referring to the one (or ones) speaking, spoken to, or spoken about. See **5**.

personification   The attributing of human characteristics to nonhuman things (animals, objects, ideas): "That night wind was breathing across me through the spokes of the wheel."   —WALLACE STEGNER

persuasive writing   A form of writing intended chiefly to change the reader's opinions or attitudes or to arouse the reader to action. See **33a**.

phrasal verb   A unit consisting of a verb plus one or two uninflected words like *after, in, up, off,* or *out* (see **particle**) and having the force of a single-word verb: We *ran out* on them.

phrase   A sequence of grammatically related words without a subject and/or a predicate. See **1d** and **2a**. Gerund, infinitive, and participial phrases are also called *verbal phrases* (see **verbal**).

plagiarism   The use of another writer's words or ideas without acknowledging the source. Akin to theft, plagiarism has serious consequences and should always be avoided. See **34e(1)**.

plural   More than one. Compare **singular.**

point of view   The vantage point from which the subject is viewed. See also **27e**. It also refers to the stance a writer takes—objective or impartial (third person), directive (second person), or personal (first person).

positive   See **comparative, comparison.**

possessive case   See **case.**

predicate   A basic grammatical division of a sentence. A predicate is the part of the sentence comprising what is said about the subject. The *complete predicate* consists of the main verb and its auxiliaries (the *simple predicate*) and any complements and modifiers: We **chased** the dog all around our grandmother's farm. [*Chased* is the simple predicate; *chased* and all the words that follow make up the complete predicate.]

predicate adjective   The adjective used as a subject complement: The bread tastes *sweet*. See **1c** and **4b**. See also **linking verb.**

predicate noun   A noun used as a subject complement: Bromides are *sedatives*. See **1c** and **5f**. See also **linking verb.**

predication   The act of stating or expressing something about the subject. See **faulty predication.**

prefix   An added syllable or group of syllables (such as *in-, dis-, un-, pro-*) placed before a word to form a new word: *disposed–indisposed*. A prefix ordinarily changes meaning.

premise   An assumption or a proposition on which an argument or explanation is based. In logic, premises are either major (general) or minor (specific); when combined correctly, they lead to a conclusion. See **31e**. See also **syllogism.**

preposition   A part of speech that links and relates a noun or noun substitute to another word in the sentence: The dancers leapt *across* the stage.   [The preposition *across* connects and relates *stage* (its object) to the verb *leapt.*] See page 15 for a list of words commonly used as prepositions.

prepositional phrase   A preposition with its object and any modifiers: *in the hall, between you and me, for the new van.*

present and past participle   See **participle.**

prewriting   The initial stage of the writing process, concerned primarily with planning.

primary source   In research or bibliographies, the source that provides unedited, firsthand facts.

principal parts   The forms of verb that indicate the various tenses: the present (*give, jump*); the past (*gave, jumped*); and the past participle (*given, jumped*). See **7a**.

process analysis   A rhetorical strategy either to instruct the reader how to perform a procedure or to explain how something occurs. See **32d(3)**.

process, process writing   See **writing process.**

progressive verb   A verb phrase consisting of a present participle (ending in *-ing*) used with a form of *be* and denoting continuous action: *is attacking, will be eating.*

pronoun   A part of speech that takes the position of nouns and functions as nouns do. See **1c, 5, 6b, 28**. See also **noun** and the separate entries for the types of pronouns listed below.

> PERSONAL PRONOUN   **She** and **I** will drive to Conway.
> RELATIVE PRONOUN   Jack is a person **who** enjoys life.
> INDEFINITE PRONOUN   **Each** of us played against **somebody.**
> INTENSIVE PRONOUN   **I myself** am an agronomist.
> REFLEXIVE PRONOUN   Jane enjoyed **herself** at the fair.
> DEMONSTRATIVE PRONOUN   **This** is closer than **that.**
> INTERROGATIVE PRONOUN   **What** is it? **Who** said that?

proofreading   Checking the final draft of a paper to eliminate typographical, spelling, punctuation, and documentation errors. See **8c** and **33g**.

proper adjective   See **adjective.**

proper noun   See **noun.**

purpose   A writer's reason for writing. The purpose for nonfiction writing may be predominantly expressive, expository, or persuasive, though all three aims are likely to be present in some measure. See **33a**.

See also **expressive writing, persuasive writing,** and **referential writing.**

qualifier   Any modifier that describes or limits: *Sometimes* movies are *too* gory to watch. Frequently, however, the term refers only to those modifiers that restrict or intensify the meaning of other words. See **intensifier.**

quotation   Repeated or copied words of another, real or fictional. See **16a** and **34e.**

reciprocal pronoun   One of two compound pronouns expressing an interchangeable or mutual action or relationship: *each other* or *one another.*

redundant   Needlessly repetitious, unnecessary.

referential writing   Writing whose chief aim is to clarify, explain, or evaluate a subject in order to inform or instruct the reader. Also called expository or informative writing. See **33a.**

reflexive pronoun   See **pronoun.**

regular verb   A verb that forms its past tense and past participle by adding -*d* or -*ed* to the present form (or the stem of the infinitive): *love, loved; laugh, laughed.* See **7a.**

relative clause   An adjective clause introduced by a relative pronoun: the suits *that they wore.*

relative pronoun   A noun substitute (*who, whom, whose, that, which, what, whoever, whomever, whichever, whatever*) used to introduce subordinate clauses: He has an aunt **who** *is a principal.*   [adjective clause introduced by the relative pronoun *who*] OR **Whoever** *becomes treasurer* must be honest.   [noun clause introduced by the relative pronoun *whoever*] See **5b, 5c,** and **6a(6).**

restrictive   A word, phrase, or clause is restrictive when it limits the word referred to by imposing conditions or by confining the word to a particular group or to a specific item or individual: Every student *who cheats* will be removed from the class.   [The restrictive clause *who cheats* imposes conditions upon—restricts—the meaning of *every student.* Only those students *who cheat* will be removed.] See **12d.** See also **nonrestrictive.**

revision   Part of the writing process. Writers revise by rereading and rethinking a piece of writing to see where they need to add, delete, move, replace, reshape, and even completely recast ideas.

rhetoric The art of using language effectively. Rhetoric involves the writer's **purpose (33a)**, the consideration of **audience (33a)**, the discovery and exploration of a subject (**33b** and **33c**), its arrangement and organization (**33e**), the style and tone in which it is expressed (**33a**), and the form in which it is delivered (**8**, **33a**).

rhetorical question A question posed for effect without expectation of a reply: Who can tell what will happen?

rhetorical situation The relationship between the writer and the audience that determines the appropriate approach for a particular situation.

run-on sentence See **fused sentence.**

secondary source A source that analyzes or interprets **primary source** material.

sentence A grammatically independent unit of expression. A simple sentence contains a subject and a predicate. Sentences are classified according to structure (simple, complex, compound, and compound–complex) and purpose (declaratory, interrogatory, imperative, exclamatory). See chapter **1**.

sentence modifier An adverb or adverb substitute that modifies the rest of the sentence, not a specific word or word group in it: *All things considered,* Middle America is a good place to live.   OR *Yes,* the plane arrived on time.

sexist language Language that arbitrarily excludes one sex or the other or that arbitrarily assigns stereotypical roles to one or the other sex: A secretary should keep *her* desk tidy. [Compare: Secretar*ies* should keep *their* desks tidy.] See **6b**, **19j**.

simile The comparison of two dissimilar things using *like* or *as.*

simple tenses The tenses that refer to present, past, and future time.

singular One. See **number.** Compare **plural.**

slang The casual vocabulary of specific groups or cultures, usually considered inappropriate for formal writing. Occasionally, slang can be effective if the writer carefully considers purpose and audience. See **19c**.

software Computer programs, such as in word processing, that enable the user to perform specific tasks.

space order A concept often used to organize descriptive passages. Details are arranged according to how they are encountered as the observer's eye moves vertically, horizontally, from far to near, and so forth. See **32d(2)**.

split infinitive The often awkward separation of an infinitive by at least one adverb: *to* quietly *go*. See **infinitive.**

squinting modifier A modifier that refers to either a preceding or a following word: Eating *often* makes her sick. See **25a**.

standard English See **edited American English.**

stipulative definition A definition that specifies how a certain term will be used within a certain context. See **23e**.

style An author's choice and arrangement of words, sentence structures, and ideas as well as less definable characteristics such as rhythm and euphony. See **27d**.

subject A basic grammatical division of a sentence. The subject is a noun or noun substitute about which something is asserted or asked in the predicate. It usually precedes the predicate. (Imperative sentences have subjects that are implied, not stated.) The *complete subject* consists of the *simple subject* and the words associated with it: *The woman in the gray trench coat* asked for information.   [simple subject—*woman;* complete subject—*the woman in the gray trench coat*] Compare **predicate.** May also refer to the main idea of a piece of writing.

subject complement A word (or words) that completes the meaning of a linking verb and that modifies or refers to the subject: The old car looked *shabby*.   [predicate adjective] *The old car was an eyesore.* [predicate noun] See **1b, 4b, 5f.** See also **linking verb.**

subjective case See **case.**

subjunctive mood See **mood.**

subordinate clause See **clause.**

subordinating conjunction See **conjunction.**

subordination The use of dependent structures (phrases, subordinate clauses) that are lower in grammatical rank than independent ones (simple sentences, main clauses). See **24**.

suffix An added sound, syllable, or group of syllables placed after a word to form a new word, to change the meaning of a word, or to indicate grammatical function: *light, lighted, lighter, lightest, lightness.*

summary A concise restatement briefer than the original. See **34e(4)**.

superlative degree See **degree.**

syllogism A three-part form of deductive reasoning. See **31c**.

synonym A word that has a similar meaning to another word.

syntax Sentence structure; the grammatical arrangement of words, phrases, clauses.

synthesis **Deductive reasoning** whereby a writer begins with a number of instances (facts or observations) and uses them to draw a general conclusion. See **31e**.

tag question A question attached to the end of a related statement set off by a comma: She's coming, *isn't she?* See **3a**.

tense The form of the verb that denotes time. Inflection of single-word verbs (*pay, paid*) and the use of auxiliaries (*am paid, was paid, will pay*) indicate tense. See **7**.

thesis The central point or main idea of an essay. It is one of the main ways an essay is unified (see **unity**). A clearly focused and specific thesis statement helps the writer make all the other elements of the essay work together to accomplish the writer's purpose. See also **33d**.

tone The writer's attitude toward the subject and the audience, usually conveyed through diction and sentence structure. Tone affects the reader's response.

topic The specific, narrowed idea of a paper. See **subject.**

topic sentence A statement of the central thought of a paragraph which, though often appearing at the beginning, may appear anywhere in it. Some paragraphs may not have a topic sentence, although the main idea is clearly suggested.

transitions Words, phrases, sentences, or paragraphs that relate ideas and provide coherence by linking sentences, paragraphs, and larger units of writing. Transitions may be expressions (words or phrases such as *moreover, first, nevertheless, for example,* and so on) or structural features a writer uses such as parallelism or repetition of key words and phrases. When they link larger units of writing, transitions may take the form of sentences or even brief paragraphs. See **32b**.

transitive A type of verb that takes an object. Some verbs may be either transitive or intransitive depending on the context: They *danced* [transitive] the polka. They *danced* [intransitive] all night. See **verb** and **intransitive.**

truth In deductive reasoning, the veracity of the premises. If the premises are true, the conclusion is true. An argument may be true but invalid if the relation between the premises is invalid. See **31b**. See also **validity.**

understatement Intentional underemphasis for effect, usually ironic. See **20a**. See also **hyperbole.**

unity All the elements in an essay contribute to developing a single idea or thesis. A paragraph is unified when each sentence contributes to developing a central thought. See **32a** and **33d**.

validity The structural coherence of a deductive argument. An argument is valid when the premises of a syllogism are correctly related to form a conclusion. Validity does not, however, actually refer to the truthfulness of an argument's premises. See **31b**. Compare **truth.**

verb A part of speech denoting action, occurrence, or existence (state of being). Inflections indicate tense (and sometimes person and number) and mood of a verb. Verbs may be either transitive or intransitive. See **1a** and **7**. See also **inflection, mood, voice, transitive,** and **intransitive.**

verbal A nonfinite verb used as a noun, an adjective, or an adverb. Infinitives, participles, and gerunds are verbals. Verbals (like finite verbs) may take objects, complements, modifiers, and sometimes subjects: Sarah went *to see a movie*. [*To see,* an infinitive, functions as an adverb modifying the verb *went*. The object of the infinitive is *movie*.] See **gerund, infinitive, nonfinite verb,** and **participle.**

verb phrase See **phrase.**

voice The form of a transitive verb that indicates whether or not the subject performs the action denoted by the verb. A verb with a direct object is in the *active voice*. When the direct object is converted into a subject, the verb is in the *passive voice*. A passive verb is always a verb phrase consisting of a form of the verb *be* (or sometimes *get*) followed by a past participle. See **7**, **29d**.

> ACTIVE VOICE   The batter **hit** the ball.   [The subject (*batter*) acts.]
> PASSIVE VOICE   The ball **was hit** by the batter.   [The subject (*ball*) does not act.]

Speakers and writers often omit the *by*-phrase after a passive verb, especially when the performer of the action is not known or is not the focus of attention: Those flowers *were picked* yesterday. We just heard that a new secretary *was hired*.

word order The arrangement of words in sentences. Because of lost inflections, modern English depends heavily on word order to convey meaning.

Nancy gave Henry $14,000.   Henry gave Nancy $14,000.
Tony had built a garage.   Tony had a garage built.

word processing   An electronic method of producing text. The writer
performs a number of computer operations, such as inserting, deleting,
moving, blocking, and so forth, in order to facilitate writing.

writing process   The various activities of planning (gathering, shaping, and organizing information), drafting (setting down ideas in
sentences and paragraphs to form a composition), revising (rethinking,
reshaping, and reordering ideas), editing (checking for clear, effective,
grammatically correct sentences), and proofreading (checking for correct
spelling, mechanics, and manuscript form). The writing process determines no set sequence of these activities but allows writers to return to
any activity as necessary.

COPYRIGHTS
AND
ACKNOWLEDGMENTS

Copyrights and Acknowledgments

INDEX

Boldface numbers and letters refer to rules; other numbers refer to pages; an asterisk (°) marks entries of special dialectal interference.

Index

Index

Index

Index

Index

Index

Index

Index

Index

subject (*continued*)
  predicate and, 2–3
  unstated or understood, 5
subject complement, 7–8, G-34
  adjective as, 14, **4b**: 47–48
  case of, **5**: 56; **5f**: 63–64
  for emphasis, 274
  multiple, 57
subject of composition
  exploring/focusing, **33c**: 355–62
  finding, **33b**: 353–55; **34a**: 393–94; **35a**: 496
subject-first sentence, 281–82
subjective case, G-14
  after *than* or *as*, **5b**: 59–60
  compound constructions and, **5a**: 57–58
  for appositive, 57–58
  for subject complement, 56, **5f**: 63–64
  for subject of verb, 56
  who, in clause, **5b**: 58–59
subjunctive mood, 80, 82, **7c**: 91–93
  alternatives, 91
  for wish or condition, **7c**: 92
  forms, **7c**: 91–92
  if or *as if* clauses, **7c**: 92
  shift to indicative mood, 259
  should, would, 92
  that clauses, **7c**: 92
  would have for *had*, **7c**: 92–93
subordinate clauses, 16, 21–22, G-15
  markers, list of, 244
  misused as sentence, **2b**: 33–34
  modifiers, 24–25
  nouns, 23–24
  subordination and, **24a**: 244–46
subordinating conjunctions, G-17
  adverb clause and, 24–25, 130
  list of, 22–23
  removal of, 33
  subordination and, 243–44
subordination, G-34
  combined sentence and, **24a**: 242–44
  coordination and, **24**: 241–47

faulty or excessive, **24c**: 246–47
  for stringy sentence, **24b**: 244–46
  for variety, 280
subordinators, 22
subplot, 509
subtitle, **17d**: 169; 428, 471
such, 171
  as intensifier, **22d**: 232
  in broad reference, **28c**: 266–67
such as, punctuation with, **17d**: 169
such that, **22d**: 232
suffixes, G-34
  adding, in spelling, **18d**: 185–88
  adjective-forming, 13, 44
  adverb-forming, 44
  -d, -ed, 77, 82
  hyphen after, **18f**: 190
  noun-forming, 12
  -s, -es, 66, **18d**: 187–88
  verb-forming, 12
summary, 416–17, 496, 542, G-34
superfluous commas
  between subject and verb, **13a**: 141–42
  between verb and object, **13a**: 141–42
  coordinating conjunction with, **13b**: 142
  items in series with, **13c**: 143–44
  nonparenthetical words, **13c**: 142
  restrictive elements with, **13d**: 142–43
superlative degree, **4c**: 48–51; G-19, G-34. See also *comparison*.
superscript number, 464
suppose to, supposed to, 83°
sure, surely, **4a**: 46
syllabication, **18f**: 191, 197
syllogism, **31e**: 298–99
symbolism, 502, 526
synonyms, 197, G-35
  as appositives, 239
  awkward usage, **21d**: 226–27
  in definition, **23e**: 239; 338–39
syntax, G-35
synthesis, G-35

Index

ESL INDEX

Entries in this index identify topics basic to ESL usage. Boldface numbers and letters refer to rules; other numbers refer to pages.

ESL Index

MLA Documentation Style

This index refers to items in the parenthetical citations, the works cited list, and the student papers in chapters **34** and **35**. The italics indicate the page on which a given form is illustrated in a paper.

APA Documentation Style

This index refers to items in the parenthetical citations, the reference list, and the student paper in chapter **34**. The italics indicate the page on which a given form is illustrated in a paper.